OUR FIRST SEVENTY-FIVE YEARS: A MEMOIR

How the Cuban Exile Shaped the León-Cordero Family

COLECCIÓN FÉLIX VARELA # 62

EDICIONES UNIVERSAL, Miami, Florida, 2021

Consuelo and Jesús León

OUR FIRST SEVENTY-FIVE YEARS: A MEMOIR

How the Cuban Exile Shaped the León-Cordero Family

Copyright © 2019 by Consuelo and Jesús León

First edition, 2015 (internal)
Second edition, 2021 by

EDICIONES UNIVERSAL
P.O. Box 450353 (Shenandoah Station)
Miami, FL 33245-0353. USA
(Since 1965)

e-mail: ediciones@ediciones.com
http://www.ediciones.com

Library of Congress Catalog No.: 2020950061
ISBN-13: 978-1-59388-317-1

Text composition: María Cristina Zarraluqui

Cover design: Luis García Fresquet

All rights are reserved.
No part of this book may be reproduced or
transmitted in any form or by any means, electronic
or mechanical, including photocopying machines, tape recorders
or computerized systems, without the written permission
of the author, except in the case of brief quotations
embodied in critical articles or in magazines.
For more information:
ediciones@ediciones.com

Dedicated with all our love to
our children and grandchildren
- Consuelo Beatriz
- Cristina del Carmen
- Lorenzo Javier
- Consuelo Alina
- Ethan Daniel

Contents

Prologue 9
Book I – Raíces ("Cuban Roots") 13
   Hometowns 13
   Family background and early years of Chelo and Jesús............ 19
   Last years in Cuba 56

Book II – Cataclysm: Our World Was Turned
                Upside Down!.. 61
   Revolution.. 61
   From Cuba to Philadelphia and Momence 67

Book III – Renaissance: Beginning of a new life 85
   Miami 85
   High School 93
   College 104

Book IV – Family... 115
   We finally get married! 115
   Start of our married life 122
   Family Christmas celebrations 124

Book V – Home!.. 135
   Book V – Part I – Atlanta 1969-1974 135
   Book V – Part II – Atlanta 1975-1983 152
   Book V – Part III – Atlanta 1983-1993 179

Book VI – Success! 213
   Book VI – Part I – Madrid 1993-1996....................................... 213
   Book VI - Part II – Maryland 1996-2008 240
   Book VI – Part III– Atlanta 2008-2019 279

Epilogue... 315

Postscript... 323

A few family photos 325
Appendices 341
    Appendix I – A brief introduction to Cuba 343
    Appendix II – Our Parents 351
    Appendix III – León-Cordero Genealogy 359
    Appendix IV – León-Cordero-Bills Family Milestones 369
    Appendix V – Anecdotes and interesting information 381
    Appendix VI – Excerpt of Argentina Marta Núñez
                  Berro's History 389

Prologue

The morning of October 10, 1960, was a typical Cuban fall day, awash with beautiful sunny blue skies and excellent temperature, perfect for the short flight to Miami. October 10, a major Cuban national holiday celebrating the beginning of Cuba's first War of Independence in 1868, meant there was little traffic on the Carretera Central as the León-Núñez family traveled to Camagüey Airport, approximately 70 miles west of their hometown where Jesús and his siblings were to catch a flight to Miami. Jesús was very familiar with the Tunas-Camagüey trip because he and his brother Ticó had made this trip many times while they attended a boarding school in Camagüey. What Jesús did not know was that he was not to see Cuba for a long time— it has been more than fifty years since he last set foot in his homeland. A few months later, on June 19, 1961, Chelo went through a similar experience when she left Cuba, flying from Havana's airport to Miami. Chelo was an only child traveling alone to a new country to live with strangers until her parents could join her. She, unlike Jesús, had never being separated from her family and had not experienced being on her own in a boarding school. Like Jesús, Chelo has not been back to Cuba in more than fifty years.

    We had no idea that our world was about to be turned upside down and our lives transformed from that of a tranquil Hispanic society into the lives of poor, politically exiled immigrants. We reminisce with amazement and gratitude at our struggles and successes and see in our story enough material for a television miniseries: the failure of our first attempt at a romance that eventually flourished; witnessing a medical miracle in our family; taking a big risk moving the family first to Europe and later to Maryland; Jesús being a suspect in France for an execution style double murder; and Jesús hospitalized in an intensive care unit of a Miami hospital with a mysterious illness on the eve of the wedding of his oldest niece MariCarmen.

These and many other events are part of the story of our lives, a story of love, perseverance, struggle and triumph. This book is a narrative of our lives, the lives of Jesús León Núñez and Consuelo L. Cordero Redruello, "Chelo." It recounts our childhood and early teenage years in Cuba and the pains of exile, our romance and how we forged a new life and built a family in the United States of America after the Cuban Revolution.

Our purpose in writing this memoir was to provide a summary of our life's history for our children and especially for our grandchildren. All human history is unique and ours recounts biographical facts and personal difficulties that we experienced leaving Cuba as teenagers without our parents, our struggle with a new culture, family separation, poverty, and the uncertainty of the unknown. This is a "coming of age story," a love story narrating how, in each other, we found our ideal mate, how we built a beautiful family and developed professional careers as we struggled through political, economic, and cultural challenges. It narrates our life experiences from our early years in Cuba to our retirement in the USA. It has been a life of dedication and sacrifice, but also a life blessed by a loving family and a rich community who taught, supported, and helped us through it all.

There are thousands of stories of struggle that resulted from the Cuban Diaspora. We know first hand the difficulties experienced by our parents, by Jesús' siblings, and by other relatives and friends. Each of their stories is worth telling for they confirm the resilience of the human spirit.

The memoirs are organized in a chronological order and we have made every effort to be accurate. However, we did not spend too much time verifying economical, historical or geographical details that only serve as framework and background to our life's history. Our desire was to make the book readable. We used a few sources about the history, geography, and the social-economical-political development of Cuba that we found useful— these are referenced in the footnotes. We are very thankful to all who helped us with facts and reviewed parts of the manuscript.

Two important points about the memoirs. First, most readers will find that these memoirs have a lot more details than might be considered necessary— we intentionally included many details in order to paint an expansive picture of our lives, especially for our grandchildren. Second, the document was not intended as and is not a work of literature— it is a summary of our lives, written in a simple narrative style. We ask the readers to forgive us for grammatical, syntax and any other errors.

We begin with a brief review of our lives in Cuba to provide a backdrop essential to understanding who we are, then narrate the difficulties we faced when we first came to the United States. We relate how we met, fell in love, then out of and back in love, married, raised a family, and achieved many successes at the personal, matrimonial, family and financial levels. And, yes, we will describe the unusual events that added spice to our life. But, first things first, let's start at the beginning, in Cuba, when the sun shined and our lives were uncomplicated.

Book I – Raíces ("Cuban Roots")

Hometowns

Unlikely and improbable are the words that would characterize the probability that Chelo and Jesús would marry had they stayed in Cuba. Their world traversed very different orbits separated primarily by geography, family traditions, schools, friends and social circles. Their only connection was the relationship between mutual cousins, Vicente and Bertica. Their hometowns could not be more different. Jesús lived in Victoria de las Tunas, a small town, in the easternmost Cuban Province, Oriente, while Chelo's hometown was the capital of Cuba, a large urbane metropolis.

Cuba

By 1940 Cuba had a population of more than four million people, a new constitution— the Constitution of 1940 — a new president, Fulgencio Batista, a military commander that led two coups. The first coup was in 1933; he was then elected President in 1940 and after serving his term, staged a second coup in 1952 and became a dictator until he fled Cuba on the wee hours of New Year's Day in 1959. Batista allowed the establishment of mob-influenced/mob-controlled casinos in many of the large hotels that catered to American tourists. Cuba in the 1950s was a country of contrasts. Cuba had an unstable political system with poor administrative structures but was, in some respects, a relatively advanced country. Data from the UN Statistical Yearbook, the Statistical Abstract for Latin America, and the Bureau of Inter-American Affairs, US Department of State, illustrates the economic and social situation: In the 1950s Cuba was, socially and economically, a relatively advanced country, certainly by Latin American standards and, in some areas, by world standards. Cuba's infant mortality rate was the best in Latin America— and the 13th lowest in the world. Cuba also had an excellent educational system and impressive literacy rates in the 1950s. Pre-Castro Cuba ranked third in Latin America in per capita food consumption.

"Cuba ranked first in Latin America and fifth in the world in television sets per capita. Pre-Castro Cuba had 58 daily newspapers of differing political hues and ranked eighth in the world in number of radio stations."[1] The economy depended on exports of sugar, cigars, and on an expansive tourist industry. It was most commonly American tourists who came to enjoy beautiful beaches, entertainment, low prices, gambling, American style hotels, and a currency that was pegged to the US dollar. In addition, there was no visa requirement, easy access with frequent flights from major US cities to La Habana and a daily ferry from Key West in which you could drive up with your car for personal use in Cuba. In 1960 the metropolitan La Habana region had approximately 1 million inhabitants. Over 70% of the Cuban people were ethnically white with about 12% black, 15% mulatto and less than 1% of Asian descent.[2]

Cuba was organized administratively after it gained its independence into six provinces starting in the West with Pinar del Rio, followed by the Province of La Habana the home of Cuba's capital, and the provinces of Matanzas, Las Villas, Camagüey and Oriente. A traveler driving east from La Habana on what was in the 1960s, the main Cuban Highway, La Carretera Central, would cross all the provincial capitals starting with the city of Pinar del Rio in the West and ending in the city of Santiago de Cuba in the East. Driving from the Province of La Habana on this highway, one passed near the world-famous Varadero Beach in Matanzas; then, to Las Villas Province, the site of the ill-fated Bay of Pigs invasion; next was Camagüey a province rich in cattle and sugar cane; last, the easternmost province of Cuba, Oriente, was the birthplace of many heroes

---

[1] See http://ctp.iccas.miami.edu/FACTS_Web/Cuba%20Facts%20Issue%2043%20December.htm for extensive details of Cuba's socio-economic conditions in the 1950s.
[2] Wikipedia: http://en.wikipedia.org/wiki/Cuba

of Cuban History, also of Fidel Castro's family, and the home of the León and Núñez families.

La Habana

The Spanish Conquistadores named present Habana as San Cristobal de La Habana. The words Habana and Cuba come from the language of native Cubans ("Indians") who lived in the island before the arrival of the Spanish Conquistadores. The city was founded in the early 16th century by the Spanish Conquistador Diego Velázquez and became a major strategic port for the Spanish Empire. La Habana's natural harbor is too narrow for many of today's ships but perfect for ships of the 15th to 19th centuries. The city was the geographically perfect location for the assembly of ships to travel between Spain and its American colonies. Ships sailed into or out of Havana together in a convoy, coming from or going to Seville, Spain. The section of the city built by the Spaniards is now called "La Habana Vieja" (literally, "Old Havana"). Over time the city added suburbs with colorful names like Marianao, Almendares, El Cerro, El Vedado, Miramar, and La Vibora.[3]

The city of Havana was the birthplace of notables like José Raúl Capablanca, World Chess Champion from 1921 to 1927; Ernesto Lecuona, a prolific composer; Celia Cruz, the Queen of Salsa; and, José Martí, poet, writer and intellectual leader of the Cuban Independence movement. La Habana had all the trappings of metropolitan cities with a symphony orchestra, famous ballerina Alicia Alonso, several professional baseball teams— one was the AAA League Cuban Sugar Kings— several luxury hotels and good restaurants, the world-famous Tropicana night club, wide avenues, a number of exclusive private clubs, a historical and excellent university (founded in 1728) and a large number of very good private schools, most under the direction of Catholic religious orders – Jesuits, Marists, Christian Brothers, Escolapios, Dominican sisters, Carmelites, Salesians. During the 1950s, the Augustinian order

---

[3] See Appendix I for a short introduction to Cuba.

founded a Catholic University, Santo Tomas de Villanueva, with a less politicized environment than the University of Havana although with fewer degree offerings.

This city of Havana was the birthplace and hometown of Chelo. She lived in the old section of Havana, on the corner of San Lázaro and Genios streets, one block south of the famous Malecón promenade along the harbor in the old city. Her living quarters belonged to her grandparents, Francisco (Pancho) Redruello and Consuelo Berdasco, immigrants from El Vidural village in Asturias, Northern Spain. They had come to Cuba as part of the one million Spanish immigrants that arrived between 1900 and 1930.[4] Pancho was a hardworking man who established a very successful "Bodega"— a combination of grocery, lunch counter, and bar. The bodega was a couple of blocks from "El Castillo de San Salvador de la Punta" where members of the Cuban Navy were stationed. La Punta was one of the two fortresses protecting the channel entry into the bay of Havana, the other being the distinctive Morro Castle. Pancho's Bodega was a popular place for Cuban Navy personnel stationed at La Punta Fortress, where they often met at the bodega for a beer, sandwich or "galleta preparada" with friends after work.

In Havana, the Carnival was held annually like the Rio de Janeiro and New Orleans celebrations before Ash Wednesday. The Havana Carnival lasted four weeks and included, in addition to balls and costume parties, parades with floats and convertibles full of young men and women. There were also "comparsas" (groups organized by neighborhoods or associations who would wear colorful rumba dresses and dance the parade route to their own special conga music). Each comparsa had a special name like "Las Jardineras" and "Los Dandys" The comparsas danced through the streets of Havana and Chelo was able to watch them from her bedroom balcony. On several occasions, Chelo with three of her best friends rode in a convertible car as part of "El Paseo del Carnaval" held on Sunday afternoons.

---

[4] Wikipedia, op. cit.

Tunas

Victoria de las Tunas is about 375 miles east of La Habana but, for all practical purposes, Tunas is in a different galaxy when one compares the political, economical, cultural and social life of this small town with that of the capital.

Driving east into Oriente Province from Camagüey, brought the driver to Victoria de las Tunas, a city located in an area known geographically as the Camagüey-Tunas-Holguín "sabana"— the English word savannah, meaning a treeless plain, is derived from this Spanish noun. This savannah had a rich, fertile soil great for cattle grazing and for growing sugar cane. It boasted several of the world largest sugar refining mills such as the Delicias and Chaparra mills, and many cattle ranches including a number of ranches owned by León Family members with colorful names like Palmarito and Santa Rosa. Although inland, Tunas is not far from the location of Christopher Columbus first landing in Cuba on October 28, 1492.

Today, Tunas has grown to become the capital of one of the new provinces created by Castro's Government in 1976 as part of a reorganization of the provincial administration. However, at the time of Jesús departure from Cuba in 1960, Tunas was a small town built in the tradition of the Spanish villages with the parish church, St. Jerome, in the center of the main square. Around the main square were the city hall, a few small hotels and cafeterias, and a variety of small stores. A few minutes walk from the main square is another smaller public square, El Parque Maceo, named for Antonio Maceo, a hero of the Wars of Independence; El Parque Maceo was a couple hundred feet from the León house. Jesús and his siblings played and rode bikes at the Maceo Park as children. Tunas was home to many León family members and several of Jesús' relatives lived near his house.

Because Tunas was a small town, Jesús walked or biked everywhere. There were no traffic lights, not even where the Central Highway crossed the center of the town by the main square and the City Hall. Tunas had limited educational facilities as there were only a couple of private elementary schools, one high school and one business school that prepared students with basic business skills. The size of Tunas' telephone switchboard was a proxy for the size of the town. The telephone number at Jesús' home and Rigoberto León's pharmacy was a party line with the number 113, so that 113-1 was the home number and 113-2 the pharmacy's number.

Although education and other services were limited in Tunas, the quality of medical services was one of the bright spots of the city in the 1960s. Medical services were limited until the early 1950s when a young group of doctors came into town and founded a full service clinic, Nuestra Señora de Loreto. These doctors provided basic and specialist health care including major surgery. Before the arrival of the clinic doctors, there was essentially only primary care and the quality of this care was inconsistent and depended on the particular doctor selected.

In Tunas, almost everyone knew everyone else in town, which was a blessing and a curse— all pranks and misbehaviors were reported to your house immediately. On the other hand, people visited each other frequently, especially after supper staying long enough to savor a cup of Cuban coffee and share the latest news and gossip. Town residents often met and interacted socially at open-air concerts, after Sunday Mass, and in activities sponsored by one of the social clubs (there were three for white people: El Liceo, La Colonia Española and el Club de Leones; and one club for blacks). Entertainment for the locals was limited to the already mentioned weekly concerts, a few movie theaters and special events such as the annual carnival.

Once a year Tunas held a "carnival" that lasted for a week or so. The carnival in many Cuban towns was a mixture of the Spanish "Romería" and the French "Mardi Gras." It consisted of costume parties, general revelry, eating, drinking, dancing and other festivities. However, the carnival was not held on the days before Ash Wednesday but following the custom of the Spanish Romería, during the week celebrating the patron saint of the town.[5] In Tu-

---

[5] The celebration of the carnival around the date of the city's patron feast day is why Fidel Castro's revolutionary movement was called the 26 of July Move-

nas, the carnival concluded on September 30, the feast of St. Jerome, the patron saint of the city.

Tunas' economy was based on cattle ranching and the seasonal activities of the sugar refining industry. Cattle ranching was a year-around activity but not so for the sugar industry. Sugar cane was cut during the "zafra," a period of 4-5 months in the early part of the year. It was cut by hand with machetes and sent to the sugar mills for processing. The persons that worked in the zafra were employed for a few months of the year and had to scramble to earn a living the rest of the year.

Family background and early years of Chelo and Jesús

Chelo's grandfather, Francisco Manuel "Pancho" Redruello, was originally from El Vidural, a picturesque hill village in the region of Asturias, Spain. He immigrated to Cuba at the age of fourteen and returned to Spain at age twenty-four to marry his cousin Consuelo Berdasco[6] and together they moved to Cuba to raise a family. Pancho and Consuelo had six children, three boys and three girls. The two oldest boys contracted and died of the "Spanish Flu" influenza at a very young age while traveling in a ship with their mother and their sister Carmen to Spain in 1918. Chelo's aunt, Generosa ("Tata"), was born in 1919 at their ancestral home in El Vidural, Spain. Pancho, Consuelo, Carmen and Generosa returned to Cuba where Consuelín, Chelo's mom, was born in Havana on April 13, 1921. The third boy, Paco, died of colon cancer at the age of thirty-three in 1956. The death of the oldest two boys left a lasting impact on Consuelo but it was clear to Chelo that the death of the youngest boy, Paco, was devastating to her grandmother who wore black in his memory for the rest of her life.

---

ment. Fidel and his group attacked the Moncada barracks in Santiago de Cuba on the early hours of the day following the feast of the city's patron saint, Santiago, the biggest day of the Santiago Carnival.

[6] Consuelo María del Carmen Berdasco Garrido.

The three sisters, Carmen, Generosa and Consuelín lived long lives and two of them formed families. Carmen married a Galician immigrant, Vicente Fernández Pérez, and had three children: Vicente, Adolfo and Virginia ("Mimi"). Carmen, Vicente and their children lived in the Marianao District of La Habana until the untimely death of Vicente senior in January 1959; Generosa remained single and lived with Consuelín most of her life, first in La Habana and later in Miami.

Consuelín met Lorenzo Cordero Salcines, a tall and handsome member of the Cuban Navy, at Pancho's Bodega and later married him. Cordero or "Lore," as he was known by most of his friends and family, was born on November 28, 1912, in the upscale Vedado district of La Habana, the son of a Spanish immigrant from the Santander region, Marcelino Cordero Alcalde, and of a first-generation Cuban lady, Leopoldina Salcines Beci. At the time of Cordero's birth, the family was affluent but they lost the majority of their fortune during the depression of the 1930s. Cordero had five sisters and two brothers: Rosarito, Manuelita ("Tita"), María Eloisa ("Cuyo"), Estela, and Margot; his two brothers were Marcelinito (who died as a young boy) and Rafael ("Nano"), the youngest of the family. Margot, Estela and their children left Cuba during the 1960s and lived in Miami the rest of their lives. Cordero attended school through secondary education at the Escuelas Pías of El Cerro (Havana). He was close to his siblings and their progeny, visiting them often. Cordero loved all sports but especially baseball at which he excelled: he played organized baseball for the Cuban Navy and eventually at the semiprofessional level.

Cordero and Consuelín were married on January 16, 1944, and Chelo was born in La Habana on Thursday, the 28th day of December 1944, the feast of the Holy Innocents, at the Clínica Católicas Cubanas, a particularly Cuban form of HMO. American health professionals call this type of clinic common in Cuba a "medical home." Families paid a monthly fee to a particular clinic and used it for all their healthcare needs. Many members chose a clinic because of family or ancestry connections: for example, most of the members of the Covadonga Clinic were Spanish people from Asturias; others chose their clinic because of gender or type of care: the Clínicas Católicas Cubanas provided healthcare services for children and women only.

Chelo relates her early years in a very personal way: "I was a healthy, robust baby, weighting almost 10 pounds at birth. My mother Consuelín was a petite woman; it is hard to believe that she could have carried such a big girl. My dad, on the other hand, was a well-built, tall and full-bodied man."

"It is a peculiar and interesting fact that I was born on Holy Innocents Day, the equivalent of April Fools' Day in the United States. However, there is a big difference in significance and meaning between the Cuban and the American concept of tricking or playing a joke in a person's life. For us, Cubans, when we want to fool a person, we call him/her "inocente." In other words, we consider the person to be child-like, innocent, naïve. On the other hand, the Americans call the person a fool. The American usage has always struck me as somewhat derogatory especially because I was born on a day that bears the fool implication. Anyway, regardless of the difference in cultural meanings, my father was tricked on the day I was born. He thought that family and friends were joking with him when they told him that I was a girl. Like most men of his generation, fathers wanted their first-born to be male. Nevertheless, the fact that I was a girl proved to be a great treasure to my dad. I know for sure that I brought plenty of joy, pride, and happiness to my dad, and I had the great blessing and fortune to enjoy his love, guidance, wisdom and companionship for 62 years of my life. It is noteworthy to mention that later in my life, my mom and aunt Tata reminded me of my dad's early disappointment. I know they did not mean to offend; they just wanted to tell me that they loved me from the very first day of my existence. The incredible thing is that over the years, my father and I treasured a very special connection.

Chelo continues, "I have to admit that I was a very blessed child. Both of my parents loved, protected and cared for me immensely, each in his/her own way and personality. My mom was the "resolvedora" (problem solver) type; she made sure that I had everything I needed. She would go out of her way to provide for my safety, health and security. For example, she would set her alarm, get up, wake me up and stay with me while I studied at the early hour of five in the morning. She also researched and located clippings and other materials that I needed for my school projects and compositions. My mom's energy and disposition were unparalleled. She went out of her way to help others and she was a very task-oriented person. She would never give up a task until she completed it successfully."

"My dad, on the other hand, was the affectionate type, he showered me with hugs and kisses, and often told me how great I was. My dad, one of the persons I have loved the most, showed me, through his actions how to express love. He was the epitome of a perfect gentleman: nice, pleasant, handsome, well groomed and mannered, kind, friendly, lovable, diplomatic, jovial, happy, and more. When I was a little girl, I recall my dad calling me by different names as he was coming home. One of his favorite nicknames for me was "my monita peluza."[7] Heavens know why he gave me this title! I didn't look like a monkey and I was not hairy. Even though the phrase sounds weird and kind of odd, I really liked it and looked forward to him calling me by this name. I remembered stopping whatever I was doing and running to meet him with a big hug and kiss whenever I heard him calling me. What an awesome experience!"

While Chelo did not have the privilege of meeting her paternal grandmother Leopoldina who died in her early fifties of a heart attack, due to high blood pressure, Chelo learned a lot about her paternal grandmother from her dad's stories. According to her dad, she was an exemplary mother, always attentive to her children's needs and affection. Chelo's dad recalled the many times that she would wait for him when, as a teenager, he would stay out late to about midnight. Abuela Leopoldina was an excellent cook and Cordero shared with Chelo some of her recipes; for example,

---

[7] This is quite difficult to translate to English. Monita means little monkey, something that might be taken as scornful. Peluza is a word used to describe hair or lint. A non-literal translation that illustrates its meaning could be a phrase such as "my little cutie pie" or "my dear little sunshine."

adding papitas (potatoes) to the picadillo (the Cuban typical ground beef dish) and adding plantains to either the frijoles colorados (red beans) or carne con papas (beef stew, substituting the plantains for the potatoes). Many years later, after she was married, Chelo treasured every time that Cordero compared her cooking to his mother's because "my dad looked up to his mother and I could tell by his narratives that he loved her immensely."

Chelo did know her paternal grandfather, Marcelino, very well. He was a short, temperate, well-groomed, attractive blue-eyed guy with excellent manners and a distinct personality. Abuelo Marcelino liked to talk and his conversations were very interesting because he knew a lot of Cuban history and was a great storyteller. He lived in a house near Mazorra, the hospital for demented people in La Habana. Chelo recalled visiting his house once or twice when he was sick. She remembers him always wearing an impeccable long-sleeved white guayabera with a hat, and the smell of cologne. Every Wednesday morning abuelo Marcelino came to visit Cordero and Chelo at their house in La Habana and he stayed for lunch. He always brought a white bag,"un cartuchito blanco," full of candies and chocolate. To this date, more than sixty years later, Chelo recalls how the cookies, and chocolates looked and tasted! Because lunch was the main meal in Chelo's household, huge amounts of food appeared on the table every day. Today, Chelo often wonders how people were able to work, study, and function after these large meals.

Chelo was christened Consuelo Leopoldina María Inocenta Cordero Redruello on the 18 of February 1945 by Father Juan José Lobato at the Monserrat Parish Church. Her four names represented family and cultural traditions. Consuelo is the common family name on the maternal side— both her mother and grandmother first names were Consuelo; Leopoldina is for her paternal grandmother; María is a name used by many Hispanic Catholic families to honor the Blessed Virgin Mary; and Inocenta because she was born on Holy Innocents day. Her godparents were Francisco Redruello Berdasco (maternal grandfather) and Rosario Cordero Salcines (aunt on her father's side of the family).

After her christening, Chelo lived with her grandparents, Pancho and Consuelo, her parents, her aunt Generosa and her uncle Paco in a house with address San Lázaro 101. The house was located on a corner bounded by Genios and Industria streets, one block south of the Malecón[8] and three blocks from the La Punta Fortress at the entrance to the Havana Harbor. Pancho's Bodega was on the first floor with entrances to the bodega from both San Lazaro and Genios streets. Walking up the stairs, the Redruello Berdasco household was on the left with neighbors on the right of the stairs landing. The house had a living room and a "saleta," the later a less formal sitting room, a dining room, the kitchen, four bedrooms for the family and one bedroom for the live-in maid. There was only one bathroom for everyone in the household. Each bedroom had a balcony and there was a large terrace at the back of the house. Consuelo, Pancho and Paco slept in one of the rooms, Cordero and Consuelín in a second room and Chelo and Generosa in another room. This was adjusted in early 1959 when Carmen, Vicente, Adolfo and "Mimi" moved into the house after the death of Carmen Redruello's husband. Carmen and her children moved into Chelo and Generosa's room because this room gave them some autonomy. Chelo and Generosa moved to what had been the living room and the "saleta" became the living room. Needless to say, this was somewhat crowded because like most houses in Cuba, there was only one bathroom. The living arrangement of Chelo's family is an example of common Hispanic practice to live in an extended family group. The extended family living experience has its benefits and drawbacks. One of its advantages is the built-in baby sitter and the support system. However, there is lack of privacy, and everyone has a say and an opinion on everything. Now, having lived more than 47 years in a small family circle, husband and children, Chelo thinks it would be hard to return to the extended family household style.

---

[8] The Malecón is a beautiful roadway with large sidewalk along the seacoast from the entrance to the Bay of Havana to the Vedado District.

The neighbors on the right of the stairs were three sisters, Fina, Celia and Mercedes García. Fina had two sons while Celia and Mercedes never married. Celia spoke English well and worked for Frigidaire, an American company. Another sister, Mary, worked for Westinghouse and married a US Navy Sailor and together they had a son, Jack Bell. The sisters had two nieces, Elena and Susana, whose parents, Tomasín and Hortensia, lived in a farm in Artemisa about 50 miles west from Havana. The girls went to school in Havana and lived with their aunts. The girls' parents seldom came to Havana but their daughters visited them every Sunday and spent the summers with their parents. Chelo loved to visit this farm with the girls even though it was very rustic— there was no running water, one had to take a bath using water in pans, and one had to use a mosquito net over the bed at night.

Chelo's household was run by Chelo's grandmother, Consuelo, and she adhered to Spanish not Cuban traditions. Chelo was a second generation Cuban and she grew up in a Spanish household run by immigrants— her grandmother kept her Spanish citizenship to her death— and so she only ate Cuban food when outside of her home, at a friend's house or at Tarará during the summer. Instead, the home cooking at her house was distinctly Spanish with dishes like Fabada Asturiana and Cocido Madrileño designed for cooler weather but served in the very hot climate of Cuba. There were also Pulientas (corn flour with milk) and Frixuelos (Asturian version of the crepes). Pancho ate the Asturian version of the "sopa de ajo" (garlic soup) every night.

During the week, the daily routine for the Redruello household began with breakfast followed by the departure of everyone except abuela Consuelo. Pancho went to the bodega, Cordero to his Navy job, Consuelín to the Café Pilón, Generosa to La Época Department store and Chelo to school. Abuela Consuelo remained with the maids and the assistant cook because she was the principal cook. Lola was a live-in maid, the assistant cook, washed dishes and ran errands. Another maid was in charge of cleaning and a third one was responsible for washing and ironing. Chelo remembers two major changes to this routine: the first happened with the long illness of Chelo's uncle Paco and the second with the arrival of Carmen and her children. Carmen did not work so she stayed at the house but her children Adolfo and Mimi went to school. Vicente, the oldest, went to work during the day at the Núñez Bank and went to the secondary instituto (state high school) in the evening. As was the custom in Cuba, all eleven residents came to lunch everyday and everyone ate this meal together. At night everyone, except Pancho, ate dinner together. Pancho would eventually come home from the bodega when his schedule permitted and Consuelo would serve him the "sopa de ajo."

When Chelo was a little girl, Cordero used to take her to the park to play or to the Malecón to ride skates or "carriola" (a two-wheel contraction with a steering mechanism that was propelled by pushing with one foot). Sometimes the girls next door accompanied them. Because Consuelín worked on Saturday mornings, on Sunday Chelo and her parents would go out sometimes to visit Cordero's siblings (Nano, Rosarito, Margot or Estela) and their family or go out with Cordero's friends to lunch at El Centro Vasco or El Pollo Pampero or some other place.

As was common in the middle and upper class Cuban households, Chelo did not do nor did she know how to do any household chores— she did not even hang her clothes. Cooking, washing, ironing, cleaning and other household chores were primarily the responsibility of the servants. Although Consuelo actively directed and helped with the cleaning, this was probably due to the genetic disposition of all Redruellos to cleanliness. The ignorance on how to do basic household chores, such as making a bed, would come to haunt Chelo and most other Cuban children when they reached the USA. They were not prepared to handle the chores typical of the American household.

Chelo continues her recollection of her first few years: "Like many people, I do not recall much of the very early years of my life. I was raised mainly by my maternal grandmother, my abuela Consuelo, whom I called on many occasions, "abuelera," a term very endearing to her. My mom and aunts always told me she was very strict and hard to get to know; however, my childhood years with her were very happy. She showered me with lots of love and affection. Since my mom worked outside the home my abuela was always there for me. She bathed, cooked and fed me as a baby and child. She taught me to play Spanish card games such as Brisca, Tute, Subastado, and also enjoyed playing Parcheesi with me. By the way, parchís, as we call this game, is a Cuban household fun activity. It was probably my grandmother who taught me the Lord's Prayer and the Hail Mary. She was the person that took me to Church every Sunday morning at eight o'clock to attend Mass. It was with her that I participated in Holy Week processions, Stations of the Cross, and prayed the rosary. She definitely influenced my Catholic experience." Abuela Consuelo, Chelo and her uncle Paco were the only members of the household that attended church regularly.

As was the custom in Cuba, Chelo was prepared for and received her First Holy Communion with her schoolmates at the American Dominican Academy. She had the privilege to receive her First Holy Communion from the then cardinal of Cuba, Cardenal Manuel Arteaga, at the school's Coronela campus on May 6, 1952.

There were a few weekly visitors to the Redruello household: Cordero's father, Marcelino, on Wednesdays; Celestino, Carmen's godfather, would always come for lunch on Thursday; Pepe, Consuelo's cousin who also owned a Bodega came every Sunday afternoon; Manolo, another relative of Consuelo who also owned a bodega, stopped by once a week. Chelo recalls Celestino's appetite and remembers her grandmother Consuelo warning him about his eating and that his reply to her was always: "Mujer, si muero, muero farto" ("Woman, if I die, I die sated"). Occasionally there were visitors or family members from Spain who stayed in the house. Chelo remembers that abuela Consuelo's relatives were the godparents of her uncle, aunts and mom: Celestino of Carmen, Panchín and Soledad of Consuelo, and Arduras of Paco. Panchín and Arduras lived in Spain and they visited the family in Havana from time to time staying in the house for several weeks when they came.

Pancho owned a big bodega, a facility that combined a grocery store with a luncheon area and a bar with standing room only. Pancho's bodega was not only the main family business, it was the center of life at the San Lazaro and Genios house. Pancho owned, directed and, at times, worshiped the bodega, practically living there even though he had several employees; Chelo remembers the names of three of them: Manolo, Pepe and Antonio. Pancho was at the bodega from daybreak to closing. The bodega was open all the time— he once served customers through a small door in the middle of a hurricane! Consuelo had to phone him several times every day to ask him to come for lunch and dinner while Lola brought Pancho a "merienda," the mid-afternoon snack that consisted of a "café con leche." Pancho was known for his frugality. To quote Chelo: "My mom and aunts, Tata and tía Carmen, used to tell me how hard it was for them to buy a pair of shoes or get anything from him. They had to make a few trips to the bodega to convince him to give them the money; many times, they got tired and gave up causing my abuela to end up sewing their clothes. It is hard to believe that this same man would give the food and goods of his bodega to his clients on credit but resist paying for his family's material needs. My mom liked to work at the bodega and was there often to help her father. Her task at the bodega was to prepare the notices to the customers requesting the payment of their IOUs. One of the bodega's employees would then take the IOUs to the customers. The mission of collecting what was owed to Pancho was seldom accomplished. Because of the easy credit to his customers, my dad used to call him, 'Pancho, the benefactor of San Lázaro Street.'"

Chelo's parents were also industrious like Pancho. Cordero was a member of the Cuban Navy and Consuelín worked for the Pilón Coffee Company, also known as "La Flor de Tibes," a coffee packaging and distribution company. She was the assistant to the cashier in charge of collecting the money from all salesmen and making sure that the purchases and money balanced. She was very good at her job since she excelled in math and consequently, enjoyed her job tremendously. She was very hard working, like her parents and always ready to run errands for others. Cordero and Consuelín were able to build a couple of houses in Havana that they rented out for income and retirement, houses that Castro confiscated. Unlike women of her era, Consuelín never learned to cook, sew, iron or do other household chores. Even when she immigrated to the United States in 1961, she never learned to do these tasks. She thoroughly found pleasure in doing other things like shopping, going to the beauty parlor and running errands outside the house for the entire family.

Generosa worked at a department store called La Época. She was the manager of the scarves, wallets and handkerchiefs department. She was and still is very meticulous and detail oriented with beautiful penmanship and fine motor skills. Tata used to dress like a princess: all her clothes were beautifully tailored and hand-sewn. Chelo still remembers her embroidered linen blouses; clearly she had a refined taste for good clothes and expensive jewelry, something that had to change when she came to live in the United States. Consuelín, unlike Tata, never showed an interest in clothes or fine jewelry. Chelo's uncle, Paco, the youngest of her mom's siblings, and according to the sisters, Consuelo's favorite child worked as a clerk in a law firm. He was easy-going, pleasant and good-natured. He died of cancer when Chelo was twelve years old, and his illness really impacted the family life. Chelo's abuela stayed in his hospital room for over one year and cared for him until he left this world. Everyone did what they could to cater to Paco's needs during his illness: Tata bought him a television set so he could watch his favorite programs at the hospital; Chelo's mother took him lunch and dinner every single day from home so he would not have to eat hospital food, and the rest of the family visited him frequently. He was the most religious and spiritual of the Redruello children and, at his deathbed, he told his mother to be at peace because he was going to be with God. After his death, Chelo's abuela became sick and was very sad. Chelo remembers trying to entertain her because she knew that Paco was a very special person in her grandmother's life; Consuelo yearned for Chelo's company and consequently they became very close. She was extremely affectionate to Chelo, kissing and hugging her all the time, and she expected in return that Chelo do the same for her. Chelo returned her grandmother's love whenever she could with actions like combing her hair, which she thoroughly enjoyed, and playing games when Chelo was not busy with her studies.

On her father's side, Chelo remembers that his sisters Margot and Estela resided in three different locations, first in the Luyano District when Chelo was a child, then in Tarará Beach which is about 13 miles east of Havana and later in the La Vibora District. The Tarará house was very nice but it was inconvenient for school and so they rented a house in La Vibora during the school year. Margot and her husband Ramón Agulló owned the Tarará house and they lived there with their three children: Margarita, "Monchi" (Ramón) and Roberto. Estela, her husband Armando and their three children, Teresita, Estelita and Armandito lived with Margot. Ramón was the owner of the Agulló Soap Factory in Havana.

Chelo started school after her fifth birthday. She was enrolled in a Catholic school established and directed by American Dominican Sisters of St. Catherine de' Ricci that had two locations in Havana: a day school in central Havana (Vedado) and a boarding school at La Coronela, a neighborhood about 5 miles from the center of La Habana. Why go to an American school in Cuba? Consuelín had struggled with English during her education and did not want Chelo to have this problem.

Almost all of the primary education and the majority of the secondary education in Cuba were imparted in private schools. There were a number of public high schools, "institutos," but these were few and located only in larger cities. Tunas, for example, did not have an instituto, the nearest one being in Holguín, 50 miles away. The institutos were the only educational institutions that could provide official certification that a person had satisfied the requirements to enter a Cuban university. Students at private schools had to take and pass examinations graded by the instituto's subject matter teachers in order to obtain the official state certification.

La Habana and many Cuban cities and towns had private schools, many offering primary and secondary education while others offered only primary education. The majority of the private schools were under the direction of a religious order of the Catholic Church although there were a number of non-religious schools, most notably Baldor in La Habana, an excellent coed secular school. There were a few religious, non-Catholic schools, like the "Colegio Los Amigos" (Friendship School) of the Quakers in

Holguín, the school that Estela León, Jesús' cousin attended. Bertica (Estela's sister), Vicente, Adolfo and Mimi (Chelo's cousins) attended Methodist schools in Havana, Buena Vista and Candler College, respectively. Additionally, there were schools that taught a number of the subjects in a language other than Spanish so that students would be somewhat fluent in a second language. Among these foreign language schools were two Catholic schools: The American and French Dominican Schools.

Chelo attended the Vedado School of the American Dominican Academy (ADA). Like many private schools, it offered education from Kindergarten ("Pre-Primario") to twelfth grade. The ADA was an all-girls school, a characteristic of Catholic schools in Cuba, which were mostly all-boys or all-girls. The students at private schools in Cuba had to wear a uniform that did not change from generation to generation so that everyone knew the student's school by the uniform one was wearing. Chelo's uniform consisted of a black jumper with a white, short-sleeved, linen blouse. She also had a gala uniform that included a blazer, a long-sleeved white linen blouse, and a beret (beanie, bonnet); the gala uniform was only worn for special occasions. Since she, like all other girls in the school, attended the same school for her primary and secondary education, friendships bloomed over the years and Chelo cherished and met later with her former schoolmates regularly over the years.

Chelo was an excellent student with a complete dedication to do well; she always earned the best grades and the prize for excellence in the majority of her subjects. Throughout her elementary school she was ranked first in her class and in high school she was always among the top three students. She was so obsessive about her grades that Cordero used to tell her he was worried about her health. Cordero thought she was going to get sick for studying too much since Chelo used to get up very early in the morning to review before every test. Cordero used to kid her saying that he would frame a report card that showed a grade of D or F, but, of course, that never happened! Chelo recounts, "The only time that I recall in my life that 'Pipo' (the nickname I called my dad) got really mad at me was when he believed that I was going to go crazy because I was studying too much. So he threw my books from the balcony. My dad also got mad at my mom for being my accomplice since she also got up early with me whenever I had to study. My mom also made sure that all my assignments had the best picture cutouts and decorations. She went to many stores to find the perfect ribbons, stickers and photos for my 'masterpieces.' Of course, my reports were always exhibited, and the teachers used my notebooks, compositions and posters as examples to my classmates of excellent work."

The rhythm of daily life for most students in Cuba was punctuated with a two-hour break at midday with many children returning home for their lunch, although some students paid extra to stay and eat at school. The distance from Chelo's house to the ADA was about three miles and the time required to go to school depended on the traffic. Chelo's transportation to school during part of her primary school was on a school bus. Because of the bus route, Chelo was the last one to be dropped off before lunch and the first to be picked up after which means she had to hurry to eat lunch; for this reason, for part of her elementary school, a hired car (the driver was named Silverio) would take her to and bring her back from school. For high school, however, the class schedule was different with a short morning break so Chelo carpooled with two other girls. In fact, the ADA high school followed the American high school curriculum so that at graduation one received a high school diploma, while girls who wanted to receive the Cuban bachillerato (high school) diploma had to attend one of the public institutos or another private school in order to complete the course work required.

On returning from school, except for Wednesdays when Consuelín had the afternoon off, Chelo's grandmother would greet her and prepare her "merienda". On Wednesdays, Chelo and her mother would go to the ten-cent-store (F. W. Woolworth) situated in the center of the shopping district, about one-half mile from their house, also very near the church of Nuestra Señora de Monserrat where Chelo went to Mass with her grandmother. Chelo would eat a club sandwich and a sundae for merienda! On other days, Chelo would walk with Lola to a nearby Chinese ice cream parlor that made excellent ice creams with tropical fruit flavors such as Mamey, Guanabana and Mango. On Wednesdays, after the merienda, Consuelín would go to the beauty parlor and when Chelo reached her teenage years, she began to have her nails done at the same beauty parlor.

Chelo completed her sophomore year in the ADA before having to leave Cuba. High school classes at the American Dominican School were taught in English. Going to an American School and becoming fluent in English was a great gift for Chelo when she arrived in the United States: Who was to know how useful learning English proficiently was going to be? Later in Miami and Momence, Illinois, it was a lifesaver. During her sophomore year, in 1959, she celebrated her fifteenth birthday with a Mass and breakfast at her school. Celebration of a girl's fifteenth birthday was, in the Cuban tradition, the equivalent of a debutant ball— the recognition that the girl was ready to participate in social activities.

Jesús was born on October 23, 1944, in a private residence on Morales Lemus Street in the city of Holguín, Cuba, about 50 miles east of Victoria de las Tunas. He was baptized on November 12 by his godfather, Father José Lence, at his parents' house, Morales Lemus 64, and inscribed in the San José Parish of Holguín. His godmother was his maternal aunt, María del Carmen Núñez Berro, a brilliant and forceful person who lived next door to the León-Núñez family in Holguín.

Jesús was a third generation Cuban on both sides of his family tree. His great-great grandparents had come from Spain, one great-great grandparent from the Galicia region of Spain and the others from the Canary Islands. His father, Rigoberto Amado León Díaz, was the thirteenth child of Benjamín León and Luisa Díaz and had been born in the family house in the small village of San Agustín de Aguaras. Near San Agustín were several of the León family ranches, Miguel León's Pharmacy and the Trabanco-León General Store. All of Rigoberto's siblings lived in the Tunas-Holguín region. Rigoberto and his brother Miguel had studied pharmacy and both married professional women, Rigoberto to Argentina Núñez, a teacher, and Miguel to Berta González, a pharmacist. Jesús had a large number of León first cousins, a number so large that the family held three "León Cousins reunions."[9]

Jesús' mother, Argentina Marta Núñez Berro,[10] was born in a cattle ranch on the Cauto River, near the village of Tiguabos, not far from the historical city of Bayamo. She was one of seven surviving children of Manuel Núñez and Carmen Berro, both teachers and rancher owners. The surviving children were two girls, María del Carmen and Argentina, and five boys, René, Germán, Regilio, Manuel, and Rubén. María, Argentina and Rubén earned university degrees, María earned five degrees.

At the time of Jesús' birth, María lived in Holguín but she later moved to La Habana. Rubén, a pharmacist, lived in Holguín with his wife Lila and his two daughters, Lilita and Ileana. A common denominator of the Núñez Berro men was multiple marriages. Regilio, who lived and eventually bought all the shares of the family ranch near Tiguabos, had eight children from three marriages; all his children lived with him at the ranch. German lived in Bayamo, was employed by the telegraph company and had two sons, Germancito and Arturito, each with a different wife. Jesús' uncle Manolo lived in Holguín until he left Cuba in 1961; he was married twice and fathered more than seven children, five with her first wife, Anita, two with his second wife, Guillermina, and several with women near Tiguabos. Another uncle, René, had chosen to emigrate to the USA in the 1940s and first lived in New York City and later moved to Miami. René had three wives and at least five children: two girls, Nilda and Bertha, from his marriage with Camelia and three children, America, Barbara and Renecito, from his second marriage to Marina. In his old age he married one more time. Rubén remarried many years after Jesús left Cuba. All the children of these marriages got along with their step siblings, except the children of Manolo, who never met each other.

---

[9] The first reunion was in Tunas and the other two in Miami. The last two had more than 200 participants each. Carmen Luisa told us that at one time she counted 120 León cousins.

[10] Appendix VI has Argentina's notes about her very interesting family history.

Rigoberto and Argentina were married in December 20, 1943, and lived in Holguín until 1948, when they moved to Victoria de las Tunas where they resided until the family's departure to the USA. Jesús' brother, Rigober<u>tico</u> (Ticó) was also born in Holguín, on February 1, 1946, a little bit over fifteen months after Jesús. Ticó and Jesús were close in age but had different personalities, and since both had inherited the stubbornness of the Núñez genes, they often fought (fist fights) while growing up. Ticó, because of his genetic makeup and probably to differentiate himself from Jesús, was always a rebel: throughout his life, given a choice, he would choose a path that was different from that of others regardless of the difficulty or rationality.

Jesús had reasonably good health except when, as a toddler, he was afflicted with an infection that caused fever and skin swelling all over his body. The cure to this infection was to remove his tonsils and adenoids, an operation that was done before his second birthday. After this surgery, Jesús had good health suffering only from occasional common colds and the measles when he was fifteen years old. In the USA he contracted meningitis in Philadelphia at sixteen, chickenpox at twenty-eight, pneumonia at thirty-four while working in Iran, and polymyalgia rheumatica at fifty-eight years of age. As a small child, Jesús had problems drinking cow's milk and he was given milk from a goat named "Marta" that was kept around the house to be milked regularly. There is a photo of Jesús and the goat taken during a summer vacation they spent in Gibara, a beach in Oriente Province, a few kilometers west of the location where Columbus first landed in Cuba. The family considered "baños de mar" (ocean bathing) a healthy part of life, and because they lived inland, they made it a point to spend time at the beach during the summer months.

Jesús' dental issues started when he was about ten years of age when he fell on the "zaguán" (service entrance to the house), hitting his mouth and damaging one of his front teeth. His parents took him to La Habana to a dentist near El Malecón who did a root canal without anesthesia— Jesús has never forgotten the pain of that root canal. The tooth was saved and Jesús did not have a "hole" in the front of the mouth, but because of the time that passed before the root canal, the tooth became darker than the others around it. This tooth was part of a painful dental experience for Jesús including the extraction of a wrong tooth, a canine instead of a molar, the unauthorized preparation for a five-tooth bridge when only a three-tooth bridge was necessary, and gum issues that Jesús blamed on this last procedure.

Argentina related an interesting anecdote about Jesús when in Holguín at an early age: One day Jesús "disappeared" and could not be located, neither at his house nor at his aunt María del Carmen's house next door. Argentina and others searched for him and eventually found him staring at the altar of their parish church— he had walked alone the two blocks from the house. The fact that Jesús went to the parish church indicated the respect and fervor that he felt for the Catholic faith, a faith he had witnesses in his parents, both devout and active Catholics.

The house in Tunas where the León family moved upon arrival from Holguín was spacious and originally consisted of a living room, dining room, kitchen, four bedrooms and one bath. The last two bedrooms opened into an interior courtyard where the kitchen was located. Rigoberto and Argentina modified the house by enclosing the courtyard so that from the dining room and the last two bedrooms one could walk into a hallway. Next to the hallway and connecting to the kitchen, they built a dining area for daily meals. In the hallway were several Cuban rocking chairs, a small television set with its stand, and at the end a built-in work desk. This area had a door with a secure lock opening to the patio area. The house, located at Maceo 108, was also the home of Argentina's mother, María del Carmen Juliana Berro Reyes ("Carmen"), who was a retired teacher and although she was wheelchair bound, she maintained the strong personality of the family women.

In the back of the house were three patios, the maids quarters, the clothes wash area, Carmen and Mary's "casita," a four-room brick-and-mortar playground house, an "aljibe"[11] which was used to store fresh water, and a well with a wind driven pump—

---

[11] Aljibe is a word derived from the Arab for underground water cistern.

the water from the well was used for washing and cleaning and the water from the aljibe for cooking. Drinking water came from bottled gallons delivered regularly to the house.

The first patio, built over the aljibe, was a small tiled-floor-patio area about 40 feet long by 20 feet wide with had a hand operated pump to draw water from the aljibe. This patio eventually had a very tall cement wall, over 20 feet tall, to prevent Jesús and Ticó throwing stuff (balls, toys) into the Corella's yard next door. The Corella family was peculiar: three sons lived with their mother; they had no social life nor did they interact with their neighbors or even with other family members. They complained about Jesús and Ticó so much that Argentina had the high wall built next to their patio; on top of the wall she added a three-foot wire screen. Separating the patio with the aljibe and second patio was a three-feet high stucco wall. The second patio was covered mostly with grass except for a cemented oval track used for tricycle and bicycle riding. This was the main play area for the León kids and in it there was playground equipment ("cachumbambé, columpio and canal"; that is, seesaw, swing and slide). At the end of this patio, on one side was the casita and on the other end the servants' quarters. The third patio was accessed through a door that separated the casita from the servant's quarters. The well was in the third patio and so were the washroom and the space to wash, dry and iron clothes.

Argentina directed the household activities while maintaining a full-time position as a teacher at the Holguín Institute of Secondary Education where she taught History and Geography. Since Holguín is about 50 miles from Tunas she commuted to and from Holguín using the Santiago-Habana bus service, arriving back home in time to supervise the children and give direction to the service staff. When Argentina was not home, Abuela Carmen was in charge and this arrangement worked well until her death in 1953. Afterwards, Argentina delegated a good bit of the daily activity and household supervision to Juana Hierrezuelos until Juana emigrated to New York in the mid 1950s in order to better provide for her family. The service staff who helped care for the household included Juana who did the washing and drying, a cook, one person to clean the house and another person who took care of the children and assisted with household chores. Juana started as the woman in charge of the washing and ironing for the León family, later she was in charge of the household while Argentina worked, and eventually became a bona-fide member of the family known as "abuela Juana or abuela Yaya" by the León-Núñez grandchildren.

Rigoberto was a pharmacist who owned and operated an old-style pharmacy located very near the house and he walked to and from the pharmacy on Lucas Ortiz Street.[12] The Cuban pharmacist duty was to dispense medicine and provide advise on drugs and general health issues but the pharmacies did not sell general items. There were several clerks in the store who were known as "dependientes." The pharmacy was open six days a week during normal business hours and once every fortnight it was the "farmacia de turno" (the duty pharmacy). The duty pharmacy had to be ready to dispense medicine during a twenty-four hour period to take care of emergencies. On these days Rigoberto would sleep at the pharmacy. One of the pharmacy clerks, Pepín, was an excellent employee and a very nice person. He was entrusted, from time to time, to transport one of the León children on his bicycle.

Rigoberto and Argentina were both university graduates, committed professionals and devout Catholics, but otherwise, they had very different personalities. Rigoberto was intelligent, punctual, believed in tidiness and organization, was a little insecure, and not a disciplinarian. He was respected in the community as a business and professional man, a person of integrity and values. Argentina was intellectually brilliant, a Type A personality that commanded attention and respect everywhere, was not afraid to tackle anything, taught her children to be self-sufficient, and was the disciplinarian in the house. She loved books and reading, believed in traveling and visiting family, demanded complete dedication and performance from those around her. As a disciplinarian, Argentina

---

[12] The pharmacy was located at Lucas Ortiz 407 according to the Cuban Telephone Directory published December 1949.

was known as either "the general" or the "commandant"— she was feared by her children and other family members. She was also the spiritual guide to many of her nephews and nieces and to a number of other young adults. In the early 1950s, she was elected to the Tunas City Council— a huge accomplishment for a woman at that time in Cuba. Here are two anecdotes to illustrate the depth of Rigoberto and Argentina's care and commitment to others. Upon the death of Vicenta Revuelta, a close family friend from Bayamo, Rigoberto bought her pharmacy to keep it operating until José Manuel Revuelta completed his pharmacy degree. He then re-sold the pharmacy to José Manuel at the purchase price. The second anecdote is about Juana: When Juana decided to leave Cuba, she went to see Argentina and asked for advise; Argentina gave her advise, helped with the paperwork, loaned her money and promised Juana to keep an eye on her youngest son Juanito, who stayed behind in Cuba. A few years later, when we were in the USA, Juana repaid this assistance with great generosity.

As mentioned earlier, Rigoberto and Argentina were practice-ing Catholics. Argentina's parents did not practice the Catholic faith but she was touched by God and became a true Christian apostle. Rigoberto was a member of the Agrupación Católica Universitaria, ACU, a Marian Congregation founded in La Habana in 1931 by a Galician Jesuit priest, Father Felipe Rey de Castro. Rigoberto and Argentina participated in retreats regularly, and were active in the Catholic community— Argentina organized annual evangelization missions and Rigoberto founded the local chapter of the Knights of Columbus. Jesús remembers his father saying morning prayers in the house before leaving for work every day. He remembers how his parents treated everyone with dignity, regardless of ethnic, social or economic status, how his father would start his day with prayer, how his mother organized missions and helped direct works of charity. Jesús also remembers that they took him to the celebration of the Proclamation of the Dogma of the Assumption[13]. The celebration consisted of an out-

---

[13] The dogma was proclaimed on November 1, 1950.

door Mass on a temporary altar on the Central Park of Tunas. Although Jesús was too young to understand the significance of the celebration, he could tell from the enthusiasm of his parents that this was something especial, and to this day, he remembers that special Mass.

Jesús' younger siblings Carmen Luisa, Mary Carmen and Enrique Luis ("Henry") were born while the León family lived in Tunas. Carmen and Mary were born in La Habana on February 6, 1949, and September 8, 1951, respectively, and Henry in Tunas on June 20, 1955. Henry was born at the Clínica de Nuestra Señora de Loreto (Our Lady of Loreto Clinic). This clinic was founded by a group of doctors with different specialties— cardiology, pediatrics, internal medicine, orthopedics and obstetrics/gynecology. The clinic was financed by the Freire Family of Camagüey whose son was the OB/GYN and whose father was a devotee of Our Lady of Loreto. The father requested that the clinic be named after the Blessed Mother under the title of Our Lady of Loreto.

For the first few years of Jesús life, his days revolved around playing, sleeping and eating. The meals followed the Cuban custom of a light breakfast— cereal or "café con leche and esponge rus bizcochos" (similar to lady fingers); a full meal at lunch— steak, rice, beans, plantains, dessert; a light afternoon repast— the merienda; and another full meal in the evening. As a child, he played with Ticó in the backyard or accompanied by one of the household staff in the Maceo Square Park.

Jesús started first grade just before his 6th birthday in September 1950, at the Colegio Verbo Encarnado School (CVE) in Tunas. To Jesús, going to school was fun and exciting because he loved reading and learning. The CVE School was located about five blocks walking distance from the León-Núñez house. The school was under the direction of the Congregación de Religiosas del Verbo Encarnado[14] whose nuns had other schools in Cuba, including

---

[14] Religious Sisters of the Incarnate Word, a congregation founded in France at the end of the 16th century. Most of these nuns left Mexico because of the persecution of Catholics after the 1910 Mexican Revolution.

one in the Almendares District of La Habana. The nuns were dedicated to teaching and had established a good school in Tunas with enough boy and girl pupils to fill one classroom per grammar school grade. With Argentina's help, the sisters started offering high school classes during their last couple of years in Cuba.

Jesús has fond memories of the CVE School and of the nuns, recalling the Mexican-style piñata parties with kids trying to smash the piñata while blindfolded, and the mad scramble to grab the candies that would pour out of the piñata when it finally busted open. The CVE sisters as well as other religious congregations were expelled from Cuba by Fidel Castro's government after the Bay of Pigs invasion on the pretext that most of them were not Cuban nationals. Fidel Castro used the invasion as the opportunity to close the Catholic schools and to throw out many of the priest and religious that had been working in Cuba for decades in order to remove one part of the largest and most competent opposition to his regime. The regime has continued to persecute the Catholic Church in Cuba, directly and indirectly punishing Cubans who openly participate in Catholic activities.[15]

The nuns of the CVE loved our family, and especially Argentina, who was one of the major supporters of the school and the nuns' activities in the city. Argentina and Rigoberto would present gifts to the school on special occasions. For example, they gave the school an organ for the chapel in thanksgiving for Jesús First Holy Communion. The nuns demonstrated their love for the community with educational and spiritual programs, and they also loaned their dormitory at the school to hold spiritual retreats for women. The school facilities included the nuns' dormitory, a

---

[15] The following quotation is from the US Department of State "International Religious Freedom Report 2009" for Cuba: "The Government continued to exert control over all aspects of societal life including religious expression. The Ministry of the Interior continued to engage in efforts to control and monitor religious activities and to use surveillance, infiltration, and harassment against religious groups, religious professionals, and lay persons." see the section on "Restrictions on Religious Freedom" at http://www.state.gov/g/drl/rls/irf/2009/127386.htm

chapel and a large open courtyard encircled by classrooms. The courtyard was used for civic activities every Friday, for occasional piñatas, and from time to time to show an open-air movie. There was also a sandy field used for physical education and games.

All the León-Núñez children attended the CVE School for some part of their education. Jesús was a student there until the beginning of the fifth grade. He received his First Holy Communion in the Chapel of the Colegio Verbo Encarnado on March 25, 1952, the Feast of the Incarnation, the feast day of the CVE nuns. This sacrament, a pivotal one in the life of every Catholic, was a very special occasion for the family. Rigoberto and Argentina asked the nuns to allow Jesús' godfather to be the celebrant for his First Holy Communion and they were also allowed to come to the altar with Jesús, flanking him on each side, for his reception of communion.

Jesús' school day was similar to Chelo's and to almost every grammar student in Cuba. Pepín or an elder cousin took him to school in the morning where he attended classes all morning except for a break at midmorning, the "recreo" period. Then, at noon, off to the house for lunch and to listen to the "Villalobos" radio serial episodes (the adventures of three heroic brothers). After lunch, it was back to school for more classes, and often, physical education in the late afternoon. In addition to the regular classes, Argentina believed that a well-educated person should know about music so Jesús and Ticó were enrolled in piano classes. This ended up being somewhat of a wasted effort as neither Jesús nor Ticó had the interest, inclination or talent to play music. Nevertheless, Jesús did learn about the history of music, had an introduction to piano and to the practice time required to learn how to play this instrument.

The family sat together for dinner every night but Carmen Luisa and Mary did not join the "big" table until they knew how to feed themselves using appropriate utensils. Rigoberto sat at the head of the table with Argentina to his right, Jesús to his left and Ticó at the other end of the table. The food at the León-Núñez house was unmistakably Cuban: "congrí oriental" (red beans and rice), steak, "picadillo," "carne ripiada," pork, fried plantains, yucca and avocado. Jesús knew nothing of Spanish cuisine until he met Chelo. Most of the items cooked in the house came from one of the groceries located near the house except during Jesús' last two years in Cuba, when the milk and meat came from the family ranches— a steer would be killed every week or so and the meat distributed to several León households.

There were a number of callers to the León house every day: in the mornings trade persons delivered groceries, bottled water and milk; employees brought beef from the family cattle farm once a week; Jesús' cousins, Ana María, Alicia and Grecia, who lived two houses away, came and went several times a day. Lunchtime involved arrival and departure of Rigoberto and school age children, and most evenings there were visitors that came to drink Cuban coffee and recount the day's events. One regular visitor in the evenings was Professor Rodríguez, a teacher and friend of the family, who tutored Jesús and Ticó one summer when both of them did not attain the grades expected of them.

Jesús, unlike Chelo, attended more than one school in Cuba. When he was in the fourth grade, the school nuns recommended Jesús to Father Cavero, SJ, a Jesuit priest who visited Tunas at the time. Father Cavero was the director of an experimental recruiting approach by the Jesuits: they set up the Loyola Apostolic Academy in the Coronela district of La Habana to house and educate boys who showed potential to become future Jesuits. Father Cavero interviewed candidates and invited those that he thought qualified to join the Loyola Apostolic Academy. When Jesús was interviewed, Father Cavero showed pictures of the Academy and the many activities available there: horseback riding, trips to the beach, boys playing sports and table games; in short, boys having fun— needless to say, Jesús agreed to join the Academy!

Students at the Loyola Apostolic Academy lived in a house that was set in a large plot of land. The house had dormitories, a chapel, a dining room and a study area. The boys were taken to the Belén School in the morning to attend class, had lunch in a special dining room at the school, and at the end of the day, returned to the Academy house. There was daily Mass in the evening and students were required to participate and to learn how to be altar boys, using Latin for all prayers. In addition to Father Cavero, there was a young Jesuit brother who assisted with the students' activities. One activity Jesús remembers was a "mango fight"—the boys hurled mango fruits at each other. Jesús was struck by a mango in the eye and had a swollen face for several days. Jesús remembers reading the Iliad and the Odyssey and having a lot of fun at the Academy. However, it soon became apparent that Jesús did not have a vocation for the priesthood, so after the summer, Jesús left the Loyola Apostolic Academy and became a boarding student at Belén for the 1955-56 and 1956-57 school years.

Belén had the reputation of being Cuba's best school for boys. The Jesuits founded Belén in 1854 and the school offered grades K-12 with regular "bachillerato" (high school) and "comercio" (business) program options in high school. Belén had a large campus with a distinctive building,[16] a large number of boarding students and a full program of athletics. There is a long list of distinguished alumni from the school. This list includes Roberto Goizueta, Coca Cola's CEO; Dr. José Ignacio Lasaga who was the student with the best academic record in the history of the University of Havana; José Ignacio Rivero, the director of the best newspaper in Cuba; Manuel Artime and Rogelio González Corso, leaders of the Bay of Pigs Invasion and of the Cuban underground against Castro, respectively; the founders of the Agrupación Católica Universitaria. Our least favorite Belén alumnus by far was Fidel Castro.

Jesús and later Ticó were boarding students at Belén for a couple of years. Each boarding student had a number that was stitched in his clothing to insure easy identification— Jesús' number was 255 and Ticó's was 32. Coming from a small town and a sheltered life, Belén was a life changing experience for Jesús. While at Belén, he had the first fight with another boy, he took up smoking (forbidden as you may imagine), learned how to play basketball under the direction of "Capy" Campuzano, learned how to play baseball, played his first game of soccer on a team that included a priest playing with his cassock, and "escaped" from Belén a couple

---

[16] For more on Belén's history see the school's website, www.belenjesuit.org.

of times. One of the times he "disappeared" from the school became somewhat legendary— he and two other students departed on a Saturday morning and were gone all day until that night: they went to the movies, shopping, and hung around the Marianao area. One of the students was expelled from Belén partially as a result of this escapade, but also because of his attitude. Jesús and his other companion were penalized but both were courteous and served their punishment without complaining or "talking back" to the Jesuit priests.

Jesús completed the fifth and sixth grade at Belén, the later called "Ingreso" in Cuba as it was during this year that one took the state administered entrance examination to enter the high school program in Cuba. The Marianao Institute of the Cuban Ministry of Education gave this exam to Belén students. Jesús and Ticó would have probably completed their high school education at Belén but because of the Cuban Revolution, and particularly due to the uncertainty that was created during an assassination attempt on the Cuban dictator, Fulgencio Batista, their parents decided to transfer them to a school closer to their home. The assassination attempt occurred on the 13 of March 1957 and was carried out by University of Havana students. On that day the Cuban Army was mobilized with tanks on major streets while worried parents came to pick up their children from school early. Rigoberto and Argentina decided that their children were too far away from them, and at the end of the academic year. They enrolled both of them as boarding students at the Pious School ('Escolapios') in Camagüey, a city located about one and one-half hour drive from Victoria de las Tunas. The short distance made travel less problematic because while a student in Belén Jesús occasionally flew alone from Havana to Tunas on a DC-3 airplane that landed on a grassy field in Tunas.

Jesús went on to complete the first three years of the five-year Cuban high school program at the Escolapios. He took the required state official subject examinations twice a year from teachers of the Camagüey Institute. Jesús has fond memories of his time in the Escolapios as the Pious School was known, but the changes from Belén were significant: the school was much smaller— Belén had over 1,000 students while the Escolapios had, in Jesús estimation, less

45

than 250; the academic reputation, the athletic achievements, the cosmopolitan nature, the societal influence were significantly different. Belén excelled as a premier school while the Escolapios was weaker in every category. Most of the boarding students at the Escolapios came from small towns in Camagüey and parts of Oriente provinces. The Escolapio priests came to Cuba from the Catalonia region of Spain but were no match to the Jesuits in academic excellence or inspiring a drive to greatness.

Summers in Cuba were wonderful

Oh! How Chelo and Jesús miss the great beaches of Cuba! The northern coast of Cuba is blessed with a number of beautiful beaches. The best known of these is Varadero, a world famous beach that attracts many tourists to enjoy the crystal-clear waters and beautiful sand of this 13 miles long natural wonder. Varadero is approximately 90 miles east of Havana and is connected to it by the Via Blanca, a 4-lane highway that makes it easy to make day trips to Varadero. Along the Via Blanca but closer to La Habana were a couple of public beaches and several private resorts where many of the Cuban middle and upper middle class spent the summers while some families lived in them year around. These beaches started a few kilometers from Havana and included Tarará, Santa María del Mar, Boca Ciega, Guanabo and Jibacoa. Access to the private resorts was limited to property owners, renters and their guests.

Chelo and Jesús enjoyed access to some of these private resorts even though their parents did not own property in any of them. Tarará Beach played an important role in Chelo's social life; she has wonderful memories of the beach and of the many friends whom she met there. Jesús' family often rented a house in one of the other resorts: Boca Ciega, Guanabo and Jibacoa. Chelo was a summer guest at her aunt Margot and her husband Ramón's residence in Tarará. Chelo started to go to Tarará when she was around eleven years of age and continued to enjoy the summer vacation at the beach with her cousins until the summer of 1961. Margot's house was a large house by Cuban standards, having 5 bathrooms, something rare in Cuban houses. There were three servants including a full time cook. The residents included Ramón,

Margot and their three kids: Margarita, Monchi and Roberto; and Margot's sister Estela with her husband Armando and their children: Teresita, Estelita and Armandito. Estelita was a great companion of Chelo.

A typical day for Chelo at Tarará started with breakfast. Afterwards, the young people congregated at the beach for sun, swimming and conversation. Later, they went home for lunch and to play games: canasta, dominos, Ping-Pong, etc. At mid-afternoon they went to the club for a snack (merienda) and then played tennis or squash,[17] or went horseback or bicycle riding. On most evenings, there would be a "guateque," an informal party with music and dancing. This type of party was sort of spontaneous requiring little organization and was a lot of fun. You knew that every evening people would gather for a guateque and the details about each party were passed around very quickly among the friends. The only major change to this schedule was on Sundays when attendance to Mass was practically mandatory, considering that almost everyone was Catholic. Another change for Chelo was the different cuisine because the Agulló family ate Cuban food instead of the Spanish cuisine common at her grandmother's house.

Cordero and Consuelín would come to see Chelo every Wednesday and Sunday but they did not stay at the house. Chelo's father, Cordero, was a favorite with the young people at Tarará. He took them horseback riding, taught them shot put and baseball and organized sports activities for them. He also accompanied the young people in walking tours, on the sand, from Tarará to Santa María del Mar.

In addition to Tarará, Chelo enjoyed other summertime activities. She went to Artemisa to the farm of her next door's neighbors. She also traveled to very near the eastern tip of Cuba ("Remates de Guane") in the Province of Pinar del Rio where her father's family owned a farm and where her aunt Manuelita ("Tita") lived. On the

---

[17] Squash was a popular game played in Cuba, using a tennis racquet and tennis balls, and played on a court similar to the Jai Alai court with three tall walls.

way to the Guane region, they visited the beautiful Valle de Viñales[18] in the central part of the province. They passed by a number of beautiful bays and near the heart of one of the best tobacco farming areas of the world, Vueltabajo, where the leaves of some of the best cigars in the world come from. They also occasionally went to Varadero in what was considered a long trip that had to be planned carefully. One had to check the car and maybe change the oil, and prepare lunch for the two-hour, ninety-miles highway trip. On her way to Varadero, Chelo and her family sometimes visited the Yumurí Valley, a beautiful and scenic valley full of Palma Reales (Royal Palms) that is located a few kilometers south of the highway not far from the City of Matanzas.

The last two weeks prior to the beginning of each school year, Chelo would spent time reviewing her studies and doing some preparatory school work. She would also spend time with her next-door friends, Elena and Susana, and with her abuela playing Parcheesi, card games and talking.

Jesús spent his summers in a mix of activities, including time at the beach and also at a cattle ranch, either at Tiguabos or San Agustín. There was one significant difference to Chelo's beach experience because Jesús' family rented a house for a month at a different beach every year: One summer they were in Boca Ciega, another in Guanabo, a third at Jibacoa. Many family and intimate friends joined the León-Núñez for the month at the beach. Jesús' aunt María del Carmen Núñez Berro, her husband Felix Cepero Bonilla and their children, Felix Manuel, Marta and "Bebi" (Rosa Elodia) spent the whole month with them. Uncle Felix was, like Cordero, a favorite of the children: he taught the León-Núñez children how to swim, to fish with a net and a pole, to study the stars, to learn about nature and fishes like manta rays. The children swam at least twice a day and played sports and games almost every day except when going horseback riding or exploring a nearby town or climbing hills.

---

[18] This valley is a UNESCO World Heritage site. It has beautiful hills called "mogotes."

Tiguabos was a very special place for all the Núñez family and for many of the children of the Núñez clan— a place for family reunions, for playing with cousins, for horseback riding, and other family activities. The word Tiguabos comes from the Native Cubans. There was an early settlement of native Cubans in this location that grew into a small village with a few houses along the road near the Núñez-Berro cattle ranch, a ranch that abutted the Cauto River, Cuba's largest river, between the towns of Cauto Embarcadero and Cauto El Paso.[19] The ranch was about 530 acres (16 Cuban "caballerias") and had been the home of Jesús grandparents on his mother side, Manuel Núñez and Carmen Berro and also the birthplace of Argentina.[20] Manuel and Carmen built a small but successful ranch and raised their seven children there. Argentina took her children to spend a couple of weeks in Tiguabos on many summers, their visit often coordinated with that of other Núñez-Berro family members. The homestead had an old wood house that had suffered the ravages of time, and because of this, the grownups did not allow any of the children to go up to the second story as they felt that it was not safe. Regilio, Argentina's brother had stayed in the farm and purchased from his siblings, their shares of the ranch, and thus became the sole owner of the ranch. He added a kitchen, a daily dining area and a storage area, all of wood walls with a packed dirt floor. Regilio owned a small gasoline-run generator that provided electricity in the evenings for lights and so that the family could listen to the radio.

A typical day at Tiguabos started before dawn when some of the visiting children would get up to help milk the cows, a task that was done manually. The milk from the cows was placed on large containers and carried by mules a few miles to the town of Cauto del Paso from where it was sent to the Nestlé plant near

---

[19] If you enter coordinates 20.566667, −76.78333 (20° 34' 00" N, 76° 47' 00" W) in Google Earth it will take you to the approximate location of the Village of Tiguabos. The ranch was on the Cauto River less than one mile east of this village.

[20] Argentina's story in Appendix VI describes how her family acquired the property.

Bayamo. Jesús remembers bringing a glass with brown (unrefined) sugar and Cuban coffee to the milking area, placing the glass underneath one of the cow's teats and milking the cow to make café con leche that was warm and ready to drink. The children spent the rest of the day at the ranch playing, horseback riding, climbing trees and swimming and bathing in the Cauto River. Since there was no bathroom facility at Tiguabos you had to bathe at the river, and for other necessities you walked to the outhouse ("el excusado") a couple hundred feet from the house itself. From time to time, the visiting children would do some minor chores around the ranch— chucking corn, feeding the hens and dogs, or cleaning a small garden. It is interesting that the León-Núñez children did not miss modern amenities and adjusted to the basic living conditions there. In addition to the outhouse and bathing at the Cauto River, all the water that was used at the house had to be brought every day by mules from the river and the water used for cooking and drinking had to be boiled. Furthermore, there were a limited number of beds so Jesús sometimes had to sleep in a hammock. During one of the trips, Jesús and one other cousin had to walk a little less than one mile every night to sleep in a house in the Tiguabos Village. Nonetheless, the León-Núñez kids loved Tiguabos and looked forward with anticipation to every visit.

Reflecting on Jesús and Chelo's Cuban summers, it seems like reading something extracted from a fiction novel: there were lots of boys and girls, there was swimming at the beach, games, sports, parties, horseback and bicycle riding, good food, lots of family and friends, great weather, lots of fun for everyone. Ah! Castro. In addition to the loss of freedom, the disjointing of families, Castro is also guilty of causing our families to lose the great summer vacations. That is one more sin that Castro will have to atone for!

Argentina wanted her children to know Cuba so she arranged vacation trips to many of the important historical, geographical or cultural Cuban sites: Santiago de Cuba, the Viñales Valley in Pinar del Rio, the Yumurí Valley in Matanzas, etc. One particular trip that the family made several times was to the El Cobre Sanctuary near Santiago de Cuba, the location of the statue of Our Lady of

Charity, the Patroness of Cuba, that was found in the Bay of Nipe by the three "Juanes" in 1612. Since the family did not own an automobile, Rigoberto contracted a driver, Labrada, to drive the family on these trips. The family stayed at the Hospedería (a hostelry) located next to the Sanctuary that was owned and operated by the Catholic Church. The family attended Mass in the Sanctuary and visited Santiago de Cuba, San Juan Hill, and the tomb of José Martí, Cuba's Independence hero and poet.

Havana was another regular place the León-Núñez family visited during many summers, and while there, the family stayed at the house of María and Felix in the La Vibora District of La Habana. Felix was a math teacher at a school nearby and also gave tutoring classes in a classroom built in the basement of their house. To the family children, he was the teacher par excellence, very patient, especially when he taught the León-Núñez how to swim, fish, and when he explained topics in astronomy and natural sciences. Felix loved sports and watched many sports, particularly baseball and boxing. Jesús remembers watching the live transmission of Don Larsen's 1956 World Series perfect game with Felix. While in Havana, the León children would often go to the beach at one of the many private clubs in La Habana such as El Comodoro.

It should be clear by now that Argentina made an effort to nurture family ties organizing activities with other members of her family often. Since many León family members lived in Tunas, there was little need to organize family reunions as we saw each other often. The Cepero-Núñez family spent many Christmases in Tunas with the León-Núñez family, and we saw Rubén Núñez's family often because they lived in Holguín, about one hour away from Tunas. Their children, Lilita y Eneida were close to the León-Núñez family and played with them often in Tunas and Holguín. The tradition of family get together resumed years later in the USA with annual Christmas and summer family gatherings in Miami and Marco Island, respectively.

During the part of the summer spent in Tunas, we often went to La Llanita beach, a beautiful virgin beach that was reached by small ferryboats from the Puerto Padre port, about one-hour drive from Tunas. There were limited facilities at the beach but the sand and water were wonderful, on par with the best that Jesús has ever seen. Summer in Tunas also included hanging out with the Villoch brothers ("Bebo" and "Niño"), playing in the park or in our back yard. As the boys grew older, Jesús would also bike all over town to play baseball, to swim naked in a river near the town, and body building with weights one summer at the house of Manolito Rodríguez, the son of Professor Rodríguez.

The last years Chelo and Jesús spent in Cuba would have normally been very important years to both: the teenage years, the parties and the teenage boy-girl interaction; the years when teenagers begin their growth into adulthood. These important years were impacted by the historical events in the island nation: the last year of Batista's dictatorship, the beginning of Castro's revolution, the scramble to leave Cuba when the revolution turned Communist and becoming exiles in the USA.

Jesús indicates that, for him, this period of transition was most clearly defined beginning the summer of 1958. During that year there had been an increase in the intensity of the armed rebellion against Batista, both in the countryside and in subversive actions in the cities (a type of terrorist activity that included exploding bombs in public places). Oriente Province, in particular, saw a large increase in fighting, and Rigoberto and Argentina thought it might be safer to keep the children away from the area. Thus, at the end of the 1957-58 academic year, in mid June, the family went to La Habana and from there to Jibacoa Beach where they had rented a house for the month of July. Jibacoa, was a private beach resort community located about 30 minutes east of La Habana wherein about two-dozen families owned houses, used mostly during the summer months. The resort had four small beaches: "Aguas Muertas" (literally dead water, so called because it had extremely tranquil seas), the Artist Beach (very picturesque), another beach where a small river flowed to the sea and one beach with a rough cliff to one side that was not very popular with the residents. The house rented by the family was large and spacious and it accommodated the León-Núñez family, the Cepero-Núñez family minus Felix Junior who was in Atlanta, and a number of other family and friends who stayed there for shorter visits.

Every one enjoyed the summer at Jibacoa. Jesús ran into friends he had from Belén including "Jutía" Hernández, the Capy Campuzano family, and parts of the Comella family (their parents had 18 children). There were sports including volleyball, kickball, horseback riding, hiking up a small hill with cousin Victor, "Happy," hiking a few kilometers to the Hershey Sugar Mill, a one-day trip to Varadero Beach, etc.; the children participated in all the activities. The daily schedule included mornings and late afternoons swimming at the beach. After lunch, while waiting the necessary time to return to the beach— no one was allowed to swim within two hours after a meal so the kids played word games, "prendas," or table games.

In August, after the month at the beach, Rigoberto, Argentina, Jesús and Ticó left Cuba for a trip to the USA while Carmen Luisa, Mary and Henry stayed with the Cepero-Núñez family in La Vibora. Argentina had wanted to go to Brussels for the 1958 World's Fair but Rigoberto wanted to visit the USA first— who would have thought that the León kids would be back in the USA in just over two years?

The trip was highly educational with the opportunity to learn more of the English language and something about the American way of life. There were visits to see a number of family members who lived either permanently or temporarily in the USA. The León family took a ferry from La Habana to Key West— a daily boat in which you could transport your car from Cuba to Key West or vice-versa for Americans traveling to Cuba. René Núñez, Argentina's brother, met the family in Key West, drove them to Miami and hosted them at his house as the family spent several days sightseeing. From Miami, the family traveled by Greyhound bus to Tampa in order to visit one of the places where the Cuban patriot José Martí had worked to raise funds for Cuban independence. In Tampa, the family went to dinner at the famous Columbia restaurant in Ybor City, a restaurant featuring Cuban food and Flamenco dancing since 1905.

The next stop of the trip was to Tallahassee and from there to Atlanta, Georgia, all by Greyhound bus. In Atlanta, the family stayed at the Atlanta Hotel in the downtown area. There were several reasons to visit Atlanta: first, Felix Manuel Cepero Núñez was an architectural student at Georgia Tech where he had been sent to protect him from the repression under Batista's regime; and second, Atlanta was the location of Argentina's favorite novel, Gone With the Wind. We arrived in Atlanta at the end of the academic term at Georgia Tech, and as soon as Felix Manuel was done with his studies, the family rented a car. With Felix Manuel driving, we left Atlanta to begin a tour of part of the USA heading to Washington, DC. There were overnight stops in Greenville, SC, and Greensboro, NC, and on the third day a stop for lunch at Fredericksburg, Virginia, where the family spent, unscheduled, the rest of the day. There was a parade in Fredericksburg that day, and while there, the Leóns discovered that this town is a treasure of American history, especially of the US Civil War. Rigoberto was reading the life of Abraham Lincoln and was very happy to walk the historic sites.

After arriving in DC and visiting its monuments, we headed for Philadelphia to visit Leticia, niece of Rigoberto, daughter of Mingo and María León. Two years later, Leticia and her family opened her house to seven relatives fleeing Cuba including Tico and Jesús. Here is a story of generosity and love from someone who had been, for the most part, ignored and abandoned by her family after she had married the "wrong" guy. In 1958, Leticia lived in a small rented place with three of her sons, Aristides (Ray), Ramiro and George; a fourth son had died a few years earlier in an automobile accident while serving in the US Military; her daughter had gone to Cuba and stayed with her grandparents where she was educated, married and lived until her exile.

From Philadelphia we went to New York City, a great city full of sites to see, things to do, places to visit, and on top of that, we were able to see Juana, our cousins Nilda and Bertha Núñez, René's daughters, and José Manuel Revuelta. Juana had emigrated to New York a few years earlier with the help of Rigoberto and Argentina— a move that would allow her to provide greater financial help to her children. José Manuel, like Felix Manuel, had been sent to the USA because of the repression in Cuba, especially the danger to young adult males. The Revuelta family lived in the Bayamo area and they were very close to the León-Núñez family, in many ways closer than some family members.

From New York we went to Niagara Falls with a brief visit to Canada, and after dropping off the rental car in Buffalo, we took a train back to Atlanta where we stayed at the very nice Biltmore Hotel on Fifth and West Peachtree Streets, within walking distance of the Georgia Tech campus. Jesús and Ticó attended their first college football game— a game they did not understand— but watched Georgia Tech defeat the University of Miami. After a few days in Atlanta we returned to Miami where we spent a number of days in René's house before flying back to Havana.

Castro's insurgency had spread through several parts of Cuba, making travel to our hometown dangerous. Rigoberto and Argentina decided to stay in Havana to protect the family. For the next three months, the León-Núñez family camped at the Cepero-Núñez house. There were twelve of us living in a four bedroom flat with one bath.

While in Havana, Ticó and Jesús went to school at the Academia Alfa, a private school where Felix Cepero taught Mathematics. Jesús remembers Felix making a statement that foresaw things to come when he scolded Jesús, publicly, for not giving full effort in class saying that Jesús needed to work hard because "... ranch land can burn, cattle die, houses be destroyed ..." Felix could not have known that the ranch lands, cattle, houses and the pharmacy were going to be expropriated by the Castro totalitarian regime in a couple of years. Jesús completed the first semester of his second year of the Cuban high school at the Alfa Academy. He remembers the oral final exam for the Anatomy class when one of the members of the examination panel picked a human bone at random from a box and Jesús had to identify and describe the bone!

The family was in Havana on New Year's Day when Batista fled Cuba, ushering the victory of Castro's revolution. On January 8, 1959, Argentina, Rigoberto, Ticó and Jesús went to the house of Berta González, widow of Miguel León and mother of Bertica, the future wife of Chelo's cousin Vicente. Her house was on Columbia Avenue, the route to be taken by Castro and his troops as part of their triumphal entrance to Havana. Jesús saw Fidel pass on a Jeep less than 15 feet from him. A few weeks later, the family returned to Tunas to begin the last twenty months of their lives together as a family in their hometown.

Last years in Cuba

Tunas seemed smaller to Jesús after the six months away from the city but he was happy to be back home and to return to his school. The 1958-59 academic year was shortened because of the revolution and all students had to retake the first semester exams. Jesús completed the second and third years of the Cuban bachillerato in June 1959 and 1960, respectively. The years 1959 and 1960 were very special for Jesús: biologically, he had grown to his full adult size although emotionally he was a teenager exploring and learning about life and manhood. These years were peaceful and happy years, the typical calm before the storm.

The León-Núñez family summer schedule changed during these two years although they still visited family in Tiguabos, went to the Sanctuary of Our Lady of Charity and to Santiago de Cuba but the family did not rent a summerhouse at the beach. Jesús spent several weeks during these summers in San Agustín de Aguaras, the birthplace of his father, a village about one-hour drive from Tunas, at the house of his paternal aunt Lilia and her husband Daer. Daer was a cattleman who managed his family cattle ranch and also the ranch of the León-González family (Berta, Estela, Miguelito and Bertica). Berta, who was a pharmacist, kept the pharmacy that Miguel León owned in San Agustín; she hired a pharmacist to operate the pharmacy since she lived in Havana. Jesús went to San Agustín in part for vacation and in part for learning about cattle ranching— he learned how to brand and dehorn cows, worked a little bit in the fields with some of the field hands, particularly with a field hand nicknamed "Patines" who was very close to Daer's family. In San Agustin, Jesús learned to play pool, dance to the music of a small country organ, once joined an impromptu local party, mastered the art of horseback riding, and visited the site of a local "santero"[21] who had become famous and had visitors from all over Cuba searching for healing.

René Núñez's family came from Miami to visit us during the 1959 and 1960 summers; while in Tunas, Manolo Núñez came from Holguín to visit with René's family. Jesús met Manolo's son, Manolito, for the first time on one of these occasions. During Jesús' last two summers in Cuba, he also spent some time with Vicente Fernández, the future husband of Bertica León. During his extended stay in La Habana, Jesús had met Vicente and he saw him again in Tunas and in San Agustín. Vicente, Miguelito, Bertica and a friend of Miguelito traveled from Havana during these summers to spend a couple of weeks visiting family in Tunas and Holguín and they stayed at Daer and Lilia's house in San Agustín.

An anecdote that illustrates Jesús and Argentina's personalities took place in June of one of these two summers. Argentina went to administer final exams to high school students near the Delicias and Chaparras sugar mills, about 40 miles from Tunas. Jesús asked to go with her and to go visit his boarding school friends who lived nearby. Argentina consented and when they arrived in town, Jesús went looking for his friends. Well, they lived in a "colonia" (a plantation where sugar cane was grown and harvested) more than one hour away from the city. When he arrived at their home, the mother insisted that he stay more time with them. Now, Jesús had no permission to stay, no clothes or personal effects. They tried to contact Argentina who, by this time, had finished giving her second set of exams and departed for Tu-

---

[21] Santero is the priest of the Santería Religion. According to Wikipedia, "Santería is a system of beliefs that merge the Yoruba religion (brought to the New World by slaves imported to the Caribbean to work in sugar plantations) with Roman Catholic and Native Indian traditions. These slaves carried with them various religious traditions, including a trance for communicating with their ancestors and deities, animal sacrifices and sacred drumming. In Cuba, this religion tradition has evolved into what we now recognize as Santería." http://en.wikipedia.org/wiki/Santeria

nas. Jesús stayed with his friends for three days— the family washed his clothes daily and he enjoyed his visit tremendously.[22] Argentina was obviously not worried about Jesús ability to survive but when he got home he was completely grounded for one week, allowed out of the house only to go to church.

The rest of the last two summers, when he was in Tunas, were filled with activities. Playing cards at the Liceo club, buying his first suit (in Camagüey), going to his first, and several more, semiformal dances, joining the Club de Leones which had a pool and tennis courts, and an occasional escapade to the Llanita beach. Jesús had learned to dance in 1959— Bertica was the first to give him lessons in 1958, but in 1959 he had professional training in preparation for a school pageant where he was part of a group that danced a Danzón, a Cha Cha Cha, and a Conga.

The last two years in Cuba were the time frame when Jesús became socially active with girls, went to a lot of parties, enjoyed the Cuban Carnivals of Tunas and Camagüey. In Camagüey, Jesús had met a number of girls at the school pageant and they invited Jesús and some of his friends to join them at carnival parties. Jesús remembers going with them to a Saturday party at the Camagüey Athletic Club that had four orchestras, a party that started in the early afternoon with two orchestras, and after a break for dinner, continued with the two other orchestras playing until the wee hours of the next morning. By the way, to attend the party, Jesús and his friends had escaped the boarding school in the early afternoon and returned in the dawn hours of the next day.

The carnivals of Tunas lasted about eight days and ended on September 30, the feast day of Saint Jerome, the patron saint of Tunas, and we partied every night. Jesús started every evening "arrollando," dancing on the main street of the city to conga music behind one of the several conga groups that dressed in special cos-

---

[22] One thing he learned about the Colonia lifestyle is that breakfast was the main meal of the day: rice, beans, meat, plantains, avocado and dessert. The men working the field ate this large meal in the morning, took a sack lunch for later in the day and did not return to their house until the evening.

tumes. The conga parade lasted for more than one hour and when it finished Jesús would go home to shower, change and join his friends in one of the many parties going on in the city. The girls of our social group did not participate in the conga parade, as this was not considered appropriate for "nice" girls. The girls from our social group were ready to party beginning around ten every night, the time when the orchestras of the upscale social clubs started playing. One of the organizers of the parties was Jesús' cousin Ketty, the daughter of Berta León, who later was part of the group that left Cuba together with Jesús in October of 1960. The carnival parties would last until two or three in the morning, and after the party, we escorted the girls, as a group, to their homes. Jesús and some of his friends would continue partying on many nights until five or five-thirty in the morning— Jesús remembers one night dancing in the Central Park at five-thirty in the morning. The day after his last carnival in Cuba, Jesús slept all day, got up after five in the afternoon, had some dinner and went back to sleep.

Cuban people like to dance and although Tunas was a small town, there were parties almost every week. Some were organized at one of the social clubs or by the young people at their homes or by their youth club, "Alegre Juventud" (Happy Youth), and held at the Liceo. Jesús has many good memories of his friends from that era. Unfortunately, the Cuban Revolution caused such a dispersion (diaspora) of the Cuban people that he became disconnected from them, in time and space, and he rarely, if ever, saw any of these friends over the next fifty years— another of the unpleasant consequences of the revolution.

Jesús knew he was going to the USA in October so he went to many parties during his last few weeks in Cuba up to and including his last weekend in Cuba. The fact that Jesús knew he was leaving Cuba was significant since families of people departing Cuba kept this a secret— you found that "so and so" left to the USA days after their departure. In any case, Jesús danced away the last few hours before departing Cuba on that fateful and beautiful Monday morning of October 10, 1960.

During the summer of 1959, Chelo recalled going to the famous Cuban seamstress Elena Llansó to have fittings for her 15th year old debutante. She was supposed to have a "quinceañera" party during the 1959-1960 winter, but due to the uncertainty and unrest caused by Castro's regime, her party and that of other of her friends were not given. Instead of a party, Chelo celebrated her 15th birthday with a Mass at her high school (the American Dominican Academy) and a breakfast at the famous "El Carmelo" restaurant located near the school. Her family and many of her friends shared the Mass and breakfast with Chelo.

Unlike Jesús, Chelo was totally unaware that she was going to leave Cuba. She was informed of her departure a few days before she boarded the airplane for the trip to Miami.

Book II – Cataclysm:[23]
Our World Was Turned Upside Down!

Revolution

Castro's triumph, in January 1959, ushered a period of hope among the great majority of Cubans who yearned for personal freedom, democracy and normalcy after suffering the Batista dictatorship for seven years. Unfortunately, this was not to be, and within a few months, Castro's regime began to eliminate the political opposition, to squeeze the Catholic Church, to expropriate assets, and to limit personal freedoms.

We will not attempt here to give a history of Castro's revolution— there are hundreds of books that review every aspect of the Cuban Revolution,[24] but it is important that we mention a few facts to explain the predicament and decisions taken by our parents to send us, barely teenagers, by ourselves, to the USA in 1960 and 1961.

Castro stated in January 1959 that the "revolution was as green as the Cuban Royal Palm tree" and promised elections within a reasonable time. He asked a respected member of the judiciary, Manuel Urrutia, to serve as President while he took the title of Prime Minister. In early 1959, the government started to prosecute members of Batista's government using mostly kangaroo court trials, many televised nationally, with the verdict almost always the

---

[23] One of the entries in the online Merriam-Webster dictionary defines cataclysm as "a momentous and violent event marked by overwhelming upheaval and demolition; broadly: an event that brings great changes."

[24] See for example, www.library.nyu.edu/lat-amer/cuban.doc, or the Cuba Transition Project of the University of Miami, http://ctp.iccas.miami.edu/.

same: death by the firing squad, and with many of the spectators shouting "paredón, paredón."[25]

In June, the government enacted the Agrarian Reform Law. Most Cubans welcomed this law because of the belief that it would help to improve the lives of the peasants, giving them the opportunity to farm their own land. The law was implemented arbitrarily and inefficiently targeting many productive tracts of lands and creating anxiety among many Cubans. The government followed this law with a number of policies that caused nervousness to many Cuban people and to the Cuban Catholic Church. The Church started a campaign to influence the government including pastoral letters from some of the Cuban Bishops, and in November 1959, the Church organized a massive Congress of Catholics from all over Cuba that traveled to Havana to demonstrate their allegiance to the Catholic Church.

During the same time period we saw a number of people forced out of the Cuban government: Urrutia, the respected president "resigned"; Huber Matos, one of the twelve men that reached the Sierra Maestra with Castro, was imprisoned. Camilo Cienfuegos, another of the early twelve and a popular figure with Cubans "disappeared," mysteriously, on a flight from Camagüey to Havana— nothing was ever found of the airplane!

The government continued to announce and implement "socialists" (communist) policies and one of these was a declaration about the proper education of children according to revolutionary principles. The declaration about "the proper education of children" was very troubling to many families and soon after the announcement, there was a rumor that the Cuban government planned to send some children to the Soviet Union for "education" there. Many Cuban families knew that during the Spanish Civil War, the Spanish government had shipped a number of children to Russia without their parents consent, to educate them in the "proper socialist environment" and many Cuban parents wor-

---

25 Paredón is the Spanish word for "big wall" and those convicted were lined against this big wall for their execution.

ried that this would happen to their children. Two other events increased the fear that the Cuban government might want to send Cuban children to Russia to be educated. The first, in December 1960, was the break of diplomatic relations between Cuba and the USA; the second event was that right after the failed Bay of Pigs Invasion in April 1961, Castro's government closed all Catholic Schools and expelled from Cuba the majority of priests, nuns and members of religious orders.

As a result of the increase in Communist policies by the Cuban regime and the fear of losing control of their children's education, many Cuban families began to send their children out of the country in 1960. This exodus became a flood in 1961, after the failure of the Bays of Pigs Invasion in April of that year. Several of Jesús' schoolmates and friends from Tunas departed during the summer of 1960. Rigoberto and Argentina had begun planning to send their children to the USA in 1960. Cordero and Consuelo planned Chelo's departure in 1961. Similar decisions were made in the home of thousands of Cuban families during the early 1960s, decisions that must have been gut wrenching: sending children alone to a foreign country to protect them from their countries' government. We, now parents and grandparents, are still in awe of the courage and fear that drove our parents to take such a drastic course of action.

Chelo and Jesús left Cuba and were received in Miami, Chelo by Consuelo's boss at Café Pilón, Oswaldo Rosette, and Jesús by an uncle. Along with Chelo, Jesús and his siblings, many thousands of Cuban children arrived in Miami in the early 1960s. In fact, over fourteen thousands Cuban children arrived in Miami and were in the care of the Catholic Church through the Pedro Pan program[26] until their families arrived from Cuba. Chelo and Jesús were part of the more than half-million (10% of the total population of Cuba) that arrived in South Florida during the early part of the Cuban Diaspora.

---

[26] See www.pedropan.org for information about this extraordinary program.

Because of its proximity to Cuba and its travel connections, the city of Miami was the primary destination for Cubans fleeing the Communist dictatorship. Miami has always been the most important site for Cuban exiles. It is, therefore, appropriate that before we discuss our particular experiences, we write a few words to describe Miami in the 1960s and how the flood of exiles that arrived there in the 1960-1980 period changed the city.

In 1960 the population of metropolitan Miami was about 1.5 million,[27] increasing to over 5 million in 2000, a three-fold increase in forty-years. In that time frame there were huge changes to the economy and the social makeup of the city. In 1960, Miami was a town with a dominant Anglo-Saxon population, a repressed black minority (concentrated in two major neighborhoods: Overtown and Liberty City), a Jewish community in Miami Beach with a large number of retirees, and few Hispanics. The economy was dependent on tourism with two high seasons: the "rich" winter months and the "convention" months of the summer and, consequently, there were few jobs available outside the tourist industry, especially out of season. The now famous South Beach area consisted in 1960 of a number of old, mostly neglected hotels, many of which closed after the winter season. These hotels were so inexpensive that many families, including Jesús' uncle Manolo Núñez, lived in this area year around.

Data from the 2000 census shows that 34% of the population of the city of Miami was Cuban, 67% spoke Spanish as their first language, versus 26% for English and 5% for Creole. Cubans in Miami now dominate the politics, and many of the business and social institutions of the city. Today, the city is still a magnet for tourism with a major cruise port, several beaches and the trendy and popular South Beach. It is also a financial center, the headquarters of a number of major corporations, the location of Latin American headquarters for many companies, the site of several universities and the home of four professional sport teams (Dolphins, Heat, Marlins, Panthers).

---

[27] Most of the info here is from wikipedia.org/wiki/Miami

Cubans traveling to Miami in the early 1960s flew on regularly scheduled commercial flights until the Cuban Missile crisis in October 1962. Then, in 1965, Castro opened the port of Camarioca[28] for people who wanted to travel to the US. This caused a chaotic flotilla of boats and ships ferrying many Cubans to Miami. As a result, the US and Cuban government agreed on an organized program called the Freedom Flights. These flights started in December 1965 and lasted until 1971, bringing over 600,000 Cubans, according to a Time Magazine article of September 13, 1971. The city of Miami did not have the economic capacity in the early 1960s to absorb this large number of new comers and this resulted in the relocation of many families to other parts of the United States.[29] Most of the Cubans arriving in Miami had become poor overnight, did not speak the language nor understood the culture. Newly arrived exiles scrambled to find a place where to live, many staying with relatives or friends, creating many crowded houses.

Farewell to Cuba

Rigoberto and Argentina had taken steps to plan the possible departure of the family from Cuba— a departure they thought would be temporary, in keeping with the history of previous self-exile by Cubans fleeing another bad government regime. Jesús' parents insured that each of their children had a valid passport and a US tourist visa. They purchased open-tickets (which could be used anytime) from Cuba to Miami using a travel agency owned by Ricardo Correoso, who was married to Rigoberto's niece Lydia León. Rigoberto and Argentina had coordinated their departure with Rigoberto's nieces, Berta León, who was also planning to send her two daughters to the USA.

Every October 10, Cuba celebrates a major national holiday to mark the anniversary of the beginning of Cuba's First War of

---

[28] See the USCG website for summary of this boat lift, www.uscg.mil/history/uscghist/camarioca1965.asp

[29] Miami experienced another large influx of Cubans in 1980 with the Mariel boatlift that brought around 125,000 persons to South Florida.

Independence from Spain. On this feast day in 1960, a beautiful Monday, the León-Núñez children left Cuba. Early that morning, the León-Núñez family left Victoria de las Tunas and headed towards the city of Camagüey, driving west for 67 miles along Cuba's Central Highway. They arrived in the city, checked into the Grand Hotel where the children changed clothes before heading to the Ignacio Agramonte Airport, located a few miles north of the city. This airport was used in 1960 for both military and commercial flights, a few domestic flights and an occasional international flight. By the year 2000, the airport handled over seventy thousand passengers per year.[30]

The León-Núñez children were booked on a regular commercially scheduled Pan American Airways flight that departed Kingston, Jamaica, and made a stop in Camagüey on its way to Miami. The ages of the León-Núñez children leaving should serve as a reminder of the angst and fear our parents felt in sending us to a foreign country. Jesús was two weeks shy of his 16th birthday; Ticó was 14 years; Carmen Luisa 11 years; Mary had just turned 9 years old; and, Henry was 3 months past his 5th birthday. Traveling to Miami with them were their cousins Ketty and Bertica Gallardo León and Bertica's husband Manolo García; Bertica and Manolo had been married for a couple of weeks and were about to begin their new life together in a new country, without jobs or money.

After checking in at the airport, the León-Núñez children were escorted by the security personnel to a separate area where they checked all their bags, searching for jewelry and US currency. The security personnel interviewed a number of the children. They wanted to know why they were traveling. The children were prepared with an answer: "to visit an uncle and cousins in Miami." The León-Núñez clan was able to take a large amount of luggage because they left Cuba before the government started to make travel to the USA difficult. The actual flight to Miami was une-

---

[30] www.azworldairports.com estimates the airport handled eighty-thousand passengers in 2002.

ventful— Jesús does not remember it at all. Upon arrival in Miami, the immigration officer in passport control asked the reason for the trip; when he heard we were leaving because of the Cuban Government he gave each of us an "indefinite" visa status. This visa allowed us to stay in the USA as long as we wanted and gave us the right to work or study while in the country. In Miami, Manolo, Bertica and Ketty went to stay with their aunt Lalita and her family while the León-Núñez kids went with their uncle René Núñez who had come to receive them at the airport.

From Cuba to Philadelphia and Momence

And so began the exile for Jesús, his siblings and his cousins. Chelo's Calvary was to begin a few months later. We will describe some of the difficulties we experienced but you should understand that it is not possible to describe all the anguish and difficulties that we suffered. First of all, there was the pain of family separation, the first time for all of us; the uncertainty and the difficulty of arriving in a country with a different culture, language, and educational system; we had no money; we did not know how to take care of ourselves as we had never made a bed or washed clothes or prepared lunch. It would take about one year for the families to be reunited, several years to adjust emotionally and logistically to the new country, and more than ten years for us to achieve a lit bit of financial stability— obviously nothing like what we had in Cuba, at least not for many more years.

As related earlier, part of the León family had stayed at René's house in 1958. The first visit to their house was a visit by tourists planning to stay a few days only. The León family arrival in 1960 was very different. René's household included his wife Marina, and their children America ("Tata"), Barbara and Renecito ("Macho"). They lived in a three-bedroom ranch house in Miami Shores. Suddenly, five kids are added to the house, kids unprepared for the American way of life: the León children did not know how to do any household chores, and, furthermore it was not known how long the children would be staying with them. The addition of five children would have taxed the best of hostesses and since Marina was not a good hostess, she made it clear to René that the children had to leave soon. And so began the second separation of the León-Núñez family: Ticó and Jesús were sent to their cousin Lalita's house, Carmen Luisa and Mary to their uncle Manolo Núñez's house and Henry was sent back to Cuba.

Jesús has many memories from the short time he spent at René's house: first visit to an American Supermarket, observing the school bus protocol on the street, viewing the movie "Psycho" on Jesús' birthday and walking back from the theater on the center of the street because of the fear induced in us by the movie, and watching a very exciting world series. However, there was no discussion or planning for what to do while waiting. Meanwhile, Manolo and Bertica García had tried very hard, and unsuccessfully to find work in Miami while staying at Lalita's house, and they decided to try their luck in Philadelphia, a city Bertica knew because she spent time as a student there when she was a teenager. Rigoberto and Argentina arranged for Jesús and Ticó to move into Lalita and Ortelio Del Forn's house, and although Ticó and Jesús were there for only a couple of weeks, the experience was unique, odd, and rare. Ortelio worked in an office in downtown Miami and he, his wife Lalita, and their three boys lived in a rented house in southwest Miami. The family had a limited budget but additionally, Ortelio was a penny-pinching person and Ticó and Jesús felt his tightfisted approach especially at the dinner table: the number of plantains per person was calculated before hand and one was not allowed to exceed the "plantain quota." One night during their stay at their house, Jesús woke up and found himself in front of the refrigerator eating something— he had walked there in his sleep propelled by hunger; a lock was later added to the refrigerator! Now, the need to economize is understandable but, on the other hand, Jesús' parents were paying the Del Forn family a set amount per day to help economically while Ticó and Jesús stayed with them. Jesús and Ticó were also asked to help with household chores like mowing the lawn at a rental house they were going to move into where the weeds and grass were knee high. Lalita did take the time to take Jesús and Ticó to the Coral Gables High

School so that they could investigate how to register in school while waiting for the expected return to Cuba.

The environment at the Del Forn house suffocated Jesús and Ticó's lives. Their parents decided to explore other possibilities, so after a few days,[31] they were sent to Philadelphia to lodge with Leticia, her family and Manolo, Bertica and Ketty. Ortelio deposited Jesús and Ticó on a Greyhound bus for a thirty-six hours journey from Miami to Philadelphia. Manolo García was waiting for them at the Philadelphia bus station and took them to Leticia's house. Leticia was now married to Carmelo Nazario, a jovial and generous person, and they had rented a three-story house on the corner of Howard and West York Street. The first floor of the house was converted to a small grocery store ran by Nazario and Leticia with help from the household; the third floor was still inhabited by the previous tenants and was not available for use by the family until the spring of 1961. This meant that initially, ten persons and later eleven with the arrival of René Fuentes, had to squeeze into one floor. Manolo, Bertica and Ketty slept in the living room; Nazario, Leticia, her three sons, Ticó and Jesús slept in beds or sofas in the kitchen-dining room, family room and two bedrooms. And, of course, there was only one bathroom for all of us!

Jesús is sure that God must have Leticia and Nazario in a special place in heaven because their generosity was incredible. Leticia's immediate family in Cuba had ostracized her because she married against her parent's desires. In the US, Leticia had struggled to meet the basic needs for the family when her husband abandoned her. Then, there was Nazario, who was not Cuban and did not know any of the people arriving from Cuba. The three sons, Aristides (Ray), Ramiro, and George, had to make major sacrifices in order for us to live in their house. Leticia's generosity reminds Jesús about the poor widow in Mark's Gospel, Chapter 12, verses

---

[31] Ticó and Jesús were in René Núñez's house on Jesús' birthday, October 23, and in Philadelphia before Election Day, November 8; Ticó and Jesús were at Lalita's house less than two weeks. Thus, about two weeks in René's house and less than two weeks in Lalita's house.

41-44, who "...out of her poverty has put in everything she had, her whole living." Bertica, Manolo, Ketty, Ticó and Jesús lived with Leticia and Nazario for several months until little by little, we were able to move out. Manolo, Bertica and Ketty were the first to move out, in the spring of 1961, when both Manolo and Bertica found employment and were able to pay for their own place. During the summer of 1961 Jesús and Ticó moved to Miami to join their mother and siblings.

Carmen Luisa and Mary went to stay with their uncle Manolo Núñez, who had become distant from his sister Argentina because she supported the family from his first marriage, but when he decided to leave Cuba, he visited Argentina and offered to care for Carmen Luisa and Mary until Argentina could join them. Manolo and his family had visited Miami Beach on several occasions staying at a small apartment hotel on Ocean Drive just north of 12 Street, across from the beach, and he knew the hotel owners well. When he arrived in Miami from Cuba, he checked into this hotel and stayed there for many years. He negotiated a good deal with the hotel owners and lived essentially rent-free on a small apartment in exchange for working for the hotel doing odd jobs and taking care of the front desk for several hours every day. Today this hotel is part of South Beach's Art Deco boutique hotels; most of them are refurbished old hotels including the one where Manolo and his family lived. However, in 1960 these old hotels had a small clientele and most of them closed after the winter season was over. Carmen Luisa and Mary lived with Manolo's family until the summer of 1961 when Argentina came to stay permanently in Miami. The ambiance and daily life for Carmen Luisa and Mary was different and somewhat odd: they had not met Manolo, his wife Guillerma, their children Guillermita and Manolito, or Guillermita's husband, Hector. The hotel environment was unusual, Miami Beach was full of retirees, many of them Jewish. Manolo's family life style was also different from the León-Núñez family; one particular major difference was that Manolo's family did not go to church at all. On the other hand, Manolo and his family provided a caring environment for Carmen Luisa and Mary. As a result, the León Núñez children became close to Manolo and his family so that years later they chose to go to the beach near Manolo's apartment in order to visit with them before or after the beach.

Philadelphia

Jesús and Ticó lived in Philadelphia for nine months. The name of the city of Philadelphia derives from the Greek and means, the City of Brotherly Love, and even though they had difficulties adjusting to the new surroundings, Ticó and Jesús have fond memories of Philadelphia.

Leticia's house was located in a blue-collar working class section of Philadelphia, on an old house that was respectable in 1960 but that by 2009 had deteriorated to look like a war zone. The house was located at 2400 North Howard Street on the corner of York Street directly across from a neighborhood bar. The house was located close to a station for the elevated portion of the Market subway line that ran over Kensington Avenue. The house was two blocks from our Catholic Parish, St. Boniface (now closed), a few blocks from the hospital where Jesús was a patient later on, and close to many shops and groceries on Kensington Avenue, including Kelly's Korner, a large grocery where Jesús worked part time.

Although Ticó and Jesús had only met Leticia briefly during the summer of 1958, the fact that Bertica, Manolo and Ketty were staying with Leticia helped Jesús and Ticó to adjust to their new environment. Jesús remembers arriving in Philadelphia just before the 1960 presidential election held on the eight of November that saw John F. Kennedy, 43 years of age, become the youngest elected and the first Roman Catholic president. Since the weather was already cold in Philadelphia when Jesús and Ticó arrived, and since most of their clothes were only suitable for Cuba's weather not Philadelphia's winter weather, Argentina had arranged to "borrow" a couple of trousers and one overcoat from one of the parish priests from Tunas. In addition to being cold, the winter of 1960-61 had a lot of snow, with the first snow falling just before Christmas, and later that winter, there was a snow storm that paralyzed the city for three days, requiring Jesús and Nazario to walk in the snow for about three miles to buy milk for the house. That winter was the first winter since 1888 that had more than one storm with 10 or more inches of accumulation.[32] The first snow opened a door to new experiences for Ticó and Jesús: the beauty and peace when the snow is falling, the temporary cleanliness of snow-covered streets, playing in the snow with snowballs and snowmen, but also the drudgery of shoveling snow and removing ice from sidewalks, the increased difficulty in walking and occasional slippage and fall, and the ugliness of dirty snow after a couple of days of traffic.

Leticia was thoughtful and organized, and she helped Jesús and Ticó get ready for school and work in Philadelphia. First, she requested and obtained financial support from St. Boniface's Parish for Ticó and Jesús to attend Northeast Catholic High School, and she also took them to the Social Security Administration to apply and receive social security cards. Jesús, due to his ignorance of the American culture submitted an application with multiple errors. In addition to a mistake on the year of his birth, shown as 1942 instead of 1944, probably a transcription error, the social security records had his last name and that of his parents all wrong. Jesús was raised in the Spanish culture where one uses two last names: one from the father and one from the mother. And hence, the social security records for Jesús showed the following information (no accents or tilde over the n): First name: Jesus; Middle name: Leon; Last name: Nunez. Similarly, his parent's names appeared as Rigoberto Leon Diaz and Argentina Nunez Berro with Leon and Nunez as their respective middle names and Diaz and Berro as their respective last names. Jesús corrected the records while living in Maryland some forty-five years after his initial inscription into the Social Security system. Regardless, registering for high school and the inscription into the Social Security system were the first baby steps for Jesús and Ticó as they began a new phase of their lives.

---

[32] From www.nbcphiladelphia.com/news/breaking/Its-Officially-the-Snowiest-Winter-in-History-84065947.html, about the 2009-10 winter, the snowiest Philadelphia winter season in recorded history.

Northeast Catholic High School was about one-half block from the Torresdale & Kensington avenues metro station, five stations away from the York Avenue station near Leticia's house, so it was very easy to go to school every day. The school was under the direction of the Oblates of Saint Francis de Sales (O.S.F.S), and was at one time, the largest Catholic high school in the world with over 4,700 students enrolled. In the fall of 1960, it had a student body of about 3,000, with many teachers but not one of the teachers spoke Spanish! The school did not offer Spanish as a language option and the only people who spoke Spanish were a few Hispanic students, none of which were on Jesús' classes, forcing him to learn English to survive. Jesús remembers a few of the courses in which he was enrolled: Junior English where they were reading Jane Eyre, great English literature but Greek to Jesús; Chemistry, where the teacher wrote chemical reactions on the board but Jesús did not understand what was going on; Senior Math— very interesting but the language barrier was too high: what did "locus of points mean?" Some of the Junior students went out of their way to help Jesús by first "renaming" him "Frank" since the use of the Lord's name was something beyond their comprehension,[33] taking him to learn to bowl where they taught him the use of the verb "to try," taking him to a Catholic school on Lehigh Avenue that held dances at least once a week— the place where Jesús learned to do the "twist" and other American dances. Memories from the school year include singing "Jingle Bells" as students headed back to class after lunch recess in December, singing for the first time some of the standard Catholic hymns during school Mass in the auditorium, drinking American coffee ("ugh") at a corner cafe near the subway station, and learning enough English to get by.

---

[33] It seems that the Hispanic tradition to give JESUS' name to boys traces its roots to the time when the Moors were a dominant presence in the Iberian Peninsula. In Islam it is common to name children after Mohammed, the key figure in their religion. In order to counteract the Muslim Moors and to demonstrate their Christianity, it became common for Hispanic Christians to name their firstborn Jesús.

A detailed chronicle of Jesús' 1960-61 Philadelphia winter would require at least one chapter to recount the many events that occurred during this time. In December, the Cuban Government severed diplomatic relations with the USA, a bad sign! Jesús' cousin Nilda Núñez came from New York to visit Ticó and Jesús; we visited the fabulous Wanamaker's department store in downtown Philadelphia to marvel at the Christmas decorations; René Fuentes arrived from Cuba— he was the husband of "Chichi," Leticia's sister; Jesús went with Nazario to the Italian open-air Market in South Philly to buy items for the family grocery— and, when it was very cold, stopping at corner bars to get a shot of whiskey to warm ourselves; we helped Nazario and Leticia in the family grocery store; Jesús worked and earned wages for the first time ever. Then, the holiday celebrations: the first Thanksgiving in the USA— a completely new holiday to us; and celebrating the first Christmas in the USA and the first one ever away from our families. Yet, one part of our life that did not change was the practice of our Catholic faith. Manolo, Bertica, Ketty, Jesús and Ticó went to church every week, walking to St. Boniface Catholic Church at Norris Square, about two blocks from the house, a parish that was closed in 2006.

Jesús and Ticó found part-time, jobs at Kelly's Korner, a large grocery situated at 2501 Kensington Avenue, a five minutes walk from Leticia's house. Jesús' primary duties were bagging groceries and bringing grocery carts to the store from the parking lot. Bringing carts from the parking lost was particularly painful on many days during the cold Philadelphia winter— at times Jesús' hands became bluish because he did not have gloves. In addition to earning a little money, the job at Kelly's Korner was a place to practice English and to make new friends with some the other part-time workers of his age. At Kelly's Korner, Jesús met a group of boys and girls of his age who lived in the neighborhood. This group of friends was one of the social clusters that Jesús developed in Philadelphia, together with the friends from high school, a few friends he met at the weekly dances with whom he went out a few times, and friends he met at Hispanic parties. The friends from Kelly's Korner took him to a summer picnic at a New Jersey lake that was, by Jesús' standard, freezing. Not bad for someone who, a few months earlier, did not speak the language, did not understand the culture, and did not know any young persons in Philadelphia!

Jesús and Ticó spoke regularly to Carmen Luisa and Mary who were living with Manolo Núñez's family in Miami Beach, and who also seemed to be getting along with school and life in their new environment.

The spring of 1961 brought mixed news. The failure of the Bay of Pigs Invasion, in April, sentenced the exiles to a longer than planned stay in the USA. On the other hand, the weather improved, Manolo and Bertica were working and able to rent their own place and the tenants renting the third floor of Leticia's house moved out, giving the family more space. Jesús and Ticó moved to a room in the third floor that had a double bed, where they slept together, and a bathroom nearby. Ticó and Jesús had part time jobs, were adjusting to the way of life and making progress in school; that is, learning English since the 1960-61 year was a loss academically.

For Jesús, the worse was yet to come. A few weeks after the start of spring, he became seriously ill with a high fever and began to vomit. After a couple of days without improvement, Nazario and Leticia took him to a hospital where the doctor gave Jesús a medicine for his stomach, sending him home. Jesús continued to be ill so Leticia took him to the private practice of a Puerto Rican doctor. He said Jesús had a major infection and after asking about any allergies, gave him a shot of penicillin for the infection and told Leticia to take him to a hospital for further testing. Jesús got increasingly worse with very high fever, severe headaches, unable to hold any food in his stomach, and the loss of his vision every time he got out of bed to go to the bathroom. Leticia and Nazario were very worried, so Nazario took Jesús back to the same hospital, the Episcopal Hospital, located on Lehigh Avenue four blocks from the house. This time the emergency room doctors were two Hispanic men, one from Chile and the other one from Spain, to the best of Jesús' recollection. These doctors concurred that Jesús had some major infection and after running a number of basic tests decided to do a spinal tap to analyze the cerebrospinal fluid. This test was positive for meningitis, an infectious illness that consists of swelling and irritation (inflammation) of the membranes covering the brain and spinal cord. The doctors told Nazario that Jesús had to be hospitalized. There was one catch, Jesús had no money or insurance so the hospital was not enthusiastic about admitting him, but Nazario threatened to call the police if they did not admit and treat Jesús for this illness.

Jesús was duly admitted into the hospital and put in the poor's ward, a large dormitory style room with patient's beds lining each side of the room. Because Jesús had a highly infections disease, his area was blocked from the rest of the patients, using free standing fabric covered room dividers and entrance to his area was prohibited to everyone except medical personnel, who had to wear gloves and medical face masks. The medical treatment in 1960 was straight forward: massive dosage of penicillin injections in the butt (technically the Dorsogluteal site) given every two hours for the first two weeks— Jesús recalls having to sleep on the stomach because of the soreness of his buttocks. A priest from the high school came to visit Jesús within the first few days of his stay in the hospital and administered the Sacrament of Extreme Unction, not a good sign because before the Second Vatican Council this sacrament was only administered to patients who were in danger of imminent death.

Thanks to God, to Nazario and Leticia, to the Puerto Rican doctor who injected Jesús with penicillin, thanks to the Hispanic doctors that diagnosed his illness and thanks to penicillin and the treatment at the Episcopal Hospital, Jesús began to improve after about one week in the hospital. Unfortunately, the only way to test whether he was clear of the meningitis was to do a spinal tap, a painful procedure that Jesús underwent three times during this illness; the first for the initial diagnosis and the other two to test the status of the illness.

Meanwhile, Leticia called Argentina to tell her that Jesús had meningitis and had been admitted to the hospital where he was being treated for the disease. Argentina was in Havana with Henry and immediately started preparing to travel to Philadelphia as soon as possible, but traveling had become more difficult because of the recently failed Bay of Pigs Invasion. Argentina did have connections in the Government. Her sister, Jesús' godmother, María, was Assistant Secretary of Education, and her good friend Raúl Cepero whom she met while going to school in Sagua La Grande and who was María's brother-in-law, was at the time President of the Cuban Central Bank. Raúl helped Argentina and Henry get exit visas, find seats on a flight to Miami and gave her US $100 in spending money. Argentina and Henry did not return to Tunas but left directly from Havana to Miami in May 1961. By the time Argentina arrived in Miami, Jesús was no longer in critical condition. This allowed Argentina to spend time in Miami with Carmen Luisa and Mary, and also allowed her to figure out how to obtain travel tickets to Philadelphia using the Cuban re-localization program. The re-localization program was organized by the US Government to alleviate the concentration of Cubans in the Miami area; the program paid the one-way fare from Miami to any city in another state for exiles recently arrived from Cuba.

Jesús was in the hospital for four weeks, the first three in isolation and not allowed to step off the bed. After three weeks, and one last spinal tap, he was allowed to get out of bed, a difficult activity as he was weak and his equilibrium was somewhat impaired. By the time Jesús left the hospital he was weighing 125 pounds, about 50 pounds lighter than his usual weight; he was weak but alive. The hospital bill, paid, Jesús believes, by the City of Philadelphia was less than $700 for a four-week stay— compare this to the $25,000 bill forty-years later for a six-day stay at the Mercy Hospital in Miami.[34] Although Argentina did not see Jesús in the hospital because she and Henry arrived in Philadelphia after he was released, she was stunned by his appearance when she first saw him.

Argentina and Henry spent several weeks in Philadelphia as she assisted in Jesús' recovery and weighed the options for her

---

[34] Although the comparison is not apples-to-apples, the math is still stunning: Philadelphia = less than $25/day; Miami = $4,167/day; the Miami hospital was about 170 TIMES more expensive per day— talk about the increase in the cost of healthcare!

family's life in the USA because she had already decided she was not returning to Cuba. Argentina asked herself: "Should we all live in Philadelphia or Miami? Where would we live and how do we pay for food and rent?" A Philadelphia doctor told Argentina that the cold weather was a possible influence on Jesús' illness and that she should move him to a warmer climate. The doctor's input simplified her decision: the León-Núñez family would live in Miami together. She and Henry left for Miami while Jesús and Ticó stayed in Philadelphia for a few more weeks until she could raise the money to pay for Jesús and Ticó's trip to Miami. She began to organize herself in Miami, registering the family as Cuban refugees. This qualified the family for $100/month cash aid, and a once-a-month food distribution package. She rented an apartment and brought Mary, Carmen and Henry to this apartment. She raised the funds to pay for Ticó and Jesús' trip to Miami, a trip that was the exclamation point to the eight months of our passage from a sheltered life in Cuba to a new life in Miami. The trip from Philadelphia was in a four-engine prop airplane that flew through a major thunderstorm. During the storm, the pilots dove the plane at a pretty steep angle to try to escape the heart of the storm— the maneuver, although safe and logical, was scary especially as there was lightning all around the plane. In any case, with Ticó and Jesús' arrival in Miami, most of the family was together, except for Rigoberto who joined them in Miami a couple of months later, in August 1961. Coincidentally, Jesús arrived in Miami around the same time that Chelo was arriving from Cuba to start her own pilgrimage.

Chelo's departure

On Monday, June 19, 1961, almost exactly two months after the failure of the Bays of Pigs Invasion, Cordero and Consuelo took Chelo to the José Martí International Airport, located about 10 miles from downtown Havana. Cordero and Consuelo had decided to send Chelo to Miami to protect her from the increasing power of the Cuban Government.

Chelo was not prepared emotionally for this trip since she had never been separated from her family or traveled alone. After checking in and obtaining her boarding pass, Chelo underwent thorough checks of her belongings and of her person, a pat down to insure she was not taking either hard currency or jewelry with her. She was forced to remove her earrings and other jewelry and give them to her parents. Then, she joined all the passengers flying to the USA in the "pescera," literally fishbowl, the name that Cubans gave to the glass-enclosed room where family and travelers could see each other but not talk with one another, to wait for their flight to board.

The flight time from Havana to Miami was short, about forty-five minutes, but Chelo has no recollection of the particulars of the trip. "I was in a cloud," she says about the flight. Consuelo had contacted her former boss at the Pilón Coffee Company, Oswaldo Rosette, who had agreed to host Chelo with his family. Rosette picked Chelo at the Miami Airport and took her to their house where he lived with his wife and two children, a boy and a girl. The Rosette family lived in a nice house, better quarters than the living facilities of most of the new Cuban refugees. Chelo always thought that this family was very nice, asking herself: "Why did they welcome me into their home?" She hardly knew them, having met them only once in Cuba. The generosity of the Rosette family was one of the many examples of the generosity of Cubans to each other during those trying times.

While at the Rosette's, Chelo slept in the sofa. Consuelo had expected that Chelo would stay with the family until she and Cordero could leave Cuba. Unfortunately, the Rosette's were expecting other family members, who were also fleeing Cuba, and they informed Consuelo that she needed to find a place for Chelo to stay. Consuelo must have been really worried— where would Chelo go? Consuelo contacted the nuns of the American Dominican Academy, who were in Miami after being been expelled from Cuba, and asked for their assistance. The nuns, bless their hearts, were able to place Chelo at the St. Patrick's Academy for Girls, in Momence, Illinois, a suburb of Chicago.

Chelo left Miami for Chicago on July 10, the same day that her cousin Vicente was marrying Jesús' cousin Bertica in Havana, the day that the Cordero Redruello family met Rigoberto León Díaz. Chelo does not remember the details of the preparation of the trip, although she is sure that the Cuban Refugee Program paid for the airfare as part of the program to relocate Cubans out of South Florida.

St. Patrick's Academy — Momence

Once again, Chelo does not remember the particulars of the trip from Miami to Momence, one of several episodes from this time of her life that she has either forgotten or blocked from her memory. Who took her to the Miami airport? Who picked her up at the Chicago airport? How did she go from the Chicago Airport to Momence? One can only try to imagine what might have been going through her mind: Where am I going? What will this place so far from home will be like? When will I see my parents again?

Momence, Illinois, is located 50 miles south of Chicago. According to the website of the Momence Chamber of Commerce, in 2011, "The City of Momence has a population of approximately 3,200, with the surrounding Momence and Ganeer townships providing an additional 7,500 people to the immediate area. The population of Kankakee County in its entirety is approximately 103,800 residents."[35] In Kankakee County, Father LaBrie and the Servants of the Holy Heart of Mary founded St. Patrick's Academy at the beginning of the 20th century.[36] St Patrick was a high school for girls with boarding (dormitory) facilities. The nuns of this school agreed to lodge, feed and educate Chelo and other Cuban girls who were sent by their parents to protect them from Communism. These nuns who had no connection to Cuba were part of the many Catholic priests and nuns who, out of their love for Christ and their generosity, helped thousands of Cuban children who arrived in Miami alone.

Chelo who was raised in a very protected family environment and had lived in a large city in Cuba was now at a boarding school in a very small town in the midwest of the USA, a change so great

---

[35] http://www.momence.net
[36] For a short story of the school see http://www.illinoishs glory days.com/id799.html

it could be the script for an episode of "The Twilight Zone." To make matters much worse, Chelo arrived in July when all the regular students had gone home for the summer. She was therefore, the only student in the school with the rest of the school population made up of pre-Vatican II nuns, probably very holy women, who slept in the private convent-like-quarters open only to the nuns who lived there.

Chelo was assigned the third bed, counting from the entrance, in a dormitory room with about fifteen beds and <u>only one bath</u>, a bath with a tub and no shower. Chelo came from a family obsessed with cleanliness, so she took baths standing up because the tub had a ring caused by age, usage and hasty cleanings. The bedroom was in an old building with creaking wood plank floors and a fire escape ladder at the opposite end of the room from Chelo's bed. In Cuba, Chelo had shared a bedroom with her Aunt "Tata," now she was alone in this large bedroom, alone, scared and feeling abandoned. Her emotional stress was so serious that she stopped menstruating on arrival to Momence and her menstruation period did not return until her parents arrived in Miami, six months later. Thanks God she spoke English and at least was able to communicate with the nuns.

Chelo, like all Cuban girls from the middle and upper classes, was ill prepared to take care of herself in a USA household or for that matter at the St. Patrick's Academy boarding school. She did not know how to make a bed or how to wash or iron clothes. The nuns taught her how to make the bed and how to wash clothes, but since most of her clothes were made of linen, they needed to be dry cleaned or hand ironed, and because dry cleaning and hand ironing were out of the questions, many of her beautiful dresses were ruined.

Another completely new experience for Chelo during her summer in Momence was learning to babysit children. The nuns volunteered Chelo to babysit for a local Cuban doctor's family with three children, a family that helped St Patrick's Academy. Chelo had no idea how to babysit and remembers panicking when one of the children broke a milk bottle that he took from the refrigerator.

While Chelo was in Momence, Consuelo and Cordero tried to call her every week— a difficult and expensive proposition in the 1960s. And when she spoke to her parents, Chelo would cry, in despair, "sáquenme de aquí" (literally, "take me out of here"). The nuns asked Chelo to be more positive when she spoke with her parents, but she could not help feeling desperate and abandoned. Recalling those months, Chelo said: "I cried so much that my tear drops dried out..."

Chelo was the only person in the dorm for about six weeks until mid August, a few days before the beginning of the school year, when six Cuban Refugee girls arrived at the school. One of these girls, Isabel Cinta, had been a classmate of Chelo at the American Dominican Academy in Cuba. Because most of the new arrivals spoke little or no English, the nuns at St. Patrick's brought a Mexican nun, Sor María Elena, to assist them. Chelo's life at Momence improved with the arrival of other Cuban girls and even though Henry Thoreau said that, "If misery loves company, misery has company enough," in the case of Chelo and the others girls, sharing a common problem helped each other endure their misery.

With the start of the school year, and with the other Cuban girls sharing her difficulties, time seemed to move a little bit faster for Chelo. Her day began at 6:30 AM when a bell awakened the students so they could attend daily Mass at 7:00 AM and then proceed to breakfast, a large American style breakfast. Chelo was not used, and still is not used, to eating large quantities of food early in the morning and by lunch she was very hungry, only to find out that lunch was also American style: a sandwich or a hot dog or other small meal. The daily schedule was dedicated to academic work. Chelo remembers the academic subjects that semester to be Chemistry, Algebra II, American History, English, Religion and possibly Home Economics— the schoolwork helped distract Chelo from her personal problems.

Cordero and Consuelo arrived in Miami from Cuba on November 30, 1961, an event that improved Chelo's life immensely. Her parents called her upon her arrival in Miami and told her they would bring her to Miami as soon as possible. The arrival of Chelo's parents in Miami created strong links with Jesús' family, preparing the way for the eventual romance between Chelo and Jesús. When they arrived in Miami, Cordero and Consuelo's only "relations" were Bertica's sister, Estela, and uncle Rigoberto, so they decided to move near these relatives and rented an efficiency apartment on 28 Street NW near Fifth Avenue.

Consuelo and Cordero wanted to speak with Chelo regularly and this required access to a telephone, a device that few Cuban exiles' homes had in the early 1960s. At the time, Southern Bell required a deposit of $50 to install a phone in a home if you were not a US Citizen, a sum that was very large for most Cuban refugees as can be illustrated by a simple example. Most Cuban refugees received $100 cash aid and some food staples per month from the US Government; the rent for the León apartment, a decent two bedroom apartment on 30 Street near Northwest Second Avenue was $85 a month, including utilities. Hence, after paying for rent there was little money to eat, let alone to pay a deposit for a phone or for the phone service. Luckily, Jesús' uncle, René Núñez, was a US Citizen and had a telephone installed at Jesús' home.

Consuelo and Cordero came periodically to Jesús' home to place phone calls to Chelo. Long-distance calls then were made person-to-person via operators of the AT&T network, and since neither Cordero nor Consuelo spoke English they needed a person to make the calls. Jesús was the one who setup the calls and when Chelo got on the phone in Momence, he greeted her and gave the phone to her parents; Jesús became acquainted with Chelo setting up these phone calls.

Jesús had also become a good friend of Cordero for a number of reasons, particularly because of their shared love for baseball and because it was easy to become a friend of Cordero. Cordero used to brag to Jesús about his wonderful, beautiful, great daughter, the one for whom Jesús setup telephone calls from time to time. During one of these conversations, Jesús asked Cordero to show him a picture of his daughter, and upon looking at Chelo's picture, told Cordero: "I am going to marry your daughter." What possessed Jesús to make such a bold statement? Bravado, premonition? Whatever the reason, he predicted the future accurately: Chelo and Jesús became friends and were going steady by the end of the summer of 1962.

Chelo spent the 1961 Christmas in Momence and although she cannot recollect any celebration, she assumes that there would have been some sort of dinner with the other Cuban girls. Her time at St. Patrick's Academy did not leave good memories but Chelo did return to see Momence and the Academy forty years later when Consuelo Beatriz lived in Indiana. Chelo was able to see the school before its demise. By 2007, St. Patrick's Academy had become a coed elementary school of the Joliet Diocese under the leadership of laypersons before it closed at the end of the 2009-10 school year.

Book III – Renaissance: Beginning of a new life

Miami

Argentina and the León-Núñez siblings moved into an apartment at 210 NW 30 Street, a two-story four-unit building; each unit had two bedrooms and one bath. The front door of the apartment opened to a small living room with two modest pink sofas where Carmen Luisa and Mary slept. Next to the living room was an open bedroom with one double bed where Rigoberto and Argentina slept. Beyond this bedroom was the dining area and the bathroom. Henry slept in a small single bed in the dining area— this bed had a story of its own: Jesús saw the bed discarded on a street not far from a friend's house and brought the frame to the house. He painted the frame and then purchased a mattress; voilà, Henry's bed. Beyond the dining room was a small, narrow kitchen equipped with a simple gas stove/oven. At the rear of the apartment, behind the kitchen, was the second bedroom where Ticó and Jesús slept in twin beds. The apartment was small but affordable since the cost for rent and utilities was only $85 per month. On an interesting note, the owner of the building was a sergeant of the Miami Police Department, so all tenants paid the rent on time!

The León-Núñez family did not live in the two-bedroom apartment for long, soon moving about two blocks west along 30th Street. They rented the second floor of a two-story white house located across from what was then the Coca-Cola bottling plant. This house was old but larger with three bedrooms, with larger living-dining area and kitchen. It had excellent air circulation so the summer months were tolerable. We have fond memories of the "Coca-Cola house"; it was home to the family and to new arrivals from Cuba, especially Rodolfo and Lolín, Rigoberto's brother and sister-in-law; it was the location for Jesús and Chelo's wedding reception; and it was the place to host the first visit to Miami of the first León-Cordero baby, Consuelo Beatriz in June of 1968. The León-Núñez parents moved four more times in Miami: Briefly to a house in SW Miami, then to an apartment across the Orange Bowl, later to a duplex on SW 12th Avenue just south of 8th Street, and finally to a house that Carmen Luisa purchased at 1810 SW 92 Avenue.

Argentina's brother, René Núñez, lived in Miami and had been a US citizen for many years. He worked as a chef of a restaurant on Bird Road and owned the house where the León siblings had stayed upon their arrival in Miami the previous October. René helped the León-Núñez family in many ways: he provided the security deposit to Bell South that allowed us to be one of the few Cuban exile families in our neighborhood with a telephone; he gave us an old but functioning TV; and he would bring food from time to time, sometimes a fruit pie, other times ham, meat or turkey. René's help was timely because the family was definitely very poor in 1961 and 1962. The household finances only began to improve when Rigoberto started working at Jackson Memorial Hospital as a laboratory technician.

How poor was the family? Initially the cash flow coming into the household consisted of $100 per month from the Cuban Refugee Program, money from odd jobs, small gifts, and an infrequent informal money exchange whereby Rigoberto— while he was in Cuba— gave Cuban pesos to a person in Cuba and that person's family member in the USA gave the equivalent amount in US dollars to Argentina. The monthly apartment rent was $85, which left $15 for everything else. The Cuban Refugee Program provided food— excess food accumulated by the US Department of Agriculture that we collected once a month. The food consisted of dry milk (awful), powder eggs (awful), cheddar cheese (good), white beans (good), and canned meat that looked like SPAM (most of the Cuban Refugees grew tired of this meat, and to this day, will avoid eating SPAM). Our heartfelt thanks to the USA Government that allowed us to come into the country and created a program to help us survive.

After Jesús recovered from meningitis, he was able to work during part of the 1961 summer at the Deauville Hotel of Miami

Beach, serving as a busboy in a couple of conventions. The pay was minimum wage, $1.15 per hour, and the hours long. Because most of the Cuban workers did not have a car, they could not go home between shifts of activities. On more than one occasion Jesús was away from home for fifteen hours or more. Regardless, the job did provide a few dollars to help the family. In August 1961, Rigoberto arrived from Cuba and eventually found a job as a dishwasher on a hotel in Miami Beach— he went from being a professional pharmacist, the owner of a drug store and a land-owning wealthy man to start at the bottom level of a hotel kitchen in order to help the family.

During the summer, Jesús applied and was accepted into Archbishop Curley High School. Argentina had talked to the pastor at Corpus Christi Church, Father John O'Shea, and had obtained scholarships for Jesús at Curley, and for Carmen Luisa, Mary and Henry at the Corpus Christi Parochial School. Ticó attended Belen Jesuit, a well-known school in Cuba that was just starting in Miami; it opened first on space loaned to the Cuban Jesuits by the Gesu Parochial School in downtown Miami. The school was later moved to the corner of SW 8th Street and 7th Avenue in the heart of Little Havana. Today Belen Jesuit has a large campus on southwest 127 Avenue.

The beginning of the school year increased the financial challenges. Ticó and Jesús had to take municipal busses to/from school every day— the student fare was ten cents in each direction, a total of $2 per week. Unfortunately, on some days Argentina was short of the forty cents needed for the bus so she would walk around the neighborhood picking empty soda bottles to turn in at the grocery store for the two cents deposit fee: 20 bottles were needed to cover the bus fare of one day! Argentina also had to provide lunch for Ticó. Curley provided free lunch as part of the scholarship and this was the best meal Jesús had every day. Ticó became known as "Merita" by his schoolmates at Belén because his lunch invariable consisted of a sandwich made using Merita bread, Cuban refugee meat and a Merita pastry. The Merita items were bought at the company store where they sold bread and pastry at lower prices because the items were approaching their expiration date.

Finding money for the bus fare was just one of the many problems of being poor. Another was the limited food selection, a selection that was almost all based on the free refugee food the family received monthly. The limited menu selection was exacerbated because there was no money to purchase spices or vegetables to improve the taste of the food or to complement it: there was no ham or chorizo to add to the white beans and there were no greens to make a salad. As a result, the main meal was normally made of white beans and refugee meat. Argentina tried to change the appearance of the food but there was very little to be done. Towards the end of the month, the family would run out of the Cuban Refugee lard and then she had to fry with water: she put water on the skillet and when it got hot she added the meat! A couple of the children found a way to "improve" their diet: Jesús was lucky and ate well Monday to Friday at Curley; Mary would often walk across the street to the house of a friend, Mirito, and arrive conveniently near the time that they were serving dinner, and of course, was invited and accepted the invitation to join them for dinner. Mirito, a Cuban woman, was the wife of George, "Yoyi," Jewett whose father, Clyde Jewell, an Anglo-Saxon US citizen had gone to Cuba and settled in the Holguín area. He and his family became cattle ranchers and then, like the rest of us, had become exiles after Castro's revolution. The Jewell folks were delightful people and they assisted the León family whenever they could. They helped find jobs, gave members of the family a ride from time to time, fed Mary often. Clyde— we called him "Clay"— helped Jesús find a job in 1962 packing eggs at the Sun City Egg Company.

Many evenings in 1961 and 1962, the family gathered gather across the street from the apartment with other Cuban families and either talked or played word games similar to the TV game "To Tell The Truth" where you had to guess the person or occupation of the contestant with a few questions. This entertainment was actually very wholesome, educational and free.

In November 1961, Bertica and Vicente, Jesús and Chelo's first cousins, respectively, arrived from Cuba and moved into an apartment near the Leóns. Lorenzo Cordero and Consuelo Redruello, Chelo's parents, moved into an efficiency apartment a few blocks from the León house. Jesús saw them regularly, either at the grocery store that Consuelo worked as a cashier or because Jesús would bring the sports section of the Miami Herald to Cordero.

The month of December 1961 brought many blessings, including the celebration of Christmas together for the León-Núñez family and the reunion of Chelo with her parents. Consuelo and Cordero joined the León family for Nochebuena (Christmas Eve celebration) together with Bertica, Vicente, Estela (Bertica's sister), Rolando Rodríguez (Jesús' cousin), and Vicente's siblings Adolfo y Mimi. We ate the traditional Cuban Nochebuena meal of roasted pork, yucca, rice and beans. Jesús invited Brother Victor, CSC, who was the Academic Advisor and English Teacher at Curley to dinner— Brother Victor and the rest of the Curley Brothers were the guests of the CEO of Pan American Air Lines who lived in a superb house in a gated community off Biscayne Boulevard. Jesús' cousin Rolando Rodríguez had an old car and he drove Jesús to pick Brother Victor who came to share a meal with a bunch of Cubans in a small apartment; Brother Victor brought us a bottle of brut champagne— too refined for our taste at the time.

After dinner, several of us walked to Corpus Christi Church for Midnight Mass ('Misa del Gallo'), shivering in the unusual cold weather that enveloped Miami during the 1961 Christmas-to-New Year's week.[37] Attending midnight Mass on Christmas Eve was a tradition of the León family, one custom that later ceased with the arrival of young children. That evening was so cold that Cordero used newspapers to cover himself at night— there was no heat in their apartment and not enough comforters to keep him warm over night.

On Christmas Day, the Leóns were surprised to receive a special delivery package sent by Juana Hierrezuelo. She had re-

---

[37] The coldest day of 1961 was December 30, when the temperature dropped to 39 degrees Fahrenheit.

quested delivery of the package to arrive on Christmas Day. The package was full of gifts especially for the younger León children. What a beautiful gesture! Juana worked as a housemaid in the New York area and had previously sent money to Argentina to help the family. Juana obviously earned a low income and she used part of her limited income to help us have a better Christmas. Jesús often remarked, "Juana's act of love that year was the greatest gift that we received at any Christmas."

A few days later, on December 27, the day before Chelo's 17th birthday, the León family met Chelo for the first time. It is difficult today to comprehend why it took Consuelo and Cordero several weeks to raise the money to pay for her airfare from Chicago but this is another example of how poor everyone was. Consuelo and Cordero, like all Cuban refugees, arrived in Miami penniless and almost everyone they knew was in a similar situation so they had to scratch and borrow money to raise the funds needed to pay for Chelo's airplane ticket.

Consuelo had found a position as a cashier at a small grocery store on NW 2nd Ave and 32nd street. Cordero did odd jobs like picking tomatoes until he landed a full-time job working in the kitchen of the Columbus Hotel, one of the largest and best hotels in Miami at the time. He was a conscientious worker and made several good friends at the Columbus but this was for him, as for most Cuban in Miami of his generations, merely a job needed in order for his family to survive. There was little money left over from Consuelo and Cordero's jobs after paying for basic necessities, but they were able to save something. With the money they saved and the help of friends, they eventually gathered enough money to buy Chelo's airplane ticket. Chelo arrived in Miami from Chicago on December 27, 1961, a cold Miami Thursday. After going home and unpacking, Cordero brought her to the León-Núñez house to introduce her to the family. Jesús was out of the house when Chelo arrived but returned in time to meet her that evening. Chelo remembers him wearing light blue jeans and sporting an Elvis Presley hairstyle.

Many of the young Cubans in Miami decided to attend the King Orange Jamboree Parade on New Year's Eve. This parade was for many years nationally televised preceding the Orange Bowl Game that was then played on New Year's Day. The parade was free and there was nothing else to do on New Year's Eve. So off we went to downtown Miami on a cold and windy night that caused us to shiver, a night so cold that fifty years later we can still remember it well. Chelo went to the parade with her cousin Estelita and some friends from Tarará, while Jesús went with family members.

Consuelo and Cordero were living in an "efficiency[38] apartment" when Chelo arrived in Miami. Later they moved to a second-floor one-bedroom apartment (Chelo called it the "palomar," literally pigeon house) on Thirtieth Street between Fifth and Sixth avenues where Chelo, Consuelo and Cordero shared lodgings with Cordero's niece and nephew, Estelita and Armandito. Chelo's cousins lived with them while waiting for their parents to come from Cuba. The living accommodations were tight— an efficiency apartment for five adults— but there was a more pressing issue to be resolved: who was going to cook? None of the residents of the Cordero household knew how to cook, nor were they jumping at the opportunity to cook— this was done by servants in Cuba and since everyone was planning to return to Cuba soon, why should one learn how to cook? The cooking problem required a practical, affordable solution and Consuelo, a person you could count to solve problems, found a solution. She hired René, a very nice person who had worked for the family of a friend in Tarará. René was an excellent cook and he prepared the food for the Cordero family until he moved to Houston the following year. By this time the Cordero family had moved to "more spacious" quarters at a one-bedroom apartment located at 336 NW 35 Street, this being their third residence in little over one year. This apartment was part of an eight unit complex that consisted of two rows of four apartments parallel to each other, separated by about twenty feet of green space, each row perpendicular to 35 Street. Vicente and Ber-

---

[38] An apartment in which one room typically contains the kitchen, living and sleeping quarters, with a separate bathroom.

tica lived at 330, Bertha and Estela at 328, and Chelo's family at 336. The apartments were nice, clean, and close to the rest of Consuelo's family in Miami since Carmen, Vicente's mother, and her other children, Adolfo and Virginia ("Mimi") lived only about a block away, also on 35 Street just beyond NW Fifth Avenue. The apartment on 35 Street was Chelo's home during the rest of her high school and her college studies until her wedding in 1967. Cordero and Consuelo moved two more times in the next 30 years, twice to duplex units: the first one on near SW 30th Avenue and 5 Street and later to 1123 NW 34 Avenue where they lived for more than 20 years. In November 1995, they moved to a detached house at 609 SW 87th Place in the Poinciana Pointe gated community that Chelo and Jesús purchased for them.

Marta Generosa Redruello Berdasco, Chelo's aunt arrived from Cuba in 1962 and she took over the cooking duties and the running of the Cordero-Redruello household activities until she was past her Ninetieth birthday. Generosa was the next to last of Chelo's family to arrive in the United States. Fourteen years later, in December 1976, Chelo's grandmother, Consuelo Berdasco Garrido arrived in Miami.

Cooking was a problem for most Cuban families because almost every middle class family in Cuba had a hired cook, and as a consequence, very few housewives knew how to cook. Cooking was also a problem at the León house but Argentina, who did not know how to fry an egg in Cuba, learned how to cook for the family. Her lack of experience in the kitchen was only part of the problem since there was no money to buy condiments, vegetables or oil. Cuban mothers had to learn to cook and to be creative with a limited budget: How many ways can you cook white beans and canned meat? How do you give it a different flavor or look when you cannot buy tomatoes, peppers or garlic?

As we write about the first few years or our lives in the USA, we once again marvel at the dedication and sacrifices made by our parents and other Cubans of their generation. These men and women left their countries, their careers, their possessions, everything they had, to protect their children so that they would have freedom and not be indoctrinated in Castro's communist system.

In Cuba, Argentina lived a comfortable life: she was the director of a commerce school, a recognized community leader who lived in large house with several servants. In the USA, she lived in a small apartment, had to learn to cook and clean house, figure out how to scrape a few pennies for bus fares, find a job in a factory and later a soda bottling plant. Similarly, Cordero left a Navy career and property in Cuba to work in the USA at odd manual labor jobs and later in the kitchen of a hotel. Consuelo, who became a supermarket cashier in Miami, left her birth home and moved into very small apartment in a country that was completely different from her own. Rigoberto, the youngest of thirteen children, had been pampered all his life and went from well-to-do owner of a drug store and of cattle ranch land holdings to extreme poverty. In Miami he initially started washing dishes at a Miami Beach hotel, but luckily, and thanks to Guillermo Hernández,[39] he eventually found a job as a laboratory technician at the Jackson Memorial Hospital, where his work was professionally interesting and the salary reasonably better. Our parents demonstrated an immense love for us through their sacrifices giving up everything for our sake.[40]

High School

After Consuelo arrived in Miami, she took steps to make sure Chelo continued her high school education. She spoke to the nuns of the American Dominican Academy who recommended that Chelo attend Notre Dame Academy for girls (NDA) situated at northeast 62 Street near First Avenue. The school was run by the Sisters Servants of the Immaculate Heart of Mary. Along with Chelo, Carmen Luisa and Mary León as well as Chelo's cousin

---

[39] Guillermo was married to Rigoberto's niece, Ethel Patallo León. Guillermo and Ethel lived about one block from Rigoberto and Argentina's house in Tunas. Guillermo and Ethel later moved to Atlanta where they died and are buried, he in 1975 and she in 2011.

[40] See Appendix II for a little bit more information about our parents.

Mimi also attended Notre Dame Academy. Consuelo paid the tuition for the school, $15 per month, a large sum of money at the time,[41] especially for newly arrived immigrants just beginning a new life.

Chelo began the second semester of her junior year in January of 1962 at NDA where she enrolled in French, Religion, English, Chemistry, Algebra II and Government. Chelo left the efficiency apartment early in the morning and walked a few blocks to NW Second Avenue where she got on the Number 5 bus that took her to NW 62 Street, about three blocks from the school. Incidentally, Jesús used the same bus route to go to Curley, getting off at NW 50 Street to walk east to NE Second Avenue, the location of his high school.

Jesús was on his senior year at Archbishop Curley High School that academic year. On February 20, 1962, astronaut John Glenn became the first American to orbit Earth as he flew aboard the Friendship 7 Mercury capsule and on May 29, 1962, Jesús graduated from high school. It seems preposterous to suggest any form of comparison between these two events except that they both happened in 1962 and they were major achievements. The first was a major technological achievement for the US; the second was a major step for Jesús and his family as they tried to restart their lives as exiles and immigrants with an uncertain future.

Completion of high school in 1962 seems even more remarkable given that the previous year in Philadelphia Jesús was not able to complete any course work. He had been seriously ill with meningitis, had moved to Miami and had to apply and be accepted to a new school. For Jesús, the 1960-61year was wasted academically, a year of transition from Cuba to the USA, learning English, and trying to understand a new system. Chelo knew English pretty well, and because of that, she was able to make progress during her first academic year in the USA.

Archbishop Curley was an excellent preparatory high school; one of the best schools and arguably the best Catholic high school

---

[41] The monthly rent for the efficiency apartment where Chelo lived was $50.

for boys in Miami at the time and it had a cafeteria that provided good lunch fare. The school was under the direction of the Brothers of the Holy Cross.[42] The student body, before the arrival of the Cuban exiles, consisted primarily of boys from upper middle-class and rich households. In Jesús' class, for example, was Frank E. Mackle, III, from a very rich real estate development family who, among other properties, developed Marco Island. There were several Brothers of the Holy Cross teaching at Curley when Jesús was a student— it was common at the time to have several religious teachers at Catholic schools. Four of his six teachers were brothers: the teachers of Religion, Math (Brother Keric Dever, also Principal), English (Brother Victor) and Government. His other teachers (Home Room, Biology, Typing) were also athletic coaches.

Brother Victor, the Academic Advisor, prepared a special academic program for Jesús in order for him to meet the high school graduation requirements and also round out his college preparation. He was placed on the class with the advanced students and he shared several classes with them: Religion, Math and English. Jesús daily schedule started with homeroom followed by Biology (with sophomores), Religion and Advanced Math, lunch, Senior English Literature, Typing and Government (with Juniors). It is interesting that the subject that Jesús considered most useful during his senior year was typing— very valuable to type reports and later for programming and daily use as technology moved to the computer age.

There were many first experiences for Jesús during his year at Curley: going to high school football games and high school dances, scrapping to put together enough money to buy the class ring, a ring that Jesús lost in a bathroom at the University of Florida, the inability to go to any proms because of lack of money— Jesús was also invited to the Immaculata Girls School Prom but could not

---

[42] The members of the order use CSC as the abbreviation of their religious order, from the French, Congrégation de Sainte-Croix; example: Brother Kevic Dever, CSC. This order directs Notre Dame University in Indiana.

attend. He had to adjust to the USA academic approach and a continuous schedule with classes right after a big lunch: he usually felt asleep in Brother Victor's English Literature class; on the days he did not fall asleep, Brother Victor would come by and tell him to go to sleep. He had several good friends among the students: Isidro A. Díaz— who moved to California with his uncle and aunt after high school; and Roosie "Frenchie" Kwahly, a French descendant of the settlers of Haiti, whose family moved to Miami and lived near Jesús. Roosie went to Tulane University for his undergraduate and then to the University of Florida for medical school. He later practiced in the Miami-Coral Gables area but Jesús saw him only once when Roosie was in medical school in Florida. Other students at Curley included boys from the Pedro Pan program and a senior, Richard Fleming, who was the first person Jesús met who had Type I Diabetes— he was the captain of the football team, an excellent student and a very nice person.

Chelo's last one-and-one-half years of high school were uneventful. After school she went to the apartment, changed clothes and walked to the grocery store where her mother worked. Chelo did her homework and studied at the grocery store because her parents did not want Chelo to stay in the apartment alone. Although she made very good grades she was not asked to be a member of the National Honor Society because she did not participate in extra-curricular activities, an American concept that was new to her. Of course, she was disappointed at not being invited to the National Honor Society. Like Jesús, Chelo got the NDA High School ring but did not go to the prom. One of the subjects that Chelo studied during her senior year at Notre Dame Academy was French. The French teacher, a Cuban woman named Elena de Armas, was the inspiration for Chelo to purse a degree in French in College. Chelo graduated from NDA in May 1963.

While at Notre Dame Academy, Chelo met and became friends with other Cuban girls. During this time, the Cuban girls were a close-knit group eating lunch together as a group. Chelo became a member of the French club at the insistence of her French teacher, the only after school activity in which she participated. During her senior year, Chelo took part in a fashion show sponsored by the Home Economics class. All the girls were required to take this yearlong course divided into a semester of sewing and another one of cooking. During the sewing semester, senior girls had to make their own dress and then model it during the school fashion show. Chelo, like most girls, used dress patterns but still had to learn how to cut, measure and put together the dress. For Chelo, making the dress was strenuous and stressful. She remembers the navy ¾ sleeve dress she made but does not recall what happened to the dress afterwards.

¡Gracias Fidel!

Thanks to Fidel? Are you kidding? After all the pain we went through? Lorenzo Javier made the "¡Gracias Fidel!" statement often because he believes that Chelo and Jesús would not have married under normal conditions if there had not been a Cuban Revolution. Lorenzo made a good point: The Cuban Revolution caused a lot of pain and suffering but there were also a number of positive side effects that resulted because of it. The romance between Chelo and Jesús blossomed in part thanks to the revolution.[43] It is probable that they would have met in Cuba because of the marriage of their mutual cousins, Vicente Fernández and Bertica León, but geography and different social groups would have made a romantic relationship between them less likely. Bertica and Vicente were the bridge that connected Chelo and Jesús, but it was the revolution and exile that brought them together in Miami in the early 1960s and that resulted in romance, marriage and the formation of a family. Here is a brief summary of how their romance started.

Bertica is the daughter of Berta González and Rigoberto's brother Miguel. Miguel died very young of a brain tumor and eventually Berta moved from Holguín with her three children, Estela, Miguelito and Bertica, to Havana and lived in a flat on Co-

---

[43] Other "benefits" from the revolution: Learning English, widening our horizons, world-class professional opportunities, and, most important, living in a free country.

lumbia Avenue in the Marianao District. Bertica met Vicente Fernández Redruello while she was in high school and they became "novios" (steady) while they were very young. Vicente was the son of Chelo's aunt Carmen and of Vicente Fernández Pérez, who died of a sudden heart attack on January 24, 1959. After Vicente Fernández senior's death, Carmen and his children moved into the San Lázaro Street house in Old Havana where Chelo lived.

Jesús met Vicente in Havana soon after the triumph of the revolution and saw him again during the summers of 1959 and 1960 at his aunt's Lilia's house in the Oriente town of San Agustín. Vicente sported a crew cut haircut that epitomized his personality: serious and focused. Vicente wanted to learn about cattle ranching business and also to meet and get to know other members of the León family, most of whom lived in Oriente Province. It turns out that Bertica had invited Chelo to go with them to San Agustín the following summer, in 1961, a trip that never materialized because of Chelo's departure to the United States.

The Cuban government tightened its grip on Cuban society during 1960 and 1961. As we mentioned earlier, there were rumors that the government was planning to send Cuban children to the Soviet Union for education. The fear of losing their children created a near panic in many Cuban families and they started organizing the exodus of their children to the USA. Many parents sent their children to the USA on their own to stay with friends and families or as part of the Pedro Pan program.

Berta planned to send Bertica to the USA but ran into an unexpected problem: Bertica refused to leave Cuba unless she married Vicente before leaving, and since she was under eighteen years of age, she needed parental consent. Berta and Carmen consented to the wedding and Bertica married Vicente on July 10, 1961, in Havana. After their marriage, Bertica and Vicente arrived in Miami, separately, in the latter part of 1961.

After Chelo's arrival in Miami and while she was a student at the Notre Dame Academy, Jesús saw her regularly, sometimes in the morning bus going to school or at the grocery store where Consuelo worked or at her home when Jesús brought the sports section of the daily paper to Cordero. There was never more than normal conversation between them until the celebration of the 15th Birthday of René's daughter Tata in February of 1962, at a small party at René and Marina's house to which Jesús and his sisters invited Chelo to join them. Chelo wore the dress from her own fifteenth birthday party a couple years earlier and she looked beautiful, clearly recovered from her ordeal at Momence. When Jesús and Chelo danced together at that party there was a spark, an attraction for each other, the beginning of their romance.

Chelo and Jesús became boyfriend & girlfriend after Tata's party, but they did not communicate this to Chelo's parents— this secret romance was not to last very long but it sowed the seed for the more permanent relation later. Jesús saw Chelo very often since he continued to bring the daily sports page to Cordero who, incidentally, thought that Jesús' visits were to see him. Somehow the spark that led to the romance began to die out in Chelo's heart so that by early May she was not interested in continuing their relationship; this coolness became obvious to Jesús through her actions and lack of enthusiasm so that they formally ended their relationship less than three months after it had started.

Jesús was still in love with Chelo so he looked for opportunities to see her at the bus stop in the mornings, at her house, or at other places, but Chelo did not like Jesús' action and she looked for ways to avoid him. Jesús attempt to win Chelo back lasted for a couple of months until he got tired and stopped all his efforts to win her back. Well, his lack of interest was the ticket. Suddenly, Chelo became interested in Jesús and now she was the one who made an effort to see Jesús. This was not too difficult since Jesús joined the Cordero family on his days off from work to go to the beach or to the Japanese Gardens Park situated on the McArthur Causeway highway between Miami and Miami Beach.

Jesús and Adolfo Fernández, Vicente's brother, were working together on the night shift at the Dagwood Restaurant in North Miami Beach, and they rode together to work in Jesús' car, departing Adolfo's house in the late afternoon. Chelo started visiting Adolfo's house at precisely the time that Jesús arrived to pick up Adolfo in his gold 1955 Chevy Bel Air hardtop; it was now Chelo's turn to pursue Jesús. Fortunately, this romance was made in heaven and a couple of months later they reconnected. It happened in July 1962 during a trip to the beach in what is now known as South Beach, on Ocean Drive and Tenth Street. While in the water, Chelo was thrown from a beach float and as Jesús caught her, their hands became entwined and the romance rekindled.

Jesús insisted that this time there would not be a secret romance and proceeded to talk to Cordero about it. Cordero was not thrilled, it was his daughter after all, but he accepted Jesús as a "novio" (the Spanish word for boyfriend that is also used for the groom at a wedding). Part of the reason for Cordero's reluctance was the uncertainty about Cuba and their possible return there, but also that Jesús and Chelo were 17 years old, and neither was prepared emotionally, financially or otherwise to enter into a long term relationship like marriage. In fact, it took them over five years to reach the point where they would actually marry.

Jesús visited Chelo at her house nightly, spending one to two hours sitting at the sofa to talk and/or watch TV until Jesús was informed, orally or via non-verbal messaging, that it was time for him to leave. Chelo's family had moved from the "palomar" to a one-bedroom apartment at 35 Street. Since the Leóns lived on 30 Street near Fifth Avenue at the "Coca-Cola house," we could easily walk to each other's house in a matter of minutes.

What to do after high school?

Father Francisco Barbeito, SJ, associate director of the Agrupación Católica Universitaria, ACU, was fond of using a Spanish phrase that perfectly describes our confusion during the first few years in the USA: "Están despistados" (you are clueless). Most American youngsters have a very clear idea of what they are going to do after graduation from high school, whether it is going to college, taking a year off to travel, joining the military or finding a job. Chelo and Jesús were not sure what they wanted to do, although Jesús had shown an interest in college, had taken the SAT exam and investigated a couple of universities. Still, after graduating from high school he was "despistado." Jesús had planned to go to college when living in Cuba. Pursuing a university degree seemed logical for Jesús. Both Rigoberto and Argentina had university degrees, and reading and love of books were in the family blood stream. In addition, Jesús had plenty of intellectual capacity to tackle college academic work. However, the ups and downs of the previous twenty months, the lack of money, the uncertainty of Jesús' life combined with his ignorance about the American system and society resulted in Jesús drifting and not staring college until more than a year after his high school graduation. The summer after his graduation, he got a job as a busboy at the Dagwood's Restaurant located on Collins Avenue just north of 169 Street, and for the next two years he had a variety of jobs; he also became active in an anti-Castro group, joined the ACU and finally started college.

That summer Jesús purchased the used 1955 Chevy Bel Air, and in this car he and Adolfo went to work at Dagwood Restaurant daily. They worked the evening shift, starting at four in the afternoon and ending at midnight except on Fridays and Saturdays when the restaurant closed at a later hour. Jesús was a busboy with a pay consisting of daily dinner, a low hourly rate and a percent of the tips received by the waitresses, generally six to eight dollars per evening. The Dagwood job was one of about ten different jobs Jesús had in the two years between his graduation from high school and his enrollment at the University of Florida in September 1964.[44]

For Chelo, the decision of whether or not to enroll in a university was somewhat more complex since her family had no history of college education. In May 1963, she received her High

---

[44] Here is a list of the other jobs: packing eggs at Sun City Egg Company; paperboy for the Miami Herald; dish washer at the Miami Herald Cafeteria; one-day bus boy at a breakfast restaurant near the University of Miami; store clerk at Jackson Byron's in Miami during the Christmas season; sorting low-cost dresses at a Hialeah factory; busboy, window cleaner, hamburger maker, and delivering lunch for a small restaurant in Northwest Miami; bell boy, phone operator and general helper at a Miami Beach hotel on Collins Avenue near 20 Street; manufacturing small fiberglass parts for Bertram Yachts; and, a truck driver member of the Teamsters Union, at the New York World's Fair in the summer of 1964.

School Diploma from Notre Dame Academy. Upon graduation, her mother suggested that she should take shorthand and typing classes to become a secretary, and Consuelo enrolled Chelo with Concha Blanco, who was renown in Cuba for preparing future secretaries. Concha Blanco tutored students at her house located near Biscayne Boulevard not far from the eventual headquarters of the ACU. Chelo did not enjoy the secretarial classes that she took during the summer and did not want to be a secretary, but was not sure what to do next. Argentina and Jesús encouraged Chelo to go to college, but Chelo was not sure if this was for her. She went to the Gesu Convent in downtown Miami to speak with her former teachers in Cuba, the American Dominican Sisters. The sisters explained to Chelo about university studies and encouraged her to enroll at Barry College (now Barry University), a liberal arts Catholic college for women in Miami Shores.

Following her high school graduation Chelo also worked at a direct mail marketing company located near Biscayne Boulevard and NW 36 Street, part of the area that later became the Miami Design District. She worked there with her cousins, Estelita and Teresita, with members of the León family and a number of friends. This group referred to the marketing company as "la propaganda." Later that summer, Chelo was able to obtain work at the Richards Department Store located in downtown Miami— a mid-scale store that eventually disappeared. The Miami Avenue store had a famous "bargain basement." Chelo worked part-time during the academic year for Richards from 1963, until her graduation from Barry College in 1967[45] and full-time during the summer months.

In the summer of 1962, Jesús joined the Directorio Revolucionario Estudiantil, DRE, an anti-Castro group that was founded in Havana by members of the ACU among others. This group was actively involved in propaganda and underground activities against

---

[45] Coincidentally, we later learned that Carlos Navarro worked at Richards at the same time. Carlos and his wife María Victoria are Atlanta residents whom we met through Monsignor Richard López and with whom we became good friends after our return to Atlanta in 2008.

the Castro regime. The DRE achieved notoriety in the USA because of a daring attack on the Blanquita Theater in Havana in September 1962[46] and because it was the first organization that claimed there were USSR missile installations in Cuba— the presence of the missiles led to the 1962 October Missile Crisis. Jesús was part of a group of younger people led by Ricardo Rubiales, a spirited young man. The primary activity of Rubiales' team was to prepare and distribute propaganda intended to influence members of the US Congress to continue to support the anti-Castro movement. The most exciting activities for Jesús in the DRE included a class on how to clean a handgun, a firing range practice session using a M-1 semiautomatic carbine, and conversations with members of the CIA who came to investigate the DRE immediately after the Blanquita attack.

The DRE would normally be relegated to one sentence in Jesús' life history except that it was the gateway through which Jesús came to the ACU, an organization crucial to Jesús, Chelo and their family. Ricardo Rubiales invited Jesús to the ACU in 1963 and there he met two Spanish Jesuits: Father Amando Llorente, the Spiritual Director of the ACU, and Father Francisco Barbeito. The ACU had survived persecution by the Cuban government— several ACU members were executed by the regime, and during the Bay of Pigs Invasion, Father Llorente had to seek asylum at the home of the Spanish Ambassador. Father Llorente arrived in Miami in 1961 and started organizing the group, finding a place to live and for the group to meet. He and the ACU residents moved locations three times in two years, so that when Jesús started participating in the ACU, it was located in a large house near the corner of southwest 12 Avenue and 6 Street.[47]

---

[46] A daring raid undertaken by DRE members who motored a boat into the Havana Harbor and from the boat used a small cannon to shoot at the theater in August 1962 where it was believed that Castro would be speaking on that day.

[47] See José M., "Manolín," Hernández's book, The ACU At The Threshold of the Third Millennium, published by the ACU in 1999 for a concise history of the ACU.

A number of agrupados (as the members of the ACU are known) lived in the house and most of them joined other agrupados at the daily morning Mass and stayed for a breakfast of "café con leche y pan cubano." The official ACU meetings took place on Saturday afternoons. The meeting started with a study session, called "círculo," with the attendees participating as one does in a college seminar. After the círculo, there was a rosary with the exposition of the Blessed Sacrament. The meeting ended with the members singing the ACU Hymn composed by a brilliant member of the ACU, Dr. José Ignacio Lasaga, who coincidentally, had been a classmate of Jesús' mother, Argentina, at the University of Havana.

College

Chelo and Jesús finally started college during the 1963-1964 academic year. By the summer of 1963, both Jesús and Chelo had jobs, and although still struggling financially, the earning from their jobs helped improve their lives. Chelo applied, was accepted and enrolled at Barry College in September of 1963. Chelo's choice of colleges was limited. She applied only to Barry university because (1) Barry was recommended by the American Dominican nuns that Chelo knew from Cuba; (2) the University of Miami was too expensive; (3) Barry was an all-girl school; and, (4) going to a college out-of-town to live in a dormitory was inconceivable for a Cuban girl in the 1960s. Barry College was a Liberal Arts School with a strict dress code. Girls had to wear dresses with short sleeves at all times and were not allowed to wear pants. To pay the $750 tuition per academic year, Chelo took advantage of the Cuban Loan program, a program utilized by most Cubans who attended college during the 1960s and 1970s.[48] Chelo used part of the

---

[48] The following was taken from the University of California's Office of the President Accounting Manual for Student aid (see www.ucop.edu/ucophome/policies/acctman/s-772.pdf): "The Cuban Loan Program provides loans to needy Cuban students who left Cuba after 1960 and who are not yet citizens of

earnings from her part-time job at Richards to pay for books, transportation and other expenses.

Her college career was almost nipped at the bud because she received a C grade on her first English 101 exam, and of course, she thought she was not college material.[49] However, Jesús insisted she was very capable of handling the academic load, and Chelo did continue her studies. The bad grade in her first English class was not the only issue at Barry. Chelo started school intending to major in French but her first French teacher ridiculed her French accent, which led her to abandon French and switch majors to become a teacher with a concentration in Spanish. During her first semester, she enrolled in a swimming class that was held at 8:00 AM in the morning; thus, she had to get up very early to get to school on time. Every Barry student was required to take three physical education (PE) classes and Chelo later enrolled in tennis and softball classes— unfortunately for Chelo, most of the other students in these classes were PE majors who played very well. The PE courses were not an easy grade for Chelo.

The story of Chelo's education is an example of perseverance and hard work. She not only had to borrow the money to pay for tuition but she had to take two buses each way, four per day, to go to Barry. At home, she had to study in the small kitchen of her family's one-bedroom apartment. The lack of space and the fact that the kitchen was next to the small living room where Chelo and her aunt Generosa slept, made things more difficult. Chelo was always mindful not to make noises because she worried that

---

the United States. The terms for granting these loans are identical to those established by the Federal government for NDEA loans, including the 50% cancellation of loan obligation for students who go into teaching." The program allowed students to borrow up to $500 per semester or $1,000 per school year up to a maximum of $5,000 for undergraduate education. It was later extended to allow up to $5,000 maximum for graduate education.

[49] It seems that teachers in Miami at that time "assumed" that non-Americans could not do better than C quality work in English. Jesús had a similar experience at Miami-Dade Junior College with his first English class. Was it discrimination or ignorance or both?

any noise and the light from the kitchen would bother her aunt. This limitation made it even more difficult for Chelo to do her research papers.

Chelo wanted to complete her degree as soon as possible so she took a full load of classes every semester and was able to graduate after only seven semesters. Part of the requirements to receive a teaching certificate was a one-semester teaching internship at a public high school. Chelo did her internship at the Miami Edison Senior High School, located at the corner of northwest Fifth Avenue and Sixty-second Street, a few blocks from her high school, Notre Dame Academy.

Chelo graduated in January 1967 with a graduating class of 139 women: sixty-five received BA degrees, thirty-one BS degrees, twenty-five MS degrees and eighteen BS degrees in Nursing. Chelo completed her college degree with a grade point average that qualified her to be recognized as Magna Cum Laude during the graduation ceremony and on her diploma— Bachelor of Arts Magna Cum Laude. Unfortunately, Barry College screwed up. She was not recognized as Magna Cum Laude in the ceremony and her diploma did not state that she had graduated with high honors. Chelo cried after the ceremony— she had worked so hard and was very disappointed that she was not recognized in front of her parents, her future husband, her schoolmates and her friends. Chelo was the first member of her family, on both her father and mother's side, to obtain a college degree.

While going to Barry, Chelo continued working part time at the Richards Department Store until her graduation. After graduation, Chelo joined the Flager Federal Savings and Loan Association bank as a full time employee— a job she held until her wedding.

Jesús also started university studies during the fall of 1963. He had worked full time the first year after high school and was not sure how to go about going to college, but the creation of the community colleges in Florida made it possible for him to start his academic career. The Miami-Dade Junior College, MDJC, opened in 1960 and was intended to serve all Miami-Dade County residents at very low cost: A $5 application fee and no tuition. The school started with about 1,500 students and by the mid 1960s, it had nearly 15,000 students!

Jesús enrolled at MDJC and registered for Math, Chemistry, Drafting, Social Studies and English— he dropped the English class when he discovered that his teacher believed that Jesús could not receive a grade higher than C in English <u>because he was a foreign born student</u>, an experience similar to the one Chelo had in her first English course at Barry. Most of the public colleges and universities in Florida including the MDJC used a trimester system at the time. The idea of the trimester system was to allow students to graduate early by compressing the academic material of one semester (approximately 16 weeks duration) into a 13 weeks trimester. Students could register for three trimesters in one year, and hence, complete their degrees in three years instead of the usual four years. The idea was good but could, in some cases, result in burnout for students who went to school continuously.

Jesús completed two trimesters at MDJC and then, in April of 1964, accepted a job to work at the New York's World's Fair between April and August. This was a great opportunity to live in New York City, enjoy a World's Fair and save some money. He lived at the ACU New York Chapter house located at 548 west 113 Street, a four-story building that used to be a fraternity house of Columbia University.

The time Jesús spent in New York was worthwhile: the World's Fair was fabulous; New York is a great city; and Jesús got to meet many ACU members of the New York Chapter. The New York ACU house had a small chapel with the Blessed Sacrament, a living room and a small meeting room on the first floor, with dormitories in the second, third and fourth floors. Jesús worked for the Brass Rail Company, the main food vendor at the fair. Brass Rail operated several restaurants and a number of fast food locations.[50] Jesús started in one of the snack bars but, after a couple of weeks, came to the conclusion that the money he was making was not enough. He was able to transfer to another job within the company, a job that required driving a truck with supplies into the World's Fair. To qualify for the new job, Jesús obtained a New York driver's license, and maybe of more interest, he joined the Teamsters Union— New York was a closed shop state so everyone had to join the union. Deliveries to the fairground had to be made between the hours of midnight and eight in the morning so Jesús worked the graveyard shift seven days a week. He was now making good money since the hourly rate for drivers was high and he was working a good bit of overtime. A couple of months later, the company removed the overtime and then the amount he was earning became less appealing to Jesús. Eventually, he left the job and returned to Miami.

Gainesville and the University of Florida

Jesús had decided early in the 1964 calendar year to enroll at the University of Florida (UF) located in Gainesville and to live in the ACU residence there. He traveled to Gainesville with Father Llorente during that summer to visit the University and met most of the Gainesville ACU members.

The city of Gainesville was and is the home of the University of Florida, a city that has been heavily impacted by the university. According to Wikipedia, the population of the city of Gainesville was just under 30,000 in 1960, and the number of students at the university exceeded 10,000. If you add to the number of students, the faculty and staff of the institution, it is easy to see that the university population accounted for about one-third of the area's population, and the economic impact of the university to Gainesville was large. Furthermore, on football Saturdays, the attendance

---

[50] Brass Rail fast food units at the World's Fair were famous for their unusual roof designs; you can see photos of these at http://www.worldsfair photos.com/nywf64/brass-rail.htm

at the games exceeded the combined population of the city and university community.

The rationale for selecting UF to complete his studies was defined by Jesús' economic situation: It was the only school with a strong engineering school that Jesús could afford; other schools such as the University of Miami and out-of-state universities were too expensive. Additionally, there was an ACU residence in Gainesville where Jesús could live while going to school. Jesús was a student at UF and lived in Gainesville from September 1964, until the end of the summer of 1969. Jesús received two degrees from the University of Florida— a Bachelor of Science in Electrical Engineering in 1967 and Master in Systems Engineering in 1969.

Gainesville and UF were a significant change from Miami and MDJC. UF was a large school with many students, the curriculum and classes were more competitive and some courses were taught in an auditorium with over one hundred students. There were fraternities, football games and homecoming activities, intramural competition and many young people. There were also a lot of free educational and entertainment programs available to the students.[51] Gainesville was a small city and one could get to most places by walking, which was good since most of the ACU residents did not own a car. The major drawback of not owning a car was that one had to schedule trips to Miami based on car owner's planned trips.

The cost of living and the cost of going to school in the 1960s seem fictional compared to today's costs. The trimester tuition at UF was $113[52] and the housing rent for the trimester at the ACU house was $100. The Cuban Loan Program provided $500 per academic period; after paying for tuition, books, supplies and rent, Jesús had about $150 left for food and other expenses for the trimester— not a lot. Many of the Cuban students ate dinner, Monday-to-Friday, at the house of one of two Cuban ladies (Mer-

---

[51] Jesús recalls Handel's Messiah, a Trumpet Concerto, and concertos by Mantovani and Ferrante & Teicher.
[52] At the private Barry College the semester tuition was $375.

cedes and Fe) that charged $5 per week, $65 to $70 per semester. To cover expenses, Jesús worked for many trimesters as a grader in the Math Department making up to $15 a week for about 10 weeks each trimester. Since there was little money left for the rest of the meals (breakfast, lunch and weekend dinners), many ACU students traded babysitting services for meal invitations at the house of married families. Jesús, unfortunately, would tend to run out of money towards the end of the school term resulting in a decrease in food intake with the consequence that many trimesters Jesús lost between 15 and 18 pounds.[53]

The ACU Gainesville house opened officially in September 1964 with eleven residents. The number of residents at the ACU house fluctuated between ten and thirteen persons over the years that Jesús lived in the house. Additionally, there were a number of married ACU members living in Gainesville who were also students. Many of the Gainesville ACU members remain close friends of Chelo and Jesús to this day.[54] During Jesús' time in Gainesville, UF had many Hispanic students, particularly a large number of Cuban students, including many veterans of the Bay of Pigs Invasion.

Jesús lived at the Gainesville ACU house from September 1964 until his wedding in August 1967. The ACU house, a modest two-story bungalow, was located at the corner of SW 10 Street and First Avenue, two blocks from the University of Florida Campus. The house had two stories: the first floor had a living room, a library— the only room with air conditioning in the house— a kitchen, four bedrooms and one bath. The second floor had one bathroom and two large bedrooms, each with capacity for three residents. The problem with the second floor was that to access it

---

[53] Here is an illustrative example. One Saturday night, Orlando Carneiro, Jesús and another friend pooled their "financial holding." They had enough money to buy two cans of Chef Boyardee's Spaghetti & Meatballs and one loaf of bread: dinner for three!

[54] See Appendix V for the names of some of the Gainesville residents at the time.

you had to use an outdoor stairs and the access door was broken and could not be closed; hence, in winter the hallway and the bathroom were very cold. The house had a detached garage that was used as a study area and was equipped with a blackboard and student desks. The ACU rented that house from 1964 until the property was sold soon after Chelo and Jesús were married in 1967. Afterwards, the residents moved to another house located about half-a-block east from the first house.

Jesús went to Miami a couple of times each trimester, on average about once a month. The main reason for the trip was to see Chelo and visit the family, but it was also an opportunity to eat good meals and bring some food with him back to Gainesville. The trips were short, Friday to Sunday, and the trip was not too bad, driving took about five hours each way. During these visits and for almost all of Jesús and Chelo's courtship, they seldom went out to the movies or to restaurants since Jesús did not have any money.

Football was always big at UF, and during Jesús' period at the school, students could get tickets to every game. It was also easy to get a date ticket for most games except for homecoming when there were a limited number of date tickets available. Jesús remembers how he and a group of his buddies once spent the night in a queue, hoping to get date tickets to a homecoming game—and once he had the tickets he proceeded to the Engineering Building to take an exam on Electromagnetism. Once a year, during homecoming weekend, some of our girlfriends came to campus to participate in the festivities, including the football game on Saturday and a big party afterwards. Chelo came to Gainesville several times accompanied by either Cordero or Argentina and stayed in the house of one of the agrupado families.

The cadence of life for Jesús at UF was that of a normal student taking a full load every semester with a typical curricula for engineering: English, Math, Physics, Social Studies, Humanities during the first two years and then the Electrical Engineering course work. Jesús has always been very appreciative of several of the UF required classes, in particular the introductory courses in humanities and law. The two-semester humanities sequence included an introduction to Philosophy, World Religions, Literature, Opera, Classical Music and Art Appreciation. All UF engineering students had to take a course labeled "Law, Contracts and Specifications for Engineers and Scientists" that provided an introduction to legal concepts that were especially instructional and useful to Jesús. His elective courses were in Latin American Politics and French, a language he has always loved.

The ACU residents followed their individual class schedules on weekdays and in the late afternoon most would attend the 5:30 PM Mass at the St. Augustine Newman Center and then walk to dinner at Mercedes' or Fe's house. Mercedes left Gainesville during Jesús' second year at Gainesville, and then Jesús ate dinner at Fe's house. Their houses were not only the place to eat dinner but to socialize with many other Hispanic students, almost all male, until Fe and Rafael Angulo rented a larger house and offered room and board to a few Hispanic women students. On weekends the residents caught up with studies and took care of laundry and housekeeping duties. All residents were responsible to keep their rooms clean and each resident was assigned a rotating responsibility to clean one of the common areas of the house. In the evening, the residents would study or do homework until 10:00 PM, when we gathered in the living room to pray the Rosary and then take a break. After the Rosary, some of the residents walked to a nearby doughnut shop— the cost of a doughnut was five cents, a treat Jesús could not normally afford. The ACU members came together twice a week for formal meetings: the first, on a weeknight, was a "círculo," a meeting to study Catholic topics ranging from the Catholic Catechism to the documents of the Second Vatican Council. The second was on Saturday afternoon, the "Guardia," a meeting that started with praying the Rosary followed by listening to the previous week's Miami Guardia (sent to us on a reel-to-reel tape) and ending the meeting singing the ACU Hymn. There was also a meeting, usually on Saturday, for those men who were not yet full members of the ACU to discuss the history and traditions of the organization.

While living in Gainesville, Jesús attended the Second ACU Convention held in Atlanta during the Thanksgiving break of 1965 and became a full member of the ACU (a congregant) on November 27 of that year. Jesús had attended the First ACU Convention in Atlanta in 1963, soon after he entered the ACU in Miami. It was prophetic that Jesús became a full member of the ACU in Atlanta, the city where he was later to live most of his life and where Jesús mentored many young men members of an ACU student group.

Entertainment in Gainesville for Jesús was limited to free university activities; he also participated on intramural sports, especially softball, played dominos until the wee hours of the morning, and read. There was little money so going to the movies was limited, unless you could sneak in to the drive-in. He almost never went out to eat except maybe for pizza at the beginning of the semester before he ran out of money.

Jesús and the ACU Gainesville residents experienced many difficulties but also a great camaraderie: the result of living together through hard times. The residents played practical jokes on each other from time to time. Most of them were as simple and harmless as throwing cold water at a person who was showering, hiding food, waking people in the middle of the night, etc.; but a number of the pranks were significant, and in retrospect, some pranks went beyond the bounds of Christian charity. One particularly cruel prank consisted of convincing one of the residents that he had been drafted to fight in Vietnam, and therefore, was required to report to the bus depot for induction into the Army the following Tuesday. A more agreeable activity was the encouragement by ACU residents in assisting in the marriages of two of their own: Leopoldo to María, and Ignacio to Lourdes; the last one was of particular interest to the residents because Lourdes' mother, Fe, cooked and served dinner for many students including the ACU guys— we hoped to get some benefit from that relationship!

A famous Gainesville ACU event was the organization and execution of the bachelor's party for Jesús, labeled the "Orange and Blue Despedida de Soltero." The University of Florida athletic colors are orange and blue and that was the theme of the party organized by a committee led by Dr. Jorge "Pico" Marbán who was not only a good friend but Jesús' ACU Sponsor in 1965. The party was a major celebration, organized in secret by the committee. It began around noontime on a hot August Friday afternoon, near the end of the 1967 Summer Trimester when Jesús and a few residents started to clean and paint the living room of the house. There was cleaning and painting and beer and camaraderie. Jesús noticed that late in the afternoon and early evening many non-residents started to arrive at the house, including El Pico who at the time was living in Lakeland, Florida.

By early evening, there was a large crowd in the house and many people had brought beer and finger food. The organizers' plan was to saturate Jesús with enough beer so as to reduce his resistance. In order to achieve their goal, they asked a number of participants to engage in drinking contests with Jesús. The plan worked and even though Jesús did not become intoxicated, he was cooperative throughout the evening with the activities planned by the committee. Jesús was "requested" to wear a brassiere and his genitalia were painted "orange & blue." At about three in the morning the city police visited the house for the third time and threatened to call the Dean of Students if the party, particularly the noise, did not end. The noise was due to loud talking, singing, and by the screams of some people who ventured outside and were sprayed with water by someone who had climbed on the roof with a hose. Following the third visit by the police, most people left with a few going to the White Castle restaurant nearby to eat.

The celebration continued on Saturday with a large luncheon organized by the Orange & Blue Committee. Fe cooked "Arroz con Pollo" for all the attendants and the committee gave Jesús a cash gift. Two final notes about the party: Jesús did not eat the Saturday lunch— his stomach was queasy in part by the large volume of alcohol and in part by the low quality of the beer that he drank; second, the photography shop refused to develop or release many of the photos taken during the party probably because they were in bad taste.

Jesús' bachelor party was the last major event for Jesús as a single man and as a resident of the ACU House in Gainesville. Days later, after taking final exams he packed all his clothes and went to Miami to celebrate his wedding to Chelo and start a new life and a new family.

Book IV – Family

We finally get married!

It was a long journey, but after more than five years of a steady relationship, we were ready for marriage; ready is a relative word: we were both very young, 22 years of age and had very little financial means. However, we had achieved the milestone we set as a requirement for the wedding: to complete our college degrees before getting married. The fact that we were young, poor and with few prospects except our energy and education, were not even considered: it was time for the wedding!

The date was set, August 26, 1967, and the preparations done. Chelo had taken full load of classes to accelerate her graduation to January of that year. Jesús had gone to school every trimester, summers included, to complete the degree in early August of 1967. Chelo made most of the decisions regarding the wedding except two: Jesús wanted Father Llorente to celebrate the wedding and he did not want the ceremony to interfere with the ACU Guardia that took place at 6:30 pm on Saturdays. These two requirements resulted in the wedding ceremony to be scheduled for 4:00 PM at Corpus Christi Church in Miami, because Chelo's first choice of church, the Cathedral of St. Mary, required the wedding celebrant to be a priest from that parish.

Chelo paid for essentially all her wedding expenses including the wedding dress, the studio pictures, wedding flowers and household goods for her future home. At the time of her wedding, there were no wedding registries for gifts and our friends were too poor to purchase gifts. Jesús signed up his agrupado friend Tony Abella for the wedding photos. He later received an unexpected gift: an eight-millimeter home movie of the wedding ceremony made by Puchín González, a friend from Victoria de las Tunas. In January of 1967, Chelo started working full time at Flager Federal S&L and there she opened her first bank account.

She had worked part time at Richards Department Store while going to school, but now, with a full time position at the bank, she was able to save enough to buy her trousseau and pay for wedding items.

Jesús was still going to school full time so he had very limited funds to help with the wedding expenses or for the honeymoon. His approach for raising funds was threefold: (1) he asked his close friends and relatives to send cash for the wedding gift; (2) he arranged for a couple of plant trips along the planned honeymoon route— each would help to pay for part of the trip; and, (3) he took a student loan from the Organization of American States. The cash gifts from his friends were small: $5, $10, and occasionally a $20, but the sum of all these helped, and his friends in Gainesville raised over $100 cash as part of his bachelor's party. Jesús trousseau consisted primarily of a few new clothes, one new suit and a new pair of shoes; the shoes he kept and wore at his 40th wedding anniversary party.

Saturday, August 26, 1967, was a beautiful day: sunny, clear skies and hot, a typical late summer day in Miami. Adolfo, Chelo's cousin, and Jesús went to get a hair cut at Adolfo's barbershop on Flager Street and 17th Avenue. Chelo had her hair and nails done. At least two hundred persons attended the wedding ceremony at Corpus Christi Church. Chelo's father, Cordero, was very elegant in his afternoon formal wear. Minutes before he walked Chelo down the aisle, he was worried about how he looked and asked Chelo whether every piece of his clothing was properly set. The sponsors ("padrinos") of the wedding were Cordero and Argentina, as was the Cuban custom; the celebrant was Father Amando Llorente, SJ, and the two altar servers were Orlando Carneiro and Arsenio Milian, roommates of Jesús at the ACU house in Gainesville. Chelo's cousin Mimi was the Maid of Honor; Vicente and Bertica's children, Vicentico and Ileana, were the ring boy and flower girl. The ceremony followed the normal Catholic ritual with the wedding vows, the blessing and exchange of rings, the giving of "Arras" (coins) from Jesús to Chelo and back to Jesús, and the placement and removal of the "mantilla" before and after Holy Communion by Jesús' sisters Carmen Luisa and Mary. Jesús, like

Cordero, was dressed in formal afternoon wear and he wore his ACU Congregant Medal. Arsenio and Orlando were also the altar server at the Mass of thanksgiving for Chelo and Jesús' 40th Wedding Anniversary in Atlanta, a celebration attended by some who were present at the wedding.

Many family and friends attended the wedding ceremony at the church. Unfortunately, we could not afford to have a large reception— it was either the reception or the honeymoon— and there were less than 30 people at Jesús' house for Spanish Cider, "bocaditos" and cake. In addition to the immediate families, those attending the reception included Father Llorente, Rodolfo and Lolín León, who were living at Jesús' house at the time, Chelo's aunts Generosa and Carmen, Chelo's cousins Adolfo and Mimi, and a few of our friends from Gainesville with their respective girl friends— Victor Sorondo and María de los Angeles Menéndez, Ignacio Abella and Lourdes Angulo, Orlando Carneiro, Arsenio Milian, and Juan Luis Porro. Chelo gave the bridal bouquet to her friend María who married Victor one year later.

A Remarkable Honeymoon!

We had a great honeymoon! Our honeymoon would have been remarkable under normal circumstances but it was more so because we were young, inexperienced about traveling and had limited resources.

Once the wedding reception was over, we changed from our wedding attire and had Adolfo drive us to where Jesús had hidden our car in the southwest section of Miami. Jesús was afraid that his Gainesville friends would be up to some mischief with our new car. For the same reason, he had not told anyone about his wedding night plans. Argentina found out about these plans because the hotel sent a letter confirming the reservation to the house. After fetching the car, a brand new 1967 two-door Dodge Dart, red with a black hardtop, we drove to the Doral Beach Hotel in Miami Beach.⁵⁵ We had wanted to go to the Doral for the wedding night. We were trying to look sophisticated while registering at the hotel but unfortunately some grains of the rice thrown as we left the reception fell from Chelo's hair while signing the guest card! Jesús had reserved a room in the penthouse of the hotel and after arrival, he ordered two daiquiris to toast our marriage and we exchanged wedding gifts: Chelo gave Jesús a gold key chain, one he lost in a movie theater in Gainesville a year later; Jesús gave Chelo a solitaire ring. Later that night Chelo became hungry (What else is new?) and we went to dinner at the Starlight Room of the hotel, a restaurant located on the top floor of the hotel with glass windows that provided a beautiful view of Miami and Miami Beach. The restaurant was a supper club with a full orchestra that played dance music. Jesús remembers that Chelo, who claimed to be hungry, ordered Beef Stroganoff but did not eat much. He also remembers that we did not dance either.

The next morning Jesús went for a quick swim in the beach, and then we had breakfast in the hotel before departing to go to Sunday Mass.⁵⁶ The pastor of the church was Father O'Shea who had been pastor of Corpus Christi Church during the early 1960s and who had helped the family with scholarship for the León children at their elementary school and for Jesús at Archbishop Curley High School. After Mass we started our three-week honeymoon road trip.

The plan for the honeymoon was to drive north, leisurely, going from city to city with the main destination being the 1967 World's Fair at Montreal (Expo 67). The first leg of the trip took us from Miami Beach to Gainesville where we stayed overnight in order to pick up, on Monday morning, the key to our future

---

⁵⁵ According to Wikipedia, the hotel opened in 1963 on Millionaire's Row on Collins Avenue near the famous Fontainebleau and Eden Roc hotels of Miami Beach and "it was long considered the most elegant and luxurious hotel in the area."

⁵⁶ Jesús thinks they went to St. Mary Magdalen Church in Sunny Isles, a parish founded in 1965.

apartment. From Gainesville, we drove to Atlanta and there, by chance, stayed at a Ramada Inn motel in Atlanta near the corner of Shallowford Road and I-85; the hotel was located about one block from the apartment that we rented two years later when we moved to Atlanta. That night, in Atlanta, we had the first of many memorable honeymoon meals[57] at the Chateau Fleur de Lis, an excellent restaurant on Cheshire Bridge Road, a restaurant where we later dined several more times. The waiter helped us through the menu (turtle soup for the first time) and gave us several souvenirs. How did we know about this and other excellent restaurants? Chelo studied the AAA Guide books during the daily drive and selected restaurants to explore at our next stop, and even though we were inexperienced travelers, we had two things going for us: the readiness to explore new places and the use of professional guidebooks to research restaurants in the different cities. We have continued to use this approach very successfully throughout our lives while traveling to new places. The passion for excellent food served in elegant surrounding has been a constant throughout our lives, a practice that began, but was unplanned, during our honeymoon.

Leaving Atlanta, we traveled to Asheville, North Carolina, driving through parts of the Great Smoky Mountain National Park, a beautiful scenic drive but one that requires patience because of the curves and hills. The next day, Wednesday, was off to Washington, DC. The city was and is beautiful with many tourist attractions and we saw several of the monuments and buildings. That evening we ate at a French restaurant that was famous as a meeting place of politicians and business people.[58] From Washington, the road trip headed northwest through parts of Maryland and Pennsylvania to Sharon, a small city about 75

---

[57] Since we did not eat much at the Starlight Room of the Doral Hotel on our wedding night.
[58] We believe this restaurant was the Sans Souci; according to the New York Times it "... was a fashionable gathering place for the Washington elite..." (www.nytimes.com/1985/07/01/us/briefing-the-sans-souci.html)

miles northwest of Pittsburgh. Jesús had arranged for an interview on Friday, September 1, with the Westinghouse Company at their transformer plant, a one-mile long building in the outskirts of the city. The Westinghouse plant was interesting and the interview was fine, but the 40° F weather in late August was a bit cold for people coming from Florida. Because of the interview, we had to stay overnight in Sharon and that evening, after dinner, we went to the movies and watched Robert Redford and Jane Fonda in <u>Barefoot in the Park</u>, a comedy about newlyweds in New York City that appealed to us because we were newlyweds.

From the mountains to the waterfall: the next morning, after breakfast, we drove to Niagara Falls, New York, a beautiful, romantic and enchanting place. We saw and marveled at the beauty and power of nature in the Horseshoe Falls, then walked down to the deck next to the American Falls to feel the power of the water; we drove across the border to the Canadian side to be captivated by the falls once more. Canada is a wonderful, beautiful and welcoming country, and we thoroughly enjoyed our first visit there as a married couple. We drove from Niagara Falls to Montreal along the northern side of Lake Ontario and the St. Lawrence River, a 410 miles distance. In Montreal, it was necessary to find the residence of a Quebecois family where we had reserved a room for our four nights stay in Montreal. We had to stay at a private residence because there were no hotel rooms available in the Montreal area. By chance, we happened to be at the World's Fair on the busiest day of the exposition, on Labor Day, 1967. It was somewhat of an adventure finding the house before the advent of GPS in a city we did not know and the house was located in a neighborhood where the only language spoken was French. We found the house after asking for directions. The bedroom at the house was very nice with the bathroom outside; we paid about ten dollars a night for the room.

Montreal's World's Fair was superb: the ambiance, the pavilions, the food, everything! We visited most of the national pavilions, including the Cuban Pavilion and also saw several special exhibitions. We ate fancy lunches: our first chateaubriand, a superb steak at the German Pavilion and a very good and very expensive fancy hamburger at the French Pavilion. Almost every aspect of our visit to the fair was marvelous, although we had a few minutes of trepidation on our first day at the World's Fair, the busiest day of the exhibition. The fair had a very nice monorail system to transport visitors to different sections of the exhibition area and we used it often during our visit. On that Monday, we took the monorail and when we got off at our stop we left Chelo's purse in the monorail. Oh My God! The purse had money, credit cards, driver's license, and most important, the documents to get back into the USA: our Cuban Passports, Chelo's residency (green card), and Jesús' reentry permit. God was with us that day because we realized the problem immediately, and notified the monorail operators who called the next station with the information; the purse was returned to us intact— what a relief!

After two-and-one-half days at the Fair we were exhausted and took the final evening off to rest and prepare to drive back to the USA. Jesús was not a permanent resident of the USA and he had requested and obtained a reentry permit to enter back into the country. The plan was to arrive in Nashua, New Hampshire, on Thursday since Jesús had arranged for a plant trip with Sprague Electronics on Friday, September 8. The trip from Montreal to Nashua traversed beautiful country in Vermont and New Hampshire including a ferryboat ride to cross a lake. On Friday, during the interview, Jesús noticed that the Sprague plant did not use air conditioning; the weather was cool in early September. We were not enthusiastic about moving to a location with such cool weather.

The last stop on the trip was in Philadelphia where Jesús had lived earlier and where we planned to stay with Jesús' cousin Berta Gallardo, her husband Enrique, and their family, Ketty, Bertica and Manolo García. We left Nashua at mid-day on Friday after the interview was completed and drove from Nashua to Philadelphia, a drive along a number of expressways that skirted both Boston and New York City. We were in Philadelphia for a couple of days and then drove to Miami, arriving there two days later. We finished our honeymoon with a visit to Miami for a couple of days;

we stayed in a motel in the Miami Gardens area in northern Miami, visited our relatives, and then left Miami and drove to Gainesville to start our lives as a married couple.

Whenever we think back about our honeymoon, we always reiterate and relish the great experience we had. For three weeks we ate at excellent restaurants, saw beautiful sights and thoroughly enjoyed ourselves. We remember the honeymoon as a wonderful time and we are very happy that we spent our limited resources to share quality time together after the wedding. We encourage all newlyweds not to postpone the honeymoon but to have it immediately after the wedding— it is our belief that a honeymoon cannot ever be the same when you do it later, at a time distanced from the wedding ceremony.

Start of our married life

We have fond memories of the two years we lived in Gainesville. In Gainesville we started our lives as a married couple, learned to live together, and started to build our family. Consuelo Beatriz was born in Gainesville and Cristina was conceived there. We learned how to manage a household and Chelo learned how to cook. It was in this city that Chelo started her professional career as a teacher and Jesús earned a master degree in Systems Engineering. During this time Gainesville was the home of a wonderful ACU community, a group of friends so close that many people were impressed. When Argentina came to visit us there, she wrote a letter to Father Llorente comparing the Gainesville ACU group to the Christian Community described in the Acts of the Apostles.[59]

We arrived in Gainesville after our honeymoon in September 1967. We had leased a one-bedroom furnished apartment at Village 34, three blocks south of University Avenue on 34th Street, on the western end of the UF campus. We were not eligible to apply for the university's married student housing until we were mar-

---

[59] Acts 4, 32-37

ried, so we leased the apartment for one year, the minimum lease available at the time. The apartments were distributed on one-floor square-buildings, each building had four units and each apartment had a small patio that was bounded on one side by a wooden fence. The inside of the apartment had wood paneling and was very cozy. It had a living-dining room, a small, narrow kitchen that could be closed with a sliding door, a bedroom with a walking closet and a full bath.

The apartment in Village 34 was our first home together. For Chelo, this apartment was the first time in her life that she had her own bedroom (actually she shared the bedroom with Jesús but considered it her own bedroom). Here, in the bedroom, we started to make adjustments: Chelo was from a family of early-to-bed, early-to-rise persons while Jesús was heavily influenced by the Núñez tradition of reading in bed late into the night. Chelo had difficulty falling asleep while there was a light in the nightstand and Jesús told her: "you will have to get used to this"— she did!

The resolution of marital disagreements was another area of disconnect for us. Jesús was frustrated by the passivity of Chelo as he expected her to actively participate (fight back) and wanted her to become more vocal. As the saying goes, "Be careful what you wish for, because you might just get it." Well, Jesús got it: Chelo did become outspoken and confident!

Dinner at Village 34 was an adventure for the first few weeks of our lives together. Neither Jesús nor Chelo knew how to fry an egg when they got married. Chelo had never cooked or managed a household and Jesús did not have the talent or desire to learn how to cook. Chelo had a Cuban Cook Book, <u>Cocina al Minuto</u> by Nitza Villapol and she was committed to learn how to cook. We remember well one of Chelo's early experiments, an Asturian dish called "Cachelos"; Chelo thought the (red) paprika was for coloring and she overloaded the dish with the spicy condiment; Jesús, who was committed to support Chelo, ate his serving and downed a pitcher of water with it. A better experience was the dinner for Victor Sorondo and Father Sardiñas, SJ, who was visiting the ACU group in Gainesville. Chelo decided to make Caneton a l'Orange, what some would consider a little bit risky given her limited cooking experience. The food was delicious— Father Sardiñas loved it and said he had not had this dish since Cuba. Unfortunately, Chelo and Jesús had very little of the duck to eat, thanks to our inexperience. It turns out that duck shrinks whilst cooking and the size of duck that Chelo bought was enough to feed two people with a little bit of leftovers— so Chelo and Jesús ended up eating a bit of the leftovers while Victor and Father Sardiñas had a feast.

Family Christmas celebrations

In December of 1967, we traveled to Miami to celebrate Christmas. It was the first time we celebrated Christmas as a married couple and Chelo was pregnant with Consuelo Beatriz. The annual Christmas celebration is a tradition in our family, a tradition that goes back many years and fosters deeper bonds of love among all the family members. This celebration, together with the annual summer beach vacations have nourished our family relations and given our children the opportunity to build strong bonds with their cousins.

The annual Christmas celebration begins with the arrival to Miami of the out-of-town family members, and it lasts for at least a week, depending on the date Christmas falls within the month. The major event of this celebration is going together to Christmas Vigil Mass, and then the Nochebuena (Christmas Eve) festivities. Nochebuena is a tradition common to Hispanic countries; the specific food served and some details of the celebrations vary from country to country but the basic idea is common: the celebration of the birth of Christ during the night.[60]

Jesús' family had a history of getting together for Christmas, dating back to Cuba and this continued in the USA— recall the celebration of Christmas in 1961 in Miami that we described be-

---

[60] Maybe the idea of the birth of Jesus during the night comes from the story in Chapter 2 of Luke's Gospel: "In the countryside close by there were shepherds out in the fields keeping guard over their sheep during the watches of the night." Notice the last word, "night" (www.catholic.org/bible/).

fore. Likewise, Chelo's family on Cordero's side had the same tradition. Chelo always had Nochebuena at her aunt's Margot's house, Cordero's youngest sister. For the first few years after we were married, we celebrated Nochebuena mainly in Chelo's parent's house. Slowly, over a few years period, with the expansion of the family, the celebration of Nochebuena migrated to Carmen Luisa's house, and Consuelo and Cordero always came with us. The participation in the Nochebuena dinner grew over the years as our children and the children of Jesús' siblings started getting married— they often brought their significant others for dinner before they got married. Then, as they got married, they started bringing their spouse and their in-laws; Carmen also invited other close relatives (Felix Manuel, Mireya and kids; Ana María, Elio and Martica; and Nilda). She also invited Adele Chicco and Teresita Pulido who were very close to us. By the 1980s, the number of people sitting for Nochebuena dinner exceeded fifty persons.

The menu for the Cuban celebration of Nochebuena is standard and essentially the same for all Cuban households: lechón asado (roasted pig, Cuban style with lots of "mojo criollo")[61], Yucca (with its own "mojo"), rice and beans (Jesús' family likes the Congrí that has the rice cooked with red beans and chorizo), lettuce/tomato or avocado salad, and, sometimes, plantains. Jesús family, coming from the Oriente Province of Cuba, likes to serve, in addition to regular bread, "casabe," bread made from yucca that traces its origin to the Caribbean natives. To accompany the food, there is wine, beer, sodas and water. For dessert we have Spanish Turrones (nougat), figs, dates, and now we also have flans, cakes, pies and cookies.

The preparation for Nochebuena starts with logistics: Carmen Luisa rents chairs and tables that are delivered to the house. During the day on Christmas Eve, we move Carmen Luisa's living room furniture to the covered patio and set up the tables and chairs, place the tablecloths, utensils and plastic cups. The food

---

[61] We make Cuban mojo by mixing garlic, salt, pepper and oregano with lime and sour orange juice.

preparation has changed over the years as the number of people has increased. Originally, the participants cooked all the food, but lately most of the food is bought from professional caterers. Occasionally, we have roasted a whole pig using the Caja China (www.lacajachina.com).

As members of the family arrive to Carmen's house, we get together in the covered patio for drinks and conversation while the kitchen crew organizes the food for serving. When the food is ready, we move to the dining area. Before we eat, a member of the family, most of the time Jesús, says a prayer of thanksgiving. The dinner is very enjoyable even though the noise level is high due to the fifty or so Cubans in a small room with many talking at the same time. After dinner, many people move to the covered patio while cleanup takes place; at the patio we have after-dinner drinks, talk with each other and some smoke cigars. The younger persons help remove the tables and chairs and set up the living room furniture back to the right place. Then, the families, especially those with young children, start departing to prepare for Christmas at their homes.

The next day, Christmas Day, we spend most of the day opening gifts at various houses: at Paco/Mary's house, at Cordero/Consuelo's house, and at other family houses. Later on Christmas Day, we get together for a family meal. Many years ago, in the 1980s, a number of us started to go to the house of Adele Chicco's parents on Christmas evening for dinner. Their house was located in the Roads area of Miami, east of southwest 12 Avenue and south of southwest 11 Street. Jesús' parents, Carmen Luisa, Chelo, Jesús and our children shared dinner with the Chicco family, which included Adele's father, mother (Teresa) and several aunts. Adele had connected with our family because she and Mary were students at Barry at the same time. The friendship that started with Mary extended promptly to the rest of the family and Adele became a bona fide member of the extended family. A few years later, after Adele's mother died, Adele sold the house and moved to a condominium that she shared with Teresita Pulido, who then became very close to all of us. Adele and Teresita bought a house near St. Timothy Catholic Church and that became the location for the Christmas Day get together. Along the way, Adele was diagnosed with Multiple Sclerosis, a terrifying disease. As she became more ill, the tradition of the Christmas Day dinner at her house stopped, but for many years she was still able to join the family for Nochebuena. Sadly, this also had to stop when it became very difficult to move Adele. We continued to visit them regularly, especially during the Christmas season.

Our Christmas celebrations make it possible for all the family to become more intimate. We spend a lot of time together: talking, playing games, going to the movies or bowling, etc. Some years we even celebrated New Year's with a party, food, music and dancing. We return home every year reenergized after the Christmas celebration.

Our return to Gainesville after the 1967 Christmas celebration was very special because we were expecting our first child in a matter of months.

Consuelo Beatriz is born

Consuelo Beatriz (CB, "Socia," "Nona") was born on Thursday, May 30 (Memorial Day) 1968. Coincidentally, Cristina and Lorenzo were born on Thursday, as was Chelo. The odds for a person to be born on any one day of the week are one-in-seven, so the probability that all three children would be born on the same day of the week is about three in one thousand. Jesús was born on a Monday— the odd one out!

Consuelo Beatriz's birth was a major family milestone as she was the first grand child on both sides of the family. The birth and delivery were a bit of an adventure. Chelo started to have contraction pains in the wee hours of the morning on the day Consuelo Beatriz was born. When the frequency of the contraction episodes reached the prescribed interval, we left for Alachua General Hospital. However, by the time we arrived at the hospital, the contractions had disappeared so we headed back to the apartment assuming this had been a false alarm. Interestingly, as soon as we parked the car in the apartment parking lot, the contraction pains started again, and once again, we headed to the hospital. For the second time, the contraction pains stopped as we reached the hospital, and we decided to go back home. By now, it was close to five in the morning, we had been up most of the night and Jesús, but not Chelo, was getting hungry (what a surprise). So, on the way back to the apartment, he stopped at a Krystal hamburger restaurant on University Avenue where he proceeded to eat three of the famous square hamburgers. As you may guess, as soon as we reached the apartment, the contraction pains restarted. Again, we left for the hospital and as soon as we reached the hospital the contraction pains stopped once more. This time Jesús told Chelo that they were going in to have someone check her. We are glad we did that; Chelo was almost ready to give birth. We learned later that her fear of the hospital had paralyzed the delivery process. We checked in the hospital after 6 AM and Consuelo Beatriz was born at 8:24 AM, about two hours of labor and delivery for a first-time mother.

Jesús saw mother and baby and then went home to call both sets of new grandparents. Grandmother Consuelo was concerned about her daughter's health and wanted to immediately come to Gainesville so Jesús asked her if she was planning to hitchhike her way from Hialeah where she was working. She did not hitchhike to Gainesville, but on Friday night we had a full house in the small apartment and Jesús had to move to the ACU house, as there was no room for everyone.[62]

Consuelo Beatriz was a bundle of energy from the day she was born, more than any other newborn baby we have ever seen; she moved herself from one end of the little crib to the other just hours after birth while other babies barely moved. She left the hospital after a couple of days and joined her joyous family at her first house, the Village 34 apartment. Dr. Ganey, the OBGYN, pierced Consuelo Beatriz ears the week after her birth at his office. She was a very good baby and slept most of the night by the time she was one month old; Chelo followed Argentina's advice to slowly space out her feeding times adding 15 minutes every day until she was able to feed the baby every four to five hours. We do remember that Consuelo Beatriz, as a baby and for some unknown reason, cried hard every evening around seven for about thirty minutes; the crying episodes lasted several weeks.

Father Amando Llorente baptized Consuelo Beatriz in Miami, at St. John Bosco Catholic Church, on July 1, 1968. Her godparents

---

[62] Writing about this reminded Jesús about the Gran Combo song "No Hay Cama Pa' Tanta Gente" (literally: there are not enough beds for this many people).

were Adolfo Fernández, Chelo's cousin, and Mary, Jesús' sister. Consuelo had brought Chelo's Baptism "cargador"[63] from Cuba and we dressed CB with this cargador for her baptism. Afterwards, we had a celebration for the family and friends at the paternal grandparents apartment near the Orange Bowl.

After Consuelo Beatriz was born, we applied for a two-bedroom apartment in the university's married housing system. We were assigned an apartment in the Diamond Village apartment complex located near 13th Street and the towers single-housing dormitories, and also within walking distance of a large part of the campus. Diamond Village had opened in 1959 so it was in excellent condition. We moved into Diamond Village in August 1968 and Jesús experienced first-hand the obsession with cleaning of the Redruello family: Generosa used a toothbrush to clean part of the floor of the baby's room! The apartment was on a second story, had about 714 square feet of space distributed as follows: a master bedroom with large open space for use as a closet and to put a study desk, one small bedroom, one bath, a kitchen-dining area and a living room. The apartments did not have air-conditioning, but we bought a room AC unit that helped cool the apartment. The Diamond Village complex had a lot of green spaces, a laundry facility and a playground.

When we moved to Gainesville, Chelo found a job in one of the administrative offices of the Shands Medical Teaching Hospital. During the next few months she explored and applied for teaching opportunities in Alachua and surrounding counties and was awarded a position in the Bradford County High School located in Starke, a city about 45 minutes (28 miles) from Gainesville. Fortunately, she was able to join a carpool with three other teachers who lived in Gainesville, and so she had to drive only one week every month; Jesús was able to use the car the rest of the time. We did have to figure out how to care for the baby while Chelo was teaching and this became a team effort with Chelo, Carmen Luisa, Fedora and Jesús as the team members. Fedora was the aunt of Laly Rodríguez, wife of Sergio Rodrí-

---

[63] The "cargador" or Baptismal Gown is fancy garment used to dress the baby for baptism in Cuba. Consuelo Beatriz was baptized with the "cargador" that Chelo wore on the day of her Baptism.

guez, a member of the ACU who lived in Gainesville while Sergio finished his Architecture and City Planning degrees. Fedora was a superb baby sitter and took care of CB several mornings every week when Carmen Luisa and Jesús had class or work conflict. Carmen was studying for her bachelor's degree and Jesús was working on a master's degree. They arranged their schedules to take turns taking care of Consuelo. Carmen Luisa lived at the Beaty Towers dormitories, located a few hundred feet from our apartment at Diamond Village. She ate dinner with us every night during the week. Chelo was frustrated that year because she missed some of Consuelo Beatriz's firsts: her first step and her first poop sitting on the little toilet. Then and there, Chelo decided not to ever work during the first few years of any future child.

Our lives at Gainesville revolved around school, work, taking care of CB, and the ACU. Jesús participated on the ACU "guardias" on Saturday and on the formation seminars on Monday evenings. We were members of a group of married couples who met monthly with the objectives of deepening our knowledge of the faith and developing a community of people with similar interests and backgrounds. The meetings rotated among the homes of each couple in the group, and the evening program consisted of prayer (normally the Rosary) followed by a short talk on a topic of interest, and then a time for social sharing.

On most weekdays, Chelo left very early for Starke and Jesús took Consuelo Beatriz to Fedora's house, unless it was a very cold day; on cold days Fedora came to our apartment. Jesús then went to the university for classes and/or teaching. Around lunchtime, Jesús picked up Consuelo Beatriz and brought her to the apartment for lunch; Carmen Luisa often joined him for lunch. In the afternoon, Carmen and Jesús split baby-sitting duties depending on their class/teaching schedule. Chelo arrived from Starke in the late afternoon, spent time with Consuelo Beatriz and cooked the evening meal.

On Saturday mornings, we bought groceries and took care of errands. The main Saturday afternoon activity was the ACU Guardia, and during football season, attending home football games. On Sunday mornings, we went to Mass at the St. Augustine Catholic Church located next to the campus on University Avenue. Occasionally, we attended Mass at the main church of Gainesville, St. Patrick, but this church was relatively far from our house, and in any case, most of our friends attended St. Augustine. Weekends were also for social activities, which, given the budget constraints, consisted primarily of get togethers at friends house or going to the movies. On Sundays during football season we visited the Marbán family, Jorge ("Pico"), his mother Ñitica and grandmother, to watch professional football games. Pico was a famous character among the Hispanic community. He was brilliant (Ph.D. Engineering), a driver with a record of crashing into every moving vehicle with the exception of airplanes— he hit automobiles, bikes, motorbikes and even a train! Pico loved Sara Lee pound cake with cream cheese and when Chelo made him a flan he would eat the whole flan directly from the baking mold.

Since Gainesville was a university town with a large number of professionals, it was easy to find very good medical care. Chelo's OBGYN practice was excellent and she was very happy to have had her favorite doctor, Dr. Gainey, be the person who delivered Consuelo Beatriz. Consuelo Beatriz pediatrician, Dr. Dell, was probably the best pediatrician that any of our children had. When Consuelo Beatriz was a few months old, Dr. Dell noticed that CB had a tendency to turn in one of her leg and recommended we take her to an orthopedic doctor in town (Dr. Kissam, we believe) who agreed with Dr. Dell and placed a cast on Consuelo's leg with excellent results. We wish we had been able to persuade Lorenzo's doctors to do the same for him!

As a student enrolled in the Master program in the department of Industrial and Systems Engineering of the University of Florida, Jesús had a Graduate Assistantship working with Professor Paavo Valisalo in the Hybrid System Simulation Laboratory. The assistantship combined research and teaching activities; the research focused on the simulation of complex problems using Analog and Hybrid computers, tools now obsolete that have been replaced by powerful digital computers. The laboratory solved engineering problems, simulating them using differential equations. Jesús and his friend and fellow graduate student Emilio Herrero, used their research to write a paper that won The EAI Scientific Simulation Student Award in 1969. For the teaching portion of the assistantship, Jesús taught a junior level course in Analog Simulation in 1968 and 1969. During one of the trips he made with Professor Valisalo to a meeting of the Southeastern

131

Simulation Council, Jesús met Dr. Joseph Hammond of The Georgia Institute of Technology (Georgia Tech, GT) who encouraged him to apply to GT for further graduate work.

Chelo, Jesús and Consuelo Beatriz took a road trip to visit Atlanta and Georgia Tech before deciding whether or not to move to Atlanta. The trip started somewhat strangely as we were to pick Chelo's aunt, Carmen, at the Starke train station but the train had stopped in Orlando and did not make it to Starke so we proceeded without her to Atlanta and from there to Columbia, SC, to visit Vicente and Bertica. They were living in Columbia because Vicente was enrolled in the Mechanical Engineering program at the University of South Carolina. After we moved to Atlanta, we visited them from time to time and they also came to Atlanta to visit us and join us in activities such as trips to the Six Flags Over Georgia Amusement Park.

Golf became part of Jesús' weekly activities during his years at Gainesville. He played most Thursday mornings with a Colombian friend who was a Ph.D. student. The University of Florida had an excellent golf course with minimal fees for students, faculty and staff— Green fees of $1.25 (1969 prices) for the whole day and $0.50 to rent a caddy push cart to carry the golf clubs. Carlos Busot, an agrupado Ph.D. Student, gave Jesús some used irons golf clubs and Jesús bought a putter, a couple of wood clubs and an inexpensive golf club bag at the local Jordan Marsh store. Golf in Gainesville did not require lots of time, was entertaining, healthy, and inexpensive. Jesús' desire to play the game lasted until we moved to Atlanta. Jesús determined that he could not afford the time or money to play golf in Atlanta and gave up the game; Chelo later sold his clubs at the garage sale of a neighbor on Fern Creek Drive.

By the time we moved to Diamond Village, Chelo had become a good cook and the quality of her cooking continued improving over the years. We remember with fondness and a smile how Carmen Luisa used to praise her cooking every night, regardless of what Chelo cooked. It is amazing how efficient Chelo has been throughout her life, and Gainesville was no exception. She taught full-time at a school thirty minutes from home and when she arrived home, she took care of the baby, did household duties and cooked a full meal every night!

Jesús had always wanted to teach at the university level and so he planned to earn a doctoral degree. After meeting Dr. Hammond from Georgia Tech and visiting the school in Atlanta, he applied and was accepted into the Ph.D. program in 1969. Choosing a place to live in Atlanta was an interesting experience, as we will narrate later. Before leaving the Diamond Village apartment we had to either clean the apartment, pay a cleaning service to do it, or forfeit the apartment deposit— a fortune for us at that time. Chelo's mother came to help with the move and between the three of us we cleaned the apartment. Then, came the inspection from the complex manager who found a bit of soap in the master bathroom wall and some grease in the kitchen range; we cleaned these spots and got our refund back.

We rented a small U-Haul truck to take our possessions: Consuelo Beatriz's crib, high chair, the air conditioner that we later sold in Atlanta, the television set, our clothes and a few other things. We traveled to Atlanta on I-75 north with Chelo driving the 1967 Dodge Dart and Jesús the small truck. The only incident of note is that we had a minor "cooking" oil spill in the trunk of the car.

Book V – Home!

Book V – Part I – Atlanta 1969-1974

We moved to Atlanta in order for Jesús to enroll in the Ph.D. program in the School of Electrical Engineering at Georgia Tech. Our plan was to live in Atlanta for a few years, but, in fact, Atlanta became our new "hometown," replacing La Habana and Tunas. Atlanta is the city where we have lived the majority of our lives, where Cristina and Lorenzo were born, where we started our professional careers and made many long-lasting friendships. Jesús had visited Atlanta with his parents in 1958 and he became a full member of the ACU in this city in 1965. Atlanta was also the first major stop in our honeymoon trip. In a way, it seemed it was preordained for Atlanta to become the location where we would live a major part of our lives, more than thirty years. We have many memories about Atlanta. We will narrate now our lives in Atlanta from 1969 to 1993, and in Book VI our lives in Atlanta from 2008 foward.

Community living

Jesús had investigated several universities to continue his studies and selected Georgia Tech for practical and financial reasons. GT had a good program and it awarded Jesús a grant from the National Science Foundation to support his Ph.D. studies. This grant was later changed to a half-time assistantship because Jesús was not a Permanent Resident of the USA.

We were going to have to manage our budget carefully because we were going to live away from the GT campus and could only afford one car, and because Chelo was pregnant with Cristina and would not be able to work. Part of our solution was to share transportation with another couple, an interesting experiment that, looking back, resonates with the 1960s, the decade of the flower children, the hippies and communal living.

Our ACU friends from Gainesville, Luis and Lourdes Gutiérrez, were also moving to Atlanta so that Luis could enroll in the Ph.D. Program in Industrial and Systems Engineering. The Gutiérrez had two children, Luisito and Lourdes María, and a higher income since Luis was to work full-time as an engineer at the Georgia Tech Experiment Station (today's GTRI). Each family could afford only one automobile; yet, in Atlanta, it was necessary, almost essential, to have two cars per family. The solution: Luis and Jesús would share one of the cars to go to Georgia Tech and Lourdes and Chelo would share the other car to take Luisito to school, buy groceries, and do other errands. This arrangement required that the two families live relatively close to each other. During the summer of 1969, we traveled to Atlanta with Luis and Lourdes to look for apartments suitable to both families. The search for apartments was an interesting experience, to say the least. Chelo and Jesús needed a low cost apartment and did not have much difficulty finding an apartment that met the criteria of value, affordability and location at The Northgate Arms Apartments, located on Shallowford Road near the Northeast (I-85) Expressway.[64] Lourdes, on the other hand, had a hard time deciding on an apartment that would be near the León's apartment. The Gutiérrez, after some arguments, finally settled on a very nice Bradford Square townhouse apartment also located on Shallowford Road. Incidentally, the Abella family, another ACU friend from Gainesville moved into The Northgate Arms Apartments the following year.[65]

Chelo, Lourdes, Luis and Jesús shared a good bit of their lives for almost two years until the Gutiérrez moved to Maryland. The four of us learned to adjust our schedule, to share the cars for work, groceries, school, doctors visits, and everything else; as a result, we became intimate about what was cooked at each house, what clothes were bought, family plans, and who was naughty or nice. Looking back at this time of our lives, we marvel at our patience and capacity to adjust to different personalities and different priorities— as they

---

[64] The apartment address was 2773-D Shallowford Road, Chamblee.
[65] Ignacio and Lourdes moved to Atlanta in August 1970 and lived in the city until the spring of 1975 when they moved to Orlando and later to Miami.

say, "necessity is the mother of invention" or, in this case, the force for adaptability.

Luis and Jesús drove to Georgia Tech each morning in Jesús and Chelo's car. Luis used this car to go back and forth from his office to classes during the day and then, in the afternoon, Luis picked Jesús at GT for the trip back to their apartments. They used their time together during these daily trips to discuss religion, the ACU, politics, graduate school, family life, sports, and to plan the next day or days. Lourdes and Chelo would similarly spend a good bit of each day together at the groceries or the stores in Luis and Lourdes' car.

Our car sharing arrangement worked well most of the times, but there were problems occasionally. For example, during the first week of January 1970 when Jesús was taking the Preliminary Examination to enter the Ph.D. program and Consuelo Beatriz developed a high fever, Chelo called Georgia Tech and had Jesús pulled out of the exam because she needed transportation to take Consuelo Beatriz to the doctor and could not locate Lourdes. Thanks God that Chelo was able to locate Lourdes and they took CB to the doctor so that Jesús could finish the exam. CB's fever was caused by a throat infection that was treated immediately and effectively.

Georgia Tech

In September 1969, when Jesús started at Georgia Tech, the school was beginning its transformation from an essentially undergraduate institution to a research university. When Jesús started the program, there were less than twenty-five students in the Electrical Engineering doctoral program, a program that now has hundreds of students.

The Ph.D. program requirements were straight-forward: One had to (1) pass a preliminary examination to enter the program and a core/qualifying examination on the subjects of specialization; (2) take a minimum of two years of courses beyond the bachelors degree with a number of them in the fields of specialty (Control Systems, Computer Simulation and Automata Theory for Jesús); (3) demonstrate reading fluency in one language (French for Jesús); (4) submit and obtain approval of a dissertation proposal; and, (5) complete and defend the dissertation. Jesús completed all the requirements except the last two when he started to work full-time. He had selected the dissertation topic, <u>Calamity Detection in Linear Systems</u>[66], completed most of the theoretical work, and was working on the simulation portion of the research.

Georgia Tech became more than the place where Jesús took courses and did research, it was the place where he honed his leadership skills. During his first year at GT, he was elected to the Graduate Student Senate, an organization focused on graduate student issues. The following year, Jesús was elected Vice President and then President in his third year at GT. He helped improve the life of the graduate students and raised the profile of the Graduate Student Senate. Among his accomplishments were successful campaigns to increase the stipend to graduate students and to obtain bookstore discounts for holders of graduate assistantship. He also took part in the search for a new GT President, Joseph Mayo Pettit, and a new Dean of Engineering, William M. Sangster. Jesús participated in numerous campus boards and was a member of the Steering Committee for the ten-year accreditation review.

As a result of the numerous activities at Georgia Tech, Jesús was invited to join several leadership organizations including ANAK, GT's most exclusive leadership society, Omicron Delta Kappa, a national leadership fraternity, and the Executive Round Table, an organization that brought together industry executives with Georgia Tech faculty and students. Jesús' non-academic activities at Georgia Tech took time away from his research work, but on the other hand, prepared him for a leadership role in industry.

Now, that we have given a background to Atlanta, Georgia Tech, our apartment and a few notes about our shared life with the Gutiérrez, we will describe our life and activities from our arrival in Atlanta in September 1969 to our departure to Spain in September 1996. We have divided this period of our lives into three parts. The first part starts with our move to Atlanta in 1969, and ends in 1974.

---

[66] The topic required using stochastic (non-deterministic) processes to analyze statistically dependent samples received sequentially from system output to determine (detect) system failures (calamities) as early as possible.

The second part starts in 1975, a year of many first for us including buying our first house, Jesús' first professional job and our first trip to Europe, and ends in 1982. The third part begins in 1983, when Lorenzo was born and covers the ten years until Chelo, Lorenzo and Jesús moved to Madrid, Spain in 1993.

Atlanta 1969-1975

After our move to Atlanta, we spent a good part of our first few months exploring the city and settling into daily life in our apartment. The apartment was small but adequate for the family. The Northgate Arms apartment complex had more than 30 buildings and 200 apartments, and several common facilities, including two swimming pools and a laundry area. In 1969, most of the tenants of the apartments were blue-collar workers and a few immigrants— all nice, decent, hard working people. However, by the time we left the apartment five years later, there was a marked changed for the worse in the social and economic level of the apartment residents.

The apartment location provided easy access to expressways, church, schools and shopping malls. We generally entered the complex from Shallowford Road and drove to our building, a structure oriented north-to-south at the center of a courtyard with perpendicular buildings on either side. The courtyard consisted of a fairly large, open green space that separated our building from the apartment road and the parking spaces. There was a cement walkway leading from the parking area to the building. The building had eight apartments with four apartments on each of the two ends of the building, two of the four on the first floor and two on the second floor. Our apartment was on the first floor at the north end of the building. Apartments on the second level were reached using a metal stairway.

Our apartment had a living room, a kitchen, two bedrooms and one bath. The entrance door led to the living room, furnished with a sofa, a reclining chair, a center table and one end table. On the wall across the sofa we installed movable shelves with books and copies of Chelo and Jesús' diplomas. On the center of this wall we had a very nice TV that Cordero and Consuelo bought for us. The TV had a modern design with doors that folded inside the unit and it was one of the last TV models manufactured by Zenith in the USA. We kept this TV until 1993 when we sold it at a garage sale before our departure to Spain. We bought the sofa and the bedroom set at Havertys and a dinette set at Sears.

From the living room, one could walk to the kitchen area or to the bedrooms. The kitchen had a gas range/oven, a refrigerator with a top freezer, a small dinette set for six persons, and the high chair that was first used by Consuelo Beatriz and then Cristina. At the rear of the kitchen, there was a door that led to a small patio where one could hang laundry. The master bedroom furniture consisted of a double bed, a dresser and a couple of nightstands. To this, we added a small TV that we installed on a shelf on the wall facing the bed and next to the closet— Consuelo Beatriz would one day cause this TV to crash to the floor when we were out and Virgie Balbona was baby sitting. The children's bedroom had Consuelo Beatriz's bed, the crib for Cristina, a baby chest for Cristina's clothes and a closet.

Having a small apartment came handy in January 1973, when that year's winter brought an ice storm that caused us to lose power for a couple of days. We moved into the living room and heated the living room, kitchen and bathroom with the gas oven and gas burners until power was restored. During the power outage, we took turns staying awake at night while the oven was on because it was a gas oven! According to the Atlanta Journal Constitution the 1973 ice storm was "the worst storm of all."[67] The apartment complex used a common system to provide heat to the apartments and our heat came from a unit near the laundry facility but the system used fans that ran on electricity.

As part of our settling into Atlanta, we found doctors, Dr. Nodal the OBGYN for Chelo and a pediatrician for Consuelo Beatriz. That first autumn season we enjoyed the change of colors and Jesús established a reputation as an excellent student at Georgia Tech. We learned where to shop in Atlanta and joined GEX, a member-only store that was a predecessor of places like Sam's Club and Costco. We also began to meet Atlanta families.

---

[67] See A brief history of Atlanta's snow horrors, http://www.ajc.com/news/a-brief-history-of-270805.html.

Several of the persons we met in Atlanta were connected to the ACU. Father Llorente told us to contact Dr. José Balbona, a member of the ACU who lived in Atlanta, and the Balbonas invited us to dinner at their home a few weeks after our move to Atlanta. At the time, the Balbonas lived in a house in Ponderosa Estates, near La Vista Road. The following year they moved to a house on Cravey Drive that was closer to our apartment.[68] That autumn, after Sunday Mass at our parish church, Immaculate Heart of Mary, we met the Antón family, whose son, Manny, and his family were to become very close to us.

In November, we went to Miami for Thanksgiving, a long car trip for a short weekend, and we decided not to <u>ever</u> drive to Miami for the Thanksgiving weekend. In December, we again drove to Miami to spend Christmas with our families, an important tradition that we have maintained throughout our lives.

The year 1970 begun inauspiciously. As we mentioned before, in January Consuelo Beatriz (CB, "Socia," Nona) developed high fever. Two weeks later Chelo, Lourdes, Lourdes María and Consuelo Beatriz were in an automobile accident. Lourdes was driving on Juniper Street when a driver ran a red light on Tenth Street and hit them broadside. Chelo, who was on her last month of Cristy's pregnancy, was knocked unconscious. Consuelo Beatriz suffered a small cut on her face; one can still see the scar in Socia's face, a small reminder of the crash. When Chelo regained consciousness she was asked about her pregnancy to which she replied "but I am not pregnant" ... Thanks God there were no health effects to Chelo or Cristina.

The rest of the year 1970 was a lot better, especially because of the birth of Cristina on Thursday, February 5, 1970, at DeKalb General Hospital in Decatur. The night before she was born, Chelo and Jesús went to Julian and Madamina Gomez's house where Father Llorente celebrated Mass for many of the agrupado families in the Atlanta area. On Thursday morning, Chelo mentioned that she had a minor pain on her stomach, more an annoyance than any serious pain. Argentina suggested that she should check with the doctor tell-

---

[68] In 1984 we built a house within walking distance of the Balbona's Cravey Drive house

ing Chelo, "Every delivery is different." Argentina was in town with Jesús' sisters Carmen and Mary to help throughout the birth and early days of the new baby. We followed Argentina's advice and went to see Chelo's doctor who told Chelo to go directly to the hospital because she was already dilated. Unfortunately for Chelo, the doctor at the hospital that day was not her primary OBGYN but his partner. Chelo had a very painful delivery and a long recovery. The delivery process was similar to the one with Consuelo Beatriz's birth: Chelo's labor pains stopped as soon as we arrived at the hospital.

After checking into the hospital, Chelo was taken to a large room that held all the women who were in labor and Jesús was allowed to see her in the room only once before she had the baby. Because Chelo's labor pains had stopped, the doctor decided to give her Pitocin, a drug used to induce delivery. This caused a problem because Chelo was left alone— no nurse or doctor supervision— and once the Pitocin took effect she was ready to have the baby, and in fact, almost had the baby in the labor room. The whole process caused her to strain significantly and resulted in very painful hemorrhoid pain that lasted for several weeks. It took Chelo weeks to recover from the delivery; Argentina was of great help during this painful time, taking over the household duties to allow Chelo to recover. The good news is that baby Cristina was born healthy. They showed the baby to Jesús after she was born and he remembers that Cristy had a lot of hair.

Cristina was baptized on June 21, 1970, by Father Llorente and given the name Cristina del Carmen. The middle name was suggested by Argentina who told Chelo, "Why don't you name her after her Godmother Carmen?" This continued a long tradition of girls named Carmen in the Núñez family. The Baptismal Ceremony was performed on a very hot day in the sacristy of St. John Bosco's Church in Miami with her aunt Carmen and uncle Henry as the godparents. Cristy, like Consuelo Beatriz, wore Chelo's cargador (baptismal gown). We had a small reception afterwards at Rigoberto and Argentina's apartment located near the Orange Bowl.[69]

---

[69] We believe the address was 1641 NW 5 Street, Miami.

In May, we blew our budget when we joined the Gutiérrez and Raúl and Annie Trujillo for Mother's Day dinner at the Chateau Fleur the Lis, the best restaurant in Atlanta at the time. In September, Ignacio and Lourdes Abella moved to Atlanta because Ignacio had found his first professional job after college. That year we met César and Carmen Berenguer, Alberto and Margarita Bolet, Juanito and Cuqui Bereijo, Pancho and Ana María Viña, and Hector and Emma Rivas. We shared Thanksgiving dinner at the Viña apartment's community facility with the Berenguer, Bolet, Viña and Bereijo families.

In the summer of 1971, the Gutiérrez family left Atlanta for Maryland. Their departure created a transportation problem for the family. Some days Chelo kept the car and Jesús took the bus to Georgia Tech. This arrangement was difficult, but thanks to the generosity of José ("Peque")[70] Balbona the problem was solved. Peque decided that Chelo should not be left alone in the house without transportation, and he proceeded to loan us the use of his Ford Futura "until such time as you don't need it anymore," and we used this car for a couple of years until we were able to buy another car.

In December 1971, we made our annual trip to Miami for Christmas and also visited Walt Disney World in Orlando, a resort that had opened on October 1, 1971. Jesús had always wanted to go to Disneyland in Anaheim California, and when Disney opened in Orlando, we decided to go to the park the week after Christmas not knowing that this was the busiest time of the year at the park. Chelo, Consuelo Beatriz, Jesús and his siblings Carmen Luisa and Henry joined us for the trip. Cristy was little, twenty-two months so she stayed with Cordero, Consuelo and Generosa in Miami. We stayed at the Sorondo's house— the Sorondos were in Miami for Christmas— and we planned to spend one full day at Disney. Getting into Disney was an adventure in itself because of the very long queues that caused long waits to drive into the Park. Jesús drove on the left lane of I-4 until the exit, and then cut in front of a car to get into the exit lane. We made it into a Disney parking lot in time— the lots filled up and

---

[70] The word is derived from the Spanish "Pequeño," as in little one.

were closed at ten in the morning! We had left the Sorondo's house before eight in the morning, were at the park by nine o'clock and yet it took us until noon to enter the Magic Kingdom Park. We enjoyed the park and were there all day until it closed at midnight, but our day was brutal. The queues for the popular attractions like "It's Small World" and "The Haunted Mansion" were three-hours long; sometimes Jesús stood in the queue while the rest of the group went to the bathroom or bought lunch. We were able to see most of the attractions, the Christmas Parade and the fireworks. Needless to say, we were exhausted when we arrived at the Sorondo's house and slept late the next day before heading back to Miami to complete our Christmas vacation.

Our daily routine in Atlanta during our first few years was very simple. Jesús left for Georgia Tech every weekday early in the morning and returned in the late afternoon. Chelo took care of the household and later worked part time in the evening. On weekends we went shopping, did a little bit of sightseeing (with limited funds), visited friends or participated in social gatherings. We attended church at IHM regularly and joined a group of Catholic couples that met about once a month.

We got to enjoy seeing our children grow. Consuelo Beatriz and Cristina were great kids, a joy to us. They were also a source of more than a little bit of wonderment because the two girls, daughters of the same parents and of similar age, separated by only twenty-one months, were very different in their physical appearance and their personalities, and at the same time, were very close to each other.

Consuelo has been, since birth, a bundle of activity ready to explode at a moment's notice. Right after birth, she moved in her hospital crib constantly. She was always fearless, ready to explore and try new things, looking for opportunities to invent activities. She was quick to learn everything like walking and becoming potty trained. In fact, she ran at ten months bouncing a balloon ball that was connected like a yo-yo with a string to her hand. Consuelo always had a smile on her face and was a very happy child. She grew up to be a very happy person— always laughing and always looking for adventures, and she was mischievous ("traviesa" in Spanish), looking for things to do that would annoy others. For example, she would run up the iron grille steps of the stairs in front of the apartment leading to the second floor and would cry to her mother, "I am going to fall" just to see how Chelo would react because she knew her mother would be stressed. When going out with Lourdes and Lourdes María Gutiérrez, Consuelo would run to the car to sit behind Lourdes because she knew this would bother Lourdes María. On one occasion, when Chelo was ready to go to a doctor's appointment, she moved the transmission from park to neutral causing the car, with baby Cristy in the car, to roll down a few feet (cars at that time allowed moving the transmission when the car was turned off and without the key in the ignition). Consuelo B. also disappeared from the apartment on a couple of occasions while Chelo was changing Cristy and she would go to the area next to the swimming pool.

Cristy, on the other hand, was a very sweet, cautious and well-behaved child, and she grew up to be a sweet and engaging woman. As a baby, she barely moved; Chelo could change her diaper, comb her hair, add a hair bow and place her on the crib; you could come two to three hours later and find Cristina in exactly the same position. She was careful and not so adventuresome, taking her time about doing things; she would cry even before falling from her own two feet to make sure someone would come to pick her up. It took her over a year to start walking, because we think she did not feel a need to walk, the risk-to-reward ratio was too high, surely a sign of intelligence and practicality that we would understand later.

Cristy always looked up to her sister and was always ready to play with her. Consuelo Beatriz's game playing tended to be more physical: running, jumping, throwing balls and pillow fights. Cristy was reflective and patient, weighing alternatives before making a decision. Her only accident as a child was one involving her sister. One evening, Consuelo Beatriz started chasing Cristy around the small apartment living room; Cristy fell and suffered a cut in her right eyelid. We called the Balbona's who suggested that we take her to Northside Hospital. There, Cristy had a plastic surgeon, Dr. Lovic Hobby, take care of the cut. Dr. Hobby did an excellent job and he remarked on how well behaved Cristy had been during the procedure.

Cristy loved and worshiped her big sister, partly because of the age difference but also because CB was and still is a very special person. Chelo and Cristina will never forget that every time there was a birthday party at IHM School, CB would come home with half a cupcake, a cookie or whatever candy she got, to share it with her sister.

Cristy, unlike Consuelo, enjoyed playing with dolls, "casita" as we call it in Spanish. She would spend hours combing the baby doll's hair, arranging cups and saucers, while Consuelo was unraveling things craving more action. CB did not like to be dressed with bows, laces and nice shoes but Cristy always wanted to be "dressed to the nines" with all the trimmings!

Our financial situation during our early years in Atlanta was somewhat precarious as the household income was very limited. Jesús borrowed from the Cuban Loan Program to pay for Georgia Tech's tuition and books and he received a relatively small income for his work as a half-time graduate assistant at GT. Chelo was able to help with the finances as soon as Cristina was more than a few months old. Her first job was as a part-time teacher of English as a Second Language, ESL, to immigrants, primarily Cuban. The ESL classes were held at a public school near Lindbergh Plaza because many Cubans lived near this school in an apartment complex that was called "Pastorita[71]." Later, Chelo obtained a position teaching Spanish at the Berlitz Language School located near Lenox Square Mall. Chelo would leave the house around six in the evening and Jesús would take care of the girls. Every time Chelo left for work, Cristy would go to the living room window and cry because she did not want her "mami" to leave.

Chelo's income from her part-time jobs helped tremendously with our finances. We also received a lot of help from the Cordero family, especially during the early part of our family life. Consuelo and Cordero prepared care packages for us to take every time we went to Miami. The packages included some groceries, filet mignon for the girls, cigars for Jesús, and many other goodies. Consuelo bought many Dorissa dresses— fancy dresses from a clothing fac-

---

[71] The name was used to ridicule a Castro Cuban Government Housing Minister whose last name was "Pastor" and who favored large public housing project. There was a "Pastorita" in Southwest Miami also.

tory in Miami where she knew one of the workers; we could not afford to buy this quality of dress for the girls. Generosa, Chelo's aunt, cooked "Masa Real" for us, a food we all loved.[72] Cordero and Consuelo also took care of the girl's birthday parties. They drove from Miami, first to Gainesville and later to Atlanta, a full day of travel, to bring piñatas, bocaditos, croquetas, pastelitos and the birthday cake to celebrate the girl's birthdays. The cakes and piñatas were often based on a theme such as Snow White, Cinderella or Mickey Mouse.

Cordero continued to drive to Atlanta, almost always alone, until he was in his 70s. He loved coming to Atlanta and spending time with Chelo, his grandchildren and with the many friends he made in Atlanta. The Atlanta Hispanic community loved Cordero and considered him one of its own.

In September 1973, thanks to Sister Louise, a friend we met through the Atlanta Cursillo Movement, Chelo started working as a part-time Spanish teacher at St. Pius X High School. The timing of the St. Pius position was very good. Consuelo Beatriz was five years old and was starting Kindergarten at the Immaculate Heart of Mary School, IHM, on Briarcliff Road— a half-day program. Chelo asked a nice Mexican woman who lived three doors down from our apartment to take care of Cristina who was three-and-one-half years old. However, later that year, Chelo enrolled Cristina in the Briarcliff Baptist Church pre-school program. The following year, Cristy went to a Montessori school on Dresden Drive. All these schools were very close to the apartment. Cristy was eager to go to school just like her big sister so she was very happy when we enrolled her in school, and she was an excellent student. While attending the Montessori school, one day during dinner in the apartment, she pointed to one of the steaks and said: "it looks like South America"; she was right and we were astonished!

Consuelo Beatriz, unlike Cristina, had not gone to pre-school and her knowledge of English was limited to what she learned from

---

[72] Masa Real is essentially a layer of guava inside of a cake made with flour, eggs, sugar, butter, lard and a touch of vanilla. Chelo makes it from time to time and there are plenty of recipes for it in the Internet.

television programs and playing with the children of our friends. CB regularly watched Mr. Roger's Neighborhood (which premiered in February 1968) while Cristy loved Sesame Street (which premiered in November 1969). Consuelo Beatriz's limited English vocabulary impacted her first few months at school, and we think this probably caused her to have a lack of enthusiasm for Spanish. CB's limited English gave rise to at least one humorous anecdote: on one of her first days at school, when asked by her Kindergarten teacher, Sister Barbara, if she had had breakfast, she answered no because she did not know the English word for breakfast— at our house we had "desayuno." Sister Barbara called Chelo to grill her about sending her young child to school without any food!

Cristina thoroughly enjoyed her one-year at the Montessori School, but she could not wait to start IHM School in September 1975, to be with her sister. Cristy's first year at IHM School did not go so well; the teacher was a disaster and played favorites. In addition, Cristy already knew how to read and the curriculum at IHM was not up to par to the Montessori school. It was a boring year for Cristy, but she was thrilled to be with her sister. Her first grade experience was a little better but her teacher, Mrs. Pat Darden, thought that Cristy had no self-esteem. When Chelo went to see Cristy's teacher for the first parent-teacher conference, Mrs. Darden explained that when Cristy was asked to draw a picture of herself, she instead drew one of her sister, the epitome of perfection in Cristy's eyes. On hearing this, Chelo told the teacher not to worry, that she would take care of the matter. From that day forward, Chelo pointed out to Cristy that CB was not perfect after all and that everyone had virtues as well as flaws. Chelo took every opportunity to point to Cristy her good qualities and virtues, and before first grade was over, Cristy became the self-assured, confident and vocal individual that she is today.

For the next six years, both Cristy and Consuelo attended the IHM School together. IHM was our parish, the elementary school for Consuelo, Cristy and later Lorenzo, and the church where our children received most of the sacraments: Consuelo and Cristy had their First Penance, First Communion, Confirmation and Marriage Ceremonies there; Lorenzo was baptized, had his First Penance and received the preparation for First Communion at IHM.

"You People Live in a Bubble"

Sonia Guigou's cousin Maritza came to Atlanta to visit Sonia in the 1970s, and after spending a few days with Sonia and her friends, told her, "ustedes viven en una burbuja" (you live in a bubble, outside reality). Maritza referred to the intimate, loving and supporting community that we shared and that she experienced while visiting Atlanta. This close-knit community was formed through our participation in the Atlanta Cursillo Movement. The Cursillo Movement is an evangelization tool that consists of a three-day short-course and provides effective follow-up tools for sharing and support.[73]

Atlanta had a strong Hispanic presence that was strengthened by the influx of Cuban exiles in the 1960s. The Cursillo Movement in Atlanta was a catalyst that transformed a portion of this group of Hispanic people into a very special community.

The inspiration and driving force behind the Atlanta Cursillo Movement was Father Richard Kieran, an Irish native, son of a protestant mother, who was ordained a priest in 1965, in Ireland. His first priestly assignment was as parochial vicar to the Immaculate Heart of Mary Parish, IHM, in Atlanta. Father Richard represents to us, the epitome of John F. Kennedy's statement that, "One person can make a difference and every person should try." Father Richard made a huge difference in Atlanta as an educator and spiritual leader. As an educator, he was the principal of St. Pius X High School and later Secretary of Education for the Archdiocese of Atlanta. He was the pastor at several parishes in the Atlanta area, rector of the Cathedral of Atlanta, and was for a number of years, elected president of the Atlanta Senate of Priests. But more than anything else, he was the founder, director, the heart, and the leader for more than 17 years of the Atlanta Cursillo Movement. Father Richard made his Cursillo in 1966 and immediately recognized that this movement was an excel-

---

[73] Cursillo is Spanish for short course. The Cursillo Movement is a short course in how to live a Christian life. It started as a movement within the Catholic Church in Spain in the 1940s, came to the USA in 1957, and to Atlanta in the early 1960s. The Cursillo Movement has been adopted by several Christian Protestant denominations. There is plenty of information in the Internet about the Cursillo Movement and about the Atlanta Cursillo Movement.

lent lay evangelization tool. Then, with the assistance of Sister Margaret McAnoy, I.H.M., and Sister Louise Sommer, CSJ, he worked tirelessly to organize and lead cursillos that touched and transformed countless lives.

Father Richard met several Hispanics who attended Cursillo weekends. Among them were Drs. José and Virginia Balbona with whom he became very close friends. Father Richard decided to bring the Cursillo experience to the Spanish community in Atlanta and achieved this goal through three specific steps. First, he decided to learn Spanish so he could preach to the Hispanic Community. Father Richard wanted to make "himself a Hispanic to win the Hispanics" in a manner similar to the Apostle Paul.[74]

Father Richard's second step was to contact the leaders of the Miami Spanish Cursillo Movement to ask for their help— the Miami Cursillo group was ready to help in this mission. Father Richard coordinated with the people of Miami the dates, logistics and human resources to offer Spanish Cursillos in Atlanta.

Lastly, Father Richard mobilized the Atlanta Cursillo Movement lay persons, mostly Anglo members, to help organize the first Cursillo in Spanish for men, as well as a second Cursillo for men and one for women. The first Cursillo in Spanish for men was held at the Monastery of the Holy Spirit in Conyers, Georgia, in October 1972. The Miami Spanish Cursillo sent a team led by Father José Hernando, Miguel Cabrera (Lay director of the First Cursillo in Atlanta), Pepe Guerra, Lorenzo de Toro and Ramiro Tavel. The Miami team gave most of the talks in this Cursillo. The Anglo community was of great help in this and other Spanish Cursillos serving in the set-up (logistics) and the kitchen. The second Spanish men's Cursillo was held a few months later with the help of then Father, later Bishop,

---

[74] In his First Letter to the Corinthians, Chapter 9, 20-22, Paul said: "To the Jews I made myself as a Jew, to win the Jews; to those under the Law as one under the Law (though I am not), in order to win those under the Law; to those outside the Law as one outside the Law, though I am not outside the Law but under Christ's law, to win those outside the Law. To the weak, I made myself weak, to win the weak. I accommodated myself to people in all kinds of different situations, so that by all possible means I might bring some to salvation." (www.catholic.org)

Agustín Román, Pepe Guerra and Pepín Argilagos as lay director. Jesús attended the first Cursillo and worked in the team that put together the second Cursillo.

The first Spanish women's Cursillo was held in 1973 after the first two men's Cursillo weekends. Sonia Argilagos and Miguel Cabrera's wife came from Miami with Father José Hernando. The Anglo community was once again of tremendous help working in the kitchen and set-up. Chelo had attended an English language Cursillo and was part of the lay team of the first Spanish women's Cursillo.

From 1974 forward, the Atlanta community organized and directed all the Spanish Cursillos, normally one for men and one for women every year. We were both very active in the Cursillo Movement in Atlanta, each of us were lay leaders (rectors) of at least one Cursillo weekend. We also worked in the kitchen, set-up and as auxiliary and presenters in many Cursillo Weekends. Jesús was the Lay Leader of the Archdiocese of Atlanta Cursillo Movement for the year 1978-79.

We met many people through the Cursillo Movement who became very close friends. The list of these friends is very long and we will not attempt to list everyone; however, to provide an inkling of the close friends we had, here are the name of some families we met through the Cursillo: the Cimadevillas, Macias, Guigous, Saldañas and two López families. We also met and became good friends with many Anglo Cursillistas. The Cursillo Movement was a very good networking tool for us to open doors in the Atlanta Catholic community. We became close friends with Father Richard, Sister Margaret, Sister Louise and other cursillistas. Chelo was Father Richard's Spanish instructor and Sister Louise told Chelo about an opening at St. Pius X for a Spanish teacher.

The Cursillo Movement has two effective follow-up tools. One is the "group reunion" that brings together four-to-eight persons weekly. The second, the "Ultreya," brings together larger groups of persons, also in a weekly basis, and is generally organized by geographic regions. We had a Spanish speaking Ultreya that met at first at IHM and then later at Holy Cross Church. Additionally, there was a "leaders' school" that met at St. Pius X High School on Wednesday night. There, Cursillo members learned about their faith, about the Cursillo Movement and prepared to be part of Cursillo teams. We were both participants and also teachers in the leaders' school helping to organize teams and teaching on different topics of Christianity. For many years we had two group reunions, one male and one female, with the Macias, Guigous, Saldañas and Armandito and Juanita Rodríguez. The spiritual unity intensified the bonds we already had as Cuban exiles living in Atlanta. When Maritza told us we lived in a "bubble," she was referring to the closeness and sharing of members of the Atlanta Cursillo Community.

A sad note and at the same time an example of the personal witness of a man of faith occurred in 1999. While pastor in Gainesville, Georgia, Father Richard suffered a major brain hemorrhage. Following surgery, he had to retire from active ministry and experienced ongoing therapy and rehabilitation. Although a major loss to the Cursillo Movement and the Catholic Community of Atlanta, Father Richard's acceptance of his illness has been an example for all of us of what a true Christian is to be, someone who prays and believes the words of the Lord's Prayer, "Thy will be done, on earth as it is in heaven." He died on November 21, 2016, and he never forgot how to speak Spanish despite his brain illness.

Book V – Part II – Atlanta 1975-1983

After four years living in the apartment, Chelo was ready to move out. As we mentioned earlier, there was a marked decline in the quality of the tenants of the Northgate Arms Apartments. The tenants in 1969 were solid lower middle class people with good manners. Over the next three years, there was deterioration in the cultural, social and economic level of the people who moved into the apartment complex. By 1974, we had neighbors whose social behavior created a poor environment for all of us, especially for our children. The second problem with the apartment was the limited space in our small two-bedroom unit; the girls were growing, we had run out of closet space and Chelo did not know where to store things anymore. Chelo started to lose hair due to the stress caused by living in the apartment. Something had to give and it did in 1975, when we bought our first house.

The year 1975 was an excellent vintage year for the León-Cordero family; we achieved several milestones. It was Jesús' first year working full-time professionally as an engineer. It was the year that Chelo and Jesús traveled to Europe for the first time. In 1975 Cristy started at IHM School and we purchased our first house. Let's start with the job.

Jesús had started interviewing for a full-time position early in 1974 because he understood that he needed to provide better living conditions for the family. Chelo, Jesús and the girls visited Panama City during that summer in order for Jesús to interview at the Naval Coastal Systems Laboratory. Jesús received a job offer there and loved the position; it was a federal government civil service position, working on the ocean at a fine beach. However, Chelo was appalled at the limited possibilities in the city since schools, shopping, social and cultural activities were either limited or nonexistent. We also had a difficult experience at the beach that added another negative value to the city. Chelo and Jesús were caught by a severe undertow when swimming while the girls played in the sand. Chelo panicked and would have drowned except for the fact that Jesús had learned, in his lifesaver training how to deal with the undertow.[75] We obviously did reach the shore but the experience was so intense that, since then, Chelo has never swum in places where she cannot reach the sand with her feet.

Jesús had also a job interview with Martin Marietta Corporation in Orlando, and this one was much more promising. Jesús accepted their offer to start working there in 1975. Unfortunately, Martin Marietta lost a major Defense Department contract and was planning to lay off hundreds of engineers. This was not a good sign for a new employee, so Jesús decided to begin looking for a new engineering position.

Jesús started his first full-time job in December 1974, thanks to a friend, David McGill. Dave was a professor at Georgia Tech and one of the members of Jesús' Cursillo group reunion. Dave spent one day each week as a consultant for Scientific-Atlanta, "SA," a compa-

---

[75] One needs to swim at a forty-five degree angle between the shore and the undertow, and slowly one makes progress to finally reach shore.

ny that was founded by members of the Georgia Tech Research Institute in 1952. During the fall of 1974, Dave recommended Jesús to Ed Williams who was the Engineering Manager for the Electro-Products Division at SA, and his recommendation opened the door for Jesús. SA was at the time a mid-size company with annual sales revenue around twenty-million dollars, and with a few hundred employees. Jesús interviewed with Ed Williams, Dr. Larry Clayton, the company's Chief Technology Officer, and with Graham Mobley, one of the best analytical minds that Jesús has ever known. The interview was unique for several reasons. First, because of the technical caliber of the interviewers; second, because there was a lot of smoke in the room since the CTO was a chain-smoker of cigars and both Graham and Ed smoked cigarettes; and the third reason was that Jesús noticed Graham's eyebrows and ears would move irregularly up and down while he was pondering an issue. The combination of smoke and the personalities gave Jesús a feeling of a surreal atmosphere. At any rate, the outcome was that SA offered Jesús a part-time position immediately. In December, Jesús was offered and accepted a full-time position to start after the Christmas-New Year holidays. Chelo bought clothes for Jesús that would be appropriate for a professional person and Jesús was set to start his first engineering job.

Our first house

As soon as Jesús started working full-time at Scientific-Atlanta, we started looking for a house suitable for the family. We had the typical problem of young persons who want to buy their first house— the lack of cash for the down payment, closing costs, and moving expenses. On the positive side for homebuyers, there was a recession in 1974-75 that impacted the housing market and created incentives for people who wanted to purchase a new house.

We started looking for houses in areas that where near our apartment, but we soon determined that we could not afford any of the houses that we liked in the Briarcliff Road area inside of the I-285 Perimeter. Thus, we started to expand our search to areas further out of the city, and eventually, started to search in the Lilburn area, about eight miles north of the Perimeter. One Sunday, after Mass, the León family plus Abuela Juana, who had come to Atlanta to accompany

Chelo while Jesús was on a business trip to Brazil, went to see a house that was advertised for sale in the Lilburn area. The family looked at the advertised house but did not like it at all. On the way back home, the family drove through a couple of neighborhoods looking at "for sale" signs. By chance, the family drove into what was then a small neighborhood located off Harmony Grove Road, and saw a "For Sale By Owner" sign in front of an empty house. The family walked in the house, and collectively, fell in love with the house. We remember that Consuelo Beatriz and Cristy offered to contribute their savings account money to help buy the house. That evening, back at our apartment, we started to try to figure out how we were going to be able to buy the house, because the asking price for the house was higher than what we believed we could afford to pay.

The owner of the house had a contract to sell the house to another family. The contract had a contingency clause whereby the prospective buyers did not have to execute the contract until they could sell the house they were living in. This clause also allowed the owner of the house to continue trying to sell the house, and if he received a new offer, to give the "right-of-first-refusal" to the family with the original contract. Well, as we mentioned before, the USA was experiencing an economic recession that impacted the housing market. The family who wanted to buy the house in question was not able to sell their house and this gave us the opportunity to try to buy the house. Jesús called the owner of the house and explained our desire to buy the house, our financial limitations, and made the owner an offer for the house that was ten-percent below the asking price.[76] We reached an agreement with the owner of the house.[77] We then applied for a mortgage loan to buy the house. We could barely afford the house but the Decatur Federal S&L approved the mortgage loan, so we

---

[76] The asking price was $55,000 and we offered around $50,000. Later, we asked the owner to pay for all closing costs and agreed to increase the offer to about $53,500, to cover for the closing costs.

[77] The owner was also impacted by the recession so he wanted to sell the house, get some cash, and eliminate the mortgage payments on that house.

bought it. We moved into our new house, our home, at 5659 Fern Creek Drive in Lilburn, Georgia, in the summer of 1975.

We enjoyed the Lilburn house a lot because it fit our family needs and was a step in consolidating our family life and in building a financial base. The house was located on a half-acre lot at the beginning of a cul-de-sac. It had two stories, a full basement and natural woods in the back. The house had three bedrooms and two baths in the second floor, a guest/office room and bathroom in the first floor. It had a masonry fireplace and wood paneling in the family room.[78] An interesting feature of the house was that the garage had outdoor carpeting, and this made it a great playroom, except in winter, for Consuelo and Cristy. It also had a cedar closet in the basement that Consuelo Beatriz loved.

The Lilburn house was our home for nine years. Cristy and Consuelo grew from children to teenagers in that house, and Lorenzo was born while we lived in the Lilburn house. Many family members visited us at that house including Chelo's grandmother, Jesús' brother Ticó and his wife, Marta, Alexandra's mother; Jesús' younger brother, Henry, who came from Georgia Tech to stay with us many weekends, Paco and Mary Trujillo's family. While we lived there, Chelo and Jesús established themselves professionally in Atlanta, expanded our group of friends, continued our activity in the Church and the Cursillo Movement, and helped start a chapter of the ACU in Atlanta. Consuelo and Cristy continued attending IHM initially, and later went to St. Pius X High School. While in Lilburn, we met Kathi Stearns, a good friend and classmate of Consuelo Beatriz. At the Lilburn house we hosted our first Cuban-style pig roast and celebrated many birthdays.

A house that becomes a home is full of memories and this was the case for our Lilburn house. We remember the woodpecker ("pájaro loco") that decided to wake us up every morning as he banged on the wood siding next to the master bedroom. We remember Cristina walking in the patio "talking" to the trees and flowers and Consuelo's imaginary friends, Margaret and Collins. We remember Cristy and Consuelo playing in a softball league near our house. We remember St. John Neumann Parish and Jesús volunteering to

---

[78] We provide more details about each of our houses in Appendix V.

teach CCD to a group of high school sophomores— what a challenge! We remember being isolated for three days after a snowstorm.

When we moved into the Lilburn house, there were only three houses in the street. The neighbors in these houses were quiet and courteous but not overly friendly. Over the next three years, five houses were built on the remaining lots of the street. Unfortunately, these houses were of lower quality than the original three houses, resulting in a reduction of the value of our property. The neighbors that moved into the house were nice people and some had girls close to Consuelo and Cristina's age so they had occasional friends to play with. Later, a very nice Catholic family moved to the house across from our house; the lady of that house, Mary, was a favorite of our family, with whom we maintained good relations for many years after moving away from Fern Creek Drive.

The Lilburn house was in a subdivision that did not have a community pool, but a nearby subdivision, Four Winds, had made provisions for a community area with space for a pool, tennis courts and picnic tables. Chelo and Jesús became members and helped the Four Wind Association build the pool and tennis courts, because we bought, initially, two memberships in the association. When enough people joined, we sold one of our memberships. Consuelo Beatriz and Cristy received swimming lessons at this pool.

One drawback of the Lilburn house was that we had a larger commute to work and school, but the location of the house gave us the opportunity to join other church parishes. We were members of Corpus Christi Parish for a while and still remember a number of Monsignor Richard López's excellent sermons while he was assigned to that parish. Afterwards, we were founding members of St John Neumann Parish. However, our religious center of gravity remained IHM, the center of the Hispanic Cursillo Movement, the parish of many dear friends, and the elementary and middle school that Consuelo and Cristina attended.

Although 1975 was a very good year for the León-Cordero family, it ended on a sad note. Guillermo Hernández, who was married to Jesús' cousin Ethel, died of a sudden heart attack on Wednesday, December 17, while taking a siesta at his house. Jesús had known Guillermo and Ethel since he was a boy when they were his dentists in Cuba. Chelo had met them at Tarará when Guillermo went to visit his sister, Maya Citarella, who had a house there. Guillermo, Ethel and their children had moved to Atlanta and he had opened a dental practice on Briarcliff Road near North Druid Hills Road. Guillermo was the León-Cordero family dentist and we saw him and Ethel often at his office, at church and at social events. Rigoberto and Argentina came to the wake and funeral in Atlanta. We remember that the funeral was held during an unusually cold spell in Atlanta, the temperature dropped to 14 degrees on the Friday that Guillermo was buried; we were all freezing at the cemetery.

Rigoberto, Argentina, Chelo and Jesús drove to Miami the day after the funeral to celebrate Christmas with the family. Chelo and Jesús remember a humorous anecdote from that trip, a memory that illustrates how Rigoberto communicated. When telling a story, Rigoberto was prone to diverge from the main theme regularly, going on to describe related, but secondary topics. Well, Rigoberto started to relate to Chelo a trip that he took in Cuba to the city of Sagua de Tánamo, while Jesús drove and Argentina dozed off. Some time later, Argentina woke up, heard Rigoberto speaking and wrote a note to Chelo that said, "Has he reached Sagua de Tánamo yet?" Of course, he had not yet reached the city, having deviated throughout his recounting of the story. Chelo had to control herself not to burst out laughing!

Our first trip to Europe

We made our first trip to Europe during the year 1975. Father Llorente organized an ACU pilgrimage on the occasion of the Catholic Holy Year in 1975.[79] The trip was named "La Ruta Ignaciana" (Ignatius' Route) because Father Llorente wanted not only to celebrate the Holy Year but also use the occasion to visit sites that were important in St Ignatius Loyola's life. These sites included the cities of Loyola, Pamplona, Barcelona, Paris and Rome. Father Llorente made arrangements with a travel agency and obtained an extremely

---

[79] The Pope normally calls for a Holy Year those years that end in xx00, xx25, xx50 and xx75, to commemorate Jesus Christ's birth. It is a special opportunity for Catholics to pray and make pilgrimages, especially to Rome.

good price for the trip, $595 per person from New York's Kennedy Airport. The cost included all transportation and hotels, most meals, guided tours, and entrance to a number of museums and monuments. Rigoberto, Argentina and Carmen Luisa flew from Miami to New York; Chelo and Jesús flew from Atlanta to join the rest of the group, a group that numbered around 170 persons. We flew from NYC to Madrid, from Barcelona to Rome, and from Paris to NYC on a Boeing 707 of the Portuguese airlines TAP.

The group spent several days in the Madrid area visiting the city and making one-day excursions to Toledo, Avila and Segovia, El Escorial and The Valley of the Fallen. Father Llorente celebrated Mass in many of these locations including St. Teresa de Avila's Convent of the Incarnation and a chapel in Toledo's Cathedral. From Madrid, the group went to Burgos, Loyola, Pamplona and Barcelona. We learned about Spain, celebrated Ignatius Loyola's life, and deepened friendships with members of the group. In Madrid, we saw and spent time with Jesús' cousin, Félix Manuel Cepero, his wife Mireya and children.

In Rome, we made the required pilgrimage to the four major basilicas (St Peter, St Paul Outside the Walls, Santa Maria Maggiore and the Lateran Cathedral), celebrating Mass in each one, a special one at the major altar (not the papal one) in St Peter. We also attended a Papal audience in St Peter's Square. We were also able to visit many sights of both Imperial and Christian Rome. We left Rome on an overnight train that took us to Paris. We had sleeping accommodations in the train, but we were not able to sleep much because of the train's movement and noise, and also the disturbance created by members of the ACU group.

Arriving in Paris, the group boarded buses for a general overview tour of Paris. It was not the optimum time for a bus tour after the overnight train ride and many slept during the bus tour. After checking in at the hotel, our family left immediately so we could see a little bit of the Louvre Museum before it closed. We had only a couple of days in Paris, not enough to see much, but we visited Versailles, the Eiffel Tower, the Louvre, Sacre Coeur, and Notre Dame. Father Llorente concelebrated at Notre Dame with other priests the Saturday Vigil Mass on our last day in Paris. The next day, the group flew to New York from Paris via Lisbon. The Atlanta group connected in New York and flew home that evening, exhausted.

The Ruta Ignaciana was a great experience at a very low cost. In addition to the spiritual portion of the pilgrimage, we saw many sights, attended a bullfight in Madrid, experienced the Lido Cabaret in Paris, stayed overnight at a thermal spa resort in Cestona in the Basque Country of Spain,[80] ate churros late at night at the famous San Ginés Cafe in Madrid, walked the Ramblas of Barcelona and the avenues of Madrid, Paris and Rome.

Although a great experience, there were several problems with the Ruta Ignaciana trip. First, the group was too large making it difficult to coordinate. The travel agency that arranged the trip did not send anyone to assist the group so Father Llorente was forced to deal with all logistical problems. The group was not fully homogeneous because several people heard about this trip and signed up for it because it was inexpensive, a bargain. Some of the people who came for the low price were not too happy about all the religious activities. A drawback, especially in Madrid, was the quality of the hotels. In Madrid, the group was divided into four hotels. One of the hotels, the Londres, was pretty good, a couple of others were tolerable, and one, the Magerit, was inadequate. The groups assigned to the Magerit included several older people, many young ACU members, Jesús Chelo, Rigoberto, Argentina and Carmen Luisa. Chelo and Jesús remember the "limitations" of the hotel: the bed that sunk in the middle, bathroom towels that were almost transparent, no elevator to carry luggage, and food that was barely edible for the main meal of the day.[81] The hotels in the rest of the cities were mostly adequate. As is normally the case, you get what you pay for, and since we did not pay very much for the trip, we should not have expected much.

---

[80] At this hotel Carmen Luisa got stuck in the elevator between floors. She had to squeeze out the bottom part of the elevator and jump down a small distance to the floor.

[81] Several of the people assigned to this hotel left to other accommodations. Argentina, Rigoberto and Carmen Luisa, for example, moved with Félix Cepero's family. By the way, Magerit is the Arab word for Madrid.

On the positive side, we enjoyed the company of many friends including the Antón, Guigou, Ledón, and Julio Ramírez families of Atlanta. We met and became better friends with ACU members and families from Miami, Washington and other cities. The trip helped Chelo and Jesús learn about international travel, and in particular, about Spain, Rome and Paris. In Paris, we almost made it to dinner at the most prestigious restaurant in the city at the time, La Tour d'Argent. Carmen Luisa invited Rigoberto, Chelo and Jesús to dinner at this restaurant. On the way to the restaurant, Carmen Luisa experienced stomach cramps and did not want to continue. She suggested that the three of us continue to dinner without her, but obviously, we were not going to do that and returned to the hotel. Chelo and Jesús did make it to the Tour d'Argent sixteen years later!

Professional careers

Both of our careers blossomed in Atlanta, and for this reason, we will now reflect on Chelo's and Jesús' professional careers from the mid 1970s until the family moved to Spain.

In the spring of 1973, we participated in a religious study day sponsored by the Cursillo Movement held at Sacred Heart Church. At this meeting, as we mentioned earlier, Sister Louise told Chelo that St. Pius X High School was looking for a part-time Spanish teacher. Chelo followed-up on the information and was offered the job. In September 1973, Chelo started working part-time at St. Pius X High School, Consuelo started Kindergarten at IHM, and Chelo arranged for a Mexican lady who lived in our apartment building to watch Cristy while she taught at Pius.

Chelo's professional trajectory at Pius was a very successful one. Father Jim Sextone was the school Principal when she started at Pius. Two years later, in 1975, the Archdiocese named Father Terry Young to be the Principal of the school. Father Terry was an excellent administrator, someone who admired Chelo's work ethics and teaching ability. Father Terry was instrumental in making St. Pius an excellent academic institution. Chelo was soon a full-time teacher and was later promoted to be the head of the Language Department. She created several new courses at Pius including a very successful one for native Spanish speakers.

Chelo loved St. Pius, especially because of the school's success in creating a widespread sense of a Christian Community, a community focused in the development of the overall individual that went beyond imparting an excellent academic education. Many of the teachers at St. Pius became Chelo's good friends, notably among them, Father Richard López, a teacher and treasure in the Religion Department for forty years, and Rayanne Barnett, a Spanish teacher that Chelo hired and trained when she was Department Head. Rayanne later became a Catholic following Chelo's example; Chelo was the sponsor of both Rayanne and her son Donny. Later, her husband also became Catholic.

When Chelo became a full-time employee at Pius, she explained to Father Young that she had to transport and care for her daughters in the early morning, and consequently, she would not be able to take the responsibility of being a homeroom teacher. Father Terry accepted this arrangement without hesitation because Chelo was an outstanding teacher and was committed to helping every student there. Unfortunately, this arrangement became an issue with some of the other teachers at the school who felt that Chelo was receiving special treatment. Father Terry, reacting to the complaints of the teachers, called Chelo in the summer of 1981 to tell her that she would, henceforth, be assigned a homeroom. Chelo responded immediately and informed Father Terry that this was not acceptable to her because in order to be at St. Pius in time for homeroom she would have to leave her daughters alone at the IHM parking lot until the school opened. Chelo told Father Terry that she was not going to sacrifice the safety and well being of her daughters, and therefore, she would no longer be able to continue at Pius. Chelo's decision was an example of a person who knew her priorities in life and what elements of her life were not negotiable. Father Terry did not want to lose Chelo so he proposed to find someone, acceptable to Chelo, who would take care of the girls until the IHM School opened its doors in the morning. After a few conversations with Father Terry, Chelo offered him solution: Mrs. Griffin, an excellent teacher at IHM, a person who Chelo trusted would arrive early at IHM and monitor Consuelo Beatriz and Cristy. Father Terry was able to work out an agreement with Mrs. Griffin and Chelo stayed at St. Pius and accepted to have a Home Room.

Chelo continued teaching at St. Pius until December 1982, when she took maternity leave for Lorenzo's birth in January 1983. She returned to Pius in 1988, when Lorenzo started preschool. By the time she returned to full-time teaching, she had obtained a Master of Arts degree in Spanish Literature and Education from Georgia State University with a perfect 4.0 average. The final requirements for the degree were a written test and an oral examination conducted by a faculty tribunal. Chelo was very nervous as the calendar approached the date for the oral exam, developing a skin rash and losing sleep. She successfully completed the oral exam in the summer of 1988. Chelo continued at St. Pius until September of 1993 when the family moved to Spain.

Meanwhile, Jesús began his professional career with Scientific-Atlanta, SA. As mentioned earlier, Jesús started at SA at the end of 1974, joining the Electro-Products Division of the company. This division designed, manufactured, tested, and installed telemetry and tracking systems for satellite and radar systems. A major area of Jesús' course work was in Control Systems and the SA work was a very good application of his academic studies, using his knowledge of servomechanism controls. He became a systems engineer responsible for the overall project design on several interesting projects, leading the design, testing and customer acceptance for systems delivered to NASA, to the US Armed Forces, and to customers in Iran, India, Japan, Brazil and Taiwan. The projects in Iran and India were used to track and receive transmissions from the LANDSAT and METEOSAT satellites. One of the projects for the military was the design of a very accurate precision tracking system for the US Navy.

Jesús' leadership capacity was recognized by Scientific-Atlanta and he was steadily promoted in a matter of a few years from Senior Engineer to group leader to Engineering Manager to Manager of Engineering and Programs. As he progressed to higher position of leadership, Jesús decided that it would be useful to learn about business, enrolling and eventually receiving an MBA from the Executive MBA program at Georgia State University. These executive programs are now very common and there are now more than four such programs in the Atlanta area. These programs require the applicants to have a minimum number of years of work experience. In the MBA program, Jesús learned the basics of accounting, marketing and finance, which combined with his leadership experience, helped him to continue advancing in the technical and administrative management ranks.

One benefit of the SA job was the opportunity to travel widely to interesting international locations. Jesús often seized the opportunity to make side trips on his own, before beginning or after completing his work. For example, on his trip to India, he stopped in Cairo and Mumbai and then took a week of vacation to visit Calcutta (Mother Teresa), the Taj Majal at Agra, and the Himalayan city of Darjeeling. On the way back from India to Atlanta, he stopped in Amsterdam. He traveled to Iran twice and was able to visit London, Athens, the Caspian Sea, Persepolis and the city of Shiraz in Iran. Other locations that Jesús visited included Rio de Janeiro and Sao Paolo in Brazil, Caracas in Venezuela, Hong Kong, Taipei in Taiwan, Gothenburg, Karlsborg and Stockholm in Sweden, and Copenhagen. Last, but not least, Jesús taught a seminar on Antenna Measurements in Beijing, China in 1982, when China was beginning to open its door to the rest of the world. On a few occasions Chelo was able to join Jesús on a trip, visiting Japan, Hong Kong and Taipei with him.

Consuelo Beatriz and Cristina at Fern Creek Drive

Consuelo Beatriz and Cristy spent the bulk of their formative years during the time we resided at Fern Creek Drive. Consuelo Beatriz was seven years old and Cristy five when we moved to Fern Creek Drive.

Consuelo Beatriz was a dedicated and an excellent student, working hard every day on her assignments with no need of supervision or cajoling, earning excellent grades. Cristy, on the other hand, was reflective and patient, weighing alternatives before making a decision. As Cristy grew, we realized she had a photographic memory and a very quick intellect. At school, she was always one of the best students and got excellent grades. Unlike Consuelo, she did not start her homework the moment it was assigned, but she always completed it with a grade of "A" even when she did it during the TV commercials while watching a soap opera. Her quickness would show up in different occasions. Chelo was teaching CB Spanish and would ask CB questions as part of the learning; very often Cristy would chime in with the answer before CB could respond, even though she was not supposed to be learning how to read and write in Spanish. Another time, when Cristy was twelve years old and was with Chelo at the cashier's line at the Kroger Supermarket, a woman overheard them speaking Spanish and said, "This is the USA, we speak English here." Cristy turned to her and said something like, "Excuse me, but I am having a private conversation with my mother and the last time I checked, the USA is a free country, and therefore we can speak whatever language we choose. Sorry for you that you are ignorant and perhaps can only speak one language. I speak more than one and choose to speak Spanish with my mother." Cristy turned around and kept talking to Chelo, and the checkout lady looked over and smiled.

One interesting difference between CB and Cristy was about attendance at school. CB would not miss a day of school for any reason, even if she was sick. She had perfect attendance for years. Cristy, unlike Consuelo, did not mind losing a day of class, especially when Abuelo Cordero was in town. On several occasions, she would pretend to be sick in order to be with her abuelo. Cordero would pick her up and they would go for lunch to McDonald's or the International House of Pancakes and have a grand time together. When Chelo came home from Pius, she would find out that everything was perfectly fine with Cristy. After a few times, Chelo decided not to pay much attention when IHM called Pius to inform her that Cristy was sick; she knew what Cristy wanted to do.

Another difference between the two girls was their study habits. CB, like Chelo, was the perfect student. She was always ready, fully motivated, ahead of schedule and over prepared. On the other hand, Cristy was laid back and did everything at her own pace. She, like CB, had excellent grades, but she did not spend that much time studying because she was a naturally gifted girl. Chelo has heard Cristy say many times that she never developed good study-skills habits. Cristy, like Jesús, and now Ethan, does not like being told the same thing more than once.

CB and Cristy's life during the academic year while we lived at Fern Creek Drive revolved around school, extracurricular activities and friends. During the nine years we lived in Lilburn, CB completed second through eighth grade at IHM and her freshman and sophomore years at Pius; Cristy completed her whole elementary education at IHM. Transportation to school varied although Chelo was normally the one who drove them to school before heading to St Pius to teach. Chelo made arrangements to have the girls brought to St Pius to join her before heading home.

Extracurricular activities kept Chelo and the girls busy. There were ballet classes for Consuelo and Cristy— neither had a lot of innate talent for dance. Both played in a girl's softball league in Lilburn with very different styles. CB, who played first base, wanted to tag the bag whether or not she had caught the ball thrown to her. Cristy played right field and did not want to be bothered— she played softball because CB was playing— so she preferred if the ball was not hit her way; a few times, while the game was going on, she sat on the ground in right field to take a break.

Chelo placed CB and Cristy in swimming lessons at the Four Winds Subdivision Community Pool and both learned how to swim well. The community area also had two good tennis courts and some of us played there from time to time. CB learned quickly how to ride a bicycle while we lived in the apartment and Cristy learned to do this at Fern Creek Drive. However, as with almost everything in their lives, Cristy was less reckless riding a bike or swimming or playing sports than Consuelo Beatriz.

A special occasion every year was the celebration of birthdays. For some birthdays, Chelo would reserve or rent a picnic area in a park or at a private location such as Mathis Dairy in Decatur or Stone Mountain Park. Both girls had many friends in addition to their girl cousins. Many of their more lasting friends came from the children of Cuban parents in our community in Atlanta. A number of these Cuban friends were also classmates of CB and Cristy (the García-Carreras, Berenguers, Bolets). They both developed life-long friends among their classmates (Kathi Stearns, Lara O'Connor, Amy McBride). They also met and played with a handful of girls from our neighborhood cul-de-sac at Fern Creek Drive. None of the friends from the neighborhood group remained after we moved out of the house and neighborhood.

Every year we made several family outings to the Six Flags Over Georgia Amusement Park, and every two years or so, we went to the Walt Disney World Resort in Orlando. We also drove to Helen, Georgia for a day or went to visit Vicente and Bertica in Columbia, South Carolina, for a weekend. One characteristic of many of the outings was the need to manage our expenses. We had reasonable but limited financial resources and thus, when we went to Six Flags we would normally pack lunches and looked for special entry fee specials to minimize expenses. For Disney visits, we often stayed at the house of the Sorondo family in Orlando. When this was not possible, we would find a budget hotel located outside the Disney Resort area. We would visit the Magic Kingdom in one day, arriving at the park very early in the morning and departing after the park closed. We brought our lunch like we did at Six Flags. A couple of times we drove to Washington, DC, and stayed with ACU friends, like the Gutiérrez family, who lived in the Maryland area north of the city.

CB and Cristy spent part of the summer vacation with their grandparents in Miami. They would go to the beach with abuelo Cordero and their cousins and spent time playing with them. Chelo and Jesús were in Miami only part of the time because of limited vacation time. CB and Cristy also spent time with the family during Christmas. Whenever we went to an overseas vacation like the Ruta Ignaciana in 1975 and the Holy Land Pilgrimage in 1978, CB and Cristy stayed with their grandparents in Miami.

We made a concerted effort to help our daughters become fluent in Spanish. Chelo taught them how to read and write during the summer months. We spoke in Spanish at our home, emphasized the importance of the language and required that the girls speak to us in Spanish. There were consequences when they spoke in English in our presence. Jesús would ignore them when they spoke to him in English, as if no one was listening. We also penalized them with sanctions suited to their personalities— Consuelo had to pay us twenty-five cents and Cristy had to do some house or yard work when we caught them speaking in English.

Speaking of household chores, Consuelo Beatriz and Cristy helped with chores around the house, especially when Cordero was not visiting us, because Cordero helped with different household chores every day. CB and Cristy took turns helping with the vacuum and mowing the grass. Jesús did almost all the yard work at Fern Creek Drive, and because we had a fairly large front yard, mowing, weeding, reseeding and cleanup was a good bit of work. CB loved mowing the lawn, but did not enjoy as much the vacuum while Cristy was the opposite, mowing involved too much sweating in the Atlanta sun. They also helped with the dishes and kept their rooms clean and neat, especially CB, who was a cleaning and organization "nut" for most of her young life, until her last year or so at Georgia Tech. She changed her style during the co-op quarters she spent living with the León-Núñez grandparents in Miami. This was also the time she fell in love with Todd Bills, and from that time on she centered all her time and attention on her boyfriend.

We have mentioned that CB and Cristy have different personalities and approaches to life and we want to give an example of how these personalities affected their relationship to us, their parents. Jesús spent a lot of time with Consuelo Beatriz during the first year of her life and Chelo spent a lot of time with Cristy during her first three years. We are not sure that this was the main reason for their behavior toward us, we are sure that their personalities were determined somewhat by their genetic make up. Whatever the reasons, CB was dad's promoter while Cristy was mami's advocate. So, when we lived in Fern Creek Drive, CB would tell Cristy, "dad does all the hard work, the dangerous work, he goes up on the roof to clean gutters, etc." Cristy would reply, "dad does this only once a year and mom cooks, cleans, takes us to the doctor, to parties and school every day."

The Miracle

A miracle? Really? Well, yes, we witnessed a real, physical, miracle in our family!

Our lives in Atlanta, after we moved into the Lilburn house, were typical of any family of four. Chelo and Jesús worked, Consuelo and Cristy went to school, we attended Mass on Sundays, enjoyed social activities with friends, spent Christmas with our families, and took summer vacations— all very common. The year 1976, however, was going to be exceptional, a year that we shall never forget.

We returned to Atlanta from Miami after the 1975 Christmas family celebration in early January 1976, and resumed our ordinary activities. Jesús traveled to Newfoundland, Canada, for three weeks in late January to adjust a Landsat tracking system. The dates of the trip coincided with Cristy's birthday, something that happened two or three years in a row, a conflict that Cristy did not like.

Chelo scheduled tonsillectomies for Cristy and Consuelo with Dr. Leonard at West Paces Ferry Hospital in late February, and both surgeries went well. Argentina came from Miami to assist; she was very good at this, especially helping Consuelo and Cristy to swallow the first few days. The recovery for Cristy was routine but not so easy for CB. CB had a harder time swallowing and Argentina told Chelo that she spat blood on one or two occasions.

On Saturday, May 8, Father Richard Kieran celebrated a Mass wherein Consuelo Beatriz and George Balbona, José and Virginia Balbona's youngest child, received their First Communion at the IHM Parish Church. It was a beautiful ceremony that was followed by a family celebration.

The story of the miracle started during the month of May, after Consuelo's First Communion. Consuelo Beatriz complained about difficulty swallowing, and Chelo who checked the children's health regularly, looked at CB's throat and determined that there was something there that did not belong. Chelo was the only one who, at the beginning, noticed that there was a problem, so she set up an appointment with the surgeon, Dr. Leonard, who after examination of CB's throat, agreed that there was a growth in her throat and prescribed cortisone to reduce it.

Consuelo Beatriz took the cortisone on-and-off for about three months. In early September, on the day the Atlanta Catholic Community celebrated the Feast of Our Lady of Charity, the Leóns spent part of their day at the home of the Macías family in Henry County. Francisco (Paco), Carmín and Carmencita Macías had a very nice swimming pool with a water slide in their house. Reemberto and Rafael (Toti) Rodríguez, nephews of Carmín, were staying with the Macías awaiting the arrival of their parents from Cuba. We visited the Macías from time to time at their home, often on weekends when we could enjoy the pool and the camaraderie with the family and other friends. On that September day in 1976, Chelo asked Paco, who is an excellent medical doctor, to examine Consuelo Beatriz's "bola" in her throat. Paco, after looking at it, suggested we take CB back to her surgeon. The "bola" had grown to a size that caused all of us to worry. After we arrived at our house that evening, CB said she could not swallow, so we decided to take her to the emergency room at West Paces Ferry Hospital. Chelo called Rosie García-Carreras who lived near us and whose daughter Cristina was Cristy's schoolmate and asked Rosie if she could take care of Cristy that evening and take her to school the next day. Rosie agreed immediately, and after preparing Cristy's school clothes and book bag, we went to Rosie's house to drop Cristy there. As we were beginning to drive off, Rosie came running out to our car and gave us a bottle with water from the Sanctuary of Lourdes.

We drove to West Paces Ferry Hospital and took CB to the emergency room. The emergency room physician examined Consuelo Beatriz. We remember his statement to us, as clearly as if we were hearing it today: "I would not touch that with a twenty foot pole." Then he proceeded to tell us that the blob was a cluster of veins and that if the veins were not handled properly, she could bleed to death in the operating table! He further stated, "the procedure needs to be done by a surgeon, early in the morning." We left the hospital somewhat in a daze, very worried.

Arriving home, we placed CB in our bed between the two of us. We prayed, and Chelo asked Consuelo Beatriz to pray because "your prayers will be heard" quickly. CB asked if she could drink some of the water from Lourdes, so she drank some. She then stayed in bed holding the bottle with the water from Lourdes. Chelo and Jesús agreed to a plan for the next day. In the morning, Chelo took CB to St Pius with her and Jesús set up an appointment, at one in the afternoon, with the surgeon.

At Pius, Chelo did not teach very much that day. She explained to every class why Consuelo Beatriz was in the classroom and asked her students to pray for her. Consuelo Beatriz did not eat anything for breakfast nor did she have anything for lunch. However, right after Chelo's lunch period, CB who was seating at Chelo's desk said: "Mom, I can swallow." Chelo asked her to come to the window, looked closely at Consuelo's throat and to her amazement, saw that the blob had disappeared; there was no "bola" in Consuelo's throat. Jubilation, happiness, joy, a sense of thanksgiving, all these sentiments rolled by at once. She and the class prayed in thanksgiving. Chelo went to the office between class periods and called Jesús at his office.

Jesús picked CB at Pius as previously arranged and took her to Dr. Leonard's office. When Dr. Leonard examined CB, he told Jesús:

"I do not know what happened. The blob was there last night and is not there any more." Jesús replied: "I do understand what happened." Dr. Leonard had seen the blob before; he had prescribed cortisone to reduce it and he had read the emergency room doctor's report from the previous night. He just could not explain medically what had happened. **And this is precisely the definition of a miracle**. The Oxford Dictionary online defines miracle, a noun as, "an extraordinary and welcome event that is not explicable by natural or scientific laws and is therefore attributed to a divine agency."[82] We had just witnessed a miraculous cure in our family.

Chelo was so happy that she decided to go from St. Pius directly to Holy Cross Church to give thanks to God. On the way to the church she had a flat tire, but this did not bother her. What is a flat tire compared to her daughter's dangerous blob of veins in the throat? We have always been very grateful for the intercession of Our Lady of Lourdes to cure CB, and we pledged to take Consuelo Beatriz to Lourdes in the future, a pledge that we fulfilled in 2006 when all of our family, including our grandchildren Alina and Ethan, made a pilgrimage to Lourdes, France.

1976-1978

There was another important family event in 1976, the arrival of Chelo's grandmother, Consuelo María del Carmen Berdasco Garrido. She was the last of Chelo's family members to leave Cuba. Consuelo Berdasco flew to Spain to visit her family and then traveled to Miami, arriving on December 30, at 84 years of age. All the members of her family were at the airport to welcome her. These included her three daughters, her four grandchildren, six great-grandchildren, Cordero and the spouses of the grandchildren.

Consuelo Berdasco visited Atlanta during the summer of 1977. She had excellent health and could stand for a long time at the stove to make a mountain of "feisuelos," a crêpe-like thin pancake. Consuelo's feisuelos were very light and delicious. Consuelo Berdasco lived with Cordero and her daughters Consuelo and Generosa until

---

[82] http://oxforddictionaries.com/

she suffered a stroke and was moved to a full-care facility where she died on August 19, 1997, a few weeks after celebrating her 105 birthday.

The year 1978 was very busy with wonderful events. In January, we flew to Puerto Rico to join in the celebration of Manny Antón and Annette Lefebvre's wedding, a joyful and sad event at the same time because Manny's parents and sister did not attend. Cristy made her First Communion on the Feast of Our Lady of Fatima, May 13, in a celebration at IHM presided by Father Richard Kieran. In May, Jesús went to Iran, via London, to install a satellite tracking and receiving system. While in Iran, he traveled to and swam on the Caspian Sea, and visited Shiraz and Persepolis. From Teheran, Jesús flew to Tel Aviv, Israel, on the Israeli airlines El-Al to join Chelo and two busloads of people for an ACU organized pilgrimage of the Holy Land led by Father Llorente.

The pilgrimage to the Holy Land, in June 1978, was very special and Chelo and Jesús remember the enthusiasm of Father Llorente during this trip. We remember that en route from Tel Aviv to Nazareth, our Franciscan guide, Father Angel, mentioned that the mountain that we were viewing on the right side of the bus was Mount Tabor. Father Llorente exclaimed, "El Monte Tabor, stop the bus!" So, we stepped off the bus to look at Mount Tabor from a distance. His enthusiasm and wonderment were contagious throughout the trip. We visited most of the major sites mentioned in the New Testament. In the north, we went to Nazareth, the Jordan River (where we dipped our toes), the Sea of Galilee (where Jesús and Chelo bathed in very cold water and Chelo got a cold), Capharnaum (the Synagogue and Peter's house), and the sites established by tradition as the sites for the Sermon of the Mount and the Primacy of Peter (John 21). From the north, we traveled through Palestinian territory, stopping at Jacob's Well (the Samaritan woman) on our way to Jerusalem. Near Jerusalem, we stopped at Ain Karim (Elizabeth's house), went to Bethlehem and many sites in Jerusalem (The Temple, Upper Room, Mount of Olives, Via Dolorosa, the Church of the Holy Sepulcher, the traditional place for the Ascension and the Church of the Dormition of Mary). We also traveled to Jericho, to Qum Ram and the Dead Sea (Jesús bathed on the "ugh" Dead Sea water).

From Tel Aviv we flew to Malaga, Spain to visit Andalusia (Granada, Cadiz with the "La Bomba" dessert at El Faro Restaurant) and then to Madrid for a few days.

In October Jesús went to Iran, via Athens, for his second trip there that year. The difference on this trip was that the Iranian political situation in October was very tense and the government had declared martial law. Because of Jesús' self-imposed pressure to complete the job and leave the country as soon as possible, Jesús overworked himself and caused a simple cold to develop into pneumonia by the time he left Iran. Nevertheless, Jesús and a technician named Ken flew to Istanbul on Pan Am flight 001 (one of the two Pan Am round-the-world flights). Jesús was taking about 16 to 20 aspirins a day to control the fever, but fever or no fever, he took a one-day excursion to visit the city. From Istanbul, Ken and Jesús were booked to change planes in Rome before flying to New York and then to Atlanta. Jesús told Ken that he would have loved to stop in Rome since the Conclave of Cardinals was about to elect a new pope,[83] but Jesús was too sick to stop in Rome. Ken told Jesús, half-jokingly, "You have to make it through US customs on your own. If you do, I will make sure that your body arrives in Atlanta."

After arriving in Atlanta, Jesús went to see his friend and physician, Dr. Francisco (Paco) Macías, who told Jesús that he had gotten over pneumonia without any medicine, and suggested that Jesús take a week off. Jesús did and used the week to rest while listening to all nine of Beethoven's symphonies.

ACU student group in Atlanta

To add to an already special year, 1978 was also the year that a new ACU group started in Atlanta, a momentous event for the members for the ACU group, for our family and for the Atlanta Catholic Hispanic Community. We dedicate the next few paragraphs to narrate the foundation of the group and to summarize some of its milestones and activities.

---

[83] The conclave elected John Paul II a few days after Jesús changed planes at Rome's airport.

Manuel P. Antón III, Manny, the son of ACU member Doctor Manuel Antón, was the driving force for the foundation of the ACU in Atlanta. Manny, who lived in Atlanta, graduated from Marist High School in May 1978, and planned to enroll at Emory University in the fall of 1978. During the summer of 1978, Manny went on a road trip with Miami ACU members and Father Luis "Yiyo" Maderal. He then participated in the Labor Day weekend Spiritual Exercises in Miami with two other young men from Atlanta, José Batlle and Eddy Balbona (son of ACU member Dr. José Balbona). At the conclusion of the retreat, Manny asked Father Amando Llorente how they could start an ACU group in Atlanta. Father Llorente told Manny to call Jesús to help organize and lead the group.

Upon speaking with Manny, Jesús called Father Llorente and asked his advise. Father Llorente gave Jesús several suggestions: Go slow, add new members one at a time; do not mix the young students with the older ACU members residing in Atlanta; use the Catholic Catechism as the topic of study; ask the young members to help with the presentations; and start the meeting with a Rosary.

The new ACU Atlanta group met on Saturday mornings at the house of one of the members, often followed by home cooked lunch, and many times, by afternoon sporting activities. Eddy Balbona decided to drop out of the group, but we added several others. By March of 1979, the group consisted of Manny Antón, José Batlle, Alex Saker, John Alarcón, Fernando Muñoz, Jorge Guigou, Jr., and Reemberto Rodríguez. These became, to Jesús, the Magnificent Seven.[84]

Chelo became the "de facto" mother of the group to such an extent that CB and Cristy called the ACU members, "Dad's sons." In 1979, all the members of the group participated together in Spiritual Exercises directed by Father Maderal. That year, the group held the first ACU Atlanta pig roast to celebrate the arrival of Rembe's parents, brother, sister-in-law and nephew to the USA.[85]

---

[84] A reference to a 1960 movie by that name with great artists including Steve McQueen, Yul Brynner, Charles Bronson, James Coburn and Eli Wallach.
[85] The first pig roast was a learning experience. It was held at our house in Fern Creek Drive. We dug a hole in the woods of the patio, bought a pig at the At-

The ACU Atlanta group undertook apostolic activities such as teaching high school CCD classes at Corpus Christi Parish; starting, organizing and directing a weekly Catholic Spanish Radio program in Atlanta; publishing and distributing a once-a-month flyer on Catholic doctrine at IHM Church. All the magnificent seven student members became full members of the ACU ("congregants").

The ACU Atlanta group has continued to grow through the years, helping many men to find their vocations as Catholics. The ACU Atlanta members have been very successful professionally with careers in engineering, medicine, business and architecture; and they have also been excellent family members and community leaders.

The waters of Venice and the Great Wall of China

Enrique Luis León, Henry, Jesús' youngest brother came to Atlanta in the fall of 1974 to study Electrical Engineering at Georgia Tech. The León family saw Henry often for the next four years. On Friday afternoons, Henry took a Marta bus from GT that brought him to our apartment. After we moved to Fern Creek Drive, Henry took a bus that stopped near St. Pius where he would join Chelo and the girls in the ride to our home to spend the weekends with us. Chelo washed Henry's clothes and we fed him. On Monday mornings Jesús often took Henry back to Georgia Tech. Henry babysat for us on many occasions, and he was like a big brother for CB and Cristy. This arrangement continued until the fall of 1978, and then suddenly and mysteriously, Henry stopped coming to join us for weekends. We were worried that we had done something to offend Henry. It was not until the following June when we attended the GT graduation of Jorgito Guigou that we found out the reason for his absences. Henry had met Jean Marie Finison, his future wife.

In April 1980, Jesús accompanied Chelo on a St Pius X sponsored trip to Spain with five Cuban-American students, who were the children of very close Atlanta friends. The trip was an interesting experience, particularly the stress we had trying to protect four beautiful

---

lanta Municipal Market, made mojo the hard way, peeling garlic and squeezing limes and lemons, and marinated the pig. We started roasting the pig during the night and ate the pig at midday the following day.

teenager girls who attracted men like flies to sugar. Jesús vowed never to be part of a school trip if he could help it. We arrived in Spain during the Easter Weekend. Our visit to Spain included sightseeing in the Madrid area and Andalusia.

While in Madrid, we learned about the events at the Peruvian Embassy in Havana that led to the Mariel boatlift.[86] When we returned to Atlanta, the Mariel boatlift was just about to begin, an operation that resulted in a major influx of Cuban refugees to the United States, including several close members of our family. Carmen Luisa, Jesús' sister, together with René Núñez, Jesús' uncle, Teresita Pulido, a family friend, and other Cuban Americans leased a Georgia shrimp boat and traveled to Mariel to pick up members of their respective families. The group spent a month in Mariel, an adventure that requires a chapter of its own, and that Carmen Luisa might one day write. They brought to the USA seven members of our family. Carmen's objective was to bring to the USA a group consisting of Elio Leyva, his wife Ana María Núñez, Jesús' cousin, and their daughter Martica. René went to bring his oldest daughter, Nilda, and her three children, José, Tony and Camelia. The León-Cordero family from Atlanta embraced the newcomers a few weeks later in Miami.

Henry and Jean Marie Finison got married in Atlanta on December 20, 1980, the same day but thirty-seven years later than Rigoberto and Argentina's wedding day. Many members of the family came from Miami to the wedding, including Angel Trujillo and Martica Leyva, who rode in Cordero's car with "Abuela Juana," who remarked to Cordero during the trip, "Esa niña que nunca habla no ha parado de hablar en todo el viaje" ("this girl who hardly talks, has not stopped talking the whole trip"). Well, Angel and Martica hit it off and became husband and wife a few years later.

The year 1981 was typical and flew by quickly but this was not the case for 1982, a remarkable year for our family. The year started with very cold weather, with temperatures as low as five degrees Fahrenheit below zero. This caused many schools, including IHM and St Pius to close on Monday, January 11, 1982, because they could not heat the building to a comfortable temperature. On Tuesday,

---

[86] See http://en.wikipedia.org/wiki/Mariel_boatlift#Background for details.

IHM School opened but because St Pius was closed and because it was still very cold, Chelo decided to keep the girls at home. This turned out to be a very wise decision because that day was the "famous Atlanta Snow Jam of 1982."[87] It snowed during the afternoon and thousands of Atlantans were stranded on the highways. Jesús returned home in the afternoon, having left early from work and made it home safely before the worst of the storm. We were stranded in our house for the rest of the week. Jesús was finally able to get out of the neighborhood on Friday afternoon. The good news is that we did not lose power and so we spent a few days of family togetherness.

The snowstorm was just the beginning of an eventful year for our family. In the spring, Jesús went to China to give a three-day seminar on Antenna Measurements in Beijing. While in China, he stayed at the Friendship Hotel and visited famous sites including the Forbidden City, the Temple of Heaven and the Great Wall. Coincidentally, Carmen Luisa León traveled to China about the same time, and she and Jesús were able to see each other in Beijing.

A couple of weeks after Jesús left for China, Chelo also departed Atlanta, traveling as a teacher chaperone on a trip sponsored by St Pius to Italy. Chelo left Atlanta while Jesús was in China with the result that they did not see each other for several weeks. Upon her return, and to paraphrase Cordero who said, "The waters of Venice washed upon the Great Wall of China," Chelo became pregnant! When Chelo went to see her OBGYN doctor, he told her that she was at a risky age and should consider not taking the pregnancy to term. That was it for that doctor; Chelo never saw him again. She changed to a wonderful doctor and human being, Dr. Robert Kral, who encouraged Chelo throughout her pregnancy not to worry because she was a healthy woman and had previously delivered two healthy children. Chelo prayed that it would be Dr. Kral, and not his partner, to deliver her baby. Fortunately, Chelo's wish was granted.

---

[87] There are lots of stories about the snow jam. See for example, http://www.ajc.com/news/news/local/theres-no-jam-like-snow-jam/nQqrG/

In May, Consuelo graduated from eighth grade at IHM and prepared to enter St Pius X in September. During that summer, Adolfo Fernández, Chelo's cousin, had a heart attack. Consuelo Cordero called Jesús to tell him, and Jesús also talked with Rossina, Adolfo's wife. Jesús was worried about how to tell Chelo, and the potential impact of the news to the baby. God always helps and it did so here again. There was going to be an intimate picnic at Stone Mountain Park with Father Llorente who was visiting Atlanta and with Peque and Virginia Balbona. After consultation with Father Llorente and with Peque, Jesús told Chelo, who was visibly impacted but handled it very well.

It is customary to give expectant mothers baby showers to celebrate the promise of a new baby. Chelo had a traditional baby shower, but she also had a very special one with married couples of the Atlanta Hispanic Community, held in late October.[88] The shower was planned by and held at the home of Dr. José (Pepe) and Zenaida López, very good friends of ours that lived in the south of Atlanta. They engaged a common friend and well-known Atlanta decorator, Enrique Dorta, to organize a celebration with a Chinese theme, as per the "water of the Venice washing upon the Great Wall of China." In addition to Chinese-themed decorations, Enrique dressed as a "Chinese Doctor" and Zenaidita, the Lopéz's daughter, as a Chinese nurse, and the two "helped Chelo deliver" one "chino negrito" doll.[89] The party was a great success and the next day Jesús and Chelo left for San Francisco for a few days of vacation.

In December, Cordero arrived in Atlanta to help the household in preparation for the birth of our new child and Chelo took maternity leave from St. Pius. Because of Chelo's pregnancy we could not travel to Miami to celebrate Christmas, so the family stayed in Atlanta. This was the first time since 1961 for Jesús and since 1962 for Chelo that we did not celebrate Christmas with our family in Miami. We did have a peaceful beautiful Christmas Season that started with a great Nochebuena celebration at Paco and Carmin Macías' house.

---

[88] Jesús thinks it was on his birthday, Saturday, October 23.
[89] Cristy did not like this negrito doll.

Book V – Part III – Atlanta 1983-1993

Lorenzo Javier

Lorenzo was born on the Feast Day of the Epiphany ('Los Reyes Magos,') Thursday, January 6, 1983, at Northside Hospital in Atlanta. That morning Chelo woke up with a minor pain in her back, and we decided that she should see Dr. Kral as a precaution. Because we were not sure of the cause of the pain, and in order not to cause unnecessary worry, we did not tell CB or Cristy about our plans when Jesús drove them to school. We told Cordero, who was staying at our home, that we were going to visit the OBGYN to make sure everything was fine and that we would keep him posted of any developments. We then drove to Dr. Kral's office. After he examined Chelo, who was already dilating, he told us to go directly to the hospital. Northside Hospital was located near the doctor's office, and thus we arrived there in a matter of minutes.

After checking into the hospital around ten in the morning, Chelo was taken to one of the labor rooms, and, as she had experienced on her two previous deliveries, the labor process came to a halt. Jesús recalls telling Chelo that she looked like she was at the beauty parlor, reading magazines and talking calmly. The actual birth of this baby was going to be a new experience for us because for the first time, Jesús would be allowed into the delivery room to witness the birth of his son. By coincidence, Mark and Linda Kelly were also at Northside Hospital because Linda was about to give birth to their third child. Mark was a good friend and colleague of Chelo at St. Pius where he taught, coached basketball and later became Athletic Director. Linda, maiden name Buechner, was the daughter of Cursillo member friends of ours. She had babysat CB and Cristy when we lived in the apartment. Mark and Linda had two boys and wanted a girl and we remember Mark coming to chat with us from time to time to check on Chelo's progress and keep us informed about Linda's progress.

Dr. Kral was not scheduled to be at the hospital until noon that day, so Chelo, who wanted Dr. Kral to deliver the baby, was not in a big hurry. However, by early afternoon, Dr. Kral decided that he needed to help Chelo with the delivery, and he started administering

Pitocin intravenously to her. As the Pitocin started to take effect, Chelo began to experience labor contractions again. During this time, Mark Kelly came to Chelo's labor room and told her, "Linda had a baby girl. Now it is your turn to have a boy." When Chelo was almost ready to have the baby, Jesús was told to put on scrubs and meet the doctor at the door of the delivery room. Witnessing the birth of a baby is an exceptional event, and the birth of Lorenzo was a great experience for Jesús. The delivery was without complications, very straightforward. When the head of the baby was coming out, Dr. Kral remarked that the baby had black hair, not a surprise! Chelo finished giving birth and seemed to be as "fresh as lettuce" while the nurse assisting in the delivery room was sweating. Dr. Kral asked us and the nurse to hold hands and he said a prayer of thanksgiving almost immediately after the baby was born. Then, he gave the baby to Jesús who proceeded to baptize him in the delivery room; Jesús had previously baptized CB and Cristy after they were born.

CB and Cristy heard that their mother was giving birth via a St Pius announcement over its public information system. Mike Kelly had called the school to inform the administration that Linda had delivered a new baby girl, and that Mrs. León was in the delivery room about to give birth. Jesús had already called Cordero and the other family members and started to get the word out to the Atlanta community. That evening CB did not want to go to the hospital because she had to study for a vocabulary quiz the next day. However, Jesús "convinced her of the benefit (ahem)" of coming to see her mother and new baby brother. CB, Cristy and Cordero were part of the many visitors that came to the hospital that evening. There were so many friends that the nurse, at first, was convinced that we were having a party. Later, when another new mother came to share the room, she asked the visitors to depart. A group of our friends brought a fake flower arrangement that had "screw nuts" instead of flowers[90] for "Arnold," the name they used to call Lorenzo in reference to a popular TV sitcom at the time, "Different Strokes."

---

[90] Many of these friends were members of the so called "Club de las Tuercas because no teníamos madre," given our general behavior; hence, lacking a mother we "were children of machines with screw nuts."

Argentina came to Atlanta, as she did when Cristy was born, and she joined Cordero to help Chelo and the rest of the family. Lorenzo slept on a small, portable crib in the master bedroom, because Chelo breastfed him, the only child to be breastfed in our family. Lorenzo's breastfeeding was done at the request of Dr. Kral who insisted that the mother's milk was the best for the child. As a baby, we called Lorenzo by different nicknames, "Cucufate" by Argentina, "Tiburcio" by Jesús and "ET"[91] by his sisters. Cordero kept asking us, "When are you going to call him by his name?" Cordero called him Lorencito from the start. Our son Lorenzo was named after his grandfather, and thus his insistence on calling him by his name.

Father Llorente baptized Lorenzo at IHM Church on March 13, 1983, in a very special ceremony attended by family, friends and members of the ACU Board of Directors. The ACU Board had met at the Conyers Monastery during two days and concluded the meeting with a Mass at IHM. During the Mass, Father Llorente baptized Lorenzo. Lorenzo wore the cargador that Jesús had worn at his baptism in Holguín, Cuba, in 1944. Father José Fernández-Solis concelebrated and Deacon Jorge González led the music for the Mass, except at the end, when Father Llorente asked that we sing the ACU Hymn. Not many baby's baptisms are witnessed not only by the family and community, but also by the ACU Board of Directors, and ending it with the ACU Hymn. After the baptism, we went to the Atlanta Cuban Club for a celebration that was organized by Lorenzo's godparents, Drs. José (Peque) and Virginia Balbona.

Time to build a new house

The arrival of Lorenzo required us to make a decision about our housing arrangement. Before Lorenzo's birth, we were happy with the Fern Creek Drive house but the distribution of the house was impractical to accommodate the new baby. The three rooms in the second story were occupied. Chelo and Jesús had the master bedroom, and Consuelo Beatriz and Cristina had their own room. There was a room in the first floor that was used as an office/guest room.

---

[91] In reference to the movie by that name.

Our options were to finish the basement, adding a bedroom or to move to another house. We did not believe that we would recover any further investment in the house because ours was the best house in the neighborhood, and for this reason, we started our search to buy a new house closer to St Pius, to Jesús' office and to Georgia State University, GSU. Chelo was taking Master's level classes at GSU and Scientific-Atlanta had agreed to sponsor Jesús in the Executive MBA Program at GSU, a two-year program conducted at the university's downtown campus. Jesús started the EMBA Program in September 1983.

During our search for a new house, we found an empty one-half acre lot on Cravey Trail, in a very desirable neighborhood, a lot that was not on the market at the time. Jesús went to the DeKalb County Tax office (this was before the internet so Jesús had to do the search manually) and found the name of the owner of the lot, a family that lived in a house near Briarcliff Road. We made an offer and came to an agreement with the owners to purchase the lot and we took on a mortgage to finance the purchase. Our next step was to have an architect design the house, and since one of the Atlanta ACU members, Reemberto Rodríguez, was an architect, we asked him to prepare a design. Our arrangement with Rembe and Geraldina consisted of dinner invitations for them at our house in order for us discuss the plans for the house after dinner. They collected the architect's fee with free dinners cooked by Chelo, not a bad deal for us. After a couple of iterations, including one design that looked like a church to Chelo, we agreed to a design that met our housing and financial requirements.

We had to sell the Fern Creek house before we could start building the new house. We also needed to find a builder for the new house. We initially put the Lilburn house on the market using a realtor but she was not able to sell the house at the asking price. When our contract with the realtor expired, we decided to sell the house ourselves, and we reduced the asking price, removing the realtor's commission. In the meantime, we started meeting with builders and requested construction estimates from five of them. One builder quoted a very high price, another a very low price, and the other three builders quoted comparable estimates, within a few thousand dollars of each other. Chelo's mom had suggested to Chelo that we should find out who was the builder of the Lilburn house that we liked so much. And so, Jesús called the previous owner of the Fern Creek house who gave Jesús the name of the builder, Walter Chewning. Chelo and Jesús met with Walter at a cluster house he was building near Briarcliff Road. Walter was one of the three builders that bid a reasonable construction price, and we also happened to like him a lot. Consequently, we selected Walter to build our new house.

In the spring of 1984, we sold the Lilburn house to a family who agreed to allow us to stay in the house, paying rent, during part of the time that it took to build the new house at Cravey Trail. With the proceeds of the sale of the Fern Creek house, we paid off the mortgage on the lot and applied for a construction loan with Fulton Federal Savings & Loan Association. We entered into a cost-plus-fixed-fee agreement with Walter, and then opened a joint checking account wherein either Walter or Jesús could write checks. We trusted Walter, obviously. Just before we started construction, we decided to raise the height of the first story from eight to nine feet, a reasonable idea but one that almost caused a problem. The extra one-foot of height required that we add one step to the stairs. The additional step would have pushed the first step of the stairs almost to the front door, something that would have ruined the looks of the open foyer with curved stairs. Thanks God for Rafael García, SJ, an agrupado architect friend of us who came to dinner one night, and after looking at the drawings, noticed the issue and suggested that we add one foot to the depth of the house— problem solved. Rafael also suggested that we add under cabinet lights in the kitchen, a nice touch that helped brighten the area. Rafael was in Atlanta doing the Regency portion of his training as a Jesuit for the Province of New Orleans. We had known Rafael for many years and traveled with him in the ACU pilgrimage to the Holy Hand in 1978, a couple of years before he decided to enter the Jesuit novitiate.

Walter Chewning started building the house in early May 1984, and completed it at the end of November, seven months from beginning to end. As it is typical of new house construction, we made changes during the construction that caused us to overshoot our budget by about 20%. In order to come up with the additional money, we used every bit of savings and we took two personal loans, one with our bank and the other with a credit union. Among the changes we made was the addition of marble to the foyer, living and dining rooms. This was done against the advice of Enrique Dorta, our friend and interior decorator, who thought that there would be too much marble and it would make the house feel cold. Enrique later admitted that the marble floors looked really beautiful. Building the house with Walter was a delight. He is a professional, a very honest person, a committed Christian, a person who always tries to do what is right, and on top of everything else, he has a great personality so it is easy to get along with him.

We had agreed to move out of the Fern Creek Drive house in early August to allow the new owners to settle in before the beginning of the school year. So, in August, we moved into a three-bedroom unit at the Cherry Hill Apartments, located in Buford Highway south of Clairmont Road.[92] We lived a little bit like gypsies in that apartment because we took with us the minimum amount of furniture. We moved out of the apartment and into the new house at the end of November 1984. The weekend we moved into the house the weather was awful, rainy and cold. Our Atlanta friends helped us with the move into the house.

The new house was located at 2850 Cravey Trail, about three blocks from the Balbona's house on Cravey Drive, less than ten minutes drive to St Pius X High School and about twenty minutes from downtown Atlanta. The neighborhood was significantly more upscale than our previous location and we were blessed with great next-door neighbors, the Halkos family. Alex Halkos was a cardiologist, Penny a housewife who later became our real estate agent when we sold the house in 1993. Alex and Penny had four children and they were a very Greek family.[93] The Halkos attended the Greek Orthodox Cathedral and were very involved with the Atlanta Greek Community. The Halkos were one of several very nice neighbors on the Cravey Trail. For example, when the neighbors learned that we were going to build a house on the street, they invited us to the annu-

---

[92] The address of the apartments was 3510 Buford Highway. By 2013 the name of the apartment complex had changed to The Terraces at Brookhaven.
[93] How more Greek can you get than Alexander and Penelope?

al neighborhood Christmas celebration. They served appetizers at one of the houses, the entree at another and desserts at a third one.

The Cravey Trail house was built on a one-half acre lot with a semicircular drive in the front. The house had a beautiful foyer, living and dining rooms (all with marble floors), with a semicircular staircase in the foyer. On the first floor, there was also a judge paneled family room, a full and one-half baths, a laundry room and a guest/office room with a very nice bay window. On the second floor, there were four bedrooms and two baths, with one bedroom for each of the kids. On the rear of the house, we had two sets of French Doors leading to a deck and from it via a small grassy area to natural woods. One thing we learned building this house is that no matter how detailed is your construction budget, you will almost certainly exceed your budget, an experience we repeated twice later when building houses in Maryland and in Atlanta.

Father Llorente came to Atlanta to bless the house in January of 1985. Jesús organized a super bowl party for the ACU group, on Sunday, January 20, 1985, and Father Llorente celebrated a Mass of Thanksgiving at the house. Father Llorente stayed at our house that evening and the next day we woke up to the second coldest day in the history of Atlanta with a temperature of eight degrees Fahrenheit below zero. When we walked down the stairs we noted that the main floor, where Father Llorente was staying, was very cold; it turns out that the pilot light in the gas heater for that floor had gone out during the night because of low gas pressure, a result of high demand that night.

Cravey Trail becomes home

Our family achieved many milestones during our years at the house on Cravey Trail. These included high school and college graduations and marriages for CB and Cristy, master degrees for Chelo and Jesús, and the first school years for Lorenzo.

Consuelo Beatriz and Cristina's time as students at St Pius coincided with the time that Chelo took maternity leave for Lorenzo. Both CB and Cristy were excellent students and extraordinary young ladies. CB was on the principal list every term except her first one and Cristy was on the principal list her whole time at school. We remember when Sister Rita, dean of discipline, told Chelo, "Consuelo, you have perfect children." CB had started playing basketball while at IHM, and she continued at Pius, joining the girl's basketball team. Consuelo Beatriz received, at both IHM and Pius, the coach's awards in basketball because of her dedication to the team. As Consuelo approached her high school graduation, she decided to study engineering and we "explained the benefits" to CB of enrolling at Georgia Tech instead of exploring a very small school in the northeast or applying to a very expensive school, Duke, to study engineering.

Two years later, Cristina had to select a college for her studies. She had always planned to be an attorney, and now she needed to decide where she would enroll for her undergraduate degree. Cristy toyed with the idea of going to Georgetown University, and particularly the International Affairs Program, one of the two best in the country. She applied for early admission into the program, but by Christmas time, Cristy had decided she did not want to go far away from her home; instead, she enrolled in the management program at Georgia Tech.

CB initially commuted to GT using the public transit system of Atlanta, MARTA. She also enrolled in the co-op program, a program whereby the student attends classes half the year and works at a business or industry the other half. This arrangement is very beneficial because the student acquires professional experience and earns a good salary. The only drawback is that it takes an extra year to complete the bachelor's degree. Jesús had recommended the program to CB but there was one caveat— she had to find a job in a city with family or very close friends, such as the Sorondo family in Orlando. Luckily, Florida Power & Light in Miami hired CB and she was able to stay with her paternal grandparents. Since she needed a car, Jesús gave her his car, the Mazda GLC subcompact and Jesús made the trip to/from Miami with CB at the beginning and end of every work quarter— we did not feel that Consuelo Beatriz was ready to drive by herself for ten hours on a very busy interstate highway. We were right!

On one return trip from Miami, with our godson Francisco traveling with us, Jesús allowed CB to drive for a while in order for her to gain some practice, and just north of Valdosta, we barely escaped a head-on collision. A truck leaving the weight station north of

Valdosta caused the accident. The driver of the truck blocked our car and CB had to move into the median, a grassy area that was wet from previous rains. Jesús shouted to Consuelo not to apply the brakes, but she either did not hear him or did not process this information. She applied the brakes, lost control of the car that continued across the median and into the southbound, incoming traffic toward us. Jesús remembers thinking, "this is it," believing he was about to die; we should have died! We were in a very small car that weighed less than two thousand pounds, and we were headed straight towards an American four-door sedan of the Ford LTD class, an automobile weighing close to twice as much as the GLC. Well, it does not take a physics expert to determine, based on the Law of Conservation of Momentum, that the head-on collision of two cars traveling 70 mph or more would be catastrophic for the smaller vehicle and its occupants. Thanks to God and our Guardian Angels, the driver of the other car saw our car, and managed to swerve away at the last minute, so that instead of hitting their car head-on, we hit the rear of their car. The first miracle is that we did not collide head-on; the second miracle is that none of the other cars traveling in the busy I-75 highway collided with either car. In any case, both cars spun with wheels and tires coming off. The GLC ended in the ditch and the other car was partially on the highway. The GLC was a total loss and was left in the Valdosta area. The totality of injuries for the seven passengers was one broken arm for one of the ladies traveling in the other car. God was clearly looking out for us that day, not only preventing death or major injuries but also making it easy to complete our journey. Our friend and ACU member, Frank Fernández happened to be traveling south on this highway at that time. He saw us, stopped, helped us, and drove us to the airport so we could rent a car and continue our trip to Atlanta. All of the above luck or coincidence? No way!

By the time Cristy graduated from high school, she had applied and was accepted into GT, and she had decided to live in one of the student dormitories, sharing a room with her long time friend and Pius classmate, Lara O'Connor. Cristina told us that she wanted to experience the college life and asked us not to call her all the time and not to expect her to come home every weekend. We said sure, no problem, we won't bother you. Notwithstanding Cristy's intentions, her "desire to experience college" lasted only a few weeks. The glitter and grandeur of college life was not so great. She wanted to return and live at home; she did stay in the dorm that first quarter, but afterwards, she lived at home for the remaining of her studies at GT, a home where she enjoyed mom's cooking, her private bathroom and the company of her siblings.

Unlike Consuelo Beatriz & Cristina, who attended one school from Kindergarten through eighth grade, Lorenzo went to several schools, three in Atlanta, one in Spain and one in Maryland to complete his elementary and middle school education. Lorenzo, "Loro," seeing his sisters depart to school every morning, was eager to go to school himself. Chelo enrolled Loro in 1986, at the Shallowford Presbyterian Preschool program, located less than two miles from our house, a five minutes ride. Initially Chelo drove Lorenzo to and from school each day but one of our neighbors offered to car pool with Chelo. Chelo agreed and the arrangement worked for a while until the lady in question forgot about Loro one day— she brought Lorenzo and her kids to her home and left Lorenzo in her car, never bringing him home. Meanwhile, Chelo was going nuts trying to find out where Lorenzo was, calling the school and the lady of the carpool. Needless to say, that was the end of carpooling with that woman!

While Loro was at Shallowford Presbyterian, the teachers and Chelo noted that Lorenzo needed some additional assistance. Also, when Lorenzo took the entrance test for IHM Elementary School, Mrs. Moody, the teacher that evaluated Lorenzo at the time, recommended a more extensive assessment. Consequently, Chelo set out to find professional assistance. Upon the recommendation of our friend Barbara Moore, Chelo made an appointment with a developmental Child Psychologist, Dr. Barbara Dunbar, who after testing and evaluating Lorenzo, discovered that Lorenzo had some difficulties in reading, verbal communications, spatial analysis and concentrating. She recommended that Lorenzo take Ritalin[94] to help him concentrate. We also consulted Lorenzo's godparents, Peque Balbona, a psychiatrist, and Virginia Balbona, Ph.D. Psychologist, who also tested Lo-

---

[94] Ritalin is a drug used to treat, among other things, attention deficit disorder.

renzo. Peque told us that it was very easy to determine whether or not Lorenzo needed Ritalin. Peque came to our home one Sunday afternoon to administer and monitor Lorenzo's reaction to the medicine. The final input that helped us understand Loro's needs came from successive hearing comprehension tests at Emory University. Lorenzo took two of these tests. He took the first test without medication and the second after taking Ritalin. The difference in the results was obvious— Lorenzo needed to take this medicine in order to cope with his attention deficit.

The following year, 1988, Chelo enrolled Lorenzo at the Howard School, located at the time in Ponce de Leon Avenue, a school that was founded to help students with special learning needs. Lorenzo was at Howard for three years, and while there he became a good friend with a Jewish student, Neal, from a very nice family. Lorenzo and Neal played together very well. Transportation for Loro to Howard was arranged in the morning via a carpool with neighborhood children that attended Paidea, a school that was located very near to Howard. In the afternoon, we took turns picking up Lorenzo. Most of the time either CB and Cristy and sometimes Chelo or I picked up Loro in the afternoon. When Bo, as Lorenzo called Cordero, was in town, Cordero would be the first in line for picking up students and Loro got spoiled when Bo was around. One treasured experience of Lorenzo at the Howard School occurred when Lorenzo punched a bully that had been bothering him for a while. His ability to defend himself, especially from a school bully, earned Loro a trip to Toy 'R Us to select any toy of his choice.

Chelo and Jesús were also furthering their education during the time we lived at the house in Cravey Trail. Jesús finished his MBA at Georgia State University in 1985, and Chelo completed her Masters of Arts in Teaching at Georgia State in 1988, earning A's in all her courses, a 4.0 average. She had started taking courses to meet the general requirements to maintain the Georgia Teaching Certificate. At the time, the Education Department started to recommend that teachers complete a Masters degree. So she decided that she might as well sign up for the Master's degree program. The course work was lengthy, but Chelo, who was a part-time student, completed it very well. The last requirements for the degree were to take a written examination and then an oral examination in front of a panel of professors from the Spanish Department. Chelo was very apprehensive about this examination, resulting in a lot of stress for several weeks. She woke up the day of the exams with a rash. Despite the rash, she took and performed very well on the written and oral exams, thus completing the requirements for her degree.

One of the most significant events of this time period was the meeting and subsequent romance of Consuelo Beatriz and Robert Todd Bills. Todd was a Chemical Engineering student at Georgia Tech and the first person with whom Consuelo was romantically involved. He was a very good student, tall, good looking and swept Consuelo off her feet so much so that she was no longer the "perfect child," not behaving as well as she had before. She seemed to have eyes only for Todd and made every effort to make him happy, something that can be a problem, as it was for CB, when one loses perspective and surrenders one's personal freedom. One example of her lack of perspective occurred during a Homecoming week at GT. One evening, it was about midnight on a weeknight and there was no sign of CB. Chelo was anxiously concerned, worried that something had happened to CB, so Jesús got up from bed, dressed up, drove to the GT campus and located Consuelo Beatriz's blue Mazda GLC. Jesús drove back home, informed Chelo and went to sleep. We noticed (the alarm system) that CB arrived home at three in the morning, and on the next day, Jesús explained the benefits of the program to her. That is, "you can choose to live here or not, but if you choose to live in this house, then you must abide by our rules; otherwise, move out."

One of the side effects of meeting Todd is that Consuelo also met his fraternity brothers, one of whom, Joel Higgins, started to go out with Cristy and they would later marry. Joel was an excellent student, majoring in Engineering Science and Mechanics, but with the intention to enter medical school. It seemed to Jesús that his major was awfully difficult. Joel was very agreeable, made friends easy and even started going to ACU meetings. Our Greek neighbors loved Joel because of his personality and because he would mow their side of the lawn that was near our house.

After settling into the Cravey Trail house, and after Jesús finished his MBA, our lives entered a period of simple normality, the proverbial calm before the storm. Chelo and Jesús attended two combination conference/vacation programs sponsored by the Executive MBA Alumni Class. The first one was held in Montego Bay, Jamaica, and the second one in Cancún, Mexico. For the second conference, we traveled first to Mexico City, Mérida and the Yucatán Peninsula for sightseeing; this was an interesting trip that we shared with our friends Clay and Barbara Moore.

In September 1988, Chelo returned to teach at St Pius. Before leaving Pius on maternity leave, Chelo was the head of the Language Department, but now she returned as a Spanish Teacher, albeit with a newly minted Masters Degree. Meanwhile, Jesús had left Scientific-Atlanta to join a startup, and then after the startup was sold, was without a job in the spring of 1988.

In December, we flew to Boston to attend the baptism of Maritere Antón, the first child of Manny and Annette. Father Llorente baptized her in the sacristy of Boston College's chapel on a cold Friday night. That night it snowed in Boston but we enjoyed our weekend sharing with the Antóns, with Annette's uncle and aunt, with René and Tani Romero and with Father Llorente.

Three companies and two continents in four years

"A lot can happen in four years," "God works in mysterious ways," "One needs to be open to change and be flexible." These phrases could be used to describe what happened to Jesús' career in the four years from 1986 to 1990. During these years, Jesús left Scientific-Atlanta to join a startup, was unemployed, joined a second startup, accepted a job and moved to Madrid, Spain. A lot of changes, especially after he had been in only one company for more than eleven years.

Scientific-Atlanta had grown very fast and had become a large company when it ran into operational problems, not unusual for companies that grow very fast. Also, but not unusual, these problems resulted in the departure of several executives whom Jesús knew and trusted. The last straw for Jesús was when they replaced his division vice president by a person who was inconsistent and somewhat erratic. It seemed to Jesús that his new boss thought that one day, "Jesús walked on water," but then the next day "Jesús needed help tying his shoelaces." It was time to leave the company, and in February 1986,

Jesús joined Digital Transmission Systems, DTS, a start up company founded by former Scientific-Atlanta employees, as Vice President of Engineering.

DTS was a small company with less than fifteen engineers that was developing a product specifically for MCI Communications, the company that had caused the breakup of the original Bell Systems in the USA. The first product developed by DTS was very successful, the second and third, smaller product developments were also successful. Unfortunately, when DTS selected its fourth product, the company reached too far[95]— the product was a good idea but required more money and resources that DTS had or could obtain given that the economy and the telecom market had started to slow down. The result was that the Board of Directors sold DTS to a bigger company, Data Communications Associates (DCA) of Alpharetta, who wanted to expand its telecommunications systems product line. Well, a few weeks after purchasing DTS, DCA decided not to pursue this strategy, and, suddenly, DTS' products were no longer of interest to DCA and neither were its executives. In early 1989, DCA terminated all but two executives, including Jesús. DCA gave each one of the executives a reasonable severance package that included several months of pay and a contract with an outplacement service to assist them in exploring future career options. This was the only time in Jesús' professional career that he had this experience. A Human Resource friend at SA told Jesús that losing his job would be good for him in the long run, and although Jesús did not feel very good at the time, she was right.

Jesús used the time and the outplacement services to review options for his future professional life including consulting, teaching, returning to GT to complete his dissertation for the Ph.D., and starting his own business. He used the outplacement facilities for office and secretarial services and took advantage of its consulting and advising services. He took to job hunting as a full time occupation, leaving his house early in the morning and spending the day, and sometimes the evening, looking for career opportunities. He updated his

---

[95] This reminds Jesús of the WW II novel, "A Bridge Too Far." The last product by DTS was "a product too large" for the company at the time.

resume, sent countless letters, went to professional meetings, talked to his friends and looked at all advertisements. One add that appeared in the Sunday Atlanta paper in May touted the allure of a career with Alcatel in Madrid, Spain, and Jesús sent his curriculum vitae. The result of his efforts was the development of three work opportunities: to return to Scientific-Atlanta, join a small start up, Gambatte, or to move to Spain.

During the summer of 1989, Jesús accepted the position of President at Gambatte although he recognized there were major challenges with the company. Gambatte had a unique patent for secure wireless data communications and a product that demonstrated the usefulness and applicability of the concept. On the other hand, it had no money and very few people, a total of five employees, including Jesús. Jesús set out to raise funds, calling on all his contacts in the venture capital field, approaching several major potential investors, working with a New York City investment banker, and exploring joint ventures with several potential corporate partners. To no avail, it seemed that at every turn an unexpected and sudden event would blunt each opportunity, so that Jesús was heard to say in October, "looks like God does not want me to be successful in this venture."

Meanwhile, Jesús had received a telegram from Alcatel inviting him to an interview in Raleigh, North Carolina, and he accepted the invitation. Jesús flew to Raleigh, and interviewed with three Alcatel Spaniards that had traveled to Raleigh for this purpose. Alcatel Spain needed to increase its rank of middle level managers and engineers, and Jesús fit their need and was also fluent in Spanish. Thus, in August, Jesús received an invitation to visit Madrid with Chelo for a full week of interviews and to become familiar with the company and Madrid. Chelo requested a few days of leave from St Pius, and we flew to Madrid the week of Labor Day. We visited Alcatel offices in Madrid and Toledo. Jesús interviewed, during a three-hour lunch, with Carlos González-Madroño, his future boss, and with Paco Salcedo. Carlos and Paco were both director-level managers of the Spanish affiliate of Alcatel. Carlos and his wife took Chelo and Jesús to dinner at Combarro, a fabulous Galician seafood restaurant. Chelo and Jesús used part of their time to explore the city of Madrid. Alcatel Spain, ASESA, made Jesús a job offer before he departed Madrid. Jesús told Alcatel that the salary offered was inadequate for him to accept the job. The next day, Jesús and Chelo returned to Atlanta.

Jesús, following proper professional practices, sent ASESA a letter thanking them for their job offer and for their hospitality during our visit to Spain. Alcatel was still interested in Jesús and since Jesús was having trouble raising funds for Gambatte, he negotiated an increase in the offer of salary and expatriate benefits. During this time, Jesús and Chelo discussed and grappled the pros and cons of the move to Spain. On the one hand, in Atlanta, we had a very nice house; Chelo had an excellent job; Lorenzo was happy at IHM School; Consuelo had a little bit more than one year to complete her degree and had begun to plan her wedding; and Cristy was a sophomore at GT. On the other hand, Jesús was not getting any income because Gambatte could not pay his salary, other job prospects had not yet materialized, and very importantly, this was a unique opportunity to live and work in Europe. The decision was very difficult, but at the end Jesús accepted Alcatel's offer. He would go to Madrid by himself in January and determine whether or not we should move the family there depending on how he integrated with the company environment, and how well Jesús adapted to Spain's social environment. Jesús began preparations to join Alcatel in January of 1990. Jesús was going to keep Chelo informed of his experience at Alcatel and his adaptation to life in Madrid. If things went well, then Chelo would go to Madrid in the summer to investigate school and living arrangements for the family. If we moved, Lorenzo would be coming to Madrid. CB was planning to marry Todd in September and move to Indianapolis, Indiana. We were going to investigate whether and how Cristy might spend one year studying in Madrid or whether she would move in with her best friend "La Nena" for her senior year at GT.

Spain 1990 — Nothing ventured, nothing gained

Jesús had changed companies before, had worked in different cities— New York, Miami and Atlanta— and had traveled to Spain several times, but moving to Spain would be very different. He was going to have to learn how to live in a different country and work for an European company with different work rules. There were many things to learn and many adjustments to be made, many more than Jesús had imagined— finding appropriate living arrangements, making adjustments to idiomatic expressions, payroll, banking, bill payments, transportation, and to office and work relationships.

Jesús arrived in Madrid in mid January 1990, stayed initially at El Gran Hotel Colón, and was ready to start working but his boss at Alcatel Spain, ASESA, was not ready for him. He told the Human Resources manager to tell Jesús "to go see Velazquez."[96] Jesús did not get to see the Velazquez exhibition until the last week of the showing, the end of March, when he, Adolfo and Rossina spent most of the day queuing to get into the museum.

Professionally, the move was beneficial to both ASESA and Jesús. Within days of his arrival in Spain, ASESA put forth Jesús' name to be the Project Manager for a joint Spain-Belgium Alcatel project to develop a new access cross-connect (switch) for the European Market. Jesús was to learn in this project the convoluted approach to product development at Alcatel. There was fierce competition among the various Alcatel country units to lead new product developments in the belief, typically correct, that the country leading the development would then own its manufacturing. To define and agree on the product, there were meetings in Madrid, Paris and North Carolina.

Alcatel had grown as an amalgamation of national companies with local markets, local engineering, and local manufacturing, and was now trying to rationalize (streamline) the multiple product developments to optimize its engineering and marketing. The rationalization required that the national companies give up some of their previous independence, a very hard thing to do within one country, extremely difficult when the group include German, French, Spanish, Italian and Belgian national companies. The result was that most product development projects were also political fights with at least one hidden agenda at each meeting. It was completely different to Jesús' experience with his previous USA companies where once a decision was made, it was full speed ahead with one clear objective, and rarely, any hidden agendas.

---

[96] The Museo del Prado in Madrid inaugurated that January a very special Velazquez exhibition showing 79 of the 100 Velazquez paintings known to exist.

Jesús led the development of the product, completing it within one month of the promised date. He led a team of Belgium and Spanish engineers. Jesús' Spanish team included Pedro Chamero and Mounia Doukalis, hardware and software systems engineers, and Mari Carmen Peláez, the marketing lead. Jesús had to quarrel and argue with a number of people including the person who would later be his technical boss at Alcatel, Dr. Michael Rahier. The product development was successful and earned Jesús a reputation in ASESA and among Alcatel executives of someone who could lead a multinational team to develop a new product in a reasonable time.

We mentioned there were many adjustments that Jesús had to make when he moved to Spain. Let's start with the language. The Spanish people not only speak the language with a very distinct accent to that of the Cuban people, but they also use different words than Cubans to identify some objects.[97] Spaniards often use idiomatic expressions that Jesús did not know or understand.[98] One week after arriving in Madrid, Jesús went to a leadership seminar for ASESA leaders that was held near Segovia. He remembers listening to the seminar leader and remembers understanding each of the words but missing the message because the seminar leader interspersed his message with a lot of idiomatic expressions.

Jesús found a furnished one-bedroom apartment in a central location,[99] on a wide avenue with a small park in the median, very close to the Metro station, to cafeterias, bookshops, banks and restaurants. Jesús was able to walk or take the Metro to most places in the city, a necessity since he did not have a car. The apartment had a central air conditioning system that worked well except in the hottest months of the year, a small kitchen and dining area, with both the bedroom and living room overlooking the Juan Bravo Street.

ASESA, like most Spanish companies, paid its employees via bank direct deposit. It was also the norm for people in Madrid to pay

---

[97] Coche instead of carro, gafas instead of espejuelos, etc.

[98] Example: "Los tiros van por allí" which translates more or less to, "things are moving or going that way."

[99] Apartment 210 at the Juan Bravo Apartment Hotel, located in the tony Salamanca Barrio at Juan Bravo 58, near the Conde de Peñalver Street.

utilities and home expenses via automatic electronic banking. Jesús had to open a Madrid bank account, something that normally is very easy but there was a catch for Jesús— he needed a bank that would help him transfer funds, periodically, to the USA in a simple, cost-effective manner. It turns out that the employees of the first couple of large banks that Jesús visited did not know how to do this effectively. Finally, Jesús walked into a branch of Citibank near his apartment and these bankers knew exactly what to do.

After a few weeks, Jesús was reasonably organized, knew how to move around the city, visited some interesting locations,[100] went to the theater to see zarzuelas, a light operetta, and plays from the Spanish Golden Era. Occasionally, he went to the office on Saturdays and found that the whole building, a four-story building with probably two-hundred employees during the week, would be empty except for the security guards— Jesús had to turn on and off the electricity in the floor where he worked. This was very different from Jesús' work experience in the USA where it is normal to find people in the office during part of the day on a Saturday.

Jesús was hired and worked for Carlos González-Madroño, a director level executive at ASESA and a very nice person. Carlos, understanding that Jesús was alone and separated from his family, invited Jesús a couple of times to spend long weekends with his wife, Angeles, and family at his summer flat, a block away from the Mediterranean Ocean at Javea (or Xabea) in Alicante Province. Carlos cooked Alicante Paella that uses beef, pork and rabbit meat instead of the seafood of the Valencian Paella. Jesús met and enjoyed the company of several of Carlos' friends in Javea.

The first few months of 1990 were difficult for Chelo, Jesús and the family. Jesús had to adjust to life in Spain. Chelo and the children lost Jesús' company and had to learn to address issues, pay bills and do errands that Jesús would normally do. On top of the normal teaching and household activities, Chelo was in charge of planning and organizing Consuelo Beatriz's wedding in September of that year.

---

[100] The Church were Bolivar got married, the house where Cervantes lived.

Chelo and Jesús were able to see each other in February during a business visit that Jesús made to Raleigh, North Carolina. Jesús traveled to Atlanta again in the spring, and while there, his friend Manuel Canteli made him an interesting offer— Canteli would loan Jesús a car to use in Spain so that the car would be available for Canteli's use during his annual one-month visit to Spain. Jesús quickly agreed and he and Canteli drove the car, a 1970 Mercedes Benz Model 280 SE, to Charleston, South Carolina, and shipped the car to the port of Antwerp, Belgium, a trip that took about two months.

By now, Jesús was involved in several important activities with Alcatel; the first was working in the integration of the Spanish branch of Telettra, an Italian telecommunications supplier that Alcatel acquired. There were issues of organization, product and factory rationalization, and the integration of the Telettra engineers. One of the persons that came to ASESA from this deal was Emilio Gil Delicado who later worked for and became a friend of Jesús. Jesús along with Pedro Chamero began to participate in standard setting bodies, especially the European Telecommunications Standards Institute, ETSI, to define standards for products such as the access cross-connect that Alcatel was developing. One of the first meetings was in Paris and a second meeting was in Athens, Greece, in June. The date of the Athens meeting coincided with the date when Chelo was planning to come to Spain, after finishing the academic year at St. Pius. Thus, seizing the opportunity, we purchased a trip that routed Chelo's trip to Madrid with a stopover in Athens. It turned out that the Iberia flight attendants announced a strike, actually a partial work strike on the day when Chelo was flying. The strike caused inconveniences and delays to Chelo and other passengers. The flight left Miami late, the attendants did not provide any service during the flight, and her transfer flight to Athens was cancelled. Chelo finally arrived in Athens several hours late and very exhausted. The good news is that we did enjoy a couple of good days of sightseeing and good food in Athens before flying to Madrid.

After we arrived in Madrid, we set out to look at apartments and potential schools for Lorenzo because we had discussed a plan to move to Madrid after Consuelo Beatriz's wedding. We rented a car and although we did not know Madrid, we started looking into both, a "piso" to rent and a school for Lorenzo. Chelo did not like any of the schools we visited and we did not find any apartment that we really liked. Incidentally, we lost the keys to the rental car, the car was stolen and we had to report it at a police station; our first but not last visit to a Madrid Police station to report stolen goods. The rental car was insured so there was no liability to us. In any case, Chelo had come to the conclusion that she would prefer not to move to Madrid; the failure to find suitable schools and apartments helped solidify this conclusion. Cristy had told her mother that we were "abandoning" her, notwithstanding the fact that (1) Cristy was 20 years old; (2) she was about to become a junior at Georgia Tech; (3) Chelo had arranged for Cristy to stay at the home of her best friend "La Nena," and (4) we had offered Cristy to come with us and attend school in Spain for one year. Chelo felt uncomfortable moving to Madrid and Jesús did not want her to move unless she was fully on board with the idea. Thus, we decided to make the most of our time in Europe before our return to the United States.

On one of the weekends, we rented a car and drove to the north of Spain during a heat wave that sent temperatures to record highs in Galicia. We made a brief stop to see the city and have some refreshments in Lugo and then went to Santiago de Compostela where we had reservations at the magnificent Parador de los Reyes Católicos. Unfortunately, the staff at the parador was on strike and services were at a minimum— no meals, minimum cleaning of rooms and no room service. The parador did not have air condition and we had a miserable night with the unusual high temperatures. From Santiago we drove by Franco's hometown El Ferrol and along the coast to Asturias looking for the ancestral home of the Redruello family. We stopped in a small town between Navia and Luarca[101] to see if we could find Consuelo's godfather Panchín. We asked a person for Panchín and the answer was, "Oh, el vaqueiro, he lives in the store on the main highway."[102] We found the house, Panchín and his fami-

---

[101] Maybe Villapedre on highway N-634, about 10 km from El Vidural.

[102] Vaqueiro means someone who works with cows but it is also refers, in Asturias, to an interesting cultural group, "Vaqueiros de Alzada." The Redruello and Berdasco families are members of this cultural group. Researching this

ly. His daughter came with us to guide us to El Vidural where we saw Redruello's ancestral home and visited with a niece of Chelo's grandmother who resembled Chelo's grandmother. That night we slept in Oviedo and the following day we drove back to Madrid.

On another weekend, we flew to Belgium to pick up Canteli's Mercedes Benz at Antwerp and drove to Paris where Jesús had to attend a meeting at the Alcatel office in Villarceaux. Pedro Chamero, Diego[103] and a Monsieur Saint-Supéry, who was the Alcatel Product Line Manager for the product, joined Jesús. Jesús drove to the Meridian Montparnasse hotel to pick Chelo and proceeded to drive to Brussels, at a snail pace in horrific traffic in Paris' Périphérique. The following day Chelo stayed in Brussels while the others went to the Alcatel office in Antwerp to attend a project review. Jesús returned to Brussels to pick up Chelo and drive to Spain.

We drove from Brussels to Spain leisurely stopping overnight in Normandy at Honfleur, a "disgustingly picturesque"[104] town, then to Mount Saint Michele and New Rochelle, where we also spent the night. The next day, we drove to Lourdes for our first visit there. We were touched by the devotion of the pilgrims, and especially the praying of the Rosary during the Torchlight Procession. The following day we drove through the Pyrenees Mountains into Huesca, Spain and then to Madrid. We also made a pilgrimage to the Monastery of Guadalupe during a tour of Extremadura.

Soon afterwards, Chelo flew back to Atlanta to finalize the plans for Consuelo Beatriz's wedding. Chelo had taken care of almost all details of the wedding and CB was fine with whatever decisions Chelo made. Our friend Barbara Moore had offered to host the wedding reception at the Cherokee Town and Country Club and we had accepted the offer, although Chelo almost cancelled the offer because she was not treated well by the event manager at the Cherokee. How-

---

group shows fascinating information. Wikipedia, for example, mention the last names of people of this group including Berdasco and Redruello.

[103] A Packaging Engineer whose last name Jesús has forgotten.

[104] A quote from agrupado friend Javier Salmán when Jesús joined Javier and other Georgia Tech study-in-Paris architecture students in 1984 during a trip to the Normandy area.

ever, Barbara Moore took matters into her hands and we did host a wonderful reception there. A few weeks before the wedding, Chelo called Jesús to tell him about an issue with the rehearsal dinner. Todd's mother did not want to have wine with the dinner and suggested that we toast with tea. Todd had asked Chelo for assistance with the rehearsal dinner because Todd's parents lived in South Carolina and Chelo agreed to do it and found the locale, a place that allowed the renters to bring their own wine. When Jesús, who was still in Madrid, heard about this, he told Chelo to inform Todd that Jesús was not going to have a toast with tea at her daughter's rehearsal dinner and that he would buy the wine for the dinner; in the end, Todd's family paid for the wine.

Jesús stayed in Madrid until the middle of August to insure that his four-weeks vacation included Consuelo Beatriz's wedding day. This allowed him to see Madrid during the August's vacation period when a large number of the city people were gone, including newspaper's vendors. In fact, most restaurants were closed, there was little traffic, easy access to parking, and the Alcatel building was almost empty. Jesús was in Madrid during the "Fiestas de San Cayetano, San Lorenzo and La Paloma."[105] He arrived in Atlanta in time to attend a wedding shower for Consuelo organized by Andy and Selene López at their home.

Consuelo Beatriz's wedding was a wonderful affair. CB did not want an evening wedding, so the wedding ceremony was set for eleven in the morning on Saturday, September 8, the Feast of Mary's Nativity, and for Cubans, the feast day of Our Lady of Charity, Patroness of the Cuban People. The early wedding required all the women in the house to be at their hairdressers at eight in the morning. The main celebrant at the wedding was Father, now Monsignor, Richard López, a teacher at Pius and great friend of the family. Father Amando Llorente, SJ, concelebrated with Father López, and both of them celebrated Mass before the rehearsal on Friday. We wanted to celebrate Mass for CB's wedding, but Chelo did not think it was a good

---

[105] August 7, 10, and 15, respectively. The image of the Virgin that is on a church on Paloma Street is taken on procession through city streets on the Feast Day of the Assumption.

idea to have a Mass during the wedding since Todd and his family were not Catholics. The day of the wedding was hot but otherwise beautiful; the wedding ceremony and reception were wonderful, and all the family including the many who came from out of town (Miami, Delaware, Orlando) enjoyed every bit of it.

Some days after the wedding, Consuelo and Todd returned to Atlanta from their honeymoon, picked up CB's things and headed to Indianapolis. We remember standing on the door watching her leave, with tears streaming down our faces— she was no longer part of our household. It impacted Lorenzo so much that he told Cristy not to get married.

Jesús returned to Madrid in mid September and promptly told ASESA that for family reasons, he would be returning to the USA in the near future but that he would stay at least through December to help transition the project lead to another Spanish person. ASESA told Jesús to take monthly trips, at their expenses, to visit the family while he was working on the project, and he did fly to the USA every few weeks.

That August, Iraq invaded Kuwait and it became clear that the USA and its allies might go to war with Iraq, so Jesús thought it would be wise to wait for a clear understanding of the international political situation before changing jobs. The Gulf War started on January 17, 1991.[106] After the war ended, it was already approaching the spring and Jesús decided he might as well stay through the summer to complete the first phase of the project and to give Chelo, Cristy and Lorenzo the opportunity to visit Spain during their summer vacation. During the time of the Gulf War, Jesús traveled to the USA via Zurich flying on the safe and neutral Swiss Air.

Jesús used Canteli's car mostly on weekends to visit places he did not know. One trip was to Loyola, Ignacio's home, in the Basque country, a day with heavy rain and while turning on a mountain curve he and another car had a small fender bender— actually, one broken headlight in the MB. Because both cars were insured through the

---

[106] The night the war started Jesús watched it start on CNN in his room at the Alfa de Keyser Hotel in Antwerp preparing to lead a project review the following day at Alcatel Bell.

same company, the other driver and Jesús agreed to let the insurance company settle the problem. Jesús ended up replacing the headlight and a small metal ring holder on the car by himself. Having a car gave Jesús freedom, but at the same time it increased Jesús' expenses as he now paid for fuel, a parking garage and insurance.

Alcatel Spain asked Jesús to help hire Americans to be part of a special systems group. Alcatel placed advertisements in newspapers in several US cities where there were concentration of telecom companies, and after sifting through many resumes, he and Ángel Ladrón de Guevara, a human resource manager, interviewed candidates in New Jersey (we saw Nilda and her kids), Atlanta and Chicago (Jesús took Consuelo and Todd to eat excellent steaks at the Chicago Chop House). ASESA eventually hired several Americans, including David Carballal, Chuck Hutton and Tony Costa.

In April of 1991, Manolo Canteli came to Spain with his wife, father and sister, and Jesús dutifully gave him his car for use while in the country. Manolo was in Madrid for several days and later went to northern Spain and Portugal. On Friday, May 10, Manolo called Jesús and told him he was in Fatima, Portugal, and that he had found accommodations for his family and for Jesús if he wanted to join them for Pope John Paul II's trip to Fatima. The Pope went to Fatima to thank Our Blessed Mother Mary for saving his life ten years earlier. Jesús jumped at the opportunity, rented a car and drove most of the night, from Madrid to Fatima. The drive was long; Jesús was driving alone after working a full day, so he had to stop and rest several times, using the stops to sleep in the car for maybe twenty minutes each time. The next three days were wonderful, first sightseeing and then joining nearly one million people for the two-day visit of the Pope, including the celebration of Mass in the open plaza in front of the Fatima Church.

Praying at Fatima with John Paul II was one but not the only extraordinary experience for us that year. Chelo and Jesús were going to experience a most intriguing sequence of events during the summer wherein Jesús became a suspect in a double-execution style murder. When we think or talk about this affair, we always think that if we saw it depicted in a movie our reaction would be, "Look at the imagination of these writers that have to make up such a tall tale," except we actually lived it.

We had planned Jesús' return to Atlanta after the end of August. Jesús had notified ASESA of his departure and had arranged to have the car shipped from Antwerp to Charleston with the same company that shipped it to Europe the previous year. The summer started as planned with Chelo, Cristy and Lorenzo flying together to Madrid after the academic year was finished. It was Cristy and Lorenzo's first visit to Spain, so we organized a number of visits to the usual places in Madrid (the museums, the Madrid of the Hapsburg's, Castilian restaurants) and to many surrounding cities, (Toledo, Avila, Segovia, and Salamanca) and to Sevilla and Cordoba. All of us remember the trip to Andalusia because the air conditioning in the car broke on a very hot day and the four of us sweat a lot as we returned to Madrid.

After Cristy and Lorenzo returned to the USA, Chelo and Jesús drove to Portugal on Friday, July 12. We were in Lisbon a couple of days, ate at wonderful restaurants, saw the sights and then went to Fátima and to the university city of Coimbra. In Coimbra, Jesús made a wrong turn and almost drove the car down several steps, but after a few minutes of hard turning, was able to turn the car around and drive back to the right road. From Coimbra we started our return to Madrid and were very lucky to find a room available at a Pousada (like the paradores in Spain, state run inns built in many interesting buildings) at Marvao near the border with Spain, a wonderfully quaint little town that is located at the top of a mountain. The next day, Tuesday, July 16, we drove to Madrid making one stop along the way in a small town, and lo and behold, the car would not start! Nothing happened when we turned the ignition switch to the start position, and we sat there trying to figure out what to do. Luckily, after a while, the car started, and we then drove to Madrid, not turning the car off for any reason.

In Madrid we called Ricky Canteli, Manolo's son, who happened to be in Madrid enrolled in a Spanish program sponsored by Georgia State University under the direction of our friend Dr. José Montero. Ricky came to see the car and told us that the problem was probably caused by the transmission safety relay, a relay that prevents one from starting a car when the transmission is placed in the wrong gear. He said that fixing it required one to take the transmission off, a major repair. Well, the problem was that we had already arranged a trip for a company meeting in Paris the following Monday, and from there to drive to Antwerp the following day to ship the car to the USA. So we decided to take our chance with the car.

We left Madrid the following Friday, July 19, and stayed overnight at a hotel on the AutoRoute north of Barcelona. On Saturday, we went to see Gerona, an old city that Jesús had wanted to see because it was the site of a famous novel about the Spanish Civil War. From there we drove into France and we were on our way to Limoges when we stopped to buy gasoline near the city of Brive-la-Gaillarde, and as fate would have it, the car would not start. Chelo and Jesús pushed the car hopping to start it going down hill but to no avail, so we stopped on the side of the road across a "steak-frite" stand. We spoke with the owners, a very nice couple; they called a towing service that took the car to the mechanic's garage near the roadside Hotel de la Maleyrie in Donzenac. We stayed overnight at the hotel, having agreed with the garage owner that he would give us a ride to the train station and would fix our car while we were in Paris.

On Sunday, July 21, we took the train to Paris and Jesús went to his Monday meeting in Alcatel during the day, and in the evening, we had the pleasure of having a magnificent meal at the Tour d'Argent Restaurant, a three-star Michelin restaurant. We ate their specialty, duck, and drank for the first time a Montrachet Chardonnay wine. On top of that, we had a unique experience with the waiter. When Jesús ordered dessert, the waiter told him that the dessert he had ordered "did not fit his personality." Jesús asked the waiter what he would recommend, and he suggested, to our amazement, that Jesús should order a raspberry based dessert, which is what Jesús would have ordered. Chelo challenged him to tell her what dessert she should order, and he nailed it— a chocolate dessert. Amazing!

On Tuesday, July 23, we took the train back to Brive and were promptly picked up by the garage owner who had fixed the car, gave us the bill (expensive) and told us there were visitors who wanted to talk to us, two gendarmes who were standing next to our car. The gendarmes asked us a lot of questions, at first without telling us what was the reason. Later, they told us that they were "controlling" all foreigners that came by the town. The gendarmes were very polite and asked for permission to search our car. In the car they found an old Georgia automobile tag and the receipt for the exchange of pesetas to escudos that we made during our trip to Portugal— they told us to save the receipt because it was important!

After a while, two other gendarmes showed up and they asked us if we would accompany them to the gendarmerie because they wanted to have a translator to insure we were able to communicate properly. Well, this was certainly odd. By this time, Chelo was getting concerned because she wanted to fly back to Madrid the next day so she could return to Miami to finish the arrangements for Lorenzo's first communion that was planned for August 10, in Miami.

We drove to the gendarmerie, our car behind a gendarme car with the second gendarme car behind us. At the Gendarmerie de Donzenac, they kept asking more questions, this time with a woman translator present. After about four hours, they explained the reason for all the questions. Two weeks earlier, a British man and a woman from the Netherlands had been executed nearby. We asked, so what? Why do you ask us about this? It turns out that these two persons had been involved in some money scheme where several million French Francs were missing. Yes, we said; but what does this has to do with us? Well, it turns out that the company that these people founded and from which the money was missing was based in the Atlanta, Georgia area. They thought it was just too much of a coincidence that within days of the execution of the people involved, two people driving a car with Georgia license plate would show up in the same area. We are sure that while we were being investigated they checked us with Interpol— they had Jesús' passport and his Alcatel ID. Finally, they let us go, but not before Chelo requested and received a note (intended to be a safe-conduct) from the Gendarmerie at Donzenac stating that they had checked us and we were clean.[107]

When we left the Gendarmerie we drove to the steak-frite stand where our car had stalled on Saturday. We ate at the steak-frite stand and thanked the owners for their help a few days earlier. We told the French couple about our experience and they showed us a copy of the local newspaper with the story of the executed people. We left that place and started driving toward Brussels. Jesús was exhausted,

---

[107] We include a copy of the Gendarmeire's note and other information about this affair in Appendix V.

so Chelo, who was agitated by all this activity, drove most of the way until about two in the morning when Jesús told Chelo that we had to stop and rest. There were two roadside hotels on the AutoRoute to Brussels and Jesús suggested to stop on the one on our side of the road, the une-deux-trois motel and this was another interesting experience. This motel was fully automated with an electronic display, similar to those of ATM machines next to the entrance. One entered into the display a credit card, selected the nights one wanted to stay and whether or not one wanted breakfast in the morning. The machine printed a small piece of paper with the room number, the code to enter the motel and the code for the room. We entered and found that the motel did not have a toilet in the room, which was a huge problem for Chelo who did not want to use the common toilet; she was not pleased that Jesús had selected a hotel with such lack of facilities. We won't tell you where she did her basic necessity except to mention that there was a sink in the room!

We slept at the motel, got up the next morning, drove to Antwerp to deliver the car to the shipping company, took the train to the Brussels Airport, and flew back to Madrid. As you can surmise, it was a heck of a trip, stranded in the middle of France, investigated for double murder, staying at an interesting motel before finally returning to Madrid. Chelo flew back to the US in time to finish the preparations for Lorenzo's first communion.

Last two years in Atlanta

Lorenzo's First Communion was held on his feast day, Saint Lawrence, August 10, 1991, at the ACU headquarters in Miami, at a Mass celebrated especially for this occasion by Father Llorente. Lorenzo had been prepared for this celebration at IHM in the CCD program led by our friend Yolanda Magadán, because until this time, he was attending The Howard School, a non-denominational school.

Chelo had decided earlier that year that it was time to mainstream Lorenzo, and consequently, she enrolled Lorenzo at IHM School, his third school. He started second grade in September 1991; his second grade teacher, Mrs. Moody, was a wonderful teacher who helped make Lorenzo's transition to a regular school a smooth one.

Seventeen years later, Mrs. Moody was our grandson Ethan's second grade teacher.

While Jesús was still in Spain, Chelo had been looking at advertisements in the Atlanta newspaper to help Jesús find a job in Atlanta. She saw an ad by an Atlanta telecommunications company, Americom, which was looking for an engineering manager. Jesús sent them his resume, interviewed via telephone from Madrid and was told he would have the job, pending a personal interview when he returned to Atlanta. He started his new job with this company the week after Lorenzo's First Communion. Americom was a start-up that developed radios for wireless local communications.[108] EF Johnson, a company based in Minneapolis, Minnesota had bought Americom.

The Atlanta company was small, less than twenty employees,[109] and Jesús was in charge of engineering and service, and he had to make regular trips to the headquarters in Minneapolis and to the company factory, located about one hour from Minneapolis. The trips were interesting, particularly in winter. Jesús recalls one visit in October, right after the World Series, when Minneapolis had twenty-eight inches of snow. He recalls another trip in January when the TV news stated that the temperature was going to drop during the day to near forty degrees Fahrenheit below zero! He promptly changed his flight that day to leave Minneapolis before the cold front arrived.

In December 1991, we all traveled to Lafayette, Indiana, to attend Consuelo Beatriz's graduation from Purdue University with a Bachelors degree in Industrial and Systems Engineers. CB and Todd lived in a small apartment, so the Atlanta family stayed in a motel near their home. The graduation ceremony was in the evening, and we remember that it was cold and windy that evening. After the graduation, we went to dinner together to celebrate the occasion. The next day was so cold that Jesús' Mercedes diesel-powered automobile had a very hard time starting, but with the help of another motel

---

[108] Remember that this was before the advent of inexpensive cellular radios.

[109] One of the employees later hired at Americom as a salesperson was Jesús' good friend, Julio Villafañe. Julio remained with the company for several years selling the company's products in Latin America.

guest, we finally got it started. We spent a couple of days in Indiana before heading home back to Atlanta. The following month, January 1992, Consuelo Beatriz started working for Indiana Bell, part of the then Ameritech Company.[110] Consuelo and Todd then moved to Indianapolis since Todd worked there for the pharmaceutical company Eli Lily.

Cristina, meanwhile, was engaged to Joel Higgins and selected the date for the wedding to be July 25, 1992, the Feast Day of St. James the Apostle, Patron of Spain. Chelo and Cristina started the planning and preparation, and this time, Jesús was able to help with the organization since he was in Atlanta. Joel Higgins graduated from Georgia Tech in June 1991, and started medical school at the University of South Carolina a few weeks later. Cristy decided to apply to the law school at this university to start in the fall of 1992, a plan that would result in Joel and Cristina receiving their MD and JD, respectively, in May 1995. During his last year at GT, Joel was a frequent visitor at our house, substituting for Cristy to mow the lawn, becoming friends with our neighbors, Alex and Penny Halkos, and attending ACU meetings.

Cristy graduated from Georgia Tech in June of 1992, and got married in July. Cristy and Joel had an excellent rehearsal dinner, one without stress. The wedding was beautiful, held at IHM Church, with Monsignor Richard López the principal celebrant. Father Mario Di Lela, OFM, Chaplain of the GT Catholic Center concelebrated the wedding Mass. The reception was held at the Hilton Hotel located on Peachtree Industrial Boulevard in Norcross. This reception, like the one for Consuelo Beatriz, had attendance of over three hundred persons, but this was a sit down dinner followed by dancing. We had ordered a special cheesecake wedding cake from our friend Stephen, owner at the time of Classic Cheesecakes. The cake, the first wedding cheesecake that Classic Cheesecakes ever made, was so delicious that some of it disappeared in the kitchen. We discovered the next day when we attended Mass at IHM that many of our guests did not get to taste the wedding cake.

---

[110] SBC Communications acquired Ameritech in 1999 and, in 2006, purchased AT&T. Then, it changed its name to AT&T Inc.

Cristy and Joel went on a great honeymoon, flying to London and later taking a train to Paris. On their return, they went off to Columbia, South Carolina, to start their married life together and to continue their studies.

In September, Lorenzo started third grade at IHM and he handled the schoolwork well. There were three of us in the house and we were getting used to the new arrangements when Jesús was notified that Americom would be closing the Atlanta office.

Americom was a small company with a number of problems, the foremost being that it would eventually be closed and all operations would be moved to Minnesota, something that happened in September 1992, about fourteen months after Jesús joined the company. When the company announced that it was closing the Atlanta office, Jesús set out to find jobs for his engineers, calling his contacts in many companies in Atlanta. One of the friends he called, Steve Chaddick, a colleague from Scientific-Atlanta, was the Vice President of Engineering at AT&T Tridom and when Steve asked Jesús, "What about you?" Jesús replied he would have to find a job for himself also.

Steve called Jesús back and set up an interview meeting with another colleague from SA, Larry Huang, who was Vice President of Sales and Marketing at Tridom. Steve, Larry and several other friends of Jesús from Scientific Atlanta started Tridom and were part of Jesús' network of friends and connections. Jesús was hired as Director of Sales Engineering, later to include also the responsibility of Director of Marketing. Tridom's products were the hardware and software for companies that used satellite for data communications, something we do today using the Internet over telephone or cable lines. Jesús was to be at Tridom for less than one year but it was really wonderful to see how trying to do a good thing, finding jobs in Atlanta for his engineers, had landed him a new job. As they say, "no good deed goes unpunished." For Jesús, Tridom was his sixth company.[111]

Year 1992 ended and 1993 began with our lives apparently in cruise control. Consuelo Beatriz and Todd lived in Indianapolis; they were both working and had recently bought a house. Cristina and

---

[111] Scientific-Atlanta, DTS, Gambatte, ASESA, Americom and now AT&T Tridom

Joel had settled in their apartment and were doing well in their respective studies. Lorenzo was doing well at IHM, Chelo at Pius and Jesús at Tridom. We visited Cristy and Joel at Columbia and saw also Berta González, Miguelito, Estela and John.

In the spring, Rigoberto, Jesús' father, had to be taken to the hospital because he had pulmonary aspiration, the entry of food or drink into the lungs because the "food went down the wrong pipe," a problem that can become a major health issue resulting, in some cases, in death. Rigoberto was hospitalized and probably saved by Dr. Raúl Moas, a pulmonary disease specialist at Mercy Hospital in Miami. After initial recovery, Rigoberto was sent to a rehabilitation center located in the campus of the hospital. Chelo told Carmen Luisa and Argentina that she would help them and would come down and stay in Miami to pitch in.

We also knew that our good friend and ACU member, Rafael García, SJ, would be ordained to the priesthood in July. Thus, we had clear and precise plans for the summer of 1993. Chelo, Jesús and Lorenzo would drive to Miami to attend Rafael's ordination and his first Mass. Jesús would fly to Atlanta and Lorenzo and Chelo would stay in Miami to assist with Rigoberto's rehabilitation while Lorenzo stayed with his cousins. Later, in early August, we would all meet at Marco Island to spend one week at the beach enjoying the company of a number of friends, mostly ACU Gainesville guys and their respective families. The Gainesville ACU group used to spend a week together at Marco every year.

Everything was set according to our plans, but once more we were going to witness the application of the Spanish Proverb, "el hombre propone y Dios dispone[112]." We did go to Miami and attended Rafael García's ordination on July 17, 1993, and his first Mass on July 18, both at the Gesu Church. Jesús did fly to Atlanta that evening while Chelo and Lorenzo stayed in Miami as planned. So far so good, right? Well, yes, but this is when God threw us another curve ball…

---

[112] Man proposes, God disposes.

Book VI – Success!

Book VI – Part I – Madrid 1993-1996

Spain again

God's curve ball came immediately after the trip to Miami. Jesús arrived in Atlanta from Miami on Sunday evening, July 18. On Monday morning, as Jesús was preparing to go to work, the phone rang. Jesús answered and was connected with Manuel Gordillo, the second highest ranked executive in Alcatel Spain. Gordillo told Jesús that there was an important job for him in Alcatel and asked Jesús if he would be interested in flying to Europe to discuss this opportunity. Wow! Jesús wasn't expecting anything like this, so he told Gordillo to call back the next day; he needed time to think and discuss the news with Chelo.

Jesús called Chelo and discussed the conversation he had with Gordillo. Chelo thought we should explore the opportunity since we were getting a free trip to Europe— we did not expect the trip to change our lives. Thus, when Gordillo called back on Tuesday morning, Jesús agreed to fly to Paris on Wednesday, interview at Alcatel headquarters on Thursday, then fly to Madrid and meet with Gordillo on Friday morning. Chelo flew from Miami to Atlanta on Tuesday afternoon; we packed our bags and left for Paris on Wednesday.

On Thursday morning, after checking into our Paris hotel and taking a short nap, Jesús went to the Alcatel Emeriau office for a lunch interview with two Alcatel executives, Michel Rahier and an Alcatel French Vice President. Jesús had worked with Michel before, but did not know the other person. The interview was conducted over a French lunch meal in an executive's lunchroom at the Alcatel headquarters. The lunch lasted two hours with several courses, wine, cheeses, coffee, dessert and cognac— the works! That evening, we flew to Madrid, and coincidentally, there were several Alcatel Spain engineers in the flight who Jesús knew well.

We stayed for the first time at the Palace Hotel in downtown Madrid, and on Friday morning Jesús talked with Gordillo about the challenging job opportunity. Alcatel was planning to start a major new product development to be staffed with over three hundred engineers from several European countries and wanted Jesús to direct the project! This was clearly a significant opportunity and a job that would be a professional challenge. After a short visit with the Human Resources director, Jesús returned to the hotel and related to Chelo the discussions with Alcatel. We then needed to consider the offer, explore Madrid possibilities and prepare a response to Alcatel. During the next three days, we talked and reflected on the professional opportunity, visited the American School of Madrid and looked at potential neighborhoods where we could live. Chelo met a realtor who gave her information and arranged to help her if we decided to move to Spain. We also enjoyed the excellent Spanish cuisine, eating for the first time at El Landó, one of our all-time favorite Madrid restaurants. We invited Julie Carneiro, daughter of our good friends Orlando and Yolanda, to join us at El Landó. She was enrolled in a summer course directed by another good friend from Atlanta, Dr. José Montero, professor at Georgia State University.

Chelo also took the time during the weekend to prepare the set of conditions that she wanted Alcatel to meet before she would consider moving from Atlanta to Spain. On Monday, Chelo went out with the realtor while Jesús went to Alcatel to discuss the job offer and to give Chelo's "requirements" to the HR Director. The Alcatel HR Director reviewed the requirements and balked at a couple of them; for example, he told Jesús the company never gave anyone three round trips per year for the family to go back to their home country. Jesús quietly informed him he would not accept the job offer unless they agreed to all the conditions. The Alcatel HR Director told Jesús he would discuss the requirements with his superior and would let us know their decision. And so on Tuesday, we flew back to Atlanta and prepared to go to Marco Island with ACU family friends and to continue our normal life activities.

Marco Island — Decision time

Several members of the ACU Gainesville group who were now living in Miami had started to spend a week together in Marco Island every year in early August. We thought it was an excellent idea to enjoy a beach vacation and spend time with good friends, and we had joined this group a few years earlier and had reservations for the 1993 vacation.

After settling at the Radisson Hotel at Marco, Jesús called Alcatel. The HR Director told Jesús that the company agreed to our requests except the three annual round trips to the USA, and Jesús reminded him that either they agreed to every condition or the family was not moving to Spain. Jesús agreed to call him again the next day, and when he did, the Alcatel HR Director told him that Alcatel agreed to all our conditions. The Alcatel financial offer was excellent. Besides the very nice salary, a company car with gasoline and insurance paid by the company, Alcatel would pay for three annual round trips in Business Class back to the USA. Furthermore, Alcatel would pay for a very nice apartment in Madrid and for Lorenzo's school, not to mention all moving and temporary housing and food for two months until we found an apartment and our furniture arrived.

It was now our turn to "sh... or get off the pot." Chelo, in particular, had to make a difficult choice— give up her excellent job, her very nice house and her friends in Atlanta. On the other hand, the Alcatel job offered an excellent salary and a unique professional opportunity to Jesús, and Alcatel had agreed to each and every one of Chelo's demands. Jesús had told Chelo that, "this time the whole family would board the same plane to Madrid together. I am not going to move to Madrid alone first." Chelo took the plunge and decided that we should go, and looking back years later we agreed that we made an excellent decision.

We told our decision to Consuelo, Cristy and then to Lorenzo, who was not very happy about moving to Spain. We also told our family in Miami and informed our ACU family friends during a community evening meal at Marco. Most of the people were surprised by the announcement, and some bewildered by this information.

The next step was to begin preparation for the move. Chelo called St. Pius immediately so that Father Terry Young, the Principal, could find someone to fill her position. We returned to Atlanta from Marco with exactly three weeks to complete our moving preparations. Jesús gave notice at AT&T Tridom and Chelo contacted the

215

Madrid realtor and asked her to find us a place to live. We also contracted with our neighbor and realtor Penny Halkos to sell our Atlanta house and selected a moving/storage company. We divided our belongings into two groups, the first to be moved to Madrid and the second to be kept in storage by the moving company.[113] We organized a large garage sale to dispose of many items, including our old Zenith television set, Chelo's 1984 Oldsmobile Delta 88, the washer and dryer, the lawnmower, many tools, clothes and other items. Abuela Consuelo was the cashier at the garage sale and she had a blast.

In addition to clothes and furniture, we shipped Jesús' car, the 1984 MB 300SD, which was to be Chelo's car in Madrid. We also ordered appliances that would work in Europe including a GE refrigerator and dryer, a television and a VHS tape recorder.[114]

Once the moving company packed the items for storage and those for Madrid, we took a couple of suitcases and checked into the Ritz Carlton Buckhead for our last two nights in Atlanta. As "fate" would have it, one of the nights at the hotel we had dinner at their Cafe Restaurant and our server was José Fetzer who was to enter the Jesuit novitiate in 1995, and return to Atlanta as a Jesuit priest in 2009 to direct Spiritual Exercises for the ACU Atlanta group.

Settling in Madrid

Chelo, Lorenzo and Jesús arrived in Madrid on September 1, 1993. We carried a lot of luggage because we did not expect the moving company to deliver our belongings to Madrid until the end of October. There were so many bags that we almost lost one at the airport. Luckily, Jesús realized that one was missing and was able to locate it before we left the airport. We had to take two taxis to carry all the bags, and arrived at the apartment that the realtor had found for us, a

---

[113] By the way, the storage company did a poor job with our items for storage because they mixed some of our belongings with those of another family. We ended up losing some valuable items such as, for example, Lorenzo's extensive baseball card collection and some family photo albums.

[114] Jesús had learned where to order these appliances from Tony Costa, a Portuguese engineer that Jesús hired at Alcatel during his previous time there.

flat on the eighth floor of a building at Calle Juan Ramón Jiménez 2. The building location was good, about two blocks from the Santiago Bernabeu Stadium, two blocks from the Avenida Alberto Alcocer, and near the Plaza de Cuzco. The apartment had two bedrooms and two baths, a reasonable sized living room, and a very small kitchen. The small kitchen was not a problem since we did not expect to cook very much— Alcatel was going to pay for all our meals until we settled into permanent quarters.

We registered Lorenzo at the American School of Madrid, ASM, and arranged for the school bus transportation to pick Lorenzo at the Alberto Alcocer Avenue, near our apartment. Lorenzo was placed in the fourth grade with Mr. Tribe, an idiosyncratic English teacher. Lorenzo was a little apprehensive about the school, but he adjusted quickly: he loved taking the bus to school, enjoyed the teacher, and made a few friends reasonably quickly. He later joined the Boy Scouts and played little league baseball.

Chelo had a little bit more difficulty adjusting to Madrid and during the first couple of months developed red cheeks, rosacea. She tried new soaps and other things to clear her cheeks until she realized the redness was due to stress and it eventually disappeared. She also had the bad experience of being pickpocketed in a bus on Serrano Street. We had to cancel the Visa and AMEX cards and then go to the police station to report the theft. One good thing of this experience is that once we left the police station, we ate lunch at the Chaflán Restaurant, an excellent restaurant in the northern part of Madrid.

As we mentioned earlier, Alcatel paid for all our meals during our first two months in Madrid. Lorenzo and Jesús normally had breakfast in a bar-café across the street from the apartment building before walking to the school bus stop. Breakfast normally consisted of "café con leche, churros, porras or donuts." Chelo was on her own for breakfast and lunch. Lorenzo ate lunch at school and Jesús at Alcatel. Jesús and Lorenzo's lunches were of the Spanish sort with lots of food; at Alcatel, for example, the company cafeteria lunch offered a selection of two or three appetizers, a salad, two or three entrees, fruits and desserts. Appetizers included, on occasion, Paella, while entrees included items such as steak. Alcatel offered wine or beer with the food for those who desired it.

For dinner, we ate at a different restaurant every night and got to try many of the very good restaurants in Madrid, and this allowed us to make a list of favorites.[115] We also learned a lot about Spanish Cuisine. Lorenzo loved the Ibérico ham sliced by hand from the ham leg at restaurants, the croquettes from Nicolasa, and the fabada from Casa Paco.

Luis and María José Pire loaned us María José's VW car because we did not have a car at the beginning— we had to wait for Chelo's car to come from the USA and for the Alcatel company car for Jesús. Luis was a relative of Peque Balbona who we had met when he spent a year studying in Atlanta. He and his wife, María José, and their children Ines and Alfonso became close friends of ours in Madrid. We used the car primarily to look for a permanent place to live in Madrid. Chelo started looking with the lady realtor that she had met before and who had arranged to rent the temporary apartment. However, Chelo had a falling out with the realtor and from then on we looked for apartments ourselves. We saw many apartments and finally found one that we liked and had a good location. The owners of this apartment were a doctor, an ophthalmologist, and his wife who lived in Santiago de Compostela, Galicia.

The apartment had three bedrooms, three baths, a large kitchen with space for a dinette, a good sized "salón" with space for a large sofa, television and our dining room set; it also had a room that we used as a study and where we placed a sofa-bed. The apartment was located outside of the city, in Prado de Somosaguas,[116] a very nice neighborhood that was about a ten minutes drive from the American School of Madrid, and provided easy access to Jesús to go to work— Jesús traversed the "Casa de Campo"[117] every day to go back and forth from work. This was also the route we used to go to the city for shopping, dining out and going to shows or visiting friends. In the

---

[115] Among the favorites were El Landó, Nicolasa, Goizeko Kabi and El Señorio de Bertiz.

[116] The apartment address was Cierzo 10, 2-A, Pozuelo de Alarcón.

[117] A large park similar to New York's Central Park and Paris' Bois de Boulogne. Casa de Campo is situated next to the city and has a lake, a zoo, an amusement park, picnic and sports facilities, and a Madrid Metro stop.

basement of the apartment building we had space to park three cars and a storage area (the Spanish call it a "trastero"). The apartment was on the second floor of a complex with forty-eight units distributed along two buildings that faced each other across a courtyard; each of the buildings had four entrances leading to three floors with two apartments on each floor. The apartment complex was fenced, had twenty-four hour security, pool, tennis and paddle courts, basketball and soccer fields for the children.

Thus, we were ready to move to our permanent quarters when our furniture, car and other belongings arrived in October. Jesús scheduled to return Luis Pire's car and pick up our Mercedes Benz at the moving company depot. On the day Jesús was to return Luis' car, he was delayed because the Alcatel folks were washing the car and Jesús almost missed Lorenzo's school bus. That evening, Jesús returned Luis' car and the next day he went to pick up his car only to find out that the car battery was dead because the Atlanta moving company forgot to disconnect its battery in Atlanta. Other than the car battery, all our belongings from Atlanta arrived well and the move into the Somosaguas flat went without problems. We had to set up electronic payments for the rent and utilities because almost everything in Spain was paid electronically— the utility companies sent the monthly bills to the bank and the bank paid them automatically. We bought a dinette set in Madrid since we had sold the one we had in Atlanta, believing we would not have space in the Madrid flat. Alcatel gave Jesús a choice of one of several new automobiles and he ended up selecting a dark blue Audi A100, the predecessor of the A6, an excellent car that had manual transmission and space for five persons.

Penny Halkos called us in early October to discuss an offer on the Cravey Trail house, an offer we accepted after some negotiations. Thus, we had just moved into the flat when Chelo had to travel back to Atlanta to close on the sale of our Atlanta house. The timing of the closing coincided with a five-day field trip for Lorenzo's class to a farm near Madrid. The students were to learn about farm life, animals, and the basics of living in the country— a great idea. Chelo flew to Atlanta on Saturday, October 23, Jesús' birthday, to close on the sale of the house the following Wednesday. She stayed with Jorge and Sonia Guigou. On Monday, Chelo said goodbye to the Guigous and went to our house to oversee the cleaning and packing of the rest of our belongings, and at mid morning received a call that Jorge had died from a sudden heart attack! Needless to say, this was a shock, but she was able to provide emotional support to her good friend Sonia during that difficult time.

The closing of our house was uneventful and Chelo selected additional furniture to ship to Spain, including a beautiful Japanese table that was stolen at the Madrid Barajas airport. On Friday, Jesús picked up Lorenzo at the farm and joined the Pires for dinner. Chelo returned from Atlanta the following day.

On the first Sunday that we went to Mass at the mission church in our neighborhood— it was not a parish at the time— we noticed that one of the readers at the Mass looked like and spoke like a Cuban, and after Mass Chelo recognized his wife, Josefina Ganzaraín (Fina), who we had met at the farewell dinner for Armando Valladares two years earlier. Fina, who became a very close friend of Chelo, and her husband Vicente, lived nearby and they introduced us to other Cubans in Madrid including her neighbor, Mili (Milagros) who was married to a Spaniard.

Chelo joined the Newcomers Club of Madrid where she met a number of international women. Some of these women walked with Chelo and had morning coffee after dropping their respective children at school. After meeting Fina, Vicente, and the international women we were beginning to adapt to Madrid, did not feel isolated any more, and Chelo's rosacea disappeared. But we still had to learn many details about living in Spain. For example, soon after we moved to the flat, Chelo went to a market to buy foodstuff and after she was there for a while, a woman came up and asked, "¿Quién da la vez?" Chelo had no idea what this meant but soon find out that this was the informal way to keep your place in line; it means, essentially, "Who is last?"

Meanwhile, Jesús had started to settle into his job at Alcatel. He was hired to lead a large Europe-wide Alcatel project with engineers from Belgium, France and Spain. The project name was ASAN, the first letters of the product's name, Alcatel Systems Access Node. Alcatel had assigned a Systems Engineer, Michel Smouts, from Belgium and Jesús as the project lead, and placed them administratively under Manuel Gordillo of Spain and technically under Michel Rahier, a Belgian Ph.D. The Alcatel management in Belgium, France and Spain had committed the engineering manpower although the persons working on it were not yet assigned. Jesús' job was to organize and staff the project and lead the product development. He started putting together the project office, the staff that would help him manage this project, hiring first a secretary, Julia Plaza, and then the person who would become his right hand man and friend, Luis Fernández Villagrasa. Luis was married to Ana Coterillo, the daughter of a prominent Cuban family who were now living in Madrid. Jesús hired three other persons to help with the budgeting, paperwork and details of the large project with engineers in three countries.

Luis and Jesús immediately started to organize the project, working with Michel Smouts, Michel Rahier and several systems engineers to complete the technical definition of the project. He distributed the work among the groups of engineers in the three countries, defined the project management organization in each country, established a project schedule and budget, and started the product development. The three main locations for the product development were Lannion in Brittany, France, Antwerp in Belgium and Madrid, Spain. Jesús travelled to these locations, met the local management teams, learned about the strengths of each group and met a number of people with whom he became friends.[118]

A few months into the project, it became apparent to Jesús that the project was doomed because of Alcatel's internal politics. Belgium wanted to protect their big switch project; France did not want any project to interfere with either their own big switch project or with projects that impacted France Telecom; Italy wanted to modify the project to add a smaller product for the Italian market; Germany wanted a piece of the action; Spain wanted leadership of the project but wasn't sure what they would do with the resulting product. This was a recipe for disaster, and sure enough, eventually the project was abandoned.

The family spent the remaining of the year 1993, becoming adjusted to life in Madrid: Chelo with friends, Lorenzo at school, Jesús at Alcatel. In November, Cristy came to spend Thanksgiving with us and

---

[118] Particularly Pedro Fouz in Madrid and Emanuelle (Manú) in Lannion.

we did a little bit of sightseeing going to Sevilla, Jerez de la Frontera, Cadiz[119], Algeciras and Malaga. We tried to visit Gibraltar but were not to visit it because we had left our passports in Madrid. In December we went to Miami to spend Christmas and we took with us a good bit of the season's turrones to share with the family in Miami.

Madrid

Jesús spent the first part of 1994 organizing the ASAN Project, visiting the Alcatel engineering offices in Zaventem and Antwerp, Belgium, Lannion France and Vimercate Italy. He also had to deal with Alcatel's politics and periodic reorganizations. One of the reorganizations resulted in the placing of all access products under Manuel Gordillo, so Jesús became Vice President of Engineering for the Access Systems Division. The other division vice presidents included Claudio Dascal, a polyglot Brazilian that was second to Gordillo, Gerald Farrenc, a Frenchman in charge of marketing and Pablo Calvo, a Spaniard responsible for sales. Gerald and his wife Julie introduced us to the French custom of drinking champagne with aperitifs before dinner. Pablo and his wife became life-long friends and colleagues not only at Alcatel but also later at Ciena.

Jesús' responsibilities now included oversight of more than 1,200 engineers in eight cities— Madrid, Stuttgart and Hanover in Germany, Milan in Italy, Antwerp in Belgium, Oslo in Norway, Johannesburg in South Africa and Sydney in Australia. Jesús now needed to supervise project and persons in these cities and he began to travel almost every week, particularly to Germany, Italy, Belgium and France— he tried to travel to Australia only twice a year. In addition to Luis Fernández Villagrasa, Jesús' Madrid team included an excellent secretary, Julia Plaza Serrano, an accountant, Manuel García Jabardo,[120] and a couple of other engineers.

---

[119] We ate at the same restaurant El Faro where Chelo and Jesús ate during the 1978 ACU trip to the Holy Land and Spain.

[120] Manuel and his wife were guests of the Spanish Royal Family at Infanta Elena's wedding in Sevilla because she worked in the Office of the President. Some months later he brought Jesús two Cohiba cigars that were part of the

Delta Air Lines had just opened an office in Madrid to manage its operations in Spain. Jesús met the manager, Laura de Arcos, who was about to get married, so we sent her a Lladró wedding gift. One byproduct of the gift was that Delta Spain gave free upgrades from business to first class for all of the family. Jesús' secretary would call Delta Spain and informed them of our itinerary, and presto, our seats were upgraded. One of the interesting benefits of the upgrades was that Lorenzo became accustomed to eating caviar when he was only ten years old. Another was that Cordero and Argentina were able to fly first class when they came to visit us in Madrid.

We welcomed several family members to Spain during 1994. Cordero and Cristy in the spring, Argentina and Alexandra in September, Consuelo Beatriz, Todd and two of Todd's friends in October.

Cordero traveled with us from Miami after the Holy Week holidays in 1994. We made several sightseeing trips with Cordero. In addition to the usual places (Toledo, Avila, Salamanca, Segovia), we made memorable trips to visit family in Alicante and ancestral locations in Asturias and Santander Provinces. The purpose of the trip to the city of Alicante was to visit Cordero's brother-in-law's sister and the son of his nephew Monchi, Margot's son. Monchi had died of lung cancer in 1977, at age 34; Monchi's son later also died young of the same cancer. We stayed at a hotel in the center of the city and can place the date of our visit exactly because it coincided with a leg of the Vuelta de España bicycle race that ended on that city on Sunday, May 1. We had lunch that Sunday at a restaurant by the ocean. On the trip to Alicante we stopped for the mid-day meal at an excellent restaurant that specialized in game on a small city on the highway.[121]

We made a second trip to Alicante with Cordero that spring because Carlos González-Madroño, Jesús' first boss at Alcatel Spain, invited us to visit Jabea, and he cooked an Alicante style paella for us. Later in the spring of 1994, after Cristy's law school classes were over, she came to spend a couple of weeks in Spain. She joined us for

---

cigars sent by Fidel Castro to Felipe González, the President of the Spanish Government.

[121] The Michelin one-star Restaurante Las Rejas in the town of Las Pedroñeras.

a special trip to northern Spain to visit ancestral places. We took Cordero to Asturias to El Vidural, the hometown of his wife Consuelo's family. From there we went to Covadonga to visit Our Lady of Covadonga, patroness of Asturias, and we stayed at Ribadesella, a resort town in the Cantabrian Sea where one of the hotel staff was Cuban. Then, off to Santillana del Mar (according to Cristy, "the city of dogs"), to Santander where we stopped at the famous Sardinero Beach, and from there we drove to the nearby town of Torrelavega, the hometown of Cordero's father.

By summer, we were pretty well organized in Spain with Lorenzo at school, Jesús at Alcatel, Chelo with Cuban, Spanish and international friends. In June, Chelo and Lorenzo left for Miami and Jesús joined them during the annual vacation period in August. At the end of the summer vacation, Argentina and Alexandra Marta (Almar) León, Jesús' niece and goddaughter, traveled with Lorenzo, Chelo and Jesús back to Madrid.

Early in 1994, Chelo and Consuelo Beatriz had discussed the difficulties that Almar was experiencing with her living arrangements. Almar was spending her junior year of high school in West Palm Beach with Ticó and his wife Clarita, and the arrangement was causing stress and problems to Almar. Consuelo Beatriz was concerned and was trying to find a way to help Almar, and talked to Chelo about it. Chelo came up with the solution— invite Almar to do her senior year of high school in Madrid and live with us! This required the consent and participation of Almar's mother, Marta, so Chelo spoke to Marta and explained to her that we were offering this opportunity to Almar because she was Jesús' goddaughter. She further explained to Marta that this was a unique opportunity to attend one of Madrid's best schools and enjoy a new culture. Marta would only have to worry about paying for the tuition and airline ticket to/from Madrid— we would take care of all other expenses. Marta agreed, Almar liked the idea, applied and was accepted to the school, and began preparations to come to Spain. Argentina thought it would be a good idea for her to accompany Almar for the first couple of months of her stay.

After the five of us (Argentina, Alexandra, Lorenzo, Chelo and Jesús) arrived in Madrid in September, we embarked on a period of sightseeing and spiritual travels during weekends and holidays. The list of places we visited with Argentina is long and started with a trip to Lourdes, France via Burgos and San Sebastian. Argentina enjoyed Lourdes tremendously although she was not able to bathe in the Lourdes waters because we did know the procedure to be able to do it.

Another very special trip was to Fatima and Galicia Spain. We drove from Madrid to Extremadura (Trujillo and Cáceres) and then to Fatima, Portugal. From there we drove via Coimbra and Porto to Vigo, Spain where we ate an excellent meal ("Pulpo a la Gallega") at the El Castillo Restaurant that sat on a hill with a fabulous view overlooking the city and the Ría de Vigo.[122] We stayed overnight in Pontevedra and the next morning drove to Carril, the ancestral city of Argentina's grandfather, located next to Villagarcía de Arousa in the Rías de Arousa.[123] We visited the parish church and were also directed to a building where a family with last name Núñez lived— unfortunately there was nobody home. We left the Pontevedra province and drove to the famous city of Santiago de Compostela. We arrived during a downpour, but Jesús was able to drive, not park, very near to the Cathedral of Saint James the Apostle so that Argentina could visit it. We did not do a lot of sightseeing in Santiago because of the weather but departed on our way back to Madrid, stopping overnight in the city of Orense. Unfortunately, Almar missed the trip to Portugal and Galicia because her mother Marta was planning to travel to Spain that weekend— it turns out that her passport had expired and she was not able to come to Spain at that time. Almar stayed in Madrid at the house of her good friends Cecilia and Maria Eva, and their mother Juani.

We also visited Cuenca where Argentina fell down in one of the slippery streets, Avila, Salamanca, Alba de Tormes, Segovia, Ciruela and Pedraza de la Sierra. We remember a couple of interesting anecdotes from those trips. The first is that when Argentina wanted to visit a particular sight she would say to Jesús, "Chelo wants to see such and such place." Another was our visit to the picturesque hill town of Pedraza de la Sierra in Segovia Province where we ordered a

---

[122] The restaurant was closed in 2006 and the building demolished in 2013.

[123] This is one of four "lower Rías" (Rías Baixas in Galician)— inlets from the Atlantic Ocean.

meal at a restaurant that had a simple menu, roasted lamb and a tossed salad, and one had to order even number meals (two, four, etc.) Since there were five of us, Jesús ordered for six and Argentina protested that it would be too much food— well, there was nothing left of our order except the bones!

While the rest of us worked or went to school, Chelo took Argentina to many museums in Madrid. Argentina's visit was also wonderful for Chelo and Jesús because they were able to take a trip to Belgium and the Netherlands. Argentina stayed with Almar and Lorenzo who were already in school. Chelo and Jesús stayed at the Hotel Amigo in Brussels and ate at the Michelin three stars restaurant Comme Chez Soi. We then went to Bruges and Ghent in Belgium and from there to The Hague, Amsterdam and many of the picturesque small towns of the Netherlands. In October, Argentina, Almar, Lorenzo, Chelo and Jesús attended the wedding of Jesús' cousin's son, Felicín, in Madrid, one of a handful of weddings we attended where the mother of the groom was expected to wear the traditional "mantilla y peineta."[124] Another interesting note about Argentina and Cordero's trip is that both claimed they could not understand the Spanish news, and in fact, one day we found Cordero watching the news program in English on CNN!

In October we also enjoyed the visit of Consuelo Beatriz, Todd and a couple of their friends who stayed with us for several days and also traveled, with Chelo, to the south of Spain. They were in Spain, coincidentally, during Jesús' birthday, and they joined Argentina, Almar, Lorenzo, Chelo and Jesús, for dinner at Jesús and Chelo's favorite restaurant in Madrid, El Landó. The meal was magnificent as it was always at this restaurant. We remember how well Argentina ate (appetizers, one full merluza for her, a little bit of meat, and dessert). Argentina loved the "cuajada" dessert— something that feels like a plain yogurt and is normally eaten with either sugar or honey.

As we approached the Thanksgiving holiday, Argentina felt that she needed to return to Miami to help Mary and Carmen with preparations for the holiday celebrations. We tried to persuade her to stay

---

[124] See, for example, Queen Sofia's mantilla y peineta at ww.abc.es/informacion/principes-asturias/galeriaceremonia01.asp.

until December but to no avail. Later, Argentina regretted not staying longer in Spain where she was having a great time.

American School of Madrid

As 1995 started, both Lorenzo and Almar were settled in the American School of Madrid, ASM. Lorenzo spent a little bit over three years and Alexandra one year at ASM.[125] The school was excellent and provided a very good education to Lorenzo and Alexandra. The school was a good experience for all of us, and we want to take the time to describe the school, curriculum, and extracurricular activities.

ASM is located in the Carretera de Aravaca in Pozuelo de Alarcón, on the outskirts of Madrid. When we walked into the school building for the first time in 1993, we felt we could have been walking into any American school in the USA— it had the look and feel of the typical USA school, the construction and distribution of the building, the posters and announcements; in short, the AMS was very similar to any school in Atlanta.

The administration and many of the teachers at ASM were American, some lived in Spain and some were expatriates who came for the experience of living abroad. There were also a number of teachers from other countries. English was the primary language of the school, but Spanish was used freely specially by the kitchen and some other staff members. The student body was a mix of American, international and Spanish pupils. Lorenzo had classmates and school friends from Argentina, The Netherlands, Spain and the USA. Many of the USA and international students were the children of expatriates working in Spain either in private companies, at embassies or international institutions. Some Spanish families sent their children to the ASM so they would become completely fluent in English while maintaining their competence in Spanish— Spanish laws required these students to complete Spain's secondary curriculum in addition to the high school curriculum of the school. The school offered also the International Baccalaureate programs so that a student could end up with three secondary degrees at graduation, the International Bac-

---

[125] For information about the Colegio Americano de Madrid, visit their website.

calaureate, the US High School and the Spanish Bachillerato. Some ASM graduates gained admission to many of the best US universities.

The school was expensive although it had different tuition costs depending on the funding arrangement for each child. Because Lorenzo was the child of an expatriate whose company paid the tuition, Lorenzo paid the highest tuition rate— somewhere between thirteen and fifteen thousands dollars every year. Students whose parents worked for the US Embassy or whose parents paid the tuition paid a lower rate.

The class sizes were small, the teachers were good and the school offered many extracurricular activities and field trips. Lorenzo spent one week on a teaching farm learning and helping with chores. He was on a two-day field trip to Merida to visit the Roman amphitheater, circus and museum after they studied the Roman Empire in school. On this trip, Lorenzo was also taught how to eat properly, how to escort a lady to a table and how to dress appropriately.

Every student at ASM was required to take Spanish classes taught by native Spanish teachers. The school required everyone to learn Geography— what a concept! Lorenzo learned all the provinces of Spain and had to be able to place them on the map. He also learned the name and locations of countries and capitals of Africa and America. The ASM emphasized hands on learning such as building a homemade oven to bake a potato. There was a period of time every year dedicated to emphasize reading with an invited author providing guidance about authorship and Lorenzo had to prepare his "own" book, a bounded small booklet with his writing on a particular topic. Sports and extracurricular activities were a mix of USA and Spain's activities. There was Little League baseball, futbol (soccer), Boy Scouts, volleyball, basketball, and other sports and activities.

Lorenzo did well in school learning Spanish and the subject matter of his classes, and he also made a lot of friends. Alexandra did very well and would have been Valedictorian if she had been a student at the school for at least two years. She played in the volleyball team, made friends and met some interesting people. For example, one of her classmates was a member of the Mahou family, the owners of one of the largest beer brewing company in Spain. Another one was Shaila Dúrcal, now a famous singer.

A year for sightseeing

The year 1995 is memorable for many reasons. On the positive side, Cristy and Almar graduated from Law School and High School, respectively. We also enjoyed the visits of several family members to Spain; we traveled and did a lot of sightseeing; we enjoyed some of Spain's cultural and religious celebrations, including the Fallas and Holy Week.

Jesús had wanted to go to Valencia for the annual Fallas festival in 1994 but could not find hotel accommodations, and hence, Jesús made reservations eleven months in advance for the 1995 Fallas. This festival includes the building of "ninots" (doll-like figures) and "fallas" (displays) built of wood, cardboard and papier-mâché that are burned on the evening of the eve of the Feast of Saint Joseph on March 19 (a Sunday in 1995), an activity called "la cremà" in the Valencian language. Many of the fallas are medium size, but some are very large and cost more than one-half million dollars. Many local women wear beautiful "fallera" dresses and there were what seemed like endless processions, lasting hours, to bring flowers to the Virgin Mary at the Cathedral. The groups that bring flowers do it to the tune of the famous Valencia pasodoble. In addition to flowers and fire, the Fallas are characterized by noise with fireworks at all times and brass bands playing in the morning to wake people up. We saw the greatest fireworks in our life on the night before la cremà, fireworks lasting non-stop for forty minutes and with sparkling shapes that we had never seen before or since. The cremà of the large fallas is a sight to behold with the fire department spraying water on the trees, buildings and nearby structures to prevent a large fire. We witnessed the cremà of several fallas and were awed by the experience.

While in the Valencia area, we visited the Lladró factory, makers of famous porcelain pieces. We looked for bargains among "seconds," pieces that did not pass the quality control but looked perfect to us— we bought a couple of pieces at reduced prices. On our first night in Valencia we drove outside of the city to a zone of restaurants (El Palmar) that specialized in "arroces." We ate at one of them and we chose different individual-size paellas. Chelo and Almar ordered traditional seafood paellas while Lorenzo and Jesús ordered meat-based paellas that included beef and rabbit meat. The day after the cremà we drove to Madrid, spending hours in a monumental traffic jam in order to leave the vicinity of Valencia.

A few weeks later we embarked on another major sightseeing trip. Because Cristy and Joel were graduating in early May, we did not go to the US during the Holy Week holidays. Instead we used the time off from school and work to travel and sightsee. We left Madrid on Saturday, April 8, and drove via Zaragoza and Lleida to Andorra where we stayed overnight. Andorra is a duty-free country, so in the summer it is full of shoppers and in the winter it also receives many skiing visitors. The following day we drove through Andorra into France and visited the picturesque town of Carcassonne—"looks like Disney to me" commented Jesús. At Carcassonne, we had crepes for lunch in a restaurant in a quaint plaza before heading out again, in the direction of the southern part of Spain. We stopped overnight at Tarragona, a city made famous by the Romans— we had visited this city earlier with Argentina to see the Roman aqueduct.

On Monday morning we drove along the coast to Peñíscola, a picturesque town next to the sea that has a unique history. Peñíscola was the residence of one of the three popes that existed simultaneously during the "Western Schism"— he was known as Benedict XIII during the schism. His name was Pedro Martínez de Luna y Pérez de Gotor, known as Papa Luna in Spain, is considered an "antipope" in the Catholic Church, and, therefore, is not listed in the official Pope directory. The old city sits on a small hill— the name of the city is derived from a word that means a place where there are rocks. We parked near the ocean and walked up the hill of this old, but still active city, to the top of the hill where the Papa Luna lived. Afterwards, we drove to Castellón de la Plana and ate a very good paella at La Marina restaurant before heading for an overnight stay in Alicante. After checking into our hotel we heard the sounds of a band playing and loud noises from the street. The music and commotion was caused by group carrying a "Paso" (a type of float, very heavy) with a sculpture of an image from the Passion of Christ. We saw many of these in Sevilla and Ronda during the rest of Holy Week.

We left the city of Alicante and drove towards the great and beautiful city of Sevilla, visiting the city of Murcia along the way. We remember stopping for lunch in a small town on a two-lane highway and being blown over by the outstanding seafood selection they had on the menu. We arrived in Sevilla late in the day and went to our hotel— we had selected a hotel outside of the city that was a good value and provided frequent free bus transportation to the city center at the Plaza de Cuba. We spent the next two days, Holy Wednesday and Thursday, enjoying the city and its famous Holy Week processions. However, there were a large number of tourists who were there for the "show," and distracted one's attention from the religious meaning of the penitents carrying the Pasos. On Holy Thursday evening, we saw many Sevilla women wearing black dresses and black "Mantillas," a traditional sign of mourning for the upcoming death of Jesus Christ on Good Friday.

The morning of Good Friday we departed Sevilla for the small and quaint city of Ronda, located in a mountainous region about 85 miles southeast from Sevilla. The city has one of the oldest bullfight rings in Spain, an interesting canyon in the middle of the city and quintessential Andalusia architecture in the old town. We arrived in time to see a couple of processions, one with an interesting "Paso" depicting Jesus being carried in a coffin. We attended Good Friday services and Easter Vigil Mass at Nuestra Señora del Socorro (Our lady of Succor) Church in the Plaza del Socorro in the middle of the city. We stayed two nights at a very beautiful bed-and-breakfast, not far from the city center, that had excellent breakfast jams that we ate every morning— Chelo bought some to take with her to Madrid.

On Sunday we returned to Madrid, a six-hours trip, stopping briefly in Cordoba to visit the Palacio de Viana Museum that has twelve beautiful patios. We arrived in Madrid on Sunday evening, rested on Monday and resumed our regular activities on Tuesday. A few days later, we received a call from Carmen Luisa who informed us of José Luis' car accident and subsequent death in México, news that shocked and saddened us. We all felt that José was an excellent human being and he was about to get married.[126]

The spring was busy with travel and graduations. In early May, Lorenzo, Chelo and Jesús flew to Columbia, South Carolina to attend

---

[126] In fact, he had already married in a civil ceremony and was preparing for the Sacramental marriage.

Cristy and Joel's graduation from Law and Medical Schools, respectively. Rigoberto, Argentina, Cordero, Consuelo and Carmen Luisa traveled to Columbia for the graduation in a "test of endurance and love." They had booked air travel from Miami to Columbia to arrive during the evening hours the day before the commencements. But due to bad weather the flight stopped in Jacksonville, Florida, where they were informed that the next connecting flight would be in the morning, a flight that would arrive in Columbia too late to make it to the commencements. They were not going to be deterred from attending the graduation ceremonies if they could help it, so they rented a car and Carmen Luisa drove during the night— with Argentina talking to her to help her stay awake. They arrived in Columbia in the early morning, went to Estela León's house to shower and change and then to the Medical School commencement and later to the Law School commencement. After the graduations, we enjoyed a family luncheon with Joel's and our family at a restaurant. That afternoon we drove to Charleston to visit this charming and historical city. We fondly remember how Argentina stopped at every house with a historic plaque to study it while Consuelo (Chelo's mother) was itching to go to Fort Sumter because that was the place that Lorenzo wanted to visit.

Almar's mother Marta and her husband came to Madrid later in the spring to attend Almar's graduation from the American School of Madrid. We all attended her graduation and a graduation party at the house of a schoolmate.

Cristy and Joel came to Spain after their graduation. We went together to the city of Elda, in Alicante Province, to participate in the "Feast of Moros y Cristianos" (Moors and Christians), a celebration that is held in several cities in the south of Spain to commemorate the conquest of Andalusia by Moors in the 8th century and their eventually expulsion from Spain in the 15th century. The full festival lasted five days but we were there only one day and were hosted by Emilio Gil Delicado, an Alcatel engineer that Jesús had known for several years. The festival included a representation of the Moor conquest with simulated gunpowder shots and discourses by each side in the morning. In the afternoon, after a nice lunch, we saw a long parade (over three hours long) of town people dressed as Christians in front followed ("being chased") by others dressed as moors. In the evening we were guests at a private party that included food, drinks, music and dancing. We stayed at a hotel at the beach in the city of Alicante, about 35 minutes from Elda. After our return to Madrid, Cristy and Joel traveled in Spain for several days enjoying tourist sights and good food.

During the summer we made our annual trip to Miami and the beach. Chelo and Lorenzo stayed in the USA for more than two months and Jesús one month. While we were at the beach in Marco Island, Cordero called Chelo to let her know that the owner of the duplex where they lived planned to sell the unit. The implication was that Cordero, Consuelo and Generosa would have to find a new place to live— a problem. Chelo told Cordero that she would help as soon as we returned to Miami from the beach. We spent a couple of weeks looking at houses and duplexes in Miami that would be suitable for the family. Chelo eventually found, after Jesús had left for Spain, a house that would be a very good fit in a gated community off SW 87 Avenue, a community called Poinciana Point. The house sat on a minimum lot, had three good bedrooms, two baths, living, dining and family rooms, a good kitchen and a small patio. Chelo made an offer for the house that was accepted and closing was scheduled for October— Jesús attended the closing and helped with the initial moving details. Cordero, Consuelo and Generosa were installed and organized in their new homes by the time we returned to Miami for Christmas.

We continued to sightsee in Europe and to welcome family visitors to Spain that year. In October, Jesús attended the Telecom Geneva exposition, one of the largest exhibitions and marketing meetings in the telecommunications world in the last part of the 20th century. The exposition was over on October 11 and Chelo and Lorenzo flew to Geneva that evening for a spot of sightseeing. We stayed at the Noga Hilton in Geneva and departed on a rented car the next day for a four-day visit to Switzerland. The United Nations celebrated its fiftieth Anniversary in 1995 and since the UN Office in Geneva is the second largest of the four major offices sites of the UN, we decided to visit it. After a short sightseeing in Geneva, we drove to Lausanne, headquarters of the International Olympic Committee. We stayed overnight in a small hotel in Fribourg and drove the next day to Berne, the de facto capital of Switzerland. Berne has a very well preserved old town in the center of the city. Next we were off to Interlaken, the city between lakes, located in a beautiful area of the country, surrounded by mountains and beautiful lakes. Then we headed to the city of Lucerne. When we arrived in Lucerne we had to find a hotel— we did not have hotel reservations in this trip in any city except in Geneva. We found a small hotel in the outskirts of the city that had one room available although they had to bring a portable bed for Lorenzo. After sightseeing we returned to the hotel for dinner and had a delightful meal. The next morning we ate breakfast at the hotel and were astonished by the quality of the breakfast— the three of us agreed that we ate the best muesli we have ever had at that hotel; they also served homemade yogurt and many other delicacies.

From Lucerne we drove through some of the mountain areas of Switzerland to arrive at Montreux, a city on the eastern end of Lake Geneva where we stayed overnight. The following day we drove back to Geneva and flew back to Madrid. A few days later we welcomed Vicente and Bertica, our mutual cousins, who came to Spain for a three-week visit. Vicente and Bertica stayed with us in Madrid for a few days before heading out to visit several parts of Spain. We remember going with them to the famous Café San Gines on their first night in Madrid to eat "churros con chocolate." The hot chocolate is so thick at this café that the churros stay vertically when you place them in the cup. Finishing the evening with hot chocolate was too much for Bertica's stomach since they had a long day that started with their flight from Philadelphia, then getting organized and doing a little bit of sightseeing— we are not sure she recovered from the chocolate during her stay in Spain. Chelo helped them with the local tourist attractions and we all joined them for our ritual dinner at El Landó.[127] In December we traveled to Miami to spend Christmas with the family.

---

[127] A dinner that almost always had similar menu items. Appetizers waiting at the table of "pan con tomate, tomates con cebolla y Jamón de Bellota." Other appetizers included "Revuelto de huevos con patatas" and maybe other appetizers. Entrees included fish, typically "Merluza" or "Mero," and "escalopines" (sliced medallion of beef tenderloin) accompanied by "pimientos de Padrón." Dessert, normally the "arroz con leche planchado" but also had their wonderful "natillas." After dinner, Pacharán or "chupito" ("Orujo").

Madrid 1996

Our last year in Madrid was also packed with travel and activities and the major decision of whether or not to move to Maryland. One more time, God played a big part in helping us to make the right decision.

The big news of the year was the birth of our granddaughter Consuelo Alina ("Alina") on Saturday, February 10. Todd called us that day to inform and congratulate us. Chelo flew the next day to Indianapolis to help Consuelo and Todd during the baby's first weeks. Lorenzo and Jesús stayed in Madrid until the Holy Week holidays. On Saturday, March 30, Lorenzo flew from Madrid to Indianapolis while Jesús traveled to Sidney, Australia for a visit with the Alcatel Access Group there. From Australia, Jesús flew to Houston on Tuesday for a one-day business visit to Alcatel and from there to Indy to see the baby and attend her Baptism on Easter Sunday, April 7, at St. Monica's Church, with Lorenzo and Almar serving as Alina's godparents.

Argentina, Almar and Cristy also flew to Indy and they plus Chelo, Lorenzo and Jesús stayed at an Embassy Suites Hotel near Consuelo's house until after the Baptism. Later that Sunday, Chelo, Lorenzo and Jesús flew back to Spain for what was to be their last six-months there.

After their arrival in Spain, Chelo and Jesús decided to go to the famous "Feria de Sevilla" (Seville's April Fair), a weeklong celebration of bullfights and parties. Local women dress in typical Sevillana costumes and many ride carriages or beautiful horses. Every night, after the bullfight and dinner, many of Sevilla's people and many tourists descend on the fairgrounds, called "El Real," for food and drinks; many attend parties at private or company booths. Jesús' secretary had to scramble to find us accommodations on such short notice, but she accomplished it by calling the local Sevilla Alcatel sales office. Thus, we went to Sevilla to experience this big party, and although we enjoyed our visit, it is clear than in order to have a really good time at the fair you need to have friends there; we had experienced this at Elda the previous year when our friends invited us to their private party.

We made another sightseeing trip over a five-day "puente," although we do not remember if we made it in December 1995 or May 1996. In either case, Chelo bought a package vacation to Tenerife in the Canary Islands that included the airfare, the hotel, most meals and air transfers. The charter flights, the hotel and the meals were adequate and we had a chance to visit a new part of Spain, the land of several of Jesús' grandparents. The Canary Islands are a favorite for German tourists and we discovered an interesting thing about them at the beach— one member of their group gets up very early in the morning, goes to the beach, places towels in their desired locations, and then departs to return later with others from the group to sun themselves. We tried the beach, Jesús swam in it and found it not as good as the ones in the Caribbean, certainly nothing to compare to the best Cuban beaches. On another day, we rented a car to tour the island and drove by Mount Teide, the highest peak in Spain at 3.7 km, and the third-highest volcano in the world. We traveled to the Loro Park amusement park and from there to Santa Cruz de Tenerife, where we ate at a restaurant that exemplified for us the similarities of the Canary Island to Cuba in their accent, their food (rice is important) and some customs (one kiss in the cheek instead of two).

At the end of the academic year, Chelo and Lorenzo traveled to the US to spend time with the family and to attend the Centennial Olympics in Atlanta. Jesús made his second trip that year to Sidney and from Sidney flew to Atlanta where Chelo, Lorenzo, Consuelo and Jesús crashed in Cristy's two-bedroom apartment for part of the duration of the Olympics. We attended a number of sporting events; Chelo went to a Gloria Estefán concert and all of us went to Centennial Olympic Park. The weather was hot, the security tight, the events fun. This was a very interesting and exciting experience for all of us, especially being woken up by a phone call to check if we were all right because there had been a bomb at Centennial Olympic Park. Chelo flew back to Spain in early September and happened to be on the same flight as friends from Atlanta, and seated near the Infanta Elena and her then husband, on the first class cabin— Chelo introduced herself to Infanta Elena.

Time to return to the USA

Jesús had kept in contact with many USA professional colleagues while in Spain. Among those with whom he kept up were Larry Huang and Steve Chaddick who both had left AT&T Tridom and were now founders of a new telecommunications company, Ciena, in Maryland. Jesús visited them once while in Spain and saw and talked to them a couple of times in Dallas in June 1996 during the SuperComm telecom exhibit. After the Olympics and a short visit to Miami, Jesús made a stop in Washington on his way to Paris for a meeting with ACU members there. After the meeting, Jesús stayed in the house of then ACU President Ramón (Mongo) Domínguez and his wife Carmencita. Jesús had no plans for Monday morning because his flight to Paris was late in the afternoon, so he decided to call and visit his friend Steve to say hello before heading to the airport.

Upon arrival at the Ciena facilities, Larry asked him to come to his office and asked Jesús, "Are you ready to come back?" Jesús misunderstood the question so Larry clarified, "I mean to join Ciena." Jesús replied, "Are you crazy? I live like a king in Europe. Why would I come back to the USA to work as a slave in a start-up?" Well, Larry and Steve, later joined by Ciena CEO Pat Nettles, continued to press on, took Jesús to lunch at the Don Pablo Restaurant in Laurel and continued insisting, so Jesús asked Steve to send him an email explaining what Ciena would want Jesús to do if he accepted a position with the company.

A few days later Jesús received an email from Steve explaining that his position would be as Vice President, responsible for developing a new area of business focused on access products. Ciena was at the time a one-product company focusing on long-haul transport systems. Jesús told Steve that he wanted to meet the rest of the team, and for that purpose he flew from Madrid on a Friday and spent most of Saturday meeting with other Ciena key executives. At the end of the day he received a formal offer letter from Pat Nettles. That evening, Pat, Steve with Barbara, and Larry with Nancy took Jesús to dinner at O'Learys Seafood restaurant; they repeatedly kept asking Jesús, "Are you ready to accept the offer?" to which Jesús kept answering, "I have to discuss it with Consuelo and she needs to visit this area." They would then tell the waiter, "Bring another bottle of wine." Well, at a late hour, the owner of the restaurant told us politely that the restaurant had been closed for a while.

The next day, Sunday, Jesús flew back to Spain and reported to work at Alcatel on Monday. We agreed that Chelo needed to visit Maryland, find a school for Lorenzo and study the housing situation before we made the decision on whether or not to move to Maryland. Chelo flew to Baltimore and spent several days looking at schools and apartments. Her number one priority was to find a school for Lorenzo, preferably a Catholic School. She told the realtor that finding a house was a lower priority and that we would easily move into an apartment temporarily. The realtor took Chelo to a number of schools, but because the school term was halfway completed she could not find a Catholic school that would admit Lorenzo. Then, the realtor told Chelo about another school, one that was not in their list of schools to visit. They visited the school, Our Lady of Perpetual Help, OLPH, in Ellicott City, and Chelo met the Principal. Chelo and the principal of the school got along fabulously, they both were Cursillistas, they both were teachers, and the principal liked Chelo and told her, "If your son is anything like you, your son is accepted." Chelo told her that her son was not like her, but the principal admitted Lorenzo on the spot without seeing his academic profile or interviewing him.

Lorenzo's acceptance into OLPH was the key requirement in order for us to consider the move back to the USA. Interestingly, we had made a trip in late August to Norway, and during part of the trip sailing from Trondheim to Bergen along the beautiful coast of Norway, passing by fjords, inlets and stopping in picturesque towns, we had time to talk about our future. We had decided during the Norway trip, that we needed to return to the USA in the future, but we would wait until the end of the academic year. The decision to return to the USA was based on several facts: (1) almost all our family lived in the USA; (2) our parents were becoming old and we wanted to spend time with them; (3) our granddaughter had been born recently; and very importantly (4) the USA offered many more educational choices for Lorenzo— Spain had essentially one choice, ASM.

In early October Jesús told his Alcatel boss, Manuel Gordillo, that he was going to leave the company and move to Maryland to work for Ciena. Chelo started to work the logistics of the move. She told the Maryland realtor to find a furnished apartment near OLPH and she started to research moving companies— the Spanish company that moved our car and belongings to Maryland did a superb packaging job, everything arrived perfectly including the car that passed the Maryland inspection immediately after it was delivered. Meanwhile, Jesús arranged to travel to many of the sites where he had responsibilities for engineering staff (Antwerp, Stuttgart, Hannover, Vimercate) to share a farewell dinner.[128] Chelo went to the town of Puente del Arzobispo, located near Talavera de la Reina, about two hours from our apartment at Prado de Somosaguas. This area of Spain is famous for ceramics and Chelo had visited and purchased items from there before; this time, she ordered ceramic pots and containers for her future kitchen in the USA.

The movers packed our belongings on Monday and Tuesday, October 28 and 29. On Tuesday afternoon, we drove the Mercedes Benz car to the moving company facilities and then drove the company Audi to Zaragoza. The next day we drove to Barcelona because Lorenzo had not been there. We spent two and one-half days there and drove back to Madrid on Friday, November 1.[129] We slept in a Madrid hotel near the Plaza de Santo Domingo, close to La Gran Via. On Saturday, we went to the airport, left the company car in the parking lot and boarded our flights to the USA.

Postscript about our years in Spain

We end this section of our memoirs noting two items about this portion of our lives. We start by saying that our years in Spain were a blessing. We learned about Europe, Lorenzo was in an excellent school with international classmates and friends. We saw a lot of

---

[128] The dinner in Milan with the Vimercate manager was very good and another learning experience. It was a white truffle dinner and unknown to Jesús they charged for the truffle separate from the rest of the dinner. The chef selected a truffle of a size to serve five people, weighed it and at the end of the meal we found out that the price of truffle alone was $550 … for a "mushroom!"

[129] We made the trip in four hours including stops, a 600 km journey. Thus, we averaged nearly 100 mph on the very limited access, very high quality Autopista A-2.

Spain and enjoyed many of their holiday feasts and commemorations (Moros & Cristianos, Fallas, Holy Week, San Fermín, San Isidro), traveled and got to see almost all of Spain— we missed only one region, the Balearic Islands. We enjoyed the culture of Spain especially the Zarzuelas (light operettas), ate very well all over Spain, began to learn about wine and champagne, met many persons and established wonderful friendships. We enjoyed bullfights at Las Ventas de Madrid and saw Real Madrid play futbol (soccer) at the Bernabeu Stadium. On top of all these things, we were able to save money because Jesús was on an expatriate package. It was a great experience and Lorenzo especially was unhappy to leave Spain— he had the best of both worlds with school sports and activities on the one hand, and on the other hand, Spanish friends in the apartment complex where we lived.

The second point is about God's assistance with the move to Maryland. As we noted, Jesús went to Washington for a meeting of the ACU (God's work), and by inspiration decided on Monday morning to call his friend Steve Chaddick. That call resulted in a visit and an offer from Ciena to move to Maryland. God's help is also obvious in how Chelo found a school for Lorenzo. She and the realtor had visited all the Catholic schools in her list when the realtor remembered the name of another school in the area, OLPH. The principal liked Chelo and admitted Lorenzo in the middle of the academic term. Coincidences, luck, random events. Absolutely not!

Book VI - Part II – Maryland 1996-2008

New job, new city, new school for Lorenzo

We arrived at Baltimore's airport (BWI) on Saturday night, November 2, 1996, carrying fourteen pieces of luggage with enough clothes for us to survive until the rest of our belongings arrived from Spain. We needed a rental car and a taxi to transport the luggage to our hotel, the Marriott Courtyard in Columbia. The next day, after Mass, Chelo called the apartment office and found out we could move into the apartment that day. We rented a three-bedroom furnished apartment at the Ashton Woods apartment complex in Ellicott City, near the OLPH School and Ciena. On Monday, Chelo took Lorenzo to school and Jesús started at Ciena as Vice President of Access Products. After a short introduction to Ciena, he began working in the definition of a new product for the metropolitan telecommunications market.

It took us a few weeks to adjust to Maryland, an adjustment that was worse for Lorenzo because he had to start in a new school in the middle of the academic term and he did not know anyone there. He had to win over his teachers who were not too happy about getting a new student in the middle of the term. The good news is that over the next few months, Lorenzo adjusted and was able to complete his seventh grade successfully. We tend to forget how many things one has to do when one moves. The tasks included changing addresses on all accounts, registering the car to obtain new license plates, getting new drivers licenses, opening bank accounts, finding out where the stores, groceries and churches are located. We needed a new car and also to keep the rental car until the Mercedes Benz arrived from Spain. We bought a Lexus ES300 for Chelo, an excellent car that was used later by Cordero and Cristy.

When our belongings arrived from Spain, we moved to an unfurnished second-floor apartment in another section of the same apartment complex. We rented covered outdoor parking places to protect our cars. We took care of most moving tasks during November and early December. Because winters are cold in Maryland, and because the Mercedes Benz car was diesel-powered and sat outside overnight, it was difficult to start the car on very cold days. For this reason, on many cold evenings Jesús ran an extension cord from the apartment to connect to the car's engine block heater to keep it warm so he could start the car in the morning.

In February of 1997, Ciena launched an IPO (Initial Public Offering) of its stock that allowed investors and employees to sell stock and this resulted in the creation of at least twenty millionaires at the company, some becoming very rich. Since Jesús had just arrived at the company, he was not able to benefit at that time, although in later years we were able to obtain financial benefits from Ciena's success.

In 1997, Jesús continued the new product development for the metro market, but Ciena did not have enough engineers to staff this project, so he participated in the identification and purchase of a company in Atlanta that brought more than a dozen engineers into the project. The new employees became part of the Ciena Atlanta office that started that year, the first company product development site outside of Maryland. As a result, Jesús started to make regular business trips to Atlanta and this gave him the opportunity to see Cristy, Francisco and Amy often.

Meanwhile, Chelo had started to look for houses in Maryland with the assistance of the realtor that she met during her first visit to the area. We saw a few houses, but did not like any, and we were surprised about the high cost of houses in Maryland compared to Atlanta. After a while, Chelo started to look at houses on her own, abandoning the help of the realtor, exploring subdivisions in different parts of Howard County, the county with the best school system in Maryland, just in case we were not able to place Lorenzo in a Catholic High School. She discovered in one of the villages of Columbia a street of "model homes," around ten houses located next to each other, where different builders displayed model homes and where one could discuss options and prices. We also looked at lots available where we could build a house. Chelo found one lot in a nice subdivision, Hobbit's Glen, but Jesús told her that the lot was so small that, "if someone sneezed in the house next door, we would hear it in our house." Chelo then showed Jesús a larger lot, about 1.3 acres, in the Forest Glen subdivision. Chelo was not to keen on building a more expensive house on a bigger lot stating, "I do not plan to retire in Maryland." Jesús replied, "I do not know how long I am going to live," and, "you are free to live wherever you want, but I will live in a house in this lot." We did buy the lot, found a floor plan we liked in one of the models homes, and we started working out the details of a contract with that particular builder. However, after a few meetings with this builder, we decided that we did not want them to build our home— they were disorganized and sloppy. Chelo had met another builder that she liked very much, The Williamsburg Group, and we approached them with our house plan ideas. We eventually signed an agreement with the Williamsburg Group who built our Maryland house in 1998.

During this same time, Chelo started researching Catholic high schools for Lorenzo who was scheduled to start high school in 1998. Her search was methodic and personal. She called several high schools to schedule personal visits to meet with the admission director, to learn what program the school offered to assist students who may need additional help, and to get a feel for the school. Many admissions director tried to persuade Chelo to wait until the school's open house, but she would have none of that. She wanted to establish a personal contact with school administrators and to be better informed about each school before the school's open house. Her research and school visits simplified our selection of schools. We should mention that part of the difficulty is that Baltimore has many Catholic high schools, for boys only and also coed— we remember visiting five or six schools. Lorenzo eventually applied, and was admitted to three schools.

The momentous event for our family in 1997 was the death of Argentina Marta Núñez Berro, Jesús' mother. In the aftermath of hurricane Andrew in 1992, Argentina was involved in a minor traffic accident, and she had x-rays taken that disclosed a number of lumps in her body. The oncologist told Argentina that she had a dormant cancer, "a sleeping lion," and that this cancer would one day rear its ugly face. The cancer woke up and Argentina submitted to a treatment that helped postpone the inevitable. In 1997, as the disease accelerated its hold on Argentina's health, the family decided to have a large reunion in August in Marco Island. It was a beautiful time for Argentina with all her children, grandchildren, her only great grandchild Alina, many nephews and close friends who went to Marco to spend all or part of the week with her. That week at Marco with Argentina started an annual family tradition, a week when we come together at that beach every year to honor her request to keep the family united. The week following Marco Island, Carmen Luisa organized a celebration of her parents' life at her house in Miami. These occasions were the last times we saw Argentina alive. She died on September 10, 1997, five days after the death of Mother Teresa of Calcutta. Chelo and Lorenzo flew from Maryland to Miami; Jesús was in England on business when Argentina died and flew back the next day to Miami to join the rest of the family for Argentina's funeral. Jesús gave the eulogy at the Mass and we remember the title of his talk, "Argentina Marta Núñez Berro, una mujer fuera de serie," which translate to, "Argentina a unique woman in a class of her own." That year's Christmas celebration was marked by her absence, but we all came to share together her legacy and inspiration.

The next year was quite interesting for the family in many ways. At Ciena, Jesús participated in high-level negotiations with Tellabs Corporation to plan the merger of the two companies, a merger announced in June that seemed perfect for both companies. However, as the companies were working through the merger plans, the merger was called off after a series of bizarre events. At the time, this seemed to be a catastrophe for Ciena, and could have meant the demise of the company except for the fact that the company had been managed conservatively and had enough cash on hand to survive the immediate future. For our family, the demise of the company would have been a major problem financially and professionally— we were finishing a house worth several hundred-thousand dollars, Lorenzo was about to start high school, Jesús would have to find a new job with the possibility of having to move the family one more time. As we said, none of this came to pass, but the company ended up reorganizing and refocusing its effort. In November, Jesús was promoted to Senior Vice President in charge of Engineering. In the end, the failed merger with Tellabs resulted in a better and stronger Ciena company, and provided better professional and financial rewards to Jesús.

In early August, Chelo went to Indianapolis to help with the anticipated birth of our second grandchild. On the morning of August 16, Alina came to Chelo's room and asked her, "Abi, where are my daddy and mommy?" Chelo did not know, but she peaked in the garage and noticed that a car was missing. Todd and Consuelo had gone to the hospital during the night but had not informed Chelo. Early that morning, Consuelo Beatriz had delivered a healthy boy, Ethan Daniel. Chelo stayed with Consuelo Beatriz to help with the new baby just like she did after the birth of Alina two years earlier. After Chelo left Indiana, Cristy came to help her sister. Three months later, on Sunday, November 1, the Feast of All Saints, Ethan was baptized at St. Malachi's Church in Brownsburg, Indiana, with Joel and Cristy as godparents for Ethan.

As we mentioned, Lorenzo started high school in September of 1998. Lorenzo applied to Mount St. Joseph High School in Baltimore, St. Vincent Pallotti High School in Laurel, and Archbishop Spalding High School in Severn, all about twenty to thirty minutes from our new home. Chelo was very much in favor of the coed Archbishop Spalding and this was the high school Lorenzo attended for four years. What a difference for Lorenzo to attend only one secondary school instead of having to adjust to four different elementary schools. Because Chelo wanted to insure that Lorenzo successfully completed his high school education, she spent lots of time helping him throughout the four years of high school. She read his school material before hand and summarized it, so she could review the subject matter with Lorenzo. Lorenzo completed every year of high school successfully. On the other hand, Chelo's effort and approach resulted in significant amounts of tension and arguments between her and Lorenzo, a situation that modified their relationship causing Lorenzo to be somewhat defensive about comments or suggestions from his mother. Reflecting on those years, Chelo regrets being Lorenzo's tutor during high school. It would have been better to hire a tutor for Lorenzo.

In late September, we moved into our new house at 11537 Manorstone Lane in Columbia, Maryland, a very nice house with an outstanding landscaping. The house sat on a good lot and with only one house in the adjacent plots of land; the front and right sides of the house bordered a nature's preserve and on the rear of the lot there was a golf course.

The house was a traditional brick two-story house with basement. It had a long driveway, and a gorgeous[130] backyard that featured a mahogany deck and a bridge over small waterfalls that poured into a small pond near the basement entrance. The sound of the water and the view of the back were magnificent. The house had five bedrooms, three-and-one-half baths and a large bonus room in the second story. In the first floor were the living, dining, family, breakfast, laundry, pantry and kitchen plus a very nice office with three large windows. Most of the basement was finished and included one bedroom, one full bath and an entertainment area with a bar. The basement also had access to the beautiful waterfalls and pond. The house had a three-car garage, and something new to us but typical in that part of the country, an entrance for service personnel.

---

[130] The house landscape won a competition and was featured on the front page of a local landscape association magazine.

In December, Jesús was selected as National President of the ACU at the annual meeting of its Board of Directors. This was the first of many years that Jesús helped direct the ACU. We ended the year, as we normally did, traveling to Miami to spend the Christmas holidays with the family.

Ciena grows again

Early during the year 1999, as part of its rebound after the failed merger with Tellabs, Ciena decided to buy and integrate two companies simultaneously, one in California and the other in Massachusetts. Jesús was responsible for the technical due diligence of the company in Massachusetts, a company that had designed a product for the telecom access market. The closing on the purchase of the companies occurred during the spring, and Ciena organized a meeting in mid July in Rhode Island to bring together the Ciena executives with the key team members from the two recently acquired companies to plan the future of the combined entities.

That summer we hosted Alfonso Pire, the son of our good friends from Madrid, Luis and María José. Alfonso spent more than a month with us and we took Alfonso with Lorenzo to see many sights in the Baltimore-Washington area. He also joined us in a trip to a wedding planned for Saturday, July 17, at Rocky Mount, North Carolina. Jesús attended the Ciena meeting in Rhode Island and planned to fly to Raleigh, about one hour drive from Rocky Mount, to join Chelo, Lorenzo and Alfonso, who had driven from Columbia, but there was a complication. After Jesús boarded a completely full airplane that was ready to depart from Providence to Raleigh, the captain announced that the brakes on the plane were not working. Needless to say, everyone got off the plane without much complaining even though this was a Friday afternoon and it would be difficult for everyone to complete his or her travel plans. Jesús had to fly that evening to Baltimore, get up very early the next morning, drive from Columbia to Washington DC to catch a flight from National Airport (now Reagan National Airport) to Raleigh. He then drove to Rocky Mount, changed into a suit and attended the wedding of Victor Tomás Sorondo, the son of our very close friends Victor and María. Our very good mutual friends Ignacio and Lourdes Abella traveled from Miami to the wedding also. It was a joyous occasion and we enjoyed spending time with our friends long after the reception was finished. Unfortunately for Jesús, he had to fly out early on Sunday morning to attend a Sunday meeting of Ciena executives with those of another company interested in discussing business-partnering opportunities. This business meeting was also unfortunate for Chelo because she had to drive by herself back to Columbia, and also unfortunate for Alfonso because they were not able to stop along the way in any of several potential tourist or historic locations.

Telecom Geneva was held in October, and because Jesús would attend the conference, we used the opportunity to plan a trip to Prague and the Czech Republic. While at the Telecom conference, Jesús was afflicted with an influenza virus and developed a high fever. He told Chelo that he needed medicines and she brought some with her and gave it to him when they met at the Prague airport. Jesús had booked a one-week stay at the Marriott Hotel in Prague using reward points and booked Chelo's airplane ticket using Delta reward points, and this made the trip very inexpensive. We loved Prague; it is a very romantic city that loves music— there were concerts every night in one of a number of old churches, churches that the communist government had closed down as places of worship and now were used for music concerts. We went to the Opera and paid less than US $30 each for two of the best tickets in the house. We walked the city and saw all major sites; our only disappointment was the very limited selection of gourmet restaurants, a limitation that we believe has been resolved since the time of our trip. We rented a car to see a little bit of the countryside and drove to the very picturesque city of Cesky Krumlow, stopping along the way in a couple of cities. On the way back to Prague we planned to sleep at a hotel along the way but we had a major problem trying to find the hotel because it was nighttime and dark (this was before GPS became available), and we did not speak one word of Czech. We remember stopping a couple on the street and using sign language and a few words, the couple gave us some general directions and eventually we found the hotel. The hotel was simple and clean and the rate was incredible— dinner, room with bath, and breakfast for less than US $50 for <u>both of us</u>. Granted, the dinner was not in a Michelin starred restaurant and the accommodations were simple, but for the price it was an excellent deal for us. In Prague, we did a little bit of shopping, buying twelve wine glasses from the famous Czech glass industry and then flew back to the USA.

We received one major upsetting announcement during the year 1999: Cristy informed us that she and Joel were getting a divorce. Any breakup of a marriage is a sad affair and it is very painful when the dissolution involves one of your children. On a more positive note, we traveled to Miami to join the rest of the family to celebrate Christmas, and then we returned to Maryland and drove to Roanoke, Virginia to join Consuelo, Todd, Alina, Ethan and Cristy in order to celebrate the arrival of the Year 2000. Consuelo Beatriz and her family had moved to Roanoke in order for Todd to accept a promotion opportunity at a plant in the city, and Consuelo had obtained permission to work remotely. The arrival of the Year 2000 had been a major concern to people in information system because most computers had been programmed using only two digits for the year, and with the zero-zero ending of the new year, some people worried there would be significant problems with computers. Thanks God all the preparation and work of the computer programmers resolved most the issues before the arrival of the New Year. We returned safely home on January 2.

Diabetes!

The year started very auspiciously for us because the price of Ciena stock had started to climb during the summer of 1999, and by the end of the year it had surpassed its all-time high. Jesús sold some of the shares he had received as an incentive and in January we paid off the mortgage on the Maryland house and ordered two new cars for us, a Mercedes E-320 for Chelo and a Mercedes S-500 for Jesús. During the year, thanks to the continued increase in the price of Ciena stock, we achieved the first rung of financial independence: we owned a house and two brand new cars, free and clear, had money in the bank, had a good amount of Ciena stock options, and our only debt was the small mortgage on the Miami house. Bless the Lord!

In the fall, Chelo and Cristy drove to Miami so Chelo could give her Lexus car to Cordero. Cordero was very happy to receive it and to drive such a nice car. In April Lorenzo, Chelo and Jesús spent a week in Buenos Aires, a great city although at the time somewhat expensive because Argentina had pegged their local currency to the US Dollar. We visited with Ruben and Silvia Montefalcone whom we had met while living in Spain and whose son Facundo was a friend of Lorenzo. We saw every site of importance in the city, danced the tango, and ate fabulous meals featuring great cuts of Argentina's beefs. This trip was also not expensive because we used Jesús' Delta and Marriott points to pay for air travel and hotel.

This was the year that we planned to inaugurate our specially built pig roast pit to celebrate with friends during the Memorial Day weekend. We had added to our backyard a large stone BBQ near the first and largest waterfall. Behind it we had built a pit for roasting Cuban style pigs. The pit was six feet long, three feet wide and three feet deep with a drain that allowed easy cleaning. And, once again, "Men proposes and God disposes."

In early May, on a Tuesday afternoon, Chelo received a very distressing call from Consuelo Beatriz. The doctors in Roanoke had diagnosed Alina with Type I diabetes. Alina had celebrated her fourth birthday in February and Consuelo Beatriz, shaken and traumatized by the news, called to tell us that Alina was in the hospital, and she needed support from her mother. Chelo called Jesús and told him, "I am going to Roanoke immediately." Jesús replied, "Be careful driving and control yourself— we do not need you to have an accident and end up with two people in the hospital." Chelo drove to Roanoke that afternoon and went directly to the hospital where Alina was a patient. She stayed with Alina and Consuelo Beatriz until Alina was released from the hospital five days later. Those five days were very difficult and trying. Consuelo Beatriz, Todd and the rest of the family had to oversee Alina's diabetes and practice how to give insulin injections. This was very hard, for Chelo but she was determined to learn because she wanted to be able to take good care of Alina. The nurse at the hospital taught Consuelo Beatriz and Chelo how to prepare the injection and both practiced using an orange.

The week Alina was hospitalized, we had planned to welcome and have dinner with Clay and Barbara Moore, good friends from

Atlanta, who had told us that they were going to come to the Washington/Baltimore area. Clay and Barbara did come by the house, and Lorenzo and Jesús took them to dinner to Tersiguel's, a French restaurant in Historical Ellicott City, and one of our favorites in the area. On Friday afternoon, Jesús picked up Lorenzo after school, drove to Roanoke, went to the hospital and spent time with Chelo, Consuelo Beatriz and Alina. Lorenzo and Jesús slept in a motel near the hospital because some of Todd's friends and their daughters were staying at Consuelo's house. We were home the following week after Alina was released from the hospital and CB was trained on how to handle her daughter's illness.

Alina's diabetes impacted the life of everyone in the family. It took a long time for us to learn how to handle Alina's diabetes. Needless to say, we canceled the pig roast that we planned for the Memorial Day weekend— we were not up to having any kind of party or celebration. Thanks God that Alina, Consuelo Beatriz, Ethan, Cristy, Lorenzo and the two of us have been able to learn to accept and make the most of our lives working with the limitations and scares that this disease causes. We are grateful that God gave Consuelo Beatriz the courage, strength and faith to watch over Alina's diabetes.

On the early morning of June 4, the Saturday before the annual SuperComm Exhibition and also the weekend before Lorenzo's final exams, Jesús flew to Fall River, Massachusetts to attend the ordination to the priesthood of his friend and ACU member Ramón Domínguez, Jr. This was a joyous occasion for the ACU and particularly for the ACU Washington Chapter. Chelo had set aside time during the weekend and the following week to review with Lorenzo for his finals exams. Lorenzo, however, was not cooperative with his mother, probably fed up with our pressure and the stress of the final exams. This was unfortunate for many reasons, first because it caused major stress to Chelo, and second because it forced Jesús to cancel his trip to Atlanta for SuperComm so that he could be at home and help with the studies and ameliorate the tension. We believe it is probable that the approach we took to support Lorenzo and his studies caused him to be turned off about education so that later he postponed further education for a while.

To Spain and a wedding

Our Washington ACU friend, Amando Madan, invited us to his wedding in León, Spain, to a grandniece of Father Llorente, and we made plans to go to the wedding and spend one week sightseeing in Spain. Lorenzo flew to Madrid early to spend a month with Alfonso Pire in his grandparent's house in Villaviciosa de Odón, about thirty minutes southwest from Madrid. Cristy, Chelo and Jesús flew to Spain and arranged to join Lorenzo and the Pire family for dinner at our favorite Madrid restaurant, El Landó.

We rented a car and the day after the dinner we started our sightseeing, driving first to the city of Soria and then to La Laguna Negra[131] nearby, a site we had wanted to see earlier but were not able to reach on a previous trip because of heavy snow. The first evening we slept in the town of Santo Domingo de Silos, home to a well-known Benedictine Monastery whose monks made Gregorian Chants famous, and whose abbey we visited that evening for vespers. The next day we drove north to the city of Hondarribia that is on the border with France on a river that flows to the Bay of Biscay. We stayed overnight in this small pretty city. The following day we went to San Sebastian to visit the city and eat at the famous Michelin three-stars restaurant, Arzak. We were welcomed by the daughter of the Chef, ate a great meal and drank very good wine, and all of this at a very reasonable price. We stayed at the fabulous Hotel Maria Cristina and had asked for a matrimonial bed, but the hotel did not have one ready for us, so when we arrived back from dinner we found a bottle of champagne and a plate of appetizers that the hotel provided to atone for the mix-up with the bed. Our next stop was at Bilbao to visit the Guggenheim Museum— the architecture of the building is fabulous, the exhibits less impressive. We then continued on our way to León. We did not have hotel reservations for that night and kept looking in at places to stay but were not happy with any. Finally, we stopped in a mediocre hotel near a natural park. The hotel was not

---

[131] We still wonder today why La Laguna Negra received three stars from the Michelin Green Guide. The place is pretty but we missed the exceptional, "deserves a special trip," attractiveness.

very good but the ride to the lookout point nearby was interesting and exciting as you go up a narrow road with no guardrails whatsoever. From this mountain peak we drove directly to León, arriving there on Friday afternoon, the day before the wedding.

We had reservations in León at the excellent Parador San Marcos, a beautiful Renaissance hotel rebuilt on the site of a monastery that was used to provide overnight accommodations to pilgrims on the way to Santiago de Compostela. Father Llorente's nephew was one of the persons in charge of the front desk, and he gave us excellent rooms. After settling into the rooms and refreshing ourselves, we went to the center of town, a pedestrian zone that includes the Cathedral of León, a masterpiece of Gothic style, and the site for Beatriz (Bea) and Amando's wedding the next night. While walking around the center of town, we ran into a group of friends and families of the groom and bride and spent the rest of the evening with them. The next day we had breakfast, did a little bit of sightseeing and returned to the hotel to dress up for the wedding.

The wedding started at eight that evening and was concelebrated by a couple of priests that were family of the bride. Afterwards, we went to the Club de Leones for the long and delightful reception that started with cocktails while we listened to typical music of the León area. The dinner was excellent with more food than what we could eat; then, there was a break for those who wanted to enjoy a Cuban cigar. At one in the morning the dance music started, and to our surprise it was a Cuban orchestra whose lead singer was from Holguín, Jesús' birthplace. We left the party around five in the morning because we had agreed to have lunch with Father Llorente the next day and we had to travel to Madrid after the lunch. We know the party continued until breakfast time. The next morning we went to Father Llorente's hometown of Mansilla Mayor, located about 14 miles south of the city of León, visited the house where he was born and saw his very own room. We had lunch, as guests of Father Llorente in a nearby restaurant, and then Father took us to visit Roman ruins near the area.

That afternoon we drove to Madrid, a three-hour trip, and stayed at the house of the Pire family. In the evening, we walked in the Castellana Avenue, and to our surprise, saw Sonia Guigou with her brother, sister-in-law and niece, at the Terraza Cristal. What a coincidence! The following morning we drove to the airport and flew back to the USA to return to our daily lives.

The Twin Towers are destroyed

When the year 2001 started, Lorenzo was enrolled in his junior year of high school, and Jesús was responsible for the Metro Transport Division of Ciena that required him to travel often to Atlanta where the division's engineers were designing the next generation metro transport product. Ciena had entered into an agreement to purchase Cyras Systems, a company in Silicon Valley that had developed a product that would complement the transport products of Ciena. The purchase was completed in March and by May it was clear to Ciena executives that they needed to take over the management of the division. Gary Smith, Ciena's CEO, asked Jesús to become the general manager of the new Metro Switching Division and also to continue to lead the Metro Transport Division. Jesús agreed to take over the new division with one condition, all the original founders of Cyras had to depart the day before Jesús became the Division President, a condition agreed to by Gary Smith.

Jesús arrived in Fremont, California, on August 15, 2001, and took over the division the following day. The first three months as the head of this group were the most difficult months that he had ever experienced in his professional life. On the one hand, he did not know anyone at the division and had no one with whom to unburden. On the other hand, the organization, culture and business practices of the division left a lot to be desired. The founders of the company had assigned managers and directors to certain functions who, in Jesús' opinion, were not the right persons. Jesús had to work very hard, under stressful circumstances, to reorganize the division, hire new persons to lead several of the functional areas, remove persons, gain the confidence of the employees, begin to change the culture of the division, complete a key new product development on time, and maintain the credibility of the few customers of the division. On top of that, he was living away from home and traveling to and from California to Baltimore every week. The combination of these factors increased Jesús' physical and emotional stress. This was the only time in his life when his professional job affected his home life. Both Chelo and Lorenzo complained to him during the first few months on the job that he was irascible and short-tempered and that his job was impacting family life. The good news is that about four months into the job the situation improved significantly thanks to the changes that Jesús made in the division.

Ciena rented a furnished two-bedroom apartment for Jesús in Milpitas, about four miles south of the Fremont division offices. The apartment was comfortable and it provided some constancy during his stays in California. Jesús traveled to California on Monday afternoons after Ciena's executive meeting, arriving at his apartment in the evening. He flew back to Maryland on Fridays arriving home also in the evening. The travel time to California was long because the flight times exceeded five hours, and because he had to make connections, initially in Cincinnati and later in Atlanta. The other problem with Jesús' schedule was the three hours time difference between Maryland and California. Jesús decided, after a few weeks, to maintain his body in the Eastern Time Zone instead of trying to adjust twice a week to different time zones. For this reason, while in California, Jesús woke up at four in the morning, exercised, shaved and showered, ate breakfast and went to the office very early, going to Mass at seven in the morning. Jesús ate an early dinner and tried to be in bed around nine in the evening.

That summer, the son of Jesús' cousin Bertha Núñez Kavanagh, Owen-Miguel, arrived at the US Naval Academy in Annapolis, Maryland, a forty-five minute drive from our house in Columbia. During the first six weeks, "Plebe Summer," he had major restrictions on what he could do. The restrictions were relaxed a little bit when the academic year began, but for the first year, he was not allowed to travel outside a twenty-mile radius from the Academy without special permission. We saw Owen-Miguel for the first time at the Navy-Georgia Tech football game on September 8, and after the game he joined us for dinner at a seafood restaurant not far from Annapolis. Two days later, Jesús flew to California arriving at his apartment about two AM Eastern Time on the morning of September 11, 2001.

The next morning he was awakened by Chelo who called to tell him about the terrorist attack to the Twin Towers and to the Pentagon. The event left a permanent scar in the psyche of the American people. This event resulted in important changes to our behavior and thinking, changes that continue to impact us after the terrorist attack. For example, Jesús had the responsibility to lead and motivate his employees through the trauma of the moment and to remind the employees that not all Muslims were terrorists. This was very important because the employee population in this division included many persons from countries with large Muslim populations. On the other hand, Jesús was stuck in California for an undetermined period of time because the US Government grounded all civilian airplanes after the terrorist attack. Jesús had his Maryland doctor call his prescriptions to a Milpitas pharmacy because he did not know when he was going to depart from California. Ciena was a very caring company that worried about how to return home those employees that had traveled for business. They leased a small airplane to pick employees from Mexico and leased one-half of a larger plane to fly employees to the East Coast from the Oakland Airport. It turned out that Jesús was able to leave on the first commercial flight that departed from San Jose Airport after 9/11— he had reservations on the morning Delta flight to Atlanta because it was part of his regularly scheduled travel back home every week. The flight left San Jose Airport two hours late and the connecting flight from Atlanta to Baltimore was also delayed because they were missing one flight attendant— part of the turmoil of that week.

The terrorist attack made air travel more difficult everywhere in the world. On the one hand, immediately after the attack lots of people cancelled their air travel plans. Jesús remembers that during the first few weeks after 9/11, the tourist section of the airplane was almost empty while the first class section was full— many businesspersons continued to fly but leisure passengers decide to postpone their travel. This resulted in the cancellation of many flights, affecting most air travel. Thus, we did not attend Roberto Daniel Vich's wedding in October in Miami because the airline cancelled Chelo's flight. Over time, airlines reinstated some of the flights that were cancelled after the terrorist attack. Another inconvenience caused by the terrorist attack was the need to arrive at the airports one and one-half hours before the flight departed, much earlier than before the attack, in order to comply with the new security measures. Finally, the attack changed our perception of our overall safety in a world full of people willing to kill innocent civilians for some fanatical reason.

Jesús did not stop flying to California after the terrorist attack, stating, "Terrorist are not going to control my life. I will go on flying and working." However, the reduction in the number of flights and the tighter security impacted his travel life.

In November, Jesús was inducted into the Georgia Tech College of Engineering's Academy of Distinguished Engineering Alumni at a banquet in Atlanta attended by Chelo and Consuelo Beatriz. We sat at a table with Steve and Barbara Chaddick and fellow inductee Steve Alexander of Ciena.

A dramatic year!

The beginning of every New Year brings anticipation and hope to almost everyone and so was the start of 2002 for us, especially with the prospect of Lorenzo graduation from high school. The year was to bring us a bad surprise, a mysterious illness that landed Jesús in the Intensive Care Unit, ICU, of Miami's Mercy Hospital.

Early in the year, Ciena decided to acquire another company in Silicon Valley, ONI Systems, a company that has a successful product for the Metropolitan Transport business segment. The decision was the consequence, in part, of the bursting of the Internet bubble with a corresponding major downturn in the telecom business. The downturn in the business that began in 2002 was the beginning of a four-year difficult period for many telecommunication suppliers such as Ciena. The idea of the merger was to consolidate two companies so that by joining forces the combined entity would have a stronger market presence and reduced expenses. Jesús was asked to be the lead integrator of ONI Systems into Ciena, a process that extended Jesús' almost full-time stay in California through most of 2002. ONI Systems had built a very extensive campus in South San Jose, and Ciena moved its two other Silicon Valley divisions from Fremont and Cupertino to the South San Jose facilities.

Integrating the two companies required some difficult decisions that impacted personnel at both companies; one was stopping the work on one major project at each of the companies, and a second was the reduction of personnel in common functions such as accounting, legal and human resources. Unfortunately, this was also the beginning of the industry slow down due to the Internet bubble burst, and as a result, Ciena laid off hundreds of employees including many engineers. Jesús had the painful job of informing many of the engineers that the reduction in the business required Ciena to dismiss them. Jesús said that this was the most difficult job for an executive— dismissing good employees not because of their performance but because the company's income was significantly reduced as a result of market conditions.

Jesús continued to travel to California almost every week until the end of the summer when he was able to space the trips a little bit. In the spring, Lorenzo asked a girl to be his date for the Senior Prom, a party that was held at a hotel in the Inner Harbor of Baltimore. Jesús drove Lorenzo to and from the prom. A few weeks later, Lorenzo graduated from Archbishop Spalding High School in a beautiful ceremony held at the Cathedral of Mary Our Queen. Cordero came from Atlanta for the ceremony and Owen-Miguel also attended since he stayed with us for a few days that week.

Lorenzo had told us that after high school he did not want to continue studying but wanted to work. Lorenzo applied to several positions and was hired as an associate at the Lord & Taylor store in the Columbia Mall, and worked in the women's shoe department. We bought Lorenzo a Honda Civic to facilitate his transportation— Jesús had taught him to drive during the weekends. Since Lorenzo had a car and a job, we had more flexibility and decided that Chelo would go to California with Jesús after SuperComm to spend a week there before going to Miami for Jesús' niece Maricarmen Trujillo's wedding, a celebration planned for June 22. We traveled to Atlanta the weekend of June 1 and stayed there until Sunday June 9, and while Jesús worked at the exhibition, Chelo visited with friends in Atlanta and with Cristy.

Jesús began to notice some weakness in his legs during the SuperComm Exhibition, and on Sunday he stayed after the IHM Mass in Atlanta to receive the Sacrament of the Anointing of the Sick.

Chelo and Cristy were somewhat taken aback by this, but Jesús only said that this was a good Sacrament to receive.[132]

That evening we took a flight from Atlanta to San Francisco, a five-hour flight during which Jesús did not get up from his seat. Jesús was fine during the flight, but upon landing he could hardly move or bring down the carry-on luggage from the overhead storage bins. He had pain in the arms and in the legs and had to shuffle slowly through the airport to the car rental buses. The pain continued during the trip to the apartment in Milpitas, and particularly as he brought the luggage up to the third-floor apartment unit. The next morning, Jesús took two Ibuprofen pills and called his Maryland doctor. After explaining the symptom and telling the doctor that the Ibuprofen had reduced his pains, Dr. Sack prescribed a higher dose Ibuprofen and told Jesús that he was going to be out of town the following week and would not be able to see him.

Jesús was able to function reasonably well although not pain free for the next three days. On Friday, we started a weekend trip along the Pacific Coast via the Big Sur to Santa Barbara, then to Los Angeles to fly back to Atlanta. Chelo drove most of the way as Jesús had some pain even though he was taking two 600-mg Ibuprofen pills two or three times a day. The drive along this route is beautiful and we took the time to enjoy it. We stopped for dinner and overnight in the town of Morro Bay on Friday and went on to Santa Barbara on Saturday. In Santa Barbara, we had dinner with Ciena colleague Bob Craven and his wife at an Italian restaurant (great zabaglione with berries). The next morning we went to Mass and while eating breakfast called Dr. Manny Antón to ask for his opinion on Jesús' problem. He told Jesús to stop taking Lipitor, a drug known for causing muscle pains. We drove to the LAX airport, experiencing a major Los Angeles traffic jam even though it was a Sunday, and barely made our flight to return to Maryland.

---

[132] This was the second time he received this Sacrament. The first time it was in Philadelphia when he had meningitis and the Sacrament was called "Extreme Unction," and was only given, at the time, to people who were very sick or near death.

Chelo flew to Miami early in the week and Jesús planned to fly on Thursday to attend the wedding of Jesús' niece Maricarmen, and then to go on to Marco Island for our annual beach vacation. When Jesús' flight arrived in Miami, he experienced the same symptoms that he had upon arrival in San Francisco. Worse, on Friday morning Jesús could hardly walk— Chelo had to help him shower and Chelo and Lorenzo had to dress him. Manny Antón had arranged an appointment with Dr. Carlos Moas, a friend and ACU member doctor at Mercy Hospital. Unfortunately, Carlos had left on vacation so the Antón's got us an appointment with Dr. Raúl Moas, Carlos' brother. Raúl Moas examined Jesús and sent him to see a neurologist, Dr. Eduardo Ibarra. Back in Raúl Moas' office, the doctor told us that Jesús needed to go to the hospital, but Jesús protested that he came to Miami for his niece's wedding. Dr. Moas told Jesús that he was not going to the wedding but to the hospital because he was very sick and read the possible diseases that he could have: a tumor in the Cervix, Lou Gehrig's Disease, Cancer, Multiple Sclerosis or Lupus. What an awful repertoire! Jesús' reaction was to tell the doctor, "I think I should skip the hospital and go directly to the funeral home; this will save the family a lot of pain and money." "Naturally," as Lou Costello said in their famous "Who's on First" routine, we did not skip the hospital; Jesús went directly to the Emergency Room to have an MRI to determine whether or not he had a tumor in the Cervix— he did not.

Jesús was admitted into Mercy Hospital and placed in the Intensive Care Unit, ICU, the second time he was seriously sick in the United States. The first time in Philadelphia was in 1961, when he had meningitis. In Philadelphia, Jesús was in the indigent ward and in isolation for three out of the four weeks of his hospital stay due to the danger of contagion; then, his only immediate family in town was one brother and a few cousins, his only visitors were his cousin Leticia, bless her soul, and a priest who came to administer the last rites of the Catholic Church. One major difference at Mercy Hospital is that the doctors did not know what was ailing him; Manny had told us that they were going to use "differential diagnosis" to eliminate potential diseases. A second major difference with this sickness was that Jesús was surrounded by family with Chelo, our children, his siblings, cousins and others. He was visited in his room at least once a day by Manny Antón, at the time Senior Vice President and Chief Medical Officer of the hospital, who besides being a very competent doctor was close family, and also by Sister Elizabeth Worley SSJ, Chair of the Board of Trustees of the hospital. Among the many visitors at the hospital were Father Amando Llorente SJ, and many family and friends.

The Friday evening when he was admitted to the hospital, many family members came to the hospital after the rehearsal dinner to visit Jesús. Sometimes during that night, Dr. Ibarra, who was obviously researching the illness, called the hospital and requested that the nurse on duty start giving him Prednisone. Although the doctor did not know what was Jesús' illness, this drug worked very well so that by Saturday night Jesús was feeling a lot better. In fact, so much better that he told Consuelo Beatriz, Cristy and Lorenzo to go to Marco Island the next day and enjoy the beach stating, "Your mother has no choice and has to stay here; you, on the other hand, cannot do much if you stay, and we have already paid for the condominium. So, go ahead, go to the beach, we will give you daily updates of my situation." By Monday Jesús was in a regular room and the doctors were doing many tests to try to determine what caused his problems: spinal taps, bone cancer testing, X-Rays, and other tests. The six days Jesús spent at Mercy Hospital were a roller coaster of emotions for us with successive spurts of good news, no news and bad news. One of the distressing events began right after the bone cancer testing, when the nurse who conducted the test asked Jesús if he had broken his right collar bone before because the test "showed something hot" in the right shoulder. When Jesús told Manny what the nurse had said, Manny stated, "Now I am worried." Well, then we were also worried and we requested X-Rays of the shoulder area to look at the problem. It turned out that Jesús did not have cancer but the nurse had noticed something that was a different issue.[133] Jesús was released from the hospital on Thursday feeling fine and with a prescription for him to continue to take Prednisone. However, when Jesús left the hospital,

---

[133] We found months later that Jesús had Paget's disease of bone in his right shoulder bone.

the doctors were not able to give him a definite diagnosis of his illness— we had to wait until our return to Maryland for a diagnosis.

We arrived at the beach on Thursday, and because we had rented the condominium for two weeks, were able to enjoy ten days of vacation time, a vacation that came just in time after the ordeal of the hospital. When we returned to Maryland, Jesús went to see his doctor at Johns Hopkins, who after a couple of weeks referred Jesús to another doctor, Dr. William Schlott whose specialty was "complex diagnostics." Doctor Schlott asked Jesús a few questions and diagnosed the illness: "You have PMR, Polymyalgia Rheumatica,[134] and you need to see a rheumatologist, you should see Dr. John A. Flynn." Dr. Flynn was not only a rheumatologist but had a couple of specialties including internal medicine, had an MBA and was a professor of medicine at the Johns Hopkins University. Dr. Flynn helped Jesús understand the disease and reduced the Prednisone dosage slowly. PMR is a strange disease that has no known cure. The only way to determine if you are cured is for the patient to slowly reduce the amount of Prednisone taken and monitor the symptoms of the disease— if the symptoms return, then the patient must increase the dose and wait a few more weeks before repeating the treatment program. In two-thirds of the cases, the symptoms disappear; in about one-third of the cases, the symptoms continue for life. Jesús followed the treatment program until the following May when PMR departed his body for seven years. Dr. Flynn became Jesús' doctor while we lived in Maryland, and in addition to being an excellent doctor with a good sense of humor, he was easily reachable for telephone consultations during thirty-minute periods at least once a week.

Dr. Schlott remembered Jesús story about the nurse at Mercy Hospital who mentioned that his bone cancer test "showed something hot" in his right shoulder and decided to check this via a series of X-Rays of his body, and this is when he determined that Jesús had

---

[134] See the American College of Rheumatology Website for information on this disease.

Paget's disease of bone.[135] Dr. Schlott told Jesús he did not have to worry about this disease until he started experiencing pain in the shoulder.

Trouble in Cleveland

The year 2003 would have been unexceptional for our family[136] except for the deterioration during the year in the relationship between Consuelo and Todd. This was the year that Lorenzo stopped working full time at Lord & Taylor and returned to school at the Howard County Community College. We went to Marco Island in June and to Miami in May to celebrate our goddaughter Gigi Antón's First Communion. Jesús had reduced the frequency of his trips to California when, in April, Ciena announced the acquisition of Wavesmith Networks, located in Acton, MA, near Boston. Jesús was Ciena's chief integrator of new companies and he traveled almost every week for the next six months to Acton. During the fall of this year, it became clearer to us that all was not well in the Bills household, and this became more obvious in December. We flew back from Miami right after Christmas planning to celebrate the New Year with our children, grandchildren and Todd. Consuelo and Todd had moved to the Cleveland area because AT&T could not legally employ her in Virginia since the company was not registered there. Todd did come to our house for the New Year but it took a good bit of cajoling and for us to pay for his plane ticket, and while there it was clear that he was not very happy.

The next month, January 2004, per Consuelo's request, Lorenzo went to Cleveland to spend a few days with her and the kids. Lorenzo noticed Todd's absence from the house but he did not mention it to us. In the spring, we went to Ohio to attend Alina and Ethan's games. We were supposed to go directly to Alina's game, but

---

[135] One of the characteristics of his disease is an abnormal level of Alkaline Phosphate Level in blood testing.

[136] This was not the case for the rest of the world that lived through the Space Shuttle Columbia disaster, the invasion of Iraq and the blackout in the northeast of the USA and Canada that year.

because of traffic delays on the road, we went directly to Consuelo's house. There was no one at the house when we arrived and we went up to the guest room. To our surprise, we found all of Consuelo's clothes in that room— this was a sign to us that something was wrong. A few minutes later, Consuelo arrived with Alina and Ethan. Consuelo informed us that Todd had moved out of the house and taken their master bedroom furniture with him. This was somewhat of a shock to us. It turns out that Cristy was the only one who knew that Todd had left the house. Cristy told Consuelo to inform us about the situation, but Consuelo did not know how to tell us. This was a very traumatic, sad and difficult period in Consuelo's life. She had wanted her marriage to last forever— her convictions and commitments were solid. Seeing our daughter suffer was extremely hard for us.

In May, Alina received her First Communion, a very important event, so Cristy, Chelo, Lorenzo, Alexandra and Jesús traveled to Wadsworth, Ohio. The occasion was joyous, but we continued to notice that there were problems in the Bills' marriage. Consuelo was making every effort to hold her marriage together, but as the saying goes, "it takes two to Tango," and the marriage relationship kept crumbling throughout the year. Consuelo and Todd sold their house and Consuelo and the children moved to a rental house. Consuelo's idea was to keep the children near to Todd and to continue trying to save her marriage.

Meanwhile, in February Ciena announced that it would purchase two companies simultaneously, one in New Jersey, Internet Photonics, and one outside Ottawa, Canada, Catena Networks. Catena, was the second company purchased by Ciena in the Kanata suburb of Ottawa, the first one was a very small company of twenty plus employees, Akara Corporation. Jesús had led the integration of Akara into Ciena and now he had to manage the integration of two geographically and culturally different companies at the same time. This was not an easy task and it required Jesús to spend most of every week's time in either New Jersey or Ottawa.

Jesús' niece Helena organized a family reunion at our Maryland house for the 2004 Memorial Day weekend. We had eighteen guests in our house in addition to Lorenzo and us[137] and we had a great time. The out-of-town people saw some of the sights in Baltimore and Washington, and Consuelo, Cristy and Jesús took time to discuss Consuelo's marriage situation and the options available to her. In October, we went to Ohio for Grandparent's day at Ethan and Alina's school. It was a difficult trip for us, we had a long conversation with Consuelo and Todd, and it was clear that their marriage relationship was in very bad shape.

At about the same time, Jesús' father Rigoberto became very sick and was hospitalized. We flew to Miami, Chelo from Maryland and Jesús from Madrid, Spain where he was working on a project. After a week in Miami, we returned to Maryland and Madrid, and a number of days later, on November 23, Rigoberto died. Jesús flew from Madrid and Chelo and Lorenzo from Maryland. Because this was the day before Thanksgiving, flights were completely booked; Jesús had a higher priority ticket and was able to make an easy connection but Chelo and Lorenzo had to wait for a later flight. Father Llorente celebrated the funeral Mass for Rigoberto at St Timothy's Church and we buried Rigoberto next to Argentina.

Consuelo Beatriz moves to Atlanta

After almost two years of effort to try to save her marriage, Consuelo Beatriz's marriage was dissolved legally in 2005, and a few years later she received an annulment. Consuelo Beatriz contacted us to discuss potential places where she could move with her children to be close to family while maximizing her professional career with AT&T. After considering Miami and Baltimore, she decided to move to Atlanta, a very wise move, since she was raised there, had many friends in the city, and very especially, her sister Cristy lived there. Cristy suggested that Consuelo move temporarily into her house until she could find a place of her own, and Consuelo organized the move once the school term was completed. Jesús bought a movie player to entertain Alina and Ethan during the long drive to Atlanta and he

---

[137] Javi & Ginny; Alexandra, Juanjo and his mother Elda; Juanqui, Helena, Samantha and Jonathan; Francisco; Cristy; Consuelo, Alina and Ethan; Camelia and Maricarmen; Owen-Miguel and his girlfriend Amy Kiesling.

flew to Cleveland to help with their move. Consuelo drove her station wagon with the two dogs, German Shepherds Zeke and Hanna, and Jesús drove Consuelo's Audi A6 with the two children. Cristy prepared a welcome meal— Jesús asked her to buy a good red wine for the dinner. Consuelo, Alina and Ethan began preparation for a new life in Atlanta. Alina and Ethan started IHM School, in fourth and second grades, respectively, in August of 2005.

We saw Consuelo, Cristy, Alina and Ethan in Atlanta, Marco Island and Miami that year and we were satisfied that Consuelo and the children were adjusting to Atlanta and school. One result of Alina and Ethan's stay in Cristy's house was their request to move to one common house instead of separate houses for Cristy and Consuelo Beatriz. With Chelo's help, Cristy and Consuelo started to look for a house that would suit the four of them and be located closer to IHM.

In early 2006, Chelo found a house near La Vista Road that met Consuelo and Cristy's needs and approvals, a house with three levels— the top level for the Bills family, the bottom level for Cristy and the middle level a common area with the living room, dining room and kitchen. This house was only a few minutes from IHM. This was the year that Ethan made his First Communion, on May 13, and in June we went together as a family on a pilgrimage to Lourdes.

We had wanted to take Consuelo Beatriz to Lourdes to give thanks for the miracle that Our Lady of Lourdes performed on her throat when she was a child and that we related earlier in these memoirs. We traveled to Paris in three groups. Chelo and Jesús went to Madrid first because Jesús had business there. Jesús used Delta points to fly the rest of the family: Consuelo, Alina and Ethan who flew directly from Atlanta to Paris while Cristy and Lorenzo spent several days in Rome before coming to Paris. Jesús used Starwood points to pay for the Paris hotel rooms at the Meridian Etoile.

We visited many of the wonderful sites of the city: The Eiffel Tower, Les Invalides, Notre Dame, Sacre Cour, the Pantheon, the Luxembourg Gardens where Ethan played with a small boat in the fountain, the Ile Saint-Louis and many others. Consuelo, Cristy and Lorenzo went to the Louvre Museum while we took Alina and Ethan to the Paris Disney Park. Ethan loved the Metro and renamed some of the stations: Porte Maillot became "Post Office," Clemenceau "Clemensuchi," and so on.

Cristy and Loro spent three days and the rest of us four days in Paris, and then we drove on a rented van to Lourdes. The first night at Lourdes we could not participate in the candlelight Rosary procession because of a major downpour, although we joined in prayer from our hotel room. The second day we went to the baths, confession, the service for the sick and the candlelight procession. It was a unique experience for all, one that we strongly recommend to all Catholics. The following day we drove back to Paris. During the drive back to Paris, Chelo, Alina and the others played in the van making lots of noise with Consuelo Beatriz making noises that sounded like a pig; after a while, Jesús had enough of this and asked them to be quiet. At Paris, we picked part of our luggage from the hotel storage, went to dinner and almost got lost on the way to the airport. We slept, with Starwood points, at a Sheraton at the airport before flying back home. The morning of the flight homes, Lorenzo almost lost his flight in Paris because of his lateness leaving the hotel and Consuelo Beatriz's rush to get to the flight; the worse part was that Consuelo had Lorenzo's passport. Jesús had to get up— Chelo and Jesús were in a different flight— to help Lorenzo find the appropriate check-in area for his flight.

That summer Lorenzo went to México for the first time and stayed at his friend Carlos Guzmán's house in Cuernavaca. Lorenzo had met and become friends in Maryland with Carlos, a teacher from a Cuernavaca university that had a joint program with the Howard County Community College. Lorenzo made a second trip to México in the summer of 2008.

When we visited Miami after Marco Island, Chelo noticed that Cordero was not eating well and decided to bring him to our house in Maryland. Cordero enjoyed spending time with us because he was with Chelo, the love of his life, and with his grandson Lorenzo. Second, because he had more freedom at our house; and, finally, because Chelo cooked his favorite dishes and attended to his needs. During his first few weeks with us, he ate well, gained a few pounds and enjoyed a cigar with Jesús from time to time. Everything was fine until Sunday, August 20, when he started to have problems walking and going up the steps to the Church of St Jude in Baltimore. Vicente and Bertica came to spend a couple of days with Cordero and us, and Vicentico and Nancy joined them on Saturday, August 26, to help us celebrate our thirty-ninth wedding anniversary, a celebration planned to include an excellent meal and two bottles of great wine. Cordero was not feeling well in the morning and we ended up taking him to the emergency room at the Howard County General Hospital. We ate our anniversary meal in shifts. Cordero was admitted to the hospital and stayed there three nights, nights that required Vicente or Jesús to stay with him in order to translate information between him and the hospital staff. The doctors determined that Cordero had fluid in his lung, a sign that he could have a cancerous tumor. Chelo decided to take him to Miami to continue his treatment. The Maryland doctors advised Cordero not to fly in his condition, so Chelo enlisted the help of Vicente and Bertica to drive Cordero to Miami, a trip they made during the Labor Day weekend. They drove from Maryland to Columbia, South Carolina, stayed overnight at Estela and John Long's house, and then went on to Miami the next day. In Miami, Chelo took him to his doctor who stabilized him although it was clear that he was very sick.

On November 1, the Feast of All Saints, Cordero was admitted to Mercy Hospital and Jesús flew to Miami to help. His doctors at Mercy included ACU members Carlos Moas, pulmonary specialist, and Glen Barquet, cardiologist. We also saw Manny Antón, CEO of Mercy, regularly while Cordero was a patient. Jesús normally stayed overnight with Cordero, and Chelo was there during the day. Jesús almost went to Spain for a one-day business meeting leaving on Monday, November 13, but while waiting for his connection in Atlanta, Chelo informed him that Cordero would probably died in a matter of hours and Jesús decided to return to Miami. Through Cordero's illness in Miami, Chelo stayed with her beloved father. Cordero had always said to Chelo that he had asked God she would be with him the last days of his life, and God granted his wish. Chelo was at his side when Cordero died on Wednesday, November 15, the day of his mother's birthday. Another gift that Cordero experienced was the peace he had during the last days of his life and he was ready to join his family in heaven, especially his mother and younger brother Nano. Chelo will never forget his last words, "I have loved much and I have also received a lot of love." What a beautiful way to summarize his life.

Fathers Amando Llorente and Nelson García concelebrated Cordero's funeral Mass at the Mission Church of St Francis and St Clare near the ACU headquarters. Cordero, like Rigoberto, died a few days before the Thanksgiving holiday weekend, and the whole family stayed in Miami for Thanksgiving. Cordero's death was very sad for Chelo because they had a very special relationship. Chelo knew that he would always be missed but that his love would always be with her. We will always remember his dear words, his mannerism and gestures, his love for baseball, Cuba and his family. His grandchildren were his great treasures: "Nona, la gordita and Lorenzo." He was in a class by himself as a grandfather, very lovable and sweet. When Lorenzo was little he could not say "abuelo" and called him "Bo." Cordero loved this nickname and it became the name his grandchildren used to call him.

Horseback accident

Ciena held sales meeting every year, generally in November, the beginning of its fiscal year. Most of these meetings were held in warm weather locations such as Aventura, just north of Miami. In 2005 and 2006, the Ciena sales meetings were held at the Fairmont Resort near Scottsdale, Arizona. One feature of these meetings was the availability of recreation activities— golf, tennis, sun and sea bathing at the beach in Florida, horseback riding in Arizona. At the 2005 meeting in Arizona, Jesús selected the horseback riding activity since he has always loved riding horses and he is a very experienced rider. At the stables, the lady who was adjusting the stirrups of his Australian saddle decided to remove two sleeves that she believed were unnecessary— she was wrong! Near the end of the trail, while Jesús' horse was trotting, the right stirrup fell causing Jesús to fall. He hit his head on the hard Arizona clay, lost consciousness temporarily and bruised his right arm. Because he had lost consciousness, as a precaution, Jesús asked to be taken to a hospital to be checked. He was taken to the Mayo Clinic in Phoenix where he underwent CAT scans of the head and the neck. The good news, according to a young doctor was that, "we checked your head and found nothing." The hospital tended to his bruises and the doctor prescribed a strong pain medication, telling Jesús, "You will be in serious pain today and tomorrow." Jesús took one-half of the pain medication before going to bed that night and the other half in the middle of the night, but did not take more of this strong drug. One of the consequences of this incident was that later in the year Jesús injured the rotator cuff in his right shoulder, a problem that recurred several times during the following years.

Later that year, Ciena asked Jesús to stay with the company for another two years and gave him an incentive Ciena stock package. Part of the agreement included allowing Jesús to move to Atlanta, and we started preparing to sell our Maryland house. Jesús continued to travel extensively until his retirement with monthly trips to Atlanta (later Baltimore when we moved to Atlanta), Ottawa, and Boston; three annual trips to Spain; twice a year to India; assorted trips to Spokane, Washington, to Chile, to San Jose, California, and the city hosting SuperComm on June each year.

We ended the year 2006 with another funeral— Andy López of Atlanta, a friend of many years died on Christmas Day and we went to Atlanta for the funeral. Jesús was one of the speakers that gave part of the eulogy for Andy's life.

We bid farewell to Maryland

In early 2007, on a Tuesday evening[138] Jesús was at the Baltimore Airport ready to fly to Manchester, New Hampshire, to visit the Ciena engineering offices in Massachusetts, when Jesús felt unwell. He could not tell what it was, he just did not feel well, and as he approached the departure gate, he decided to cancel his trip and return home. This was the only time in Jesús' career that he felt like this and cancelled a trip. That night it snowed in Columbia so early the next morning, Lorenzo and Jesús removed the snow from the driveway and walkway to the house. Chelo left the house that morning to do some errands and Jesús stayed home and joined via conference call the meeting he had planned to attend in Massachusetts. That same morning, Lorenzo had an eye appointment in Clarksville, about three miles from our house. On the way to the Columbia Family Eye

---

[138] Probably February 14 when Columbia received almost one inch of snow.

Care's office, on a road cleared by the snowplows, Lorenzo's car went over a patch of black ice, skidded out of control and hit a power company pole. The air bag deployed and saved his life, but he suffered a concussion. Lorenzo called home and told Jesús what had happened. Jesús went directly to the scene of the accident and found the police and an ambulance there. Lorenzo's car was totaled and the power pole had to be replaced later, at our insurance's cost. Lorenzo was taken to the Howard County General Hospital, the hospital where Cordero was a patient a few months earlier. The policeman, of Hispanic background, told Jesús that Lorenzo had been speeding, but that he was not going to give him a citation because "he has probably learned a lesson." At the hospital and for several hours afterwards, Lorenzo demonstrated all the symptoms of a concussion: he did not, and still does not remember the accident, he did not know that he had called Jesús, saying things like, "What will Bo say when he hears about this?" Thanks God that by the end of the day he was essentially back to normal. One point worth noting is the fact that Jesús had canceled his trip the night before. He had never before or afterwards cancelled a trip. He had no illness that we could detect or determine on Tuesday night or later; yet he came home and was at home available to assist with this problem. Was it a premonition? Why and how? We, who have seen the hand of God often in our lives, are convinced that He gave Jesús symptoms that resulted in his returning home from the airport.

Since Loro's car was a total loss, we had to purchase another car for him so he could continue his studies. That spring we put the Maryland house on the market and Chelo started to look for a house in Atlanta with the assistance of our friend Margarita Bolet. Jesús had defined the area of Atlanta that he thought was optimal for us: a section of northwest Atlanta roughly bordered by the I-285 perimeter highway on the north, by Peachtree Dunwoody Road on the east and by Northside Drive on the west. The reason for selecting this location was to minimize the driving time: less than twenty minutes to Ciena's office; about twenty-five minutes to the airport; about twenty minutes to Consuelo Beatriz and Cristy's house; and NO NEED TO GET ON I-285!

Chelo selected several houses for a second look and for Jesús to check out. We found one that we liked and that met most of our requirements; however, we would have to add a room for Lorenzo in the basement. We had the house appraised and made an offer. After a couple of round of negotiations and the inflexibility of the owners, Jesús decided to disregard the house. Chelo continued to look for houses and also for potential lots where we could build a house. We looked at a couple of promising lots and asked our builder friend, Walter Chewning, who had built our previous Atlanta houses, for his opinion.

In one of her trips to Atlanta, Chelo saw a lot with a for sale sign in a very desirable neighborhood, and she decided to call the telephone number listed in the sign and talked to the owner of the lot, Dr. David Finkelman.[139] He informed her that they already had a contract to sell the lot. However, Chelo asked David Finkelman to take her name and phone number just in case the contract did not work out. Several weeks later, he called to tell us that the contract on the lot was to be cancelled due to a terminal cancer on the other party. We looked at the lot again during Mother's Day weekend and consulted with Walter Chewning who liked the lot and location. We bought the lot during the summer and Jesús contacted his architect friend and fellow ACU member David Cabarrocas to design the house based on specifications that we provided. While at Marco Island, in June we reviewed the first design and made two major changes. First, we changed it from a traditional house to a Mediterranean style house as Chelo wanted, and second, we requested David to move the location of the elevator and interior stairs so as not to block the view of the patio and pool. There were other changes: Cristy suggested the addition of a Cabana with a bathroom because, as she said, "otherwise you are going to have wet people coming into your master bedroom suite to use the bathroom." That suggestion was brilliant! Later, following Walter's suggestions, we added a storage room underneath the main floor laundry room, and we made the main floor ceiling height twelve feet. Because of the special design of

---

[139] To our surprise we found that he and his wife Dr. Judith Finkelman, DDS, were Mexican and spoke Spanish with a Mexican accent.

the house, David Cabarrocas suggested we ask an engineer to do the structural design. We hired an engineer in Atlanta, and afterwards, Jesús requested that they move the studs even closer than in the engineer's design to provide additional strength— this is one reason why our house turned out to be very solid.

During this time, Lorenzo completed his Associate Degree from the Howard Community College in June and decided to continue his studies at Georgia State University starting in the Fall Semester of 2007. His sisters provided lodgings for Lorenzo until we moved into our new house in March 2009.

We decided to celebrate our fortieth wedding anniversary in Atlanta in August 2007. Chelo reserved the "103 West Restaurant" in Atlanta for our celebration and Cristy, Consuelo Beatriz and Amy Trujillo sent "Save the Date" announcements to many people. We asked Father Llorente and Monsignor Richard López to celebrate a Mass of Thanksgiving before the cocktail and dinner. Father Llorente was in Spain and was not able to attend, but Monsignor López celebrated a beautiful Mass at the Basilica of the Sacred Heart of Jesus. Orlando Carneiro and Arsenio Milian were the altar servers at our anniversary Mass as they were at our wedding. Lorenzo and Alina did the readings, Consuelo Beatriz, Cristina, Lorenzo, Alina and Ethan brought the gifts, and we read the petitions. After the Mass, we enjoyed a wonderful reception and dinner with one hundred and six friends and family members who had come from Miami, Orlando, Washington, Philadelphia and New Jersey. Cristy and Manny Antón said a few words about us and Jesús thanked all that came to share with us that evening. We left the reception and went to the Ritz Carlton Hotel, courtesy of Consuelo Beatriz, and waited there for the visit by the ACU Atlanta crowd and their spouses.

A month later, we completed the plans for the new house and began the negotiations with Walter to build the house. Walter did not want to build the house because he kept telling Chelo, "Consuelo, I do not build houses anymore; I am a developer now." Chelo continued to tell Walter, "Walter you need to build our house." Walter finally gave up and agreed to build the house although he hired another builder, Chuck Magbee, to be the person in charge of the day-to-day work. We finished the details of the contract in time for Walter to begin the house construction in November after Father Llorente blessed the lot.

Father Llorente came to Atlanta in November to participate in the annual ACU Atlanta Pig Roast at the Guigou's house. We maximized his visit by organizing a Mass on Friday in honor of Virginia Balbona who had died earlier. On Saturday, we took Father Llorente to say hello to Olga Goizueta and then to bless our lot before we went to the Guigou's house for the pig roast. We also spent Thanksgiving in Atlanta and saw the Antón family who came to Atlanta as part of their family reconciliation that began the year before while part of the Antón family was with us at Marco Island. One side benefit of visiting with the Antón family was that Manny suggested a change to the landscaping plan— Ed Castro and Adam Huber of Ed Castro Landscape had prepared a very pretty plan but Manny suggested that we swap the location of the Parterre (English) Garden with the Crabapple trees so that we could enjoy the garden while at the pool or the Cabana.

A few days later, the family and a few friends gathered at the Atlanta World of Coca Cola where the J. Mack Robinson College of Business at Georgia State University awarded Jesús the Technology Leadership Award. We returned to Maryland where we had started to negotiate the sale of our house to a Pakistani family.

In March of the following year we entered into an agreement to sell the Maryland house with the closing scheduled for May. Now it was time to accelerate the preparation to move to Atlanta. Chelo went to Atlanta and spent time looking at apartments and a storage location for our furniture and other goods until our new house was completed. She signed a six-months lease for a two-bedroom unit at 421 Berkeley Run, an apartment off Glenridge Drive, located very close to the new house. She also located a good storage facility at the corner of Peachtree Dunwoody and Mount Vernon Roads, and the personnel at the storage facility recommended that we use the "Two Men and a Truck" moving company for our move. Chelo contacted several moving companies, and after comparing prices and recommendations, decided to use "Two Men and a Truck" for our move from Maryland to Atlanta.

In April, we rented a small U-Haul truck and transported to Atlanta our delicate and valuable possessions, including the Lladros, the wine refrigerator and wines, some artwork and porcelains. We delivered these items to the apartment and returned to Maryland to complete preparations for the move. We had to make a few repairs to the house in preparation for the final inspection. On Monday, May 5, the folks from the moving company arrived in Maryland and during the next two days they packed our belongings into two trucks and left for Atlanta. We spent Wednesday, Thursday and Friday nights at the Columbia Inn at Peralynna, a bed and breakfast near the house. We cleaned and prepared the house on Thursday, had the final walk through on Friday morning, and closed on the sale of the house on Friday afternoon. That night we said goodbye to Maryland with dinner at the best restaurant in Baltimore, Charleston.

On Saturday morning we left Maryland, driving both our cars with most of our clothes in suitcases. We stopped overnight in Charlotte, North Carolina and arrived in Atlanta on Mother's Day. We unloaded the cars at our apartment, and as Jesús started to back up from the parking lot to go to Mass, he had a minor fender bender with the car of another tenant— what a way to start our return to Atlanta! On Monday the moving vans came to deliver of our belongings to three locations: our apartment, a storage garage in the apartment complex, and the rest of the furniture and other items went to the storage facility on Peachtree Dunwoody Road. This completed our move to Atlanta.

Family life in Maryland

Because it is difficult to capture the nuances and richness of our family life in a purely chronological narrative, we use this chapter to celebrate the wonderful times we had with our immediate family during the more than eleven years we lived in Maryland.

During the time we lived in Maryland, we saw Consuelo, Cristina, Alina and Ethan several times a year. In addition to the Marco Island and Christmas family gatherings, Chelo, Lorenzo and Jesús traveled to Consuelo's house for visits and special occasions like Baptisms, birthdays, grandparent's days, and First Communions. Chelo, for example, attended each and every grandparent's day. Cristy came to visit us at the Maryland home regularly, often making her trips coincide with visits by Consuelo Beatriz and her children. Additionally,

Consuelo brought us the grandchildren several times for us to babysit them while she was traveling for an extended period of time for work or vacation. While we were in Maryland, Consuelo lived first in Indianapolis, then Roanoke, Virginia, later near Cleveland, Ohio, and finally in Atlanta. We drove to Indianapolis (about nine hours drive) several times before the Bills-León family moved to Roanoke.

Once they moved to Roanoke, the trip to Consuelo's house became significantly shorter, about four hours and more beautiful because we drove through parts of the Blue Ridge Mountains. On the other hand, we had to "fight" the traffic in the Washington Beltway, a stressful drive at almost any time of the day. Consuelo and the grandchildren also came to visit us often at our Maryland house. Chelo had bought many toys and prepared a playroom for the kids in the basement. We remember fondly Alina role-playing as a teacher and a waitress. She would ask you to sit while she taught you or, as a waitress, she would take your order and then deliver "food" to you. We laugh when we remember how Alina and Ethan would often "put on a show" after dinner; Alina was the organizer and director, telling Ethan what role to play. When at our home, Abi would take Alina and Ethan to different parks. Alina was always ready to do something outside the house, whether to go to the play area of a shopping mall, to a park or horseback riding; Ethan, on the other hand, wanted to stay put and not leave the house.

We enjoyed watching our grandchildren grow from babies to children. We remember the development of the personalities of our grandchildren. Alina was gregarious, outgoing, talkative, always engaging people in conversation and asking them questions— the "next Barbara Walters" was one comment made by a woman at a grocery cashier's line when Chelo and Alina were paying for the items purchased there. Ethan was lovable, observant, cautious, quieter and stubborn. Once, when he was less than three years old, he bit Alina and would not apologize. Jesús had him sit at the breakfast table until he apologized— 45 minutes later!

The year 2000 was especially significant because it was the year that Alina's diabetes flared up, as we noted elsewhere in the memoirs. Because of the onset of Alina's diabetes, we spent a good bit of time that year at Roanoke with the Bills-León family. We also traveled to Atlanta in August to celebrate Ethan's second birthday at Cristy's house in Duluth. This trip gave us the opportunity to see many family and friends in the Atlanta area; it was, in particular, the last time we saw Jesús' cousin Ethel in good health— she developed Alzheimer's disease soon afterwards. We also saw Ethel's daughter, Ethel Maria, who also has Type I Diabetes. Later that year, Cordero brought his brother "Nano" to our Maryland house for a visit, and our children and grandchildren also came to our house to meet Nano and to see their beloved Bo. We enjoyed the mini family get together and remember fondly how Alina organized "a sing and dance show" for Nano and the rest of us. Nano was captivated by Alina's beautiful blue eyes.

We experienced several scary incidents during the grandkids visits to our house. One such incident happened when Ethan was two or three years old. We used expandable children's fences to prevent Ethan from falling down our house's staircase to the basement. Well, Ethan one day pushed the fence at the top of the basement stairs— and he rode the fence all the way down the stairs. As you can imagine, this caused a commotion and Chelo rushed to determine if Ethan had been hurt— he was not, thanks God. On another occasion, we took the children to a "petting zoo" near our house. Daring Alina put her head inside the fence and was bitten by a pony. What a scare! Chelo freaked out and disinfected Alina's finger. Once again, the fright of the event was more than the consequences. Then, there was the wasp attack when Ethan was still very young. Ethan was "blowing bubbles" in the patio when he accidentally disturbed a wasp nest. Jesús remembers grabbing Ethan and running to the house at panic speed— the stings of wasps are very painful. Afterwards, Jesús went to the store, purchased a spray and killed all the wasps and also the bush!

When Consuelo Beatriz moved to Ohio in 2002, our drive to visit them became approximately six hours and in winter a little trickier. We remember visiting Consuelo's Wadsworth house for Alina's seventh birthday in February, when a large part of her driveway was iced— driving up to the house was not easy. Occasionally we flew from Baltimore to Cleveland. Consuelo enrolled Alina and later Ethan at the Sacred Heart School in Wadsworth, Ohio. On a visit by Chelo to the school she discovered that Alina and Ethan had personalities like Cristy and Consuelo when they were kids; Alina was very happy to see Chelo and jumped at the opportunity to tell the teachers that this was her Abi, a former teacher, who was visiting her— Cristy used to do the same. Ethan did not wish to be singled out or called out, and given the chance, would ignore his family visitors, just like his mother used to do

We had two great family trips during 2003, Disney World and Hershey Park. We arranged a family vacation at Disney Orlando during the school spring holidays in April. Consuelo drove Alina and Ethan to Cleveland's Airport; Chelo flew from Baltimore to Cleveland, picked up the children at the airport and flew to Orlando. Jesús flew directly to Orlando, picked a rental car, met Chelo and the kids, and then drove to the Disney World Beach Club Resort hotel. The four of us were there for six days. Cristy, Consuelo and Lorenzo joined us during the week. Jesús took Alina horseback riding one day, and since Ethan was not old enough to ride by himself, Chelo took him to ride on a pony. All of us visited the different parks and explored several of the Disney World's hotels, including the Polynesian Village and the Animal Kingdom Lodge resorts.

We had a great time at the Disney Parks with a couple of interesting incidents. Alina had begun using an electronic pump to dispense insulin into her body, but Chelo and Jesús were not familiar with the device. One day, during the midday break we took to cool off from the Disney parks, we were at the hotel pool, and Alina's glucose level was low, so Chelo asked Jesús to get an ice cream cone for Alina. While Jesús was about to get the cone, Chelo decided Alina's level was dangerously low and decided to take matter into her hands. She rushed into the ice cream parlor like a tornado, passed Jesús and everyone at the counter and shouted to the attendant, "My granddaughter has diabetes; I need a cone now and I will come back to pay later." The attendant gave her the cone without question and Jesús was left standing at the counter like a dummy.

The second interesting incident was Jesús' reaction to the "Mission to Mars" ride at Epcot. We rode this simulator right after a full meal at Alfredo's Restaurant in the Italian Pavilion at Epcot. Jesús spent part of the ride trying to assist Chelo instead of looking forward as we were instructed— well, Jesús came out of the ride "white as paper," while Ethan enjoyed the ride so much that he rode it with Lorenzo for a second time.

At the end of the 2003 summer, we took the grandchildren and Lorenzo to Hershey Park in Pennsylvania for a full day of rides and entertainment. This was the first time we noticed that Ethan was ready to enjoy all the rides. We remember getting soaked, that Ethan did not want to leave the park, that Jesús came out white as paper of a rear-facing roller coaster ride he took after lunch. We stayed overnight in a hotel near the park, and drove from there to Hagerstown, Maryland, where we transferred Alina and Ethan to Consuelo Beatriz and Todd.

Chelo, Cristy, Lorenzo, Alexandra and Jesús went to Consuelo Beatriz's house to share in the celebration of Alina's First Communion on May 8, 2004. It was a very beautiful day with only one cloud on their household— Consuelo and Todd's marriage was on the rocks.

The two of us returned to Ohio in October 2004, for the annual Grandparent's Day at Alina and Ethan's school. We had a very difficult time on this trip because Consuelo and Todd's marriage was coming to an end. Chelo and Jesús had an uncomfortable conversation with Todd and Consuelo at the rental house where Consuelo lived with our grandchildren.

We saw Consuelo and the children several times during 2005. In June, after they moved to Atlanta and at Marco Island. We also got together as a family in November when Cordero died and we all stayed in Miami for Thanksgiving. And we celebrated Christmas together. Most of our visits with Consuelo and the kids up to this time had been joyous occasions although we had a couple of scary moments at our house in Maryland, especially when Alina experienced a diabetes seizure in the middle of the night. A couple of our visits filled us with sadness as we saw Consuelo's marriage disintegrate and how much our daughter suffered.

As we related earlier, in 2006, the seven members of the León-Bills family converged in Paris for a family vacation and pilgrimage to Lourdes. Later that year, Chelo and Jesús flew to Atlanta for Grandparent's Day at the grandchildren's new school, Immaculate Heart of Mary— the school that Consuelo, Cristy and Lorenzo attended as children. We then spent the Thanksgiving week with them and saw them again at Christmas time. In 2007, the last full year that we spent in Maryland, we saw the five members of the family living in Atlanta several times: for Alina's Birthday, at Marco, for Ethan's Birthday, at Grandparent's Day, for Thanksgiving and then at Christmas.

Book VI – Part III– Atlanta 2008-2019

Retirement

Two days after arriving in Atlanta we drove to the Barnsley Resort in northwest Georgia for an exploratory meeting with the Board of Advisors of the College of Business at Georgia State University. The Dean of the college had invited Jesús to join the Board of Advisors and Jesús agreed to attend their annual retreat. The meeting was a good experience for us, and Jesús later, after another meeting with the Dean, joined this board.

We returned to the apartment and began our lives in Atlanta, a city we knew well. We moved the minimum amount of furniture to the two-bedroom unit, using one of the bedrooms for our sleeping quarters, and the second bedroom for storage and office space. In the second bedroom, we placed the wine refrigerator, our collection of pictures and paintings, the Lladros and other priced possessions, a desk unit, the computer, a temporary file storage and a printer. When in town, Jesús got up early, exercised, went to the 6:45 AM Mass at St. Brigid Catholic Church and from there to his office at Ciena. He continued to travel regularly to Acton, Ottawa, and Maryland. That spring we made a trip to Madrid and Paris, eating great meals at fabulous restaurants.[140]

During the summer it became obvious to Jesús that Ciena wanted to reorganize the engineering function and that it was time to plan his departure from the company. In September, he entered into a separation agreement with Ciena to retire at the end of October

---

[140] In Madrid at El Landó and El Paraguas. In Paris at Michelin three-stars restaurants Alain Ducasse and Le Bristol, and two-stars restaurant Le Cinq. Besides great food, magnificent duck at Le Bristol, we had the best macaroons ever at Alain Ducasse and almost as good at Le Bristol.

with a one-year package that would continue his salary and most benefits through his sixty-fifth birthday. Chelo and Jesús discussed the plans for our lives once Jesús stopped working at Ciena. We agreed that we should not change the basic rhythms of our life and that this would be best accomplished if we assumed that Jesús was still working, at least part of the time. Chelo would not have to prepare breakfast or lunch for Jesús, and she would be free to come and go as she was already doing. Jesús planned to work in his home office at least until 1:00 PM in the afternoon each day.[141] Jesús planned to dedicate about one hour every day to each of three items, the ACU, writing our memoirs, and an hour for dealing with other matters.

It was a busy summer— we had our annual Marco Island family vacation and Lorenzo went to Cuernavaca, México in July to visit his friends there. In the fall, Jesús, organized visits to all the Ciena engineering locations except India to say farewell to his colleagues before leaving Ciena. In October Jesús met with Paul Freet of Georgia Tech ventures and discussed how Jesús could help a GT professor who wanted to start a telecommunications company. Paul and Jesús agreed to meet in January to kick off this effort.

Several of our friends in Atlanta had planned a cruise to the Western Mediterranean at the end of October, and we were able to join them. This was the first of several cruises and other trips we made with friends from Atlanta. This was our second cruise, and we were surprised by the quality of the food and service on the ship, the Azamara Journey. We flew to Barcelona, had a half-day tour of the city, boarded the ship, and then we went to have lunch with an ex-Ciena colleague, Vicente Arroyo and his wife in Barcelona.[142] The cruise started on a difficult note because the sea conditions caused about half of the passengers to become somewhat seasick, but that was the only problem during the cruise. The trip took us to Tripoli, Malta, Sicily, the Amalfi Coast, Rome, Florence, Portofino and Monaco before returning to Barcelona. On the second night of the trip we celebrated Jesús' retirement with the group.

---

[141] This arrangement was based on the principle that we married "for better or worse but not for lunch."

[142] We ate a great "Lubina a la sal" in a restaurant near the Barcelona port.

During 2008 and the first three months of 2009, we spent a lot of time overseeing the construction of our new house. Chelo selected everything for the house, including the overall decoration scheme, the light fixtures, the flooring, the paint colors of the rooms and the fixtures. We worked with Walter and Chuck to decide every detail and to talk about cabinets, pool design, heating and air conditioning, and everything else that was needed to complete the house.

The most important activity in 2009 was the completion and move into the new house, our dream house. We built three houses from "scratch" during our lifetime, all three from architectural plans to meet our specific needs and desires. The last house is the best of all the houses we had owned or lived in, and although much bigger than what we need, it is a beautiful house. It was, from an economics point-of-view, the culmination of our American Dream. We have written and edited most of these memoirs from this last house, so it seems proper to us to write about it in the present tense.

The house is located in a gated community, Rose Court, in an excellent area of Atlanta, less than two miles north of Chastain Park, less than fifteen minutes from the Lenox, Perimeter and Cumberland Malls, about twenty minutes from Consuelo Beatriz and Cristy's house and downtown Atlanta, and less than thirty minutes from the airport.[143]

We moved into the house in mid March and spent the next three months "finishing" the house. For example, we had lots of problem with the wine cellar cooling equipment, problems that continued for several years, primarily because we did not have any competent company to deal with it. Chelo worked with a Colombian painter and her mother to select where to place our artwork and the family pictures. Chelo ordered a large mirror for the living room. The Colombian decorator contributed to many details of the interior decoration including a painted design over the living room fireplace. We scheduled the installation of the chandeliers for May because we did not want the chandelier crystals to get dirty with all the construction dirt. Installing the foyer and living room chandeliers was a little bit stressful because our electrician was worried about the electric motor

---

[143] We describe the house in detail in Appendix V.

to move up and down the chandelier— in the end, this turned out to be simple and straightforward.

By June, when we left for Marco Island we felt the house was in pretty good shape, so that on our return we held a BBQ to inaugurate the house with the Atlanta friends with whom we had cruised on the Mediterranean the previous year. We should mention that we had a number of startup issues with the house in addition to the problems with the Wine Cellar cooling system. We had problems caused by the sewer line from our house; we had to tear up the driveway twice to repair leaky sewer lines during our first couple years in the house. The second major problem was a "water" leak on Lorenzo's balcony that moistened the outside terrace ceiling next to the family room; it took two years to find and fix the problem: the waterproofing membrane on the large upstairs balcony became unglued and allowed water to seep below it. The solution was to remove all the tiles, remove the old waterproof membrane, install a new membrane and install the tiles again.

In addition to the move to our new house, there were other noteworthy events during 2009. Jesús started working in January with GT Ventures to assist a group that wanted to start a company to develop a wireless communication product with technology developed at Georgia Tech. Jesús spent a significant amount of time during the year leading a group of six persons preparing the business plan for the startup company. The technology was good, but the timing was very bad because the USA had just experienced the financial meltdown of several banks, and there was little funding available to finance new companies. Consequently, by the end of the year, the group abandoned the effort. Jesús moved on to work with another potential startup the following year.

Another significant activity that year for Jesús was to revitalize the ACU group in Atlanta. Living in Atlanta at the time were several of the founders of the original group and also several old-timers[144] who just needed guidance. The group resurgence was notable with the addition over the next five years of seven new congregants and

---

[144] Especially José Batlle, Jorge Guigou, Alex Saker, Gorka Zurinaga, Ramiro Rodríguez and Alfredo Trujillo.

the startup of a student group. Gonzalo Revuelta and Alfredo Trujillo became congregants in 2009 and Jesús was Gonzalo's sponsor.

This year was also the initiation of three wine and food recurring events for us, starting with the first Abella-León-Sorondo weekend reunion that brought together two married couples that have been very close to us since our student days, Ignacio and Lourdes Abella and Victor and María (Mary) Sorondo. They came to Atlanta for a weekend of activities that began with a Braves-Marlin baseball game on Friday and was followed by a lavish meal with great wines on Saturday night. The second recurring wine event started with our participation in a dinner with the Atlanta branch of the International Wine & Food Society, IW&FS, an affair held at what used to be Joel's Restaurant, and to which we were invited by our friends Bob and Lynn Moore. The third of these events was the founding of the "Atlanta Exclusive Cuban Wine Club," AECWC, in October. The Abella-León-Sorondo dinners were held in Atlanta and Miami in subsequent years. We became members of the IW&FS and normally participate in four of their dinner events every year. Pepe Irastorza and Jesús organized the AECWC and invited the Bolet and Navarro couples to join the group. This group meets four times a year rotating the host family, and its purpose is to enjoy our friendship, good food and wines, and to learn about wines.

In October we enjoyed a great ACU Atlanta tradition, the Annual Pig Roast, this year held at Al and Melba Trujillo's farm with an excellent turnout of ACU families and friends. Then, in November, we joined four Atlanta couples on an Eastern Mediterranean Cruise aboard the Celebrity Solstice that sailed from Rome to Athens, Istanbul, Ephesus, Napoli (Capri) and two Greek isles, Santorini and Mykonos. The visit to Santorini was interesting because of the weather that made difficult the boarding of the tender boats and later required the stopping of the Santorini cable car. Chelo and Jesús made it a point to visit the site of the Ephesus Council that defined Mary to be Theotokos (Mother of God) in the year 431.

A difficult year

When we talk about the year 2010, our reaction is to say that it was a very bad year. In fact, there were a lot of negative events during the year, but there were also some positive ones. The year is marked in our memories by two difficult developments: the first was the death in April of Father Llorente, and the second a significant decrease in the quality of life of Chelo's mother accompanied by an increased antagonism in our relation with Chelo's aunt, Generosa. There were other difficult events during the year that included a return of PMR, a hernia operation for Jesús, dental problems for both of us, and a fire in the Miami house.

We started the year on a positive note when we returned to Atlanta in January to prepare for the first meeting of the AECWC that was to be held at our house in January. It was a very good meeting, the first of many in which we have enjoyed our friends company, eaten very good food and learned a little bit about wines. At this meeting we tasted four good red wines, one Italian, one Spanish, one French and one American.

An exciting milestone in 2010 occurred when Father José Fetzer, SJ, recently ordained, traveled to Atlanta to direct Spiritual Exercises for the men in March. Father José had found his vocation in Atlanta where he had many friends and where he spent years working and studying. He directed an excellent retreat, and the ACU Atlanta felt it had found a spiritual director for the annual Ignatian exercises! He went on to direct Atlanta exercises the next two years before his untimely death in December 2012.

During the spring Jesús started working with another engineering professor who wanted to start a new company. He was asked by the Georgia Tech professor to be the CEO of the new company, an offer Jesús declined although he did continue helping the team to define the market, to organize the development and to identify suitable CEO candidates.

On April 28, Jesús received a call from Marty Pérez of Miami who said, "Father Llorente is dead." This news was very hard for Chelo and Jesús. Father Llorente was a friend, spiritual director and confessor who had married us and baptized our three children. He was more than the Director of the ACU— as Cardinal Sean O'Malley stated, "he was our patriarch." Jesús left for Miami the next day and Chelo joined him there later because Mimi and Roberto Vich were our houseguests that weekend. The wake was long, respectful and painful with many tears. The funeral on Monday was as it should have been for "our patriarch." Present at the funeral were Cardinal O'Malley, Archbishop Favarola of Miami, four other bishops including Agustín Román and two bishops from the Cuban Church, the Jesuit Provincial, the Miami Jesuit Superior and over thirty priests. There was standing room only at the Gesu Church, a church that has room for over one thousand persons. The celebrant of the Mass was Father Fernando Polanco, SJ, the Jesuit Provincial, and the homilist was Father Pedro Suárez, SJ, the President of Belen Jesuit and the superior of the Miami Jesuits. Jesús spoke as President of the ACU and Archbishop Favarola and Cardinal O'Malley also spoke about Father Llorente. At the end, a niece of Father Llorente gave thanks to everyone in the name of the family. The funeral Mass was streamed live via the Internet especially to Llorente's family in Spain. The funeral procession used the Dolphin Expressway and the expressway was blocked to traffic to allow Llorente's body to be borne with the respect he earned during his life.

There were two other unfortunate events during the spring; the first was a fire in the kitchen of the Miami house that caused smoke damage but no injury. We had to redo the kitchen and also paint the living room, dining room and hall. In the end, we ended up with a better-finished house and the insurance paid for a significant portion of the expense. The other inconvenient event was a cystoscopy for Chelo because a lab test found blood in her urine, a hereditary condition that Cordero had experienced several times. On the positive side, in May we celebrated Alina's eight-grade graduation from IHM School with a pool party at our house. Her graduation was a joyful milestone, and family and friends joined us to celebrate at the party.

In June, Jesús convened a weekend-long meeting of the ACU Board of Directors to reflect and then recommend to the Jesuit Provincial one or more candidates to become the Director of the ACU. Jesús said it was an intense working meeting that resulted in specific recommendations to the Provincial. This meeting set the precedent for annual summer meetings of the ACU Board of Directors. The following Saturday Jesús joined the family in Marco Island for a well deserved rest before heading back to Atlanta to prepare for a trip to the Baltic Sea.

Vicente and Bertica joined us for a Baltic Cruise vacation in August that started in Copenhagen and took us to Berlin, St. Petersburg, Tallinn, Helsinki and Stockholm. We spent a couple of days in Copenhagen and then boarded the Azamara Journey for a cruise that was blessed with almost perfect weather (except in Helsinki). Most of the ports were memorable but none compared to St. Petersburg where we spent three days and took the time to visit the Hermitage Museum twice, most of the important sites in the city (except the Peterhof Palace). We took a tour of the city and "escaped" from the ship to walk to St. Isaac's Cathedral. During the trip Jesús complained about a small pain in the legs, and he thought it might be due to the shoes that he was using; it turns out that it was a return of PMR although he did not know it at the time and did not confirm it until October.

Jesús joined the Board of Trustees of the Georgia Tech Alumni Association in August and served on the board for the next three years. In August, we held the second Abella-León-Sorondo weekend get together with a similar schedule as that of the previous year. We enjoyed another great meal and fabulous wines on Saturday night. Victor and Mary stayed until Tuesday, August 31, to accompany us and support Chelo while Jesús underwent outpatient hernia surgery, a simple procedure with no complications except Jesús' reaction to the pain killer drug Percocet— he stated that he would rather have pain than take another dose; we threw the pills in the trash. Meanwhile, Manny and Annette called to ask us to join them in Puerto Rico during the Labor Day weekend to attend Maritere's formal engagement. Unfortunately, we could not go because of Jesús' hernia surgery.

The rest of the year was also memorable for other reasons. In September, we drove to Miami in preparation to fly to Punta Cana to spend four days at the Meliá Resort. During this time Jesús continued to experience bouts of pain, some significant enough that required us to split the drive from Atlanta to Miami into two days. Additionally, he did not swim while in Punta Cana and we noticed an inflammation in his hands.

We flew back to Miami and joined the Abellas at an Enrique Chia's concert in Miami. The following day we took Consuelo to see Dr. Raúl Moas. Dr. Moas asked Chelo about Jesús. Chelo informed the doctor about Jesús' pain and the inflammation of the hands. Doctor Moas asked Chelo if Jesús was in the office and told her that he wanted to see him. Doctor Moas examined Jesús' hands and then made an appointment for Jesús with Dr. Gregory Bell, a rheumatologist, for the following day. Dr. Bell examined Jesús, ordered lab tests and prescribed a six-pack prednisone-based medicine for Jesús. The medicine was effective in reducing and almost eliminating the pain. However, the pain returned a day or so after Jesús stopped taking the Prednisone. At this moment, the light went on in Jesús' brain! It had taken almost two months for Jesús to realize that he had a relapse of PMR because the pain was milder and slightly different that the original occurrence. Jesús knew he had to see a rheumatologist in Atlanta to get a prescription to treat the problem, but the first available appointment to an Atlanta rheumatologist was in two months, a long time when you are in pain. Jesús remembered that his Johns Hopkins physician, Dr. John Flynn, had telephone consultations on Tuesdays at ten in the morning. Jesús called Dr. Flynn who, after a short conversation,[145] called the local pharmacy with the prescription. This bout of PMR was milder and also took less time to leave Jesús' body, about one year. Jesús found a good rheumatologist in Atlanta, Dr. Hayes Wilson, who monitored the course of this second bout of PMR.

Consuelo's health and the quality of her life declined rapidly during the year— she lost some of her mobility and began to have anxiety issues. Consuelo's sister Generosa was not able to appropriately care for Consuelo and became frustrated. Generosa began to complain often about Consuelo to Chelo and the complaints increased during the fall in a crescendo that was to reach a climax early in 2011. Generosa's daily tirades began to affect Chelo's emotional level and also caused us to increase the frequency of our trips to Miami— we traveled to Miami ten times during the year, most of the trips to attend to Consuelo and deal with her health and the problems in the house, including the April fire. In December, we traveled to Miami for the ACU activities and spent a week in our Miami house.

---

[145] Doctor: "Do you know what you have?" Jesús: "Yes, a relapse of PMR." Doctor: "OK, what do you want me to do?" Jesús: "I need a prescription for Prednisone since I cannot see a local rheumatologist for two months." Doctor: "How much do you think I should prescribe?" Jesús: "Ten milligrams." Doctor: "I agree."

The following week, several days after returning to Atlanta, Chelo had to make an emergency trip to Miami because Consuelo had to be hospitalized. Jesús did not join her because, at the same time, he sheared a bridge over three front teeth and he needed immediate dentist work. While in Miami, Chelo decided that she needed to hire a person to help with Consuelo, and after interviewing several candidates she hired Migdalia Isern Pérez to start working immediately five days a week. However, the problems with Generosa continued!

Consuelo Beatriz, Cristy, Alina and Ethan joined us to travel to Puerto Rico for Maritere's wedding to José Luis Vilaró. The church ceremony was planned for Sunday, December 26, the Feast of the Holy Family, at the San Juan Cathedral in the Old City. We flew to San Juan on Christmas Day, rented a van, checked into our hotel, and then went to dinner with the rest of the Atlanta group.[146] On Sunday, as Chelo was taking a shower prior to dressing for the wedding, we got an urgent call from Migdalia about problems in Miami, problems caused by Generosa's behavior towards Migdalia and Consuelo. Fortunately, Vicente, Chelo's cousin, was visiting Miami. Chelo spoke with Vicente who was able to resolve the problem and we did enjoy the wedding, a fabulous wedding— the best wedding Chelo and Jesús have ever attended. We also enjoyed the next couple of days in Puerto Rico with sightseeing, horseback riding, and excellent meals. By the way, Chelo asked Migdalia to enlist the assistance of her sister Mayda to provide twenty-four hours, seven-days a week care for Consuelo. And yet the problems persisted into 2011.

Changes in our Miami house

In January 2011, we returned to Miami and spent one sleepless night in the Miami house listening to Consuelo's cries for help. The next morning we took Consuelo to the emergency room at Mercy Hospital where a psychiatrist, Dr. Evelio Sosa, changed the prescription medicines for Consuelo and ordered a new set of medicine that began to control Consuelo's anxiety level and allowed her to sleep at

---

[146] The Antóns, Guigous, Batlles, Romeros and also Ernie and María León from Miami.

night. Generosa continued to complain daily to Chelo about Consuelo, about the caretakers and their impact on the house, with the expected strain to Chelo's life, and as a consequence, to the rest of the family.

Jesús' policy had always been not to interfere in Chelo's family issues even though he often thought that their relationships were not conducive to peaceful interactions. However, by January 2011, he was worried about the emotional and mental stress that Generosa was causing Chelo and he decided to get involved. He called Generosa and explained that her attitude had to change or she had to move out of the house. During our next trip to Miami, Jesús had a meeting with Generosa, Migdalia and Iliana, the person who bathed Consuelo daily at the time. He gave each of them a one-page document explaining the rules of the Miami house going forward and telling them that Generosa would be moving out of the house in the near future. Chelo and Jesús spent several days investigating potential housing options for Generosa but did not find a good place for her.

We returned to Miami in April to celebrate Consuelo's ninetieth birthday and organized a small party attended by Consuelo Beatriz, Alina, Ethan, Mimi, Roberto, Adolfo and his wife Rossina, Migdalia and her sister Mayda, Carmen Luisa, Alexandra and Generosa. After the party, Jesús asked Migdalia about the situation in the house and she told him that everything was fine and maybe Generosa could stay. Jesús thought this improved behavior was probably due to the threat to move Generosa out and the written document he had given her. Regrettably, this improvement in behavior was not to last and in May the problem became a Greek Tragedy with Generosa threatening to do bodily harm to people, locking herself in her bedroom and taking a large number of aspirins. Migdalia called 911, resulting in emergency and police personnel coming to the house and taking Generosa to a hospital for a three-day psychiatric evaluation.

Chelo decided that Generosa should not return to the Miami house given her violent and uncertain behavior and told Rossina to check the place that Carmen Luisa had recommended, the house where Jesús' cousin Berta Gallardo had lived for many years. Rossina was able to arrange for accommodations there for Generosa. The immediate result was peace at the Miami House with the corresponding reduction in the stress level of Chelo and the rest of the León-

Cordero-Bills family in Atlanta. The peace in the house reduced Consuelo's anxiety level, improved her appetite and led to a noticeable weight gain. On the other hand, Chelo did not see Generosa again until after Consuelo's death in 2018. One other thing that helped make life less stressful for Consuelo and us was the arrangement to have a general practitioner doctor visit Consuelo at her house regularly, eliminating the painful trip and long waits to see various doctors during our trips to Miami.

When the year 2011 started both of us had to deal with dental issues. Chelo had a molar that had to be extracted by a dental surgeon who had to rebuild the bone tissue in part of her mouth. Jesús needed to have implants to replace the bridge that he lost in December. In January, Chelo had the tooth removed and Jesús began the five-month process to have implants and a new dental bridge.

The rest of the year was, thanks God, more enjoyable with many good and pleasant activities, especially during a summer that included the annual Marco Island reunion plus trips to Punta Cana and New York City. In early June, we together with Cristy, Consuelo Beatriz, Alina and Ethan joined the Antóns, Guigous, Entenzas, Ralph and Marta Barrial, and Vicky and Juanmi, José Vilaro's mother and brother, in Punta Cana to celebrate the fifteenth birthday of our goddaughter Ana María Antón, "Gigi." The celebration actually started in Miami on a Friday night at Manny's house with a party that included most of the persons named above plus other family and friends and where Jesús gave the toast on the theme "to life."[147] Then, very early on Saturday morning, we flew from Miami to Punta Cana for a week of celebration, relaxation and sharing. When we returned to Miami we went almost directly to Marco Island for our annual family reunion and week at the beach.

The last trip that summer was to New York City where we spent six days sightseeing and then went to New Jersey for Carlos Trujillo's wedding to Lauren. All of the León-Bills clan except Lorenzo flew to NYC on Sunday morning and started our sightseeing that day. Lorenzo joined us on Tuesday since he had to work on

---

[147] Reflecting on cultural toasts such as "Salud," "Proust," "Cheers" and the Jewish toast "Leheim," to life.

Sunday and Monday. We visited the Statue of Liberty and Ellis Island, Coney Island, Chinatown, the New York Library, the MOMA and the Metropolitan Museum, Times Square, Central Park and The Plaza Hotel where we ate excellent French-style macaroons. We saw a great Broadway revival one night and another night Cristina took the two of us to dinner at Daniel's while Consuelo Beatriz, Alina, Lorenzo and Ethan went to a baseball game at Yankee Stadium. Our meal at Daniel's was memorable to say the least. At Coney Island Consuelo Beatriz, Ethan and Jesús (finally) rode the famous "Cyclone" roller coaster. We took the excellent Brooklyn Pizza tour, ate great pastrami sandwiches and excellent cheesecakes at Junior's, and enjoyed family dinner twice at Carmine's restaurant. Vicente, Bertica, Vicentico and Nancy took the train from Philadelphia and joined us for the day. On Friday, we met up with Maricarmen Vazquez (Trujillo) for part of the day including an early dinner at an excellent restaurant while Alina and Lorenzo took the train to New Jersey in order to attend the Rehearsal Dinner. Maricarmen and the rest of us took a van from the NYC hotel to the New Jersey hotel where the wedding reception was to be held. The wedding on Saturday was very pretty although we had problems getting to the church because of a mechanical problem with the bus that was to take us to the church. The reception was excellent with an enormous quantity of food that we had never seen at any other wedding— there was enough food and desserts to feed an army. At the reception we sat together with Jesús' cousin Bertha and her husband Owen Kavanagh, ate an excellent dinner and then danced to the music of a band.

 The fall of this year was also important because it marked the start of a new all-student ACU group in Atlanta thanks to the leadership of Alfredo Trujillo and Jesús. We hosted a social at our home in late August and the group met on Sunday mornings at the Georgia Tech Catholic Center. We have hosted annual socials at our house most years to welcome new students and to renew the spirit and commitment of the rest of the group. In October, Father José Fetzer, SJ, was assigned permanently to Ignatius House in Atlanta as a retreat director, a function that he performed marvelously for fourteen months. One of the first things he did in Atlanta was to celebrate Mass at the Annual ACU Pig Roast, held that year at Alfredo and

Melba Trujillo's farm. Father Fetzer's presence in Atlanta was a blessing for many, especially for the ACU group, who considered him one of its own, and with whom the group made spiritual exercises three years in a row.

Jesús had cataract operations on each of his eyes during November, a very simple procedure that improved his eyesight significantly. We continued our other regular activities of the year with four meetings of our AECWC wine club, several meals with the International Wine & Food Society, Jesús assistance to the Georgia Tech team that wanted to start a company, Chelo's monthly lunches with the "muchachitas," the ACU activities in Atlanta and Miami, and going to the Atlanta Opera.

The last of the memorable events of the year was the "pase a congregantes," (the consecration to Mary for life in the ACU) of Lorenzo and Arturo Muñiz of Atlanta. Lorenzo was the third generation León to become an ACU congregant following in the steps of Rigoberto and Jesús. This consecration was done in Miami during the annual ACU celebration of the Feast of the Immaculate Conception and was witnessed by the full León-Bills family and also Carmen Luisa. Jesús was, as expected, Lorenzo's sponsor during his consecration to the Virgin in the ACU.

Unexpected deaths

Writing our memoirs has given us the opportunity to relish many joyful and great experiences but also to re-suffer a little bit of some of the difficult events in our lives. There have been many events that created happy memories and some that left sad memories. The year 2012 left some sad memories at the end of a year by the sudden death of two very special persons: José Fetzer and Jean-Marie Finison León.

The year began like most typical years. We returned from Miami after Christmas and resumed our normal activities. Father José directed two retreats in Spanish that year. Chelo attended the women's retreat held in January. In March, father José directed his last spiritual exercises for the ACU and other men.

Our grandchildren achieved two significant milestones in May: the Sacrament of Confirmation for Alina and Ethan's eighth grade graduation from IHM School. Alina chose Chelo to be her sponsor, an honor that filled Chelo with pride. Alina selected St. Therese of Lisieux as her model saint and the whole family attended the ceremony at IHM Church on May 7. A few days later and at the same church, we witnessed Ethan's graduation— we were proud to celebrate his success in reaching this milestone.

During this time, Jesús was busy preparing for the annual ACU Board of Directors weekend meeting in June. The management and communication style of the ACU Director, Father Nelson García, SJ, had created difficulties in the administration of the organization, and to make matters worse, Father Nelson fell in April and broke some bones in his leg, requiring hospitalization and surgery. During the ACU Board meeting that summer, Father Nelson was hospitalized with blood in his cranial cavity, and the Board decided it was necessary to move the administrative responsibilities to the ACU laity, a logical idea that resulted in Jesús acquiring more responsibilities.

Lorenzo had started working at Penske Truck Rental thanks to the recommendation of friend and ACU member Tim Murphy. Because of his new job, he was not able to join us for our annual summer family reunion. We made a very special trip in early August to northeast Italy and the Adriatic with Cristy and Ana Silva. Ana is the Brazilian roommate of Consuelo Beatriz's long-term friend, Kathi Stearns. This trip started with a week driving through the magnificent Dolomite Mountain range, then to Lake Garda, Verona, Padova, Ferrara, Ravenna, Bologna, Mantova, Parma, San Marino and Modena. We had several great meals[148] and enjoyed beautiful scenery. We returned the rental car in Venice and boarded the Azamara Quest for a week cruise in the Adriatic that visited Dubrovnik, Hvar, Split, Kotor and Brindisi before returning to Venice where we spent three days sightseeing, walking and sweating in the hot and humid August. We said "arrivederci" to Venice with dinner at La Terrace of the Hotel Danieli, our hotel in Venice— it was superb!

---

[148] We remember especially the food and view of Lake Garda at La Casa deli Spiriti in Monte Baldo. We also loved the food at the Ca' Matilda "farmhouse inn" we stayed in Quattro Castella.

Upon our return to Atlanta, we hosted the second social for young students to invite new students to join the ACU student group. In September, we volunteered to teach Hispanic immigrants registered in the General Education Development, GED, program that prepared them to take tests to certify that they have achieved educational skills at the United States high school level. Chelo was asked to teach Spanish (of course) and Jesús Social Studies. The program met on Thursday night at the Marist School campus and was originally expected to serve about one hundred students but exploded to include close to seven hundred students by the second year.

We continued to have a busy calendar with monthly lunches for Chelo, quarterly AECWC wine/dinner events, several IW&FS events during the year, Atlanta Opera performances, trips to Miami every other month to monitor Consuelo's health, weekly family dinners at our home, occasional pool parties for our grandchildren and for family and friends, events at Georgia Tech that included the President's dinner, a couple of invitations every year to athletic events at the school, Jesús' mentoring of students and helping a Physics professor with a project to expand his business in optical pulse testing. In other words, we were very busy in our retirement.

Then came November, a month with the "Thanksgiving week from hell." On the first Saturday of November, we attended the Annual ACU Atlanta Pig Roast where Father Fetzer celebrated Mass and presided over the Aspirant Promise of four of the student members, the first of this group to pass this milestone. We flew to Los Angeles on Thursday, November 15, to attend our goddaughter's Ana Teresa Villafañe's recital scheduled for Saturday night. We spent two days sightseeing in the area, took Ana Teresa to dinner, went to the rehearsal, enjoyed the company of Geraldina Rodríguez, and the Macias and Villafañe families.

We flew back to Atlanta on Sunday night, packed different clothes and left for Miami on Tuesday— the plan was to celebrate Thanksgiving in Miami, something we rarely do, and then stay for the ACU Immaculate Conception celebration the following week. On Wednesday morning, the day before Thanksgiving, as Consuelo Beatriz, Cristy, Alina and Ethan were driving to Miami, Jesús' sister Mary called to let us know that Jean-Marie Finison León, Henry León's wife had died that morning of a sudden heart attack. Shock, disbelief, astonishment, and pain for Henry, Margaret, Benjamin, Nicholas and Laurence— all these feelings overwhelmed us. Because this was the Thanksgiving Weekend, it was not clear when the services or funeral were to be scheduled. In any case, the caravans from Miami started traveling to Warner Robbins the next day with six members of the León-Bills family from Atlanta driving back on Friday. We drove to Warner Robbins on Saturday to spend time with the family. That evening we had a private family viewing and prayed the Rosary for Jean-Marie. The public viewing and wake was on Sunday evening and the Mass of Resurrection and burial on Monday. Jesús gave the eulogy at the Mass remembering Jean-Marie and her openness to the family and the Cuban culture.

In less than one week we had flown from Los Angeles to Atlanta— a four hour flight, drove to Miami— a ten hours drive; drove back to Atlanta; then, we then drove two hours each way to Warner Robbins and back on Saturday, Sunday and Monday. Jesús arranged travel and accommodations (at the Antón's) for the ACU Board Meeting and the Immaculate Conception Celebration the following week.

We planned Nochebuena dinner at our home. Chelo and Jesús invited José Fetzer to celebrate Nochebuena with us and also to have dinner the Tuesday before Christmas, December 18. Chelo made the Spanish Asturian dish Fabada, a great stew of large white beans ("fabes"), Spanish Chorizo and Morcilla (blood sausages). José had never had fabada and loved it, eating two full servings. He was very excited about sharing the Nochebuena dinner with us and invited the family to join the Christmas Eve liturgy that he was going to celebrate at Ignatius House. Early on Saturday morning Maria Cressler, the Executive Director of Ignatius House, called Jesús with the news that Father José had died of a massive heart attack at the Chapel during the very early part of the day. Oh, my God! This was the second sudden death of a heart attack in less that one month for someone very close to our family.

José was not only a friend but also a member of the ACU who had joined the ACU in Atlanta and decided to become a Jesuit through the influence of Father Llorente and the Spiritual Exercises. José had directed three consecutive men retreats and organized the first Spanish retreat for women. He celebrated Mass with us at the annual pig roast and shared our dinner table on many occasions. His loss was a blow not only at the personal level but also at the ACU organizational level—José had the charisma, skills and desire to become the Director of the ACU. He was sorely missed. Jesús said that José's death was the first time that he remembered telling God, "You are not been fair to us. You may have a plan, but we do not understand it."

We had a subdued Nochebuena dinner that year at our home but were cheered by the arrival of Jesús' niece and goddaughter Alexandra and her family who were in Atlanta to spend several days staying at Consuelo Beatriz and Cristy's house.

Cristina is elected President of GAWL

Lorenzo decided to return to school to complete the requirements for his Bachelor's Degree in Marketing and he reapplied and was re-admitted to Georgia State University. He registered for two classes in the Spring Semester of the year and finished them with grades of A and A-, a good start!

One of the results of the death of Father José Fetzer was the need to redo the retreat schedule at Ignatius House. We canceled the Spanish women's retreat planned for the end of January because it was very difficult to find another Spanish-speaking retreat director in such a short time. We also had to scramble to find a priest to direct the men's retreat and were lucky that Father Jorge Rojas, SJ, a Cuban Jesuit working at Belén in Miami was available to direct the retreat. Father Rojas did an excellent job with the retreat and stayed on Monday to direct a day of reflection in Spanish for women.

In April Jesús finished reading the complete four hundred anniversary edition of Don Quijote, a book the Mary Carmen Peláez gave Jesús during one of his trips to Madrid in 2005. This hardcover edition runs 1,111 pages and was the second longest one-book novel he had read.[149] April is the peak month for pollen in Atlanta and we once again lived through the heavy layers of yellow pine pollen that covered everything in the city during this month. We had experienced

---

[149] Jesús read the 1,463 pages unabridged version of Les Miserables in the 1980s.

the spring pollen in Maryland but only in Atlanta we have seen the thick layers of pine pollen covering everything.

In May, Maricarmen Trujillo Vazquez came to Atlanta to celebrate her fortieth birthday; her trip was a gift from Consuelo Beatriz, Cristy, Francisco and Amy. Her cousins, brother and sister-in-law planned many activities punctuated by a meal at our house with great wines including the Insignia 2002 and an exquisite filet mignon. In May, we also attended the Mercer University Atlanta commencements to witness Margaret León's receiving her degree in nursing, and afterwards joined the family for lunch at our favorite neighborhood restaurant, The Brooklyn Cafe. May was also an important month for Cristy because she was sworn in as President of the Georgia Association for Women Lawyers (GAWL) at a gala on May 9. We attended the ceremony and heard Cristy's first remarks as President, an excellent presentation given with her usual first-rate organization and clarity.

Danny Sorondo got married in June and we drove to Orlando to witness his wedding, then we went to Miami and from there to Marco. We returned to Atlanta and prepared for a family trip to Vancouver and Alaska in July. The seven members of the León-Bills family flew to Seattle where we were joined by Roberto Vich and Mimi for a three-day trip to the beautiful city of Vancouver Canada and then to board a cruise ship in Seattle for a one-week trip to southern Alaska. Alaska is beautiful and worth the trip by itself, but this trip was additionally enjoyable because of the thirty-two family and close friends that joined us for the cruise. When we returned to Atlanta we discovered that our friend Sergio Magadán was seriously ill with pulmonary issues resulting in his death during the month of July.

We went to Miami in August and joined the Abellas and Sorondo for our third Abella-León-Sorondo dinner, this time at the Abella's home on a Saturday evening. On Friday, the night before the dinner, we went together to a Miami Marlins baseball game.

October was a busy month. Tommy Trujillo, Jesús' nephew that Chelo calls "Chiquito"'married Adriana on Friday, October 18, and most of the family was present to celebrate the Sacrament. The wedding and reception were wonderful and joyous with many young people attending. Tommy's brothers were groomsmen at the wedding. It was a little hard for us to believe that the baby of the Trujillo-

León family was already a grown, responsible man. The family was also very impressed by the bride, Adriana, a lovely and caring young lady.

We drove back to Atlanta to host, together with Margarita and Alberto Bolet, the Fall IW&FS dinner at the Antica Posta Tuscan Restaurant and Bar with forty-four people attending. Chelo gave the invocation, Alberto presented the wines, Carli Franceschi, the President of the Atlanta Branch, and Jesús animated the meeting. The food, selected by the Bolets and us, was superb and the wines were excellent— it was a great evening!

Ethan received the Sacrament of Confirmation in November and he asked Jesús to be his sponsor. Jesús was obviously very proud to serve in this capacity just like Chelo who had sponsored Alina two years before because our grandchildren are outstanding human beings and committed Catholics. November was the month of the Annual ACU Atlanta Pig Roast, a significant event because of the Aspirant Promise made by three student members: Alex Trujillo (grandson of Ana María, Jesús' cousin), Eddy Prieto (high school classmate of Alex) and Luis Fernández-Rocha (grandson of an ACU member of the same name).

In October, our ophthalmologist told Chelo she needed to have cataracts surgery on both eyes, and he told Jesús he needed to have a simple laser follow-up procedure (Posterior Capsulotomy) to clear the back cellophane wrapping of the artificial lens implant. Jesús had this laser clearing done in November and Chelo decided to have the surgery the following year.

We spent most of December away from our house. We arrived in Miami at the beginning of the month for the annual ACU meetings and then to take a Caribbean cruise. The ACU Board reelected Jesús as ACU president on Friday. However, the significant event was the consecration, on Saturday, of two Atlanta aspirants who became ACU Congregants, David Sotto and Francisco Trujillo. Francisco is our godson, and he chose Jesús to be his ACU sponsor for this celebration. David Sotto was the first member of the newer ACU Atlanta Student Group to become a congregant in the ACU. Paco, Mary, Carmen Luisa and Chelo attended the ceremony. The ACU weekend ended with the traditional Mass and family celebration on Sunday afternoon.

On Monday, we boarded the Celebrity Equinox cruise ship at Fort Lauderdale to begin an eleven-day Western Caribbean cruise with the Irastorzas, the Bolets, René and Rosa López. Jesús was looking forward to this trip because he needed the rest after several weeks of continued activity: Tommy's wedding, hosting the IW&FS dinner, preparing the ACU Board meeting, organizing the AECWC dinner at our house, organizing the ACU Atlanta Pig Roast, and preparing the cruise.

The cruise started with a day at sea (very welcomed relaxation), then stopped at the Cayman Islands, Cartagena in Colombia, Colón and the Panamá Canal, Puerto Limón in Costa Rica, Belize City, and Cozumel before returning to Fort Lauderdale. In Panamá we took a tour of the Canal that was worthwhile although very long and wet; long because our excursion boat had to wait over five hours for a larger ship before crossing two locks— the canal authority does not open the locks for small ships alone. To add insult to injury, it started to rain while we waited at the Pedro Miguel locks, and it rained most of the time until we arrived at the Cruise ship. Even though we did not get soaked, we did get wet.

One interesting note to mention is that Jesús received a text message while at the Panamá Canal, a message sent by a Jesús' Georgia Tech mentee stating that Steve Chaddick was relating their mutual friendship during his Georgia Tech commencement speech. Steve was the Chair of the Board of Trustees of the GT Alumni Association and was explaining to new graduates the value of the alumni network. Jesús also received a message later from David Sotto stating, "You are all over Steve Chaddick's speech at the GT commencement."

We arrived back in Miami just before Christmas and "lived like gypsies" during our short stay— we slept three nights at Carmen's house and four nights at Mimi's house but had clothes in these two houses and also at Consuelo's house. We enjoyed the family celebrations and also a get together at the Villafañe's with the Antóns, José Montero and his girlfriend, and visiting with the Antón family on Christmas Day. Chelo, Jesús, Alina and Cristy traveled to Atlanta the day before Chelo's birthday. The four of us celebrated her birthday with a dinner at the Woodfire Grill, a restaurant in Atlanta owned by a Cuban who has two aunts married to ACU members who are our friends. Consuelo Beatriz, Lorenzo and Ethan drove back to Atlanta a couple of days later.

We remember 2013 as the year of "bizarre" car problems. The first problem happened to Chelo at rush hour on a busy intersection— her car stopped for no reason at all; she called Jesús who went to where the car was and eventually he started it. There seemed to be a common problem with the Mercedes E series car of that year, and we had it repaired soon afterwards. The other two problems were "strange" accidents with the other car, the Mercedes S-500. In September, we attended the IW&FS Fall Picnic, and when we returned home, as Jesús was backing the car into the garage, the garage door suddenly came down and slammed the rear top of the car shearing the antenna and shattering the rear windshield. Lorenzo told us that there had been a brief power interruption that caused the garage door mechanism to reset exactly as we were parking the car. This accident was scary and startled us. Then, during the trip to Miami in December, parts of a truck's tire came apart and hit the driver side of the car breaking the mechanism for the side mirror. Another scary accident with the only real damage done to our savings account.

Family life in Atlanta

We include here a few additional remarks about our family life in Atlanta to complement the chronological narrative in other parts of these memoirs.

We decided to retire in Atlanta because our children and grandchildren lived there, and so it should not be surprising to read about our many family activities during the time we lived in Atlanta. We saw Consuelo Beatriz, Cristy, Alina and Ethan often, generally at least once a week. Our Atlanta house became a central location and the two of us, now freed from job related responsibilities, provided other services to our progeny including providing rides to the grandchildren. The house's wonderful backyard with pool and cabana was a magnet to bring together our family for swimming, relaxation and sharing, especially during the spring, summer and fall every year. Even more important was the fact that Chelo is an excellent cook and loved to feed the family— we hosted family dinners almost every week, typically on Sundays.

Alina and Ethan, especially Alina, used the house to host parties including Alina's eighth grade graduation and activities around her high school graduation. She also organized a get together of new St Pius X first year students (Lion's Den) at our house in early August of her senior year.

We encouraged family reunions outside the city of Atlanta. Thus, we continued to rent a condominium and host the family at Marco Island for our larger family gathering every year. We helped organize and often partly subsidized other family trips, to Paris and Lourdes in 2006, Punta Cana and New York in 2011, Vancouver and Alaska in 2013, London and a cruise to the British Isles in 2014.

Our family reunions in Atlanta often included the other family members in Atlanta: Frank, Amy, Alex J and Ryan Thomas Trujillo; Henry, Margaret, Benjamin, Nicholas, Laurence and, until her untimely death, Jean Marie; and, Alex Trujillo Leyva, who came to study at Georgia Tech and joined us for family dinners and parties. We joined Frank and Amy at their house for family events, celebrating their children's milestones.

Since moving to Atlanta, we have made it a point to celebrate together family events: birthdays, anniversaries, graduations, and awards. These celebrations were invariable around an important dinner, often at our house but sometimes at an Atlanta restaurant. The last celebration we record in these memoirs was a pool party sendoff of Alina the weekend before she left to attend, as a first year student, Fordham University in New York.

We finish writing

In 2014 we celebrated our seventieth birthday; Consuelo Beatriz said 2014 was a "year of first": Chelo got an iPhone and a new <u>red</u> car, Alina graduated from high school and started college, Ethan had his first girlfriend, and Consuelo Beatriz started a new job in a different department of AT&T.

The year began in Atlanta with cold weather, snow and ice. We had low temperatures of twelve, six and fourteen degrees Fahrenheit to start the second week of January, an omen, to be sure.

Atlantans then experienced a repeat of the Snow Jam 1982, beginning also on a Tuesday, January 28, 2014. It started snowing around the middle of the day with about two inches of total accumulation. Unfortunately, a large part of the Atlanta population decided to get on the road at the same time; according to the Atlanta mayor, over one million persons tried to leave the downtown Atlanta area within a very short window of time. The result was a monumental traffic jam with extremely long drive times for most people. It took Lorenzo more than five hours to drive home from Georgia State University, normally a twenty minutes ride. It took Cristy two hours just to exit a downtown parking lot. Our nephew Francisco slept in his office and his wife Amy slept in their son's day care center. One woman gave birth on I-285 at the Riverside Drive exit and named her baby "Grace." There are thousands of stories of people stranded or sleeping in a Wal-Mart or in strangers' houses, spending fifteen or eighteen hours on the road. All the schools in Atlanta closed for the rest of the week. At least four persons were not able to attend the Spanish men's retreat that weekend because of the impact of the snow to their work or travel. Two weeks later, on February 12, we had more snow and ice, and to avoid another traffic jam, the city was shut down for three days.

The following Saturday we flew to Washington to attend Reemberto Rodríguez Junior's[150] stateside wedding reception on February 15, returning to Atlanta on Sunday and then driving to Miami on Monday. Once we arrived in Miami, Chelo noticed that Consuelo had swollen gums and we scheduled a trip to see dentist Oscar Gómez, the husband of Tuti Revuelta, who told us that Consuelo had several abscesses that had to be treated immediately. Consuelo started taking antibiotics on Thursday and Oscar removed seven teeth or the roots of teeth in one sitting on Monday, February 24. Chelo had planned to have cataract removed from her left eye on Thursday, February 27, but postponed the surgery to assist with Consuelo's recovery. Thanks God that Consuelo recovered very well and very quickly. Oscar extracted seven more teeth or roots two weeks

---

[150] Reemberto Junior wedding ceremony was held in December in Sydney, Australia.

later, again with Consuelo recovering very quickly. While in Miami, the "check engine" warning light on the E-320 turned on. Jesús took the car to the Mercedes dealer on Monday, the same day that Oscar extracted Consuelo's teeth. After checking the car thoroughly for gasoline leaks per the computer code on Monday and again on Tuesday, the Mercedes technician stated that, "the problem was caused by the winter additives added to the gasoline in Georgia that were not used in South Florida, and this "tricked" the car computer to believe there was an engine problem." Although the explanation seemed bizarre, we decided to drive back to Atlanta on Wednesday because the car was working fine and the Coral Gables Mercedes leadership had checked the car on two consecutive days. Well, once we reached Valdosta, Georgia, and filled the tank with "Georgia gasoline," the check engine light turned off!

On the ACU front, the Jesuit Provincial for the Antilles Province designated Father Guillermo (Willie) Arias, SJ, to be the provisional director of the ACU effective the first day of February of this year. One of Father Willie's first recommendations was to propose an ACU-wide assembly to be held in June; this idea resulted in a large increase in the amount of time Jesús dedicated to the ACU for the next few months.

Jesús' car was still working well but needed repairs and maintenance costing more than two thousand dollars. The car was fourteen years old and had one hundred-eighty-thousand miles. We decided it was time to buy another car because Chelo's car was also fourteen years old with about one hundred twenty-thousand miles. Jesús researched different cars, we visited dealerships, and finally Chelo decided she wanted to buy a Lexus ES 350, a car with a 'Matador' red color. Jesús sold the S-500 Mercedes to CarMax and we bought the new car in mid March.

The family spent plenty of time during the first half of 2014 discussing two questions that related specifically to Alina. The first was how to obtain enough tickets for Alina's graduation ceremony because the allocation was limited to five tickets per graduating senior and we needed eight tickets.[151] The plan put in place was for Ethan to work as a volunteer, for Consuelo to get an extra ticket from a friend and to have Lorenzo go to the Baccalaureate Mass instead of the commencement ceremony. Nevertheless, at the end, Alina was able to obtain extra tickets and Lorenzo was able to attend the graduation. The second unknown was about the college Alina would attend. She was accepted at two very expensive schools and was in the waiting list at other colleges.

We went to Miami in April to celebrate Consuelo's ninety-third birthday and noticed upon arrival that Consuelo had a bruise in her right leg. The bruise required daily nurse attention to clean and treat it. Fortunately, the bruise healed and life at Consuelo's house went back to normal. On her birthday, Roberto and Mimi joined us to sing Happy Birthday to Consuelo and eat the birthday cake.

We returned to Atlanta to prepare our house to host Maricarmen Vazquez's family and her parents-in-law during the Easter weekend. They were going to spend the week after Easter in a cabin in the Georgia Mountains together with Paco and Mary. Ofelia and Juan Senior enjoyed their visit and we had a very enjoyable time with the Vazquez family. On Easter Sunday we got together for lunch with all the Vazquez, the rest of the León-Bills family, Paco and Mary Trujillo, Francisco, Amy and their children, and Alex Trujillo Leyva at Maggiano's Italian Restaurant.

We were ready for May, a month filled with family events and one strange health episode that we describe below. The first event was Alex J. Trujillo's First Communion and this was followed by Alina's graduation from St. Pius X High School on May 17. We attended Alex J's First Communion and then joined the family for a celebration at Francisco and Amy's house. We enjoyed Alina's graduation ceremony and the celebration that took place at the Atlanta Lawyer's Club, a short walk from the auditorium where Alina's graduation took place. Family and friends came to this celebration: Henry, Benjamin and Nicholas León, Frank and Amy Trujillo, the Stokes Family who drove from Michigan to be a part of the celebration, and

---

[151] Consuelo Beatriz, Cristy, Lorenzo, Chelo, Jesús, Todd, Alexandra (Alina's godmother) and Francisco.

John Ecuyer, a friend and colleague of Consuelo who flew from Boca Ratón.

The following week we received the great news of the birth of Ana Sofía Vilaró Antón on May 20, the daughter of José Luis and Maritere, the granddaughter of Manny and Annette. What a beautiful baby!

May was the month of Chelo's "Transient Global Amnesia," a health episode that is not supposed to have long term consequences. This was Chelo's second health issue this year; in March she had a bad case of allergy that caused her a swollen left cheek. Then, on Saturday, May 24, 2014, we witnessed and "suffered" through the Transient Global Amnesia episode. In the early afternoon, Chelo swam, did weight exercises with dumbbells and then showered. She started to dry her hair while Lorenzo and Jesús were waiting for the start of the European Champions League final game. She came to the family room at about 2:45 PM and told Lorenzo and Jesús that she did not remember what she had been doing a few minutes earlier. After Jesús asked her a couple of questions that elicited strange answers, he called Manny Antón and then took her to St Joseph's Hospital, arriving there at 3:00 PM. Manny and Jesús were worried that Chelo had some type of stroke. The emergency room staff at St. Joseph's Hospital was extremely efficient— we were there for only two hours. The emergency room doctor told Jesús upon seeing Chelo that she had a condition called "Transient Global Amnesia," a sudden, temporary episode of memory loss.[152] To say that we were scared is to put it mildly; Chelo exhibited the symptoms of a concussion, similar to what Lorenzo had after his accident in 2007. Consuelo, Cristina, Alina, Ethan and Francisco came home to provide support and tender loving care. For approximately eight hours, Chelo lost the ability to access her short-term memory and kept asking the same question over and over again.[153] Thanks God that she began to recover around 11:30 PM that night and was essentially back to normal the next af-

---

[152] See www.mayoclinic.org/diseases-conditions/transient-global-amnesia/basics/definition/con-20032746

[153] "Who took me to the hospital? Why did you take me to the hospital? Was I acting funny? How funny was I acting? Who dressed me?"

ternoon. Wow! Jesús spoke with Manny Antón several times from the outset of the episode through the following afternoon; Manny's medical expertise and his family's support were very valuable during this difficult time for us.

Jesús had been very busy since the beginning of the year organizing the ACU Assembly that was held in Miami the first weekend June. This was an important event for the ACU with the participation of more than one hundred members, the first general reunion of ACU members since 1981. Needless to say, Jesús was exhausted by the end of the assembly and looked forward to rest and recuperation during our vacations in June and July. Our vacations started with our annual Marco Island family gathering, a smaller gathering than in previous years. This was the first time in many years that Cristina and Lorenzo did not attend— Cristy because of the upcoming British Isles trip and Lorenzo because he started working on a summer internship at Roper Pumps in Commerce, Georgia. Lorenzo enjoyed the internship and learned how to apply his marketing knowledge in a company, but he had to drive one-hour each way from/to our house to the company.

In July, all of the León-Bills family— except Lorenzo— went to London on a vacation celebration. Chelo and Jesús had wanted to go on this trip for several years and postponed it on two occasions. The trip was also to celebrate Alina's high school graduation and Ethan's future graduation two years later. We spent four days in London, days filled from morning to night with a detailed sightseeing schedule. On the fifth day, Consuelo flew back to Atlanta while the rest of us went to Stonehenge and from there to Southampton to board the Ruby Princess cruise ship on a trip around the British Isles.[154] We enjoyed the trip and remember fondly that Chelo loved Guinness on draught and the English High Tea served at the ship. Ethan loves cruises because the cruise lines organize teenage activities and he, once again, found a group of young persons of his age and interests. On the other hand, Ethan was in the doghouse big time on the last

---

[154] With stops at Guernsey; Cork, Dublin and Belfast in Ireland; Liverpool; Glasgow, Inverness and Edinburgh in Scotland; and in Le Havre to visit Normandy.

day of the cruise when he was late to the tour bus causing forty-three persons to wait for twenty-five minutes until he showed up— Chelo, Cristy and Jesús were extremely unhappy and embarrassed. Ethan was partially grounded that evening.

Early in the summer, Lorenzo informed us that he was going out steadily with a young lady, Denise Gutierrez, a Mexican born Physician Assistant. He met her through the Internet during the winter months. He introduced Denise to the family and she joined us from time to time for our family dinners. During the summer, Chelo and Cristy joined the ACU Atlanta group to help the Cristo Rey Jesuit High School that opened in August. Lorenzo, Jesús and some ACU members helped move furniture donated by other schools and our family volunteered to become mentors.

Jesús had his annual physical when we returned from our British Isles Cruise. Everything was fine except the doctor mentioned that the x-rays showed a "deviation of the trachea" and wanted Jesús to have a chest CT scan with contrast. This news was a little bit worrisome; however, the results of the scan showed there was nothing to worry about— whew!

Consuelo, Cristy and Ethan drove Alina to college during the Labor Day Weekend. Alina had chosen to attend Fordham University in New York, and although Chelo and Jesús were horrified at the expected cost of Alina's education, we wished her well and desired she would have a great experience in college. The trip was a driving marathon with long spells of driving on four consecutive days, Friday-Monday. They successfully helped organize Alina's dormitory room before returning. While in New York, the four of them got together for dinner with José Luis, Maritere and Ana Sofia. Before leaving for New York, Alina edited Book V of these memoirs.

Chelo and Jesús drove to Miami at the same time that Consuelo, Cristy and Ethan were helping to accommodate Alina at Fordham. The week before our trip to Miami, Migdalia had tooth pain and also an automobile accident. The teeth problems were corrected with antibiotics and then extraction. The car accident was not major, but Migdalia was shaken up and did not want to drive for a while.

We returned as volunteers for the GED program in September, although we were only able to teach for about four weeks this fall because of the trips to Miami and Chelo's plan for cataract surgeries in November. Once again, we had to alter our plans. In September, Adolfo Fernández, Chelo's cousin who had been very close to us in our earlier years died in Miami. Adolfo had lived in the same house in Cuba as Chelo after his father died, and in Miami lived about one block from Chelo until her marriage. Adolfo and Jesús had worked together at the Dagwood's Restaurant in the early 1960s. Adolfo's November birthday was sandwiched between Jesús' in October and Chelo's in December. We went to Miami to bid farewell to Adolfo and provide support for his family.

During October, Chelo became increasingly dissatisfied with the ophthalmologist who was supposed to perform the cataract surgery, and after failing to hear from the doctor when she had some questions, decided to cancel the surgery and change doctors, this time to a doctor recommended by our internal medicine physician, Dr. Peter Díaz.

We went to Miami in October to attend the wedding of Roberto and Mimi's daughter "Tati", an opportunity for a family reunion. We celebrated Thanksgiving in Atlanta but were back in Miami in December for the ACU annual meetings. While in Miami, we were very disappointed to hear that Lorenzo would not graduate in December.

Chelo began 2015 with cataract surgeries— the right eye in January and the left one in March. In between the surgeries we flew to Rio and spent the last two days of the Carnival there before boarding an Azamara ship for a cruise to Miami. In August, we spent one and one-half days in Amsterdam and then took a Rhine River cruise from Amsterdam to Basel; we rented a car in Basel to travel in Provence, Lyon and Burgundy, and finished the trip with three days in Paris. In November we traveled to New York City to attend Alina's recognition at the Fordham's Dean List celebration, and our goddaughter's Ana Teresa Villafañe's Broadway Show, *On Your Feet*. We finished our 2015 travel with a land and cruise trip to New Zealand and Australia in November. On another note, Jesús celebrated his fiftieth anniversary as a congregant (full member) in the ACU in December.

We took a fourteen-day Southern Caribbean Cruise vacation in February 2016. Chelo and Jesús stayed in San Juan at the end of the cruise for Jesús to attend the weekly meeting of the ACU Puerto Rico Chapter. Ethan graduated form St. Pius X High School in May and prepared to begin his college studies at Georgia Tech. We returned to New York City in October to attend Fordham's Dean List recognition for Alina and we celebrated Jesús birthday while in NYC with dinner at Günter Seeger NY's Kitchen Table.

However, the most important family event in 2016 was the marriage of Consuelo Beatriz to John Ecuyer. Consuelo and John met at work, in AT&T, and developed a relationship that grew over time to lead to their marriage. John is a competent professional, a gentleman, a committed Roman Catholic man educated at Jesuit High School of New Orleans, at Tulane and Northwestern Universities. He is clearly in love with Consuelo. The wedding was a family affair in New Orleans: Carmen Luisa, Mary, Henry, several of Consuelo's boy cousins and all her girl cousins attended as did Kathy Stearns, Mary Lou, Ana Silva and the Stokes family from Michigan. Consuelo and John's wedding took place in the chapel at Jesuit High School and was followed by a reception. We were very happy to see Consuelo Beatriz married to a great guy!

The year 2017 was very special because we reached our Golden Wedding Anniversary. This was the year when Jesús completed his "bucket list" with a cruise around Cape Horn and a visit to Machu Picchu. Other travels in 2017 included a trip to Sedona and the Grand Canyon with Georgia Tech Travel and the usual trip to New York City to attend Fordham's Dean List recognition for Alina. The family's most remarkable trip happened in May when we all traveled to Italy (Tuscany, Cinque Terre and Rome) to celebrate our anniversary. We completed the celebration of our anniversary on August 26 toasting with champagne at home and then a family dinner at an Italian restaurant.

In February 2018, we traveled to Tahiti and took a French Polynesian Cruise aboard an Oceania ship: great ship, spectacular water but so-so beaches. In April all the family went to NYC to attend Alina's graduation, Summa Cum Laude, from Fordham University. Chelo and Jesús flew to Los Angeles immediately after Alina's graduation to board a Regents Seven Seas Cruise with the Bolet and Irastorza couples to the Mexican Riviera. In June Jesús went to Milwaukee to be present at ACU Washington friend and congregant Kyle Shinseki's ordination as a Jesuit priest.

In October we came to the end of an era for our family: the last of our parents, Consuelo Soledad Redruello-Cordero, died on October 27. Father Willie celebrated a beautiful Mass of Resurrection at the Prince of Peace Church in Miami followed by the burial of Consuelo next to her husband. We make a special note about the death of Chelo's parents. As her parents grew older and since we have always lived away from Miami, it was Chelo's wish and prayer to God to be at their side at the time of death. God granted Chelo's prayers and she accompanied her parents in their peaceful death.

We reached our seventy-fifth birthday in 2019 and although a difficult year for our family and for our Atlanta community it was also one that demonstrated once again the great gift we have enjoyed through our life of a beautiful family and a strong community of friends. The Atlanta community suffered the death of Rosa López in January, Gonzalo Saldaña in June, and Galo Cimadevilla in August, and we saw the health of Luisa Blanco and Sonia Guigou take a turn for the worse. In our family, Henry ("Hank") Ecuyer, the father of John died in July after battling cancer for many years. Hank was a committed Catholic, a very friendly person, and an example of a professional Christian man.

The year started nicely— in January we closed on the sale of the Miami house where Chelo's parents lived for twenty years, and we accelerated our planning to travel to Europe in April with Cristy to visit Alina in Spain. Alina had accepted a position to teach English during the September-June academic year at the Colegio de Fomento Miravalles, a girl school outside Pamplona. On the other hand, in January Lorenzo started experiencing back pains which we all attributed to his return to cross fit exercises after a two month hiatus— more on Lorenzo's health issue after we cover Chelo's and Jesús' issues.

In March, a few weeks before our trip, our dentist, Dr. Jason Myerson, told Chelo he had to replace a bridge she had on the upper right side of her mouth but that she could wait until her return from the trip to have the work done. Meanwhile, Jesús had a strong pain on his right leg and went to see Dr. Peter Díaz, our internal medicine family doctor. Dr. Díaz referred Jesús to get a sonogram at Piedmont Hospital; the sonogram was negative but the nurse suggested that Jesús visit a vascular surgeon. The vascular surgeon told Jesús he would fix the varicose veins in his legs upon his return from Europe.

Chelo's teeth were not willing to wait until her return to Atlanta. She had pain and swelling of her cheek on May 2 in Madrid; the hotel called a doctor to come see Chelo and the doctor told her she had a tooth infection. The doctor prescribed an antibiotic and an anti-inflammatory. These prescriptions took care of Chelo's problem in Europe. When she returned to Atlanta she had to have major surgery to remove the remaining portion of her tooth and prepare the mouth for implants. Jesús' problem was a lot simpler— the vascular surgeon "treated" his varicose veins in both the right and left legs the week after his return to Atlanta.

The purpose of our trip to Europe was to see Alina and to show her parts of Spain she did not know. Cristy, Chelo Alina and Jesús visited Segovia, Toledo, Cordoba, Granada, Ronda, Sevilla, Mérida, Salamanca, Pamplona and Madrid. We visited with Javier Colio, his wife Judith and their daughters in Pamplona, and with Elma Gutierrez, Juanjo and Javier's mother, in Tafalla. We had lunch or dinner with several of our friends in Madrid: Fina and Vicente, Mari Carmen, María José, Luis Fernández Villagrasa and Ana, and Father José Ignacio Rubio López but we missed Pablo Calvo and Pili because of Chelo's tooth infection. Alina returned to Pamplona and Cristy to Atlanta from Madrid while Chelo and Jesús flew to Paris for five days of sightseeing and great food.

Lorenzo's health issue turned out to be complicated and dangerous. When the back pains began, Lorenzo decided to stop exercising for a couple of weeks. However, the pain continued and actually got worse; Lorenzo went to see Dr. Díaz who thought it might be a bruised rib and asked Lorenzo to rest for a while. The pain became so bad that Lorenzo had to visit hospital emergency rooms twice, at St. Joseph's and Piedmont; he had X-Rays and a CAT Scan, one at each hospital with both tests negative. Somewhere along the line, he was told it could be Shingles— it wasn't. Dr. Díaz then send Lorenzo to get an MRI but unfortunately it was done for the lower part of the abdomen— where he was experiencing the pain— and this MRI was negative. Dr. Díaz sent Lorenzo to a pain specialist, Dr. Xu, who thought Lorenzo might have a herniated disk and prescribed physical therapy. After two weeks of therapy, the pain was getting worse and

Lorenzo began experiencing difficulty walking and had to use a cane. Dr. Xu sent Lorenzo to have more MRIs done and these MRI finally identified the problem: Lorenzo had a tumor in the spine; the doctor thought it was Meningioma, a tumor that requires neurosurgery and Dr. Xu referred him to a neurosurgeon who, unfortunately, was not in the office. The neurosurgeon's office staff told Lorenzo that his problem was not "life threatening" and he could wait until July 2 to see the doctor.

Lorenzo agreed to join us for the annual family reunion/vacation at Marco Island. The trip and the week were painful for Lorenzo and a nightmare for the rest of the family. Lorenzo flew back to Atlanta on Friday, June 28. We took him to Piedmont Emergency Room on Saturday morning; the emergency room doctor examined Lorenzo and went to check on the neurosurgeon on call; it turns out that the neurosurgeon on call, Doctor Roger H. Frankel, was at the hospital making rounds and scheduled to see Lorenzo.

Dr. Frankel saw Lorenzo and after reviewing the MRI disk that we brought with us told Lorenzo that he had two options: "(1) if no surgery, 100% invalid for the rest of his life; (2) with surgery, pretty good chance of recovery to 100% or at worse to 85-90%." Lorenzo replied, "I don't have any real option." Dr. Frankel explained the surgery and risks and answered all our questions. He believed that to reduce the risks of permanent damage, surgery should be done as soon as possible and he recommended surgery the next day, Sunday at 8:00 in the morning. Lorenzo agreed and Dr. Frankel got his team together and prepared for the Sunday morning surgery.

It turns out that Dr. Frankel (1) was not supposed to be at the hospital originally but was there because his wife made a scheduling mistake while planning the family vacation early in the year; (2) is a spine specialist— he does more spine surgery that all other Piedmont Hospital neurosurgeons combined. Dr. Frankel's presence at the hospital and expertise were God's gifts.

The surgery performed on Sunday morning, June 30, was successful; it took two-and-one-half hours instead of the estimated four hours and the doctor was able to remove the whole tumor and reposition the spinal cord. The biopsy came back with a finding of a Schwannoma benign tumor. So Lorenzo's tentative diagnoses went from muscle pain to bruised ribs to shingle to a herniated disk and finally to a tumor, originally believed to be Meningioma but turned it out to be Schwannoma.

Lorenzo was discharged on Saturday, July 6, and was admitted that day to the Emory Rehabilitation Hospital (ERH). We tried very hard to get Lorenzo into the Shepherd Center for rehabilitation—with assistance from Doctor Frankel, Amy, one of Lorenzo's workmate and Alfredo Trujillo's influence at Shepherd, but without success.

Lorenzo's stay at the ERH was successful; he did at least three hours of occupational and physical therapy every day for twenty-five days with only two days of rest. Lorenzo made excellent progress during his stay at this hospital: he strengthened his core, was able to walk over 200 feet at a time with a walker, was able to go up steps, and stand for over fifteen minutes at a time. Lorenzo was discharged from ERH on Tuesday, July 30 and returned home to continue exercises at home and as an outpatient at the Piedmont Hospital Rehabilitation. Lorenzo continued to make progress at home thanks to his good attitude and the support of the family.

As we finished writing, we noticed that although we have had reasonably good health, we had our share of rare diseases: Jesús had Polymyalgia Rheumatica (2002), Chelo Transient Global Amnesia (2014) and Lorenzo a Schwannoma tumor in the spine region (2019).

We hope we have good health for the rest of our lives. We are certain there will be plenty of interesting experiences in our future—we ask our children and grandchildren to chronicle them.

Epilogue

Passion

During dinner with Atlanta friends, while discussing Jesús' work with the ACU, one of our friends remarked that it was inspirational to see Jesús' passion for this apostolic activity. Passion, commitment and intensity are the adjectives we wish to use to summarize our lives. We are both passionate about what we do; passionate about doing the best we can, passionate about God, the Catholic Church, our country, our family, our friends, our profession.

Our passion, commitment and intensity at times caused stress to family members and friends who were very close to us emotionally. Although we did not want to be the source of stress to others, we are who we are, persons of strong beliefs for whom the quote from the Book of Revelations does not apply, "But because you are lukewarm and neither cold nor hot, I will begin to vomit you out of my mouth" (Rev. 3, 16). We are not lukewarm about anything! Passion has made our lives interesting.[155]

We have enjoyed a long, generally healthy, abundant life, a life enriched and strengthened by our faith, family and friends. Among the wonderful persons who enriched our lives were our parents, our children and grandchildren and many friends in Cuba, the USA and Spain. We do want to highlight a few persons who played a special role in our lives. Lorenzo Cordero showed us the power of tenderness, affectionate love and friendship. Argentina Núñez was a mentor and an example. Rigoberto León taught us about prayer and accepting God's will. Consuelo Redruello's work ethics and readiness to serve others were exemplary. Father Llorente and Monsignor López demonstrated how to live a holy life each day of their lives.

---

[155] In her song, "Sin Clave no hay Son," Cuban singer Marisela Varela says, "A life without passion is sad." We agree.

Our lives did not turn out anything like either of us would have envisioned as youngsters or young adults. Looking back, we have to agree with our friend Steve Chaddick's statement, "Life is nonlinear." We are happy and thankful for our life's nonlinearities that brought so much wonder, excitement and satisfaction. Let us review a couple of examples of the nonlinearities in our lives that we related in these memoirs.

A major nonlinearity and one that had some positive consequences in our lives was the Cuban Revolution. Although this may sound strange or at least peculiar to some people, we are grateful to have experienced the Cuban revolution. The fact is that because of the Cuban Revolution and exile we met, fell in love, married and built a family; we learned English, received a great education, built professional careers, cultivated wonderful friends; and we are now enjoying retirement in a beautiful house surrounded by family and friends. So we thank God that brought us together. Simirlarly we had no plans to move to Spain or to Maryland, but both moves were very rewarding for our family. We envisioned spending our retirement years in a condominium by the sea, yet we are in Atlanta and happy to be near our children and grandchildren. And sometimes little things do come to those with patience. Jesús did not ride the Coney Island Cyclone roller coaster when he was 13 years old in 1958, but he did ride it in 2011, when he was 66 years old!

By the way, the two of us did not plan to become a lot more alike to each other with the years. We did share from the start of our relationship some commonalities beyond Catholicism and a Cuban Ethnic background. We both love to travel, to enjoy great meals at superb restaurants, and to explore new places and menu items. We have maintained our different personalities, but there is no doubt that we have absorbed traits from each other. Chelo has, for example, become more assertive and more willing to take risks. Jesús has become mellower and has learned to let Chelo take the lead often. This coming together is a sign of the Marriage Sacrament as expressed in "This is why a man leaves his father and mother and becomes attached to his wife, and the two become one flesh."[156]

---

[156] Matthew 19, 5.

Wisdom

As we conclude these memoirs, we wish to share a few "pearls of wisdom" that, we hope, will help future generations to have successful life. Why and how did we have a happy and successful life? Because we understood two very important things about life: the first is that one must live according to a clear set of values, and the second that one must know how to define and measure what makes a successful life.

Having a clear value system is critical to a successful and happy life. We have always had a very clear understanding of what are the really important things in our lives and also of their priority: First, placing God at the center of our lives; second, family; third, profession; and fouth, friends. We made all our important decisions based on these priorities, whether it was to move to Spain, Maryland or to Atlanta; whether it was to work or stay home for Chelo; whether or not to spend time on a particular apostolic or civic activity. Knowing our priorities and making decisions based on these values resulted not only in making good choices but also in being at peace afterwards with the outcome.

Defining success is also critical to having a rewarding life because the definition allows one to measure the achievements of one's life. We look back with satisfaction to the successes we achieved in our lives. What was our definition of success? It is based on three components: conformity to our value system, general achievements, and impact on other persons. Number one, did we live our lives in accordance with our value system? Number two, what did we accomplish? And, number three, did we influence enough people positively to make an impact in the world we live in? Let's look at our report card.

We lived our lives pretty much based on our values and priorities. We have always been committed Catholics and tried to live our daily lives, for the most part, as true Christians, following the moral and loving teaching of Christ. With regards to the family, Chelo has done an outstanding job with all her family members: her parents, her in-laws, her children and grandchildren; it would require another chapter to narrate in detail her dedication to the family. Professionally, we both achieved success, receiving accolades from our colleagues in every career position we have held and also in the volunteer work that we have undertaken. As for friends, we have friends galore, many of them very close to us, essentially family members. It is an illustration of how we attract and maintain friends that several years ago a colleague of Jesús told him, "You go around the world collecting friends and good restaurants." Thus, we grade ourselves a solid A for the first element of our measurement of success.

We also give ourselves an A grade for our second measure of success, attaining significant accomplishments. We have a large number of family and friends that have provided us plenty of happiness. We have traveled a lot, enjoyed great food at many excellent restaurants (at last count, we have eaten at more than twenty Michelin three-stars restaurants), learned a lot about the world culture and geography. Because we were excellent professionally, worked very hard, were open to opportunities and took chances, we also achieved professional and financial success.

Last but not least is the answer to the question: How many people have we impacted positively during our lives? Well, in Chelo's case it is very clear that she influenced positively many persons because she was an excellent high school teacher for many years. She has been approached often by former students who thanked her for her impact on their lives; in fact, some students chose their college major because of Chelo's influence. She was also a role model, counselor and mentor to members of our family and to many friends. Jesús has also influenced many persons in his life at work, as a part-time teacher, and especially through the ACU where he mentors and helps in the formation of many men and their families. Jesús stated on various occasions that one of his life's goals was to impact positively one person for each year of life. We believe both of us exceeded this measure. Thus, once again, we grade ourselves with a solid A.

From the last paragraphs it is clear we have had a happy and successful life. Let us now address a couple of obvious questions for anyone who writes a memoir: Did we include all major details of our lives in the memoirs? Would we change anything if we had the chance to "do over" parts of our life? The answer to the first question is categorically no. We have selected what we believe provides a good review of our lives, but it is not practical or desirable to include most details of seventy-five years of busy lives.[157] Additionally, there are some parts of our lives that will always remain private and some that are to be shared only with our confessors.

The second question is interesting and the theme of some Hollywood movies: What if you could go back in time and change some part or parts of your life? Well, the problem with changing any item in the past is that it will result in unexpected consequences in the following years. Hence, although tempting, we will pass up making changes to our past lives.[158] Why change when we had "A Wonderful Life" with a great family, excellent friends, and attaining success?

Gratitude

As we come to the end of these memoirs we are compelled to do so in thanksgiving. We thank everyone who supported us during the preparation of the memoirs. Consuelo Beatriz, Cristina and Lorenzo helped our recollection of important events. Jesús's sister Carmen Luisa provided genetic and family information; she is the reference-par-excellence about the León-Núñez family history. Our granddaughter Alina spent many hours helping to edit the manuscript.

We are thankful for our parents who gave us their genes, educated and taught us by their example how to live in harmony with our values. We are thankful for those who helped nurture our Catholic Faith. We are thankful for the joy and support of our family and many friends.

We are very especially thankful to God for we have seen His hand many times in our lives. Chelo often mentions a Spanish Catholic song that touches her heart, "Que Detalle, Señor, Has Tenido Conmi-

---

[157] For example, we relegated to Appendix V the story of the "peculiar" circumstances that resulted in meeting Placido Domínguez and several Ambassadors from Latin American countries.

[158] We were tempted to quote extensively from Frank Sinatra's song "My Way," about living a full life, doing it our way, and also "regrets, we had a few, … too few to mention."

go[159]." Although it is difficult to encompass the full meaning in English, a translation of the title could be "What special gesture, Lord, you have shown me." The song thanks God for calling each of us to be his friend. As we reflected on our lives while writing and revising the memoirs we could see God's "detalles" over and over and over in our lives. Here is a brief summary of some of the many significant "detalles" God had with us:

<u>Born in special families</u>. We received our DNA, our Catholic faith, values, examples and motivation about how to live from our wonderful families.

<u>Meeting each other and becoming a couple</u>. God led us to each other through a somewhat convoluted path. It started with our mutual first cousins Bertica and Vicente that married in Havana and served as our initial connection although we lived in different cities in Cuba. This was followed in Miami with Jesús' role as the interpreter to make long-distance calls to Chelo when she was in school at Momence. Later, residing in close proximity in Miami and the fact that Jesús worked with Chelo's first cousin Adolfo helped to bring us together.

<u>The ACU</u>. Jesús' father was a member of the ACU but it was a friend in the anti-Castro movement that took Jesús to the ACU. The ACU has provided not only a compass in our lives and a major family apostolate but gave us a plethora of great friends who have provided great support to us. In 1978, Manny Antón and others asked Jesús to lead them in a new group in Atlanta; the ACU Atlanta became a family apostolate that has been a great blessing.

<u>Moving to Atlanta</u>. We had not planned to move to Atlanta but Jesús met Georgia Tech Professor Joe Hammond at a conference and decided to go to GT. Coincidentally, Luis and Lourdes Gutierrez, very close friends from Gainesville had decided to move to Atlanta also and we were happy to move close to each

---

[159] https://www.youtube.com/watch?v=rT4jIgKCbBM&list=RDCfI1CLiN7RE&index=2 is one many examples of this song.

other for mutual support. Atlanta and its community were great for our family.

Our professional jobs in Atlanta. Both Chelo and Jesús obtained major career positions in Atlanta out of the blue, another "detalle". We were at an Atlanta Cursillo meeting when someone mentioned that St. Pius X High School was looking for a Spanish teacher— voilà, Chelo was hired! Jesús was a graduate student and was not looking for a job when Dave McGill, Georgia Tech professor and good friend from the Atlanta Cursillo, recommended Jesús to Scientific-Atlanta where Dave was a consultant— voilà, Jesús was hired and started his professional career.

Consuelo Beatriz's miracle after his tonsil surgery. As we related earlier, upon checking CB after the "growth" in her throat disappeared, the surgeon stated, "I do not know what happened. The blob was there last night and is not there any more."

Moving to Spain. The move to Spain, in two parts, was another unexpected turn in our lives as we described in Books V and VI of the memoirs. Lorenzo, Chelo and Jesús' move to Spain was completely unexpected— God was leading us with his "detalles".

Joining Ciena and moving to Maryland. Ciena's job offer and our move to Maryland were unexpected detalles." It would be difficult for us not to believe in God's plan for us when we recount how this came to be.

Finding the Atlanta location for the house we built to retire in. This was another clear example of God's hand in our lives. We had made a good offer on another house that did not work out. However, the lot where we built the house was under contract and suddenly became available!

Dr. Frankel "happens" to be at the hospital for Lorenzo. Dr. Frankel was not supposed to be on call at Piedmont Hospital the day we took Lorenzo to the emergency room; he was there because of a scheduling mistake. Dr. Frankel is the spine specialist neurosurgeon who diagnosed the seriousness of the problem and successfully operated on Lorenzo on the following day. Luck, coincidence, fate — we don't think so!

The above vignettes illustrate how wonderful God has been to us! We pray that our children, grandchildren and their progeny will enjoy a wonderful, happy life full of success with their families and friends in their chosen profession, and very especially that they maintain the Christian faith that has been the foundation of our family life.

AMDG

Postscript

The year 2020 came upon us like a Caribbean hurricane causing many issues including a delay in printing these memoirs. 2020 has been a year without parallel in our lifetime; we thought it appropriate to add a page to the memoirs summarizing some of the major events of the year.

There were two exceptional global events during the year. The first was a health crisis produced by the COVID-19 virus pandemic and this was followed by a global economic crisis. In the USA there was additionally a societal crisis caused by systematic racism in our nation.

The pandemic impacted our immediate family directly— our grandson got the virus during the early part of the Fall Semester at Georgia Tech; thanks God that it was a mild case whose major repercussion was a temporary loss of the sense of smell. Several members of our extended family were also sick with the virus.

The pandemic compelled us to reduce to a minimum activities outside the home. These reductions included canceling our family reunion in Marco Island for the first time in over twenty years. We also cancelled a ten-day trip to Portugal that was to be followed with a twelve-day cruise of the Mediterranean. In addition, we also cancelled a trip to NYC with Cristy and our friend Dorene, a trip that was to include watching the Broadway revival of The Music Man.

The virus necessitated the "virtualization" of many activities: Consuelo, John, Cristy and Alina did most of their work remotely; Ethan attended many classes virtually; we "attended" Mass virtually from our house for more than seven months. We postponed noncritical health related activities: Jesús' had back pain starting in January that was to be treated with professional physical therapy; instead, he began in-home therapy. Jesús postponed following up on hearing aids. We did receive treatment for a couple of relatively minor health problems during the year: Chelo developed minor arthritis in her left foot's instep; Jesús had a benign skin cancer on the left nostril that was removed in August.

The COVID-19 pandemic caused major economic issues, especially the closing of businesses and the layoff of many employees. Many of the laid off persons suffered significantly: they worked hourly jobs and could not work remotely. As is generally the case, the most impacted persons and families were the most vulnerable with low incomes and limited savings. The economic fallout made it very difficult, almost impossible, for Lorenzo to find a suitable and safe job.

Chelo said a couple of times that although we ourselves did not get the COVID-19 virus, the "house" seemed to have it in spades. We had a number of problems with the house. The ice maker in the Cabana needed repair. The wine cellar water removal pump failed and the water spill damaged part of the engineered flooring in the basement. There were gas leaks: (1) in the pipe bringing gas to the pool heater; (2) on the gas meter connection; and (3) on the exhaust connection from one of the water heaters. The pool heater was damaged by corrosion and will have to be replaced in 2021. Two of our neighbors and us hired an exterminating company to remove several foxes in the area— one was caught and the others disappeared. The HVAC unit for the Master Bedroom had to be repaired. A pipe in the irrigation system burst int the front lawn. Our alarm system had to be repaired three times during the year. Last, as we remember, the garage doors had to be serviced because two of them were malfunctioning.

We pray that in the year 2021 we will have a vaccine for the COVID-19 virus leading to the beginning of a healthier year wtih improved economies for the more needy and that we, in the USA, become more cordial to one another, learning from JesusChrist to love one another a little more.

A few family photos

Marcelino &
Lorenzo Cordero

Consuelo Berdasco and
Francisco Redruello

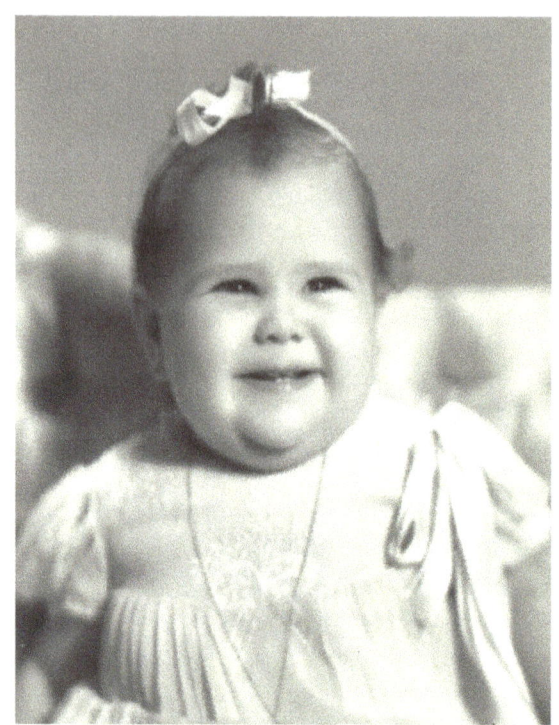

Chelo baby

Chelo child

Chelo with parents on her 15th birthday

Núñez Berro Family with Féliz Cepero, 11 April 1935
Victoria de las Tunas.
Photo taken after María and Félix's wedding

Standing (from left)

Rubén
Manolo
Argentina
Regilio
René

Sitting (from left)

Germán
María del Carmen
Manuel L. Núñez Parra
María del Carmen Berro
Félix M. Cépero

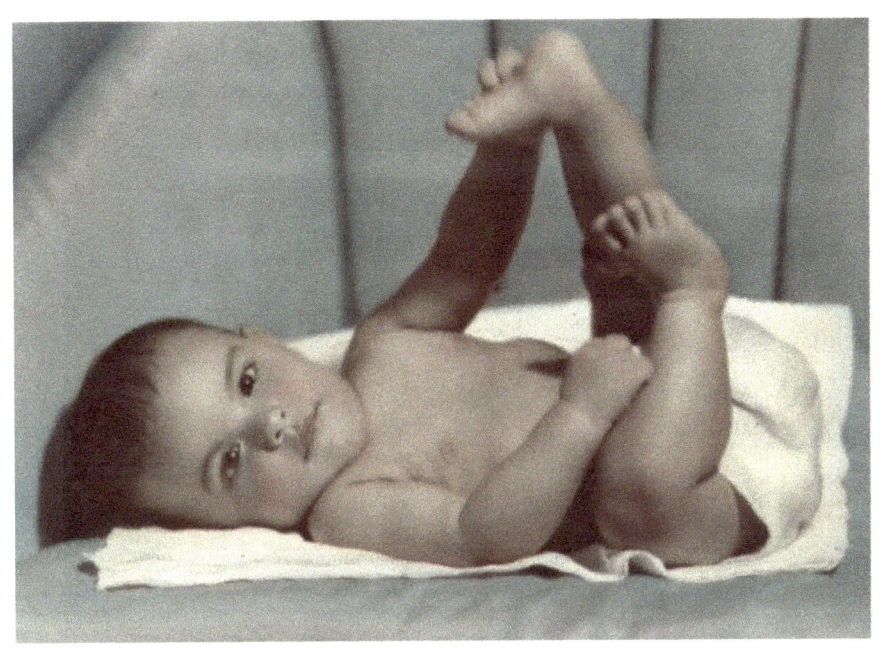

Jesús baby

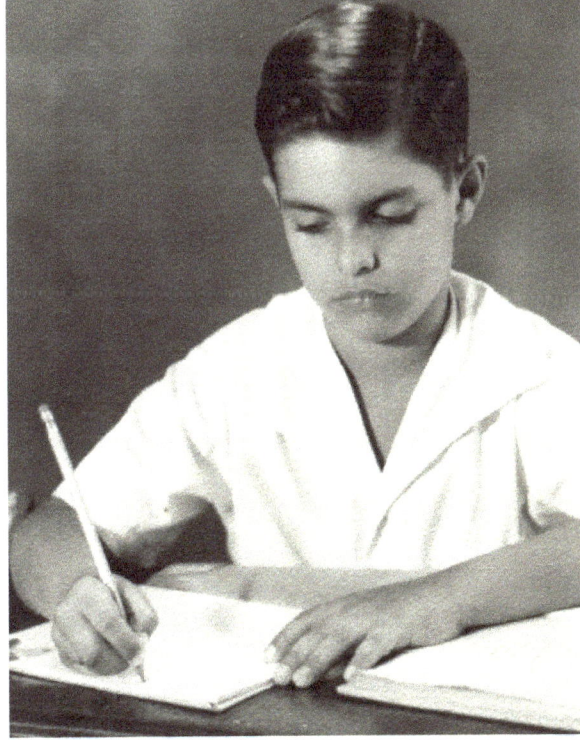

Jesús boy

León-Núñez Family
Circa 1951 (Enrique Luis was born in 1955)
From left: Rigobertico (Ticó), Rigoberto, Carmen Luisa
Argentina holding baby María del Carmen (Mary) and Jesús

St. Patrick's Academy
Momence, Illinois

Northeast Catholic
High School
Philadelphia,
Pennsylvania

Notre Dame Academy
Miami, Florida

Archbishop Curley
Miami, Florida

Cordero takes Chelo to altar

Chelo and Jesús "just married"

Chelo and Jesús with Chelo's family (Consuelo, Jesús, Chelo and Lorenzo Cordero)

Chelo and Jesús with Jesús' family (from left: Mary, Henry, Ticó, Argentina, Jesús, Chelo, Rigoberto, Carmen Luisa)

40th Wedding Anniversary

León Family 40th Anniversary

Consuelo and John's Wedding Day

Italy, May 2017
Celebrating 50 years of the birth of the family

Our Favorite House – Atlanta

Appendices

Appendix I – A brief introduction to Cuba

We are a product of the genes and education received from our parents, and of our cultural background. The cultural background is rooted in the Spanish tradition and Cuban history.

It is our intention to provide a few basic facts about Cuba for those who approach this book with little or no knowledge of the island nation. Because of the nature of these memoirs, a narrative directed primarily for our family, we have minimized the number of citations to make this appendix more readable. Most of the information on this section comes from our personal knowledge and others from basic sources such as National Geographic, Wikipedia, or from one or more of the references listed at the end of this Appendix.

Cuba is the largest of the Antilles Islands, located between the Yucatan Peninsula, Mexico, and Key West (USA). Because of its location, Cuba was for 300 years the focal point for communications between Spain and its American colonies until the Nineteenth Century when Latin American countries became independent from Spain. The area of the island of Cuba is about the size of the state of Pennsylvania, about 42,803 square miles. Before the arrival of the Spaniards, Cuba was populated by semi-sedentary natives of several tribes including the Guanacabeyes, the Ciboneyes and the Tainos.[160] Most of the native Cuban Indians died during the Spanish Conquest as a result of wars, disease or hard work. DNA from Carmen Luisa León sent to the Genographic Project of the National Geographic shows the Núñez family members are descendant of Native Americans on the woman's side of the family.[161]

Columbus visited Cuba during his first voyage, landing there on October 28, 1492, at a location in the northern coast of the Oriente Province, about 20 miles as the crow flies from the city of Holguín. Books about our history written by Cuban authors cite Columbus

---

[160] See Figueredo's book for more information on Cuban natives.
[161] Details are given in Appendix III about the León-Cordero genealogy.

saying, upon seeing Cuba: "La tierra más hermosa que ojos humanos han visto" ("the most beautiful land that human eyes have ever seen"). The Spanish started the colonization of the Americas in the island of Hispaniola and later colonized Cuba under the direction of Diego Velázquez early in the 16th century.

Cuba became a very important colony of Spain because of its geographical location and the capacity to produce cane sugar. La Habana was the port used to congregate all the ships traveling to Spain from their American colonies and for the sorting and separation of travel and shipment from Spain to the colonies. Sugar cane was a crop highly valued in Europe in colonial times and was the major crop exported by Cuba. This crop was, and still is, labor intensive and this requirement eventually led to the importation of slaves from the African Continent— a human tragedy and one with lasting influence on the Cuban culture and social context. Later, tobacco and coffee became export crops and to this day, Cuban tobacco is considered the best in the world. Eventually, cattle ranching became a large part of the agrarian economy, and in the middle of the 20th century tourism became Cuba's growth industry with most of the tourists visiting the city of La Habana and Varadero Beach.

Its geographical location made Cuba of interest not only to Spain but also to other naval powers of the time, as demonstrated by the occupation of Havana by the British during the Seven Years War. The occupation lasted less than one year but at a high price to Spain and Cuba: Spain traded the state of Florida for Havana; Cubans had to pay $15 million to the British and to bear the cost to rebuild a large part of the city. On the positive side, the invasion created a sense of nationalism in Cuba as all ethnic groups joined to fight the British. Since the occupiers allowed free trade, this helped the Cubans understand the value of free commerce and reduced their loyalty to Spain.

Cuba and Puerto Rico were the only remaining Spanish colonies in the Americas at the end of the 19th century because most Latin American countries gained their independence during the early part of that century. Cuban patriots had tried, unsuccessfully, to gain independence from Spain during various insurrections including the war known in Cuba as the Ten Years War that started on October 10, 1868. Cuban patriots started another major push for independence in 1895 and Cuba finally gained its partial independence at the end of the century when the USA declared war on and defeated Spain in 1898. As a result of this war, Cuba became independent but with a catch. First, the USA occupied Cuba for several years, and more appalling, the US insisted on the addition of the Platt Amendment to the Cuban Constitution that gave the USA the right to intervene in Cuba whenever they wanted. This amendment was abrogated in 1934. Another consequence of this war was that Puerto Rico became a protectorate— it still is today, and the Philippines became an American colony until the 1940s.

The Spanish colonization brought a number of benefits to the Americas (Catholic faith, access to European civilization and language). On the other hand, Spain did not do a very good job of building the socio-economic and especially the political infrastructure of its colonies. The legacy of Spain's approach to managing their colonies resulted in political, economic and social immaturity that continue to afflict Cuba and most of South America.[162] These were part of the reasons that explain why Cuba, like many Latin American countries, was not prepared to govern itself upon independence. To compound matters, the addition of the Platt Amendment did not do well for the self-esteem of the Cuban people.

The fact that Cuba is geographically very close to the United States influenced its relationship with the USA. On the one hand, there was general admiration by the Cubans of the USA political and economic system, and this resulted in a large flow of Cubans to the US for education and training. On the other hand, many Americans went to Cuba to invest and for vacation. US Corporations owned most of the Cuban sugar mills, the telephone company and some other companies. However, Cubans owned most of the cigar and sugar plantations and cattle ranches, and large commercial enterprises such as the Bacardí Company.

There are many other connections between the USA and Cuba. Cubans fought with the Americans during the American War of In-

---

[162] Thomas lists some of these characteristics on page 46 of his book: "centralization; reliance on a remote sovereign authority; corruption; and confusion between, or blur between, the executive and the judicial authority." Chasteen discusses other factors in Chapter 5 of his book.

dependence; Americans fought with Cubans during the second Cuban War of Independence (generally known as the Spanish-American War, inappropriately leaving out the role of the Cuban patriots). Some Cubans wanted the US to annex Cuba during the 18th and 19th centuries. Although Cuba struggled politically during the 20th century, the country made major strides in most socio-economical aspects. A review of the United Nations fact books show Cuba was one of the most advanced nations in Latin America.[163]

Finally, let us review briefly the political history of Cuba in the 20th century, the cause of Jesús and Chelo's exile to the USA. The political history in Cuba since independence is one of corrupt governments and military coups culminating in 1959 with the advent of the worst dictatorship in Cuban history— over fifty years of centralized, brutal, dictatorship by Fidel Castro. The Castro government not only limited all basic freedom but also severely damaged the Cuban economy eliminating all privately owned business and taking over essentially all private property, including people's homes. The Castro dictatorship made some positive contributions in education (Cuba has the highest literacy level in Latin America) and improvement in medical training; however, this came at a high cost: the loss of freedom was so high that close to 15% of the population left Cuba to live somewhere else— that is over one million people of a total population of about seven millions in 1960.[164] To understand the immensity of this exodus, we only need to realize that the most populous state in the USA, California, has approximately 12% of the total population of the country. Hence, the Cuban exodus was proportionally more damaging than if the whole state of California left for exile, especially because many of the early Cuban exiles included many professional, business and intellectual persons— a large part of the brainpower of the country.

---

[163] See the Cuban Transition project of the University of Miami as cited in the bibliography.

[164] Even using the average of total population between 1960 and 2005, the exodus represented more than 11% of the Cuban population.

There are many remarkable stories about the Cuban exodus and a number of them have been captured in books, films and television. One remarkable part of this exodus was the Peter Pan Program whereby parents sent their children, unaccompanied, to the USA in order to protect them from the brainwashing programs of the Castro dictatorship. The following citation is from the opening paragraphs of the official site of the Operation Pedro Pan: "From December 1960 to October 1962, more than fourteen thousand Cuban youths arrived alone in the United States. What is now known as Operation Pedro Pan was the largest recorded exodus of unaccompanied minors in the Western Hemisphere."[165]

Chelo and Jesús' story is one of thousands stories of the Cuban Exodus. They both came before their parents, although not through Operation Pedro Pan, and like many other old and young people triumphed in the USA.

A Few Key Dates in Cuban History

The following list highlights a number of dates to provide background about Cuba with a few words describing the importance of the date and associated event.

Circa 15,000 to 20,000 BC Estimated arrival in the Americas of the ancestors of the Núñez women as determined from Carmen Luisa León's DNA by the National Geographic's Genographic Project.

28 October 1492. Columbus visits ("discovers") Cuba on his first voyage to the Americas.

1513. Spanish Conquistador Diego Velazquez begins the colonization of Cuba using Hispaniola as his base. Velazquez brought Father Bartolomé de las Casas, Evangelizer of Amerindians. Diego Velazquez fought the native rebellion and burned at the stake the Cuban Indian Chief Hatuey. One of the most famous Cuban beers was named Hatuey in his memory.

---

[165] www.pedropan.org

<u>16th Century</u>. Santiago de Cuba was the first capital of Cuba until 1589 and then La Habana became the capital of Cuba and the connecting harbor of the Americas for the Spanish fleets.

<u>1868-78</u>. The "Ten Year War" was the first major war where Cubans tried to win their independence. This effort was not successful.

<u>1895-98</u>. The final war of Independence.

<u>1898</u>. The USS Maine ship blows in Havana Harbor. This was used as an excuse for the USA to enter the war. Teddy Roosevelt led the American force of "Rough Riders" who fought alongside the Cuban patriots.

<u>20 May 1902</u>. Cuba becomes almost fully independent. The US had requested that Cuba add an amendment to its constitution, the Platt Amendment, which allowed the US to intervene in Cuba. The Platt Amendment was removed in the 1930s.

<u>1952</u>. Batista takes over the government in a coup d'état.

<u>1 January 1959</u>. Batista fled Cuba in the early morning of the New Year and Fidel Castro takes over a few days later.

<u>3 January 1961</u>. US severed diplomatic relations with Cuba.

<u>April 1961</u>. Failure of the Bay of Pigs Invasion.

<u>1962</u>. October missile crisis.

<u>January 1998</u>. Pope John Paul II visit to Cuba results in a softening of Cuba's government's relationship with the Catholic Church.

Cuban Bibliography

There are thousands of books, articles, websites and blogs about the history, geography, and the social, economical and political development of Cuba. As we mentioned in the prologue, this is not intended to be an academic book but a narrative of our lives' experience. However, we did try to cite our sources whenever we quoted specific facts. Most of the information in the memoirs is based on our personal experiences and our recollections. We did use a few sources as references that we can recommend.

Two books that we especially like, as excellent sources of information are those by Hugh Thomas and John Charles Chasten. We

"Googled" and used Wikipedia liberally for references while writing our memoirs.

- **Hugh Thomas**, *Cuba: The Pursuit of Freedom*, (New York: Harper Collins, first edition 1971). The book is an excellent detailed account of Cuba, its history and culture, beginning with the English capture of Havana in 1762.

- **John Charles Chasten**, *Born in Blood and Fire: A Concise History of Latin America*, (New York: W. W. Norton & Company, 2nd edition 2006). This book provides an excellent narrative outlining the major forces shaping the Latin America of today. It is highly readable and will help understand Cuban history.

Other sources we recommend:

- **Sam Verdeja and Guillermo Martínez**, *Cubans: An Epic Journey: The Struggle of Exiles for Truth and Freedom*, (Miami: Facts About Cuban Exiles, Inc.; and, Saint Louis: Reedy Press, 2011). The book is divided into two parts. The first is about the history of Cuba. The second about the exile experience. Jesús is listed in Chapter 33, Engineering and Science.

- **Alfredo Figueredo**, *http://www.kacike.org/Figueredo.html*. Figueredo gives a lucid description of "The Indians of Cuba" a topic not widely studied.

- **University of Miami's Cuba Transition Project**, http://ctp.iccas.miami.edu/main.htm. This site is an excellent source of items about Cuba. In particular, Issue 43 of Cuba Facts gives valuable information about "Socio-Economic Conditions in Pre-Castro Cuba."

- **Biblioteca Digital Cubana**, http://bibliotecadigitalcubana.blogspot.com. This Website lists many books with data and information about Cuba.

- **National Geographic**, http://travel.national geographic.com/travel/countries/cuba-guide/. The National Geographic has published many articles about Cuba over the years. Of interest is the Cuba Guide, Facts and Photos.

- **Wikipedia**, *http://www.wikipedia.org/*, provided many useful facts.
- **CIA World Factbook**, *https://www.cia.gov/library/publications/the-world-factbook/geos/cu.html*.

Appendix II – Our Parents

We are genetically, emotionally and culturally the product of two sets of parents who raised us to be the persons we are. Our memoirs would be incomplete without an introduction, albeit brief, of our parents.

Our parents made enormous sacrifices for us. The early years of their marriage were more or less what you would expect of a new family: they married, had children, and sent their children to school. However, the Cuban Revolution not only changed their lives as it did ours, but it caused them bigger problems than it did to us. We could probably describe the struggles, challenges and difficult decisions they faced after the Cuban Revolution. On the other hand, we are not able to capture the emotional anguish and stress that they went through in those years.

Our narrative about our parents starts with a consideration of their situation before the revolution. They were middle age (40 to 50 years of age), had successful lives, and lived relatively near their extended family. Suddenly, they had to decide whether or not to send their children alone to another country in order to protect them. Then, a few months later, they came to the USA as immigrants to start a new life from scratch. They did not speak the language, understand the system or culture, and their training or career was useless in the USA.

In their memory and to honor their love and dedication, we add a few highlights about our parents in this appendix to our memoirs.

Lorenzo Cordero and Consuelo Redruello

Lorenzo Secundino Cordero Salcines was born on November 28, 1912, at the family house in El Vedado section of La Habana. His father was Marcelino Cordero Alcalde, an immigrant from the Santander region of Spain.[166] His mother, Eugenia Leopoldina Salcines

---

[166] People from this area are called "Montañenses" in reference to the mountain range running along the northern section of Spain.

Beci, was the only Cuban-born grandparent of Chelo; the other three grandparents were born in Spain and kept their Spanish citizenship until their death. Lorenzo Cordero (Pipo, Lore, Bo, Cordero)[167] was the fourth of eight children, three boys and five girls.

Cordero experienced many changes in Cuba and in his family during his lifetime. The first major change was caused by the Great Depression of the 1930s, when his father lost most of his fortune. Cordero went to school at the Catholic Escuelas Pías in Havana, but although intelligent and with an excellent memory, he was not interested in academics but in sports. Cordero joined the Cuban Navy as a young man and continued in this service until after the Castro revolution, resigning his position in 1961. Cordero's mother Leopoldina died of a heart attack when he was 22 years of age—her death left an indelible impression in his memory because he had a deep love for her. Cordero loved baseball (Cuban call this sport "beisbol"), a sport in which he excelled playing semi-professional and also for the Cuban Navy. He could watch baseball games on television all day long. He understood the game very well, knew personally many of the great Cuban baseball players, had been a baseball coach and even tried some umpiring in Miami.

Cordero and Consuelo left Cuba for Miami on November 30, 1961, and were reunited with Chelo a month later on December 27. In Miami, Cordero found a job in the kitchen of the "Top of the Columbus" Restaurant of the Columbus Hotel in downtown Miami, where he worked until his retirement. Cordero had lots of friends as he had a very easygoing and engaging personality. After retirement, he spent a few months every year with Chelo and Jesús' family and he soon became a favorite of Jesús and Chelo's friends. He was particularly fond of the Atlanta friends. Hernán Blanco, who used to call him Corderito, was one of his closest Atlanta friends. The two of them met weekly at the International House of Pancakes or at Denny's for lunch when Cordero was in Atlanta. Cordero was an

---

[167] Chelo called him "Pipo," his friends called him "Lore," his grandchildren and great grandchildren called him "Bo," and Jesús and others called him "Cordero."

excellent grandfather and enjoyed teaching his grandchildren how to play softball and baseball. He visited Chelo and Jesús in Spain in the spring of 1994 and had the opportunity to visit the town of his ancestors, Torrelavega, near the city of Santander. He also visited with the family of his nephew Monchi in Alicante. Cordero became sick during the spring of 2006 and went to live with Chelo, Jesús and Lorenzo in Maryland at the end of June of that year. He recovered somewhat and enjoyed all of July and most of August, but on Sunday, August 20, he started to feel weak. The following Saturday, August 26, 2006 (Chelo and Jesús' 39th wedding anniversary), he was admitted to the Howard County General Hospital and was in the hospital for three days. The following weekend, Vicente, Bertica and Chelo drove Cordero to Miami with a stop at John and Estela Long's house in Columbia, SC. Cordero was admitted to Mercy Hospital in Miami on Wednesday, November 1— the Feast of All Saints— and died on Wednesday, November 15— the day of his mother's birthday. He is buried in Miami at the Woodlawn Park Cemetery on southwest Eight Street.

Consuelo Hermenegilda Soledad Redruello Berdazco (Consuelín) was born on April 13, 1921. She was the fourth of the six children of Francisco, (Pancho), and Consuelo. Pancho and Consuelo had three boys and three girls. The boys died young, two from the Spanish Influenza in 1918, and Paco from cancer at age 33. The women of this family had long lives led by Consuelo Berdasco, who died at 106 years of age. Consuelín (Mima, Titi, Abuela, Consuelo)[168] attended El Centro Asturiano School in Havana. She worked in Cuba at the Flor de Tibet Coffee Company and also helped at her father's bodega in San Lazaro from time to time. In Miami, she found a job in early 1962 as a cashier at a small grocery store on NW 2 Avenue and 32 Street. Consuelo then worked for many years at the first Sedano Market, located in Hialeah and later transferred to the Sedano Market on SW 8 Street and 49 Avenue. After Sedano, she worked at a couple of other retailers until her retirement. Con-

---

[168] She was called "Mima" by Chelo, "Titi" by her nephews and nieces, "Abuela" by her grandchildren, "Abba" by her great grandchildren, and "Consuelo" by Jesús and others.

suelo received a head injury in a major automobile accident in 1967, a month before Jesús and Chelo's wedding. This head injury caused her to develop Parkinson Disease many years later. The effects of the Parkinson caused her to start losing motor skills slowly, and this loss in mobility increased significantly in 2008-09 and became worse after 2010. Consuelo was a very hard working person who loved to work interacting with customers; Chelo says, "Work was her hobby." She was always ready to be of service to us and would traverse Miami with Cordero looking for the one item any member of the family needed or requested.

Consuelo's ancestors were part of a small cultural and nomadic group from Asturias, Spain called "Vaqueiros de Alzada," consisting of persons who used to live in mountainous areas and moved locations seasonally with their cattle. Their background and cultural practices were quite interesting, particularly their inward focus among their particular subgroup. The Vaqueiros were ostracized and discriminated by valley dwellers.[169]

Consuelo and Cordero met at Pancho's Bodega on San Lazaro Street. They married on January 16, 1944, and while in Cuba, lived most of the time with Chelo's grandparents, Pancho and Consuelo in their San Lazaro house. Chelo was their only offspring.

Rigoberto León and Argentina Núñez

Rigoberto Amado León Díaz was the thirteenth child of Benjamín León and Luisa Díaz and was born on September 13, 1913, in the family house in San Agustín de Aguaras, a small village in the countryside located between the town of Tunas and the city of Holguín, in Oriente Province. Rigoberto and his brother Miguel studied pharmacy at the University of Havana where they met their future wives, Argentina Núñez and Berta González, respectively. During his university time, Rigoberto joined the Agrupación Católica Universitaria, an organization that was in tune and supported his commitment to Catholic Christianity.

---

[169] The name Vaqueiros derives from the Spanish word "vaquero" for people who take care of cows, "vacas." One can find information about this group in one of several Websites. For example, www.vaqueiros.es

After his graduation, Rigoberto opened a pharmacy, "La Farmacia León Díaz" in Victoria de las Tunas. He was the owner, pharmacist and leader of the pharmacy until he departed Cuba in 1961. Rigoberto was also part owner with several siblings of significant cattle ranch holdings that were managed together. He was a Catholic leader in Tunas, founding the local chapter of the Knights of Columbus, helping the parish and supporting apostolic activities there. Argentina said that the reason she chose him for a husband was that he attended daily Mass, and she was impressed that a professional man would be at Mass every day in the early 1940s.

When Rigoberto arrived in the USA, he, like other Cubans, made major sacrifices to support the family. His first job was as a dishwasher in a Miami Beach hotel; he went from a well-to-do professional owner of his own business to take an unskilled blue-collar job. Later, thanks to the help of Guillermo Hernández, who was married to Rigoberto's niece Ethel Patallo León, he was able to join Jackson Memorial Hospital in the position of laboratory technician, a position that allowed him to use his chemistry knowledge. Rigoberto was a stickler for punctuality, and because he did not drive or own an automobile, he depended on others for transportation to his work. He used to drive Jesús and others "crazy" asking for a ride to work more than one hour earlier than required.

After retirement from Jackson, Rigoberto spent his time praying, especially the Rosary, enjoying his children and grandchildren, and watching "novelas" on television. Rigoberto's health deteriorated when he suffered Aspiration Pneumonia in the late 1990s. This problem is caused when food, liquid or other foreign substances go into one's lungs because of a swallowing disorder. He also fell and required hospitalization and rehabilitation. Because of the Aspiration Pneumonia, Rigoberto received nourishments from a special nutrition pouch via a tube connected directly to his stomach; the pouch was placed on an "IV Pole" with four legs that he moved with him. He called the pouch and IV Pole, "la novia" (his girlfriend). Rigoberto bore his health issues with patience and conformity to God's will, he did not complain about it but lived his last years in prayerful peace. Rigoberto died on November 23, 2004.

Argentina Marta Núñez Berro was born at the family farm near the village of Tiguabos on March 4, 1916. Her parents, Manuel and Carmen were teachers— very unusual to have both parents with post-secondary education at that time and place. Argentina loved learning and was an excellent student. She was sent to study her secondary education at Sagua la Grande in the Province of Las Villas where she stayed in the house of a close family, the Ceperos, one of whom married Argentina's sister María del Carmen. Argentina continued her studies at the University of Havana earning a degree in Filosofía y Letras.

Argentina taught History and Geography at the public secondary school, the "Instituto," in Holguín, located about forty-miles from Victoria de las Tunas. She rode a Santiago-Habana bus in the morning and afternoon every day during the academic year to teach at this "Instituto." She was elected to the Tunas City Council in the late 1940s, an extraordinary achievement for a woman in a small town in that time period. During her last few years in Cuba, Argentina was the Director of a Commerce School in Victoria de las Tunas.

Argentina was an intellectual, a lover of books, a born leader, spiritual director and counselor to many of her nephews and nieces, and to other close friends including José Manuel and Ana Maria Revuelta. Argentina died on September 10, 1997; Jesús gave Argentina's eulogy at her Resurrection Mass and titled it, "Una Mujer Fuera de Serie," which translates in meaning to, "A Woman in a League of Her Own."

A measure of Argentina's extraordinary personality is that she got along famously with her daughter-in-law Chelo, stating in one occasion that, "I can live with you easily but not with Jesús." We could write more about Argentina here but refer the reader to the appendix in which we transcribed her writings about her family.

Argentina and Rigoberto León were married on December 20, 1943, and had five children. They lived briefly in Holguín and later in Victoria de las Tunas until 1961, when they departed Cuba for

Miami. In Miami, they lived in various houses and apartments[170]—their final years with their daughter Carmen Luisa.

---

[170] In an apartment on NW 30 Street and then at a house two blocks away. Later, briefly, in one floor of a house in SW Miami, then in an apartment across from the Orange Bowl, on a rented house located on SW 12th Avenue near 8th Street, and finally at Carmen Luisa's house on SW 92nd Avenue.

Appendix III – León-Cordero Genealogy

This appendix provides background information about our genealogy, our family genetic journey and a list of close relatives. The first four charts are "pedigree" charts that show the ancestry of each of our parents. We have documented the ancestry back to our great-great-grandparents for Argentina and Consuelo's families and to our great-grandparents for Rigoberto and Cordero's families. We have worked with Chelo's cousins, Vicente Fernández, Estelita Purvis and Marichu Lugo, to prepare family charts for the rest of the Cordero and Redruello families even though we do not include all the family charts here. Jesús' sister Carmen Luisa has family charts for the very large León family and also for the Núñez family. We also include a table listings the siblings, uncles and aunts of our parents.

The final two charts are "genetic journeys" for Jesús and Carmen Luisa León. These were provided by the Genographic Project of the National Geographic. Jesús' charts shows the Y-chromosome based genetic map based on the male ancestry while Carmen Luisa's chart is based on the Mitochondrial DNA and show her female ancestry.

The male ancestry traces back our genetic journey to about 75,000 years ago and shows that our male ancestry went from Africa to the Middle East and from there to northern Africa and Southern Europe. Jesús' male ancestry makes him part of "Haplogroup J2 (started with Branch M42, Branches M89, M304 and then Branch M172)." According to the Genographic Project: "The M42 branch is shared by almost all men alive today, both in Africa and around the world." The M168 Branch, "... is one of the first to leave the African homeland." The M89 is the "... marker found in 90 to 95 percent of all non-Africans."

Carmen Luisa's chart shows our ancestry beginning with the "Mitochondial Eve" approximately 150,000 years ago, with Carmen a part of "Haplogroup A." According to Carmen's DNA, one of our ancestors was a Native American. Carmen Luisa has researched and documented a good bit of our family ancestry. She found that one of our ancestors, our great-great-grandmother, María del Carmen Pérez, was born in Jiguaní, Oriente, an area with a large concentration of Native Cubans of the Taino Tribe.

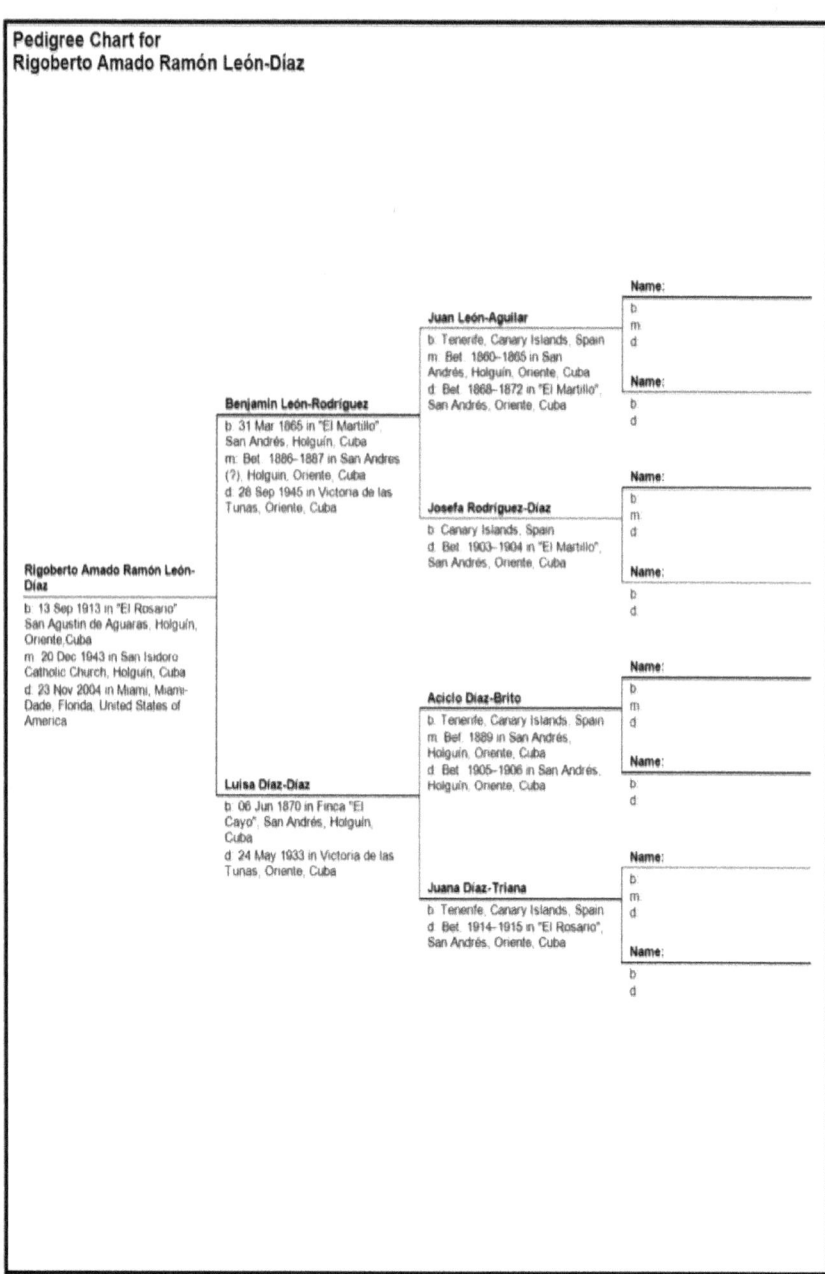

Pedigree Chart for Argentina Marta Núñez-Berro

Argentina Marta Núñez-Berro
b 04 Mar 1916 in Tiguabos, Cauto del Paso, Las Tunas, Oriente, Cuba
m 20 Dec 1943 in San Isidoro Catholic Church, Holguín, Cuba
d 10 Sep 1997 in Miami, Florida

Manuel Ladislao de la Caridad Núñez-Parra
b 27 Jun 1878 in Cienfuegos, Las Villas, Cuba
m 24 Mar 1905 in Vicana, Manzanillo, Cuba
d 17 Dec 1946 in Holguín, Oriente, Cuba

María del Carmen Juliana Berro-Reyes
b 09 Jan 1878 in Manzanillo, Oriente, Cuba
d 08 Jun 1953 in Victoria de las Tunas, Oriente, Cuba

José Manuel Núñez-González Cándamo
b 03 Jun 1841 in Santiago de Carril, Pontevedra, Galicia, Spain
m Sep 1877 in Manzanillo, Oriente, Cuba
d 16 May 1898 in Manzanillo, Oriente, Cuba

María de la Luz Parra-Oliva
b Bet 1845-1860 in Cauto del Paso Or Cauto Embarcadero, Bayamo, Oriente, Cuba
d 1934 in Cauto del Paso, Las Tunas, Oriente, Cuba

Miguel Berro-Pérez
b 30 Jul 1845 in Manzanillo, Oriente, Cuba
m 04 May 1878 in Manzanillo, Oriente, Cuba
d Bet 12-13 Aug 1898 in Manzanillo, Oriente, Cuba

María del Carmen Reyes-Pérez
b Bet 1857-1858 in Jiguaní or Manzanillo, Oriente, Cuba
d 20 Feb 1898 in Manzanillo, Oriente, Cuba

José María Núñez
b Abt 1815 in Santiago del Carril, Pontevedra, Galicia, Spain
m Spain
d Spain

Josefa González-Candamo
b Santiago del Carril, Pontevedra, Galicia, Spain
d Spain

José María Parra
b
m
d Bef 1877 in Cauto Embarcadero, Oriente, Cuba

Rosa Oliva
b
d Bef 1877 in Cauto Embarcadero, Oriente, Cuba

Miguel Berro Ortega
b Bet 1820-1823 in Bayamo or Manzanillo, Oriente, Cuba
m 1844 in Cuba
d Bet 1855-1875 in Cuba

Agueda María Pérez y Ramírez de Arellano
b 1825
d 1902 in Vicana, Manzanillo, Oriente, Cuba

José Gregorio Reyes-Torres
b Abt 1800 in Jiguaní, Oriente, Cuba
m Cuba
d 1875 in Manzanillo, Oriente, Cuba

María del Carmen Pérez
b Jiguaní, Oriente, Cuba
d Bef 1875 in Jiguaní, Oriente, Cuba

Page 1

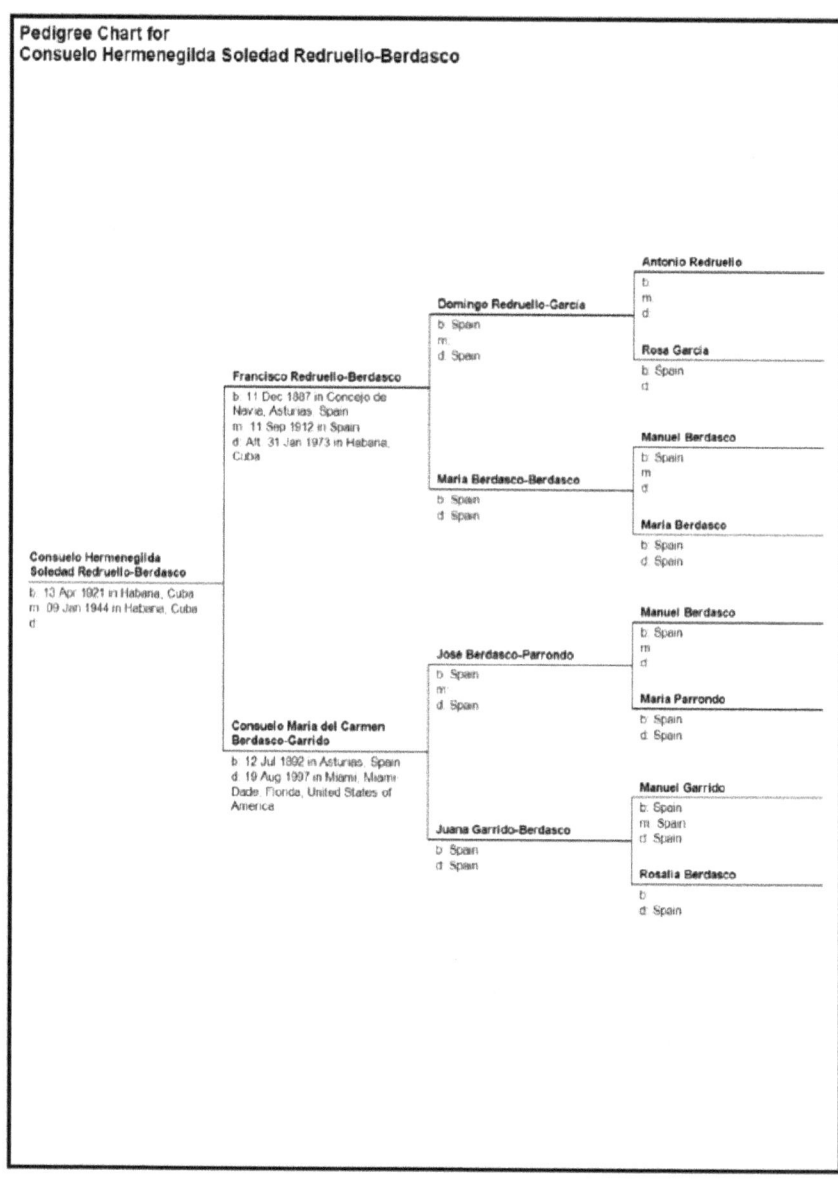

Pedigree *Chart for* Lorenzo Secundino Cordero Salcines

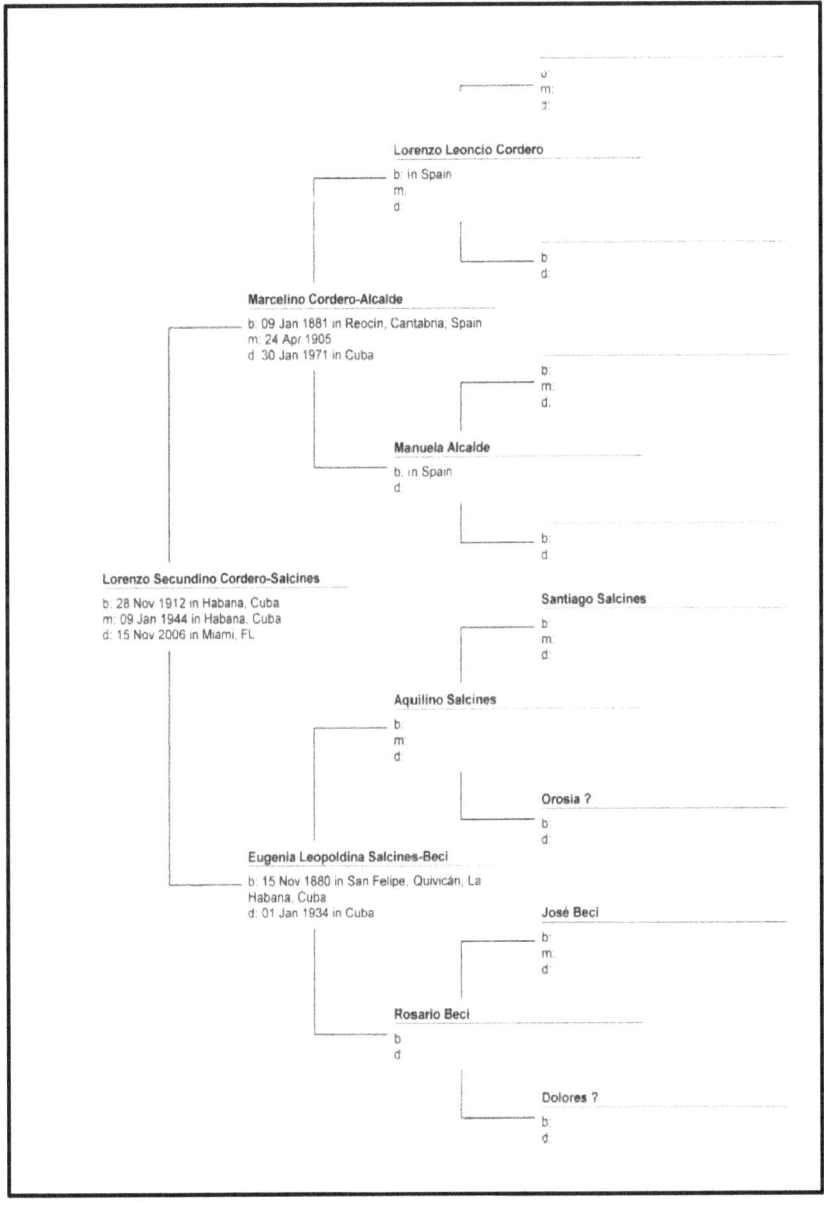

Siblings, uncles and aunts of Chelo's parents

(*) Indicates died as a child, infant or baby.

Siblings	Uncles/aunts father's side	Uncles/aunts mother's side
(Cordero Salcines)	**(Cordero Alcalde)**	**(Salcines Beci)**
Rosarito	Rafael	Orosio
Manuela (Tita)	Emilia	José
Marcelinito (*)	Lucinda	Jesús
Lorenzo Secundino		Eloisa
F. María Eloisa (Cuyo)		
Estela (Tela)		
Margarita (Margot)		
E. Rafael (Nano)		
(Redruello Berdasco)	**(Redruello Berdasco)**	**(Berdasco Garrido)**
Enrique	Juan	Manuel
Carmen Manuela	María	Balbina
Domingo	Rosa	Carmen
Generosa Genoveva		Amparo
Consuelo Soledad		Juan
Francisco		Emilio

Siblings, uncles and aunts of Jesús's parents

(*) Indicates died as a child, infant or baby

Siblings	Uncles/aunts father's side	Uncles/aunts mother's sied
(León Díaz)	**(León Rodríguez)**	**(Díaz Díaz)**
María Eladia	Sebastián	María
Encarnita	Juan	Mercedes
Pablo Benjamín	Antonia	
Juan Ramón	Loreto (*)	
Benjamín (Niño)		
Carmen		
Rodolfo		
Dolores (*)		
Dolores (Lola)		
Miguel		
Lilia		
Laura		
Rigoberto Amado		
(Núñez Berro)	**(Núñez Parra)**	**(Berro Reyes)**
María del Carmen	José Manuel (Pepe)	Miguel
Manuel de Jesús (Manolo)	Andrés	Barbara (Barbarita)
Germán Bernardo	Domingo	Manuel ("Berro")
María Grecia (*)	Rosa	Milagros
Regilio Armando		
Grecia Zoila (*)		
Orlando (*)		
René Armelliní		
Argentina Marta		
Rubén		

Genographic Project migration chart for Jesús León

Genographic Project migration chart for Carmen L. León

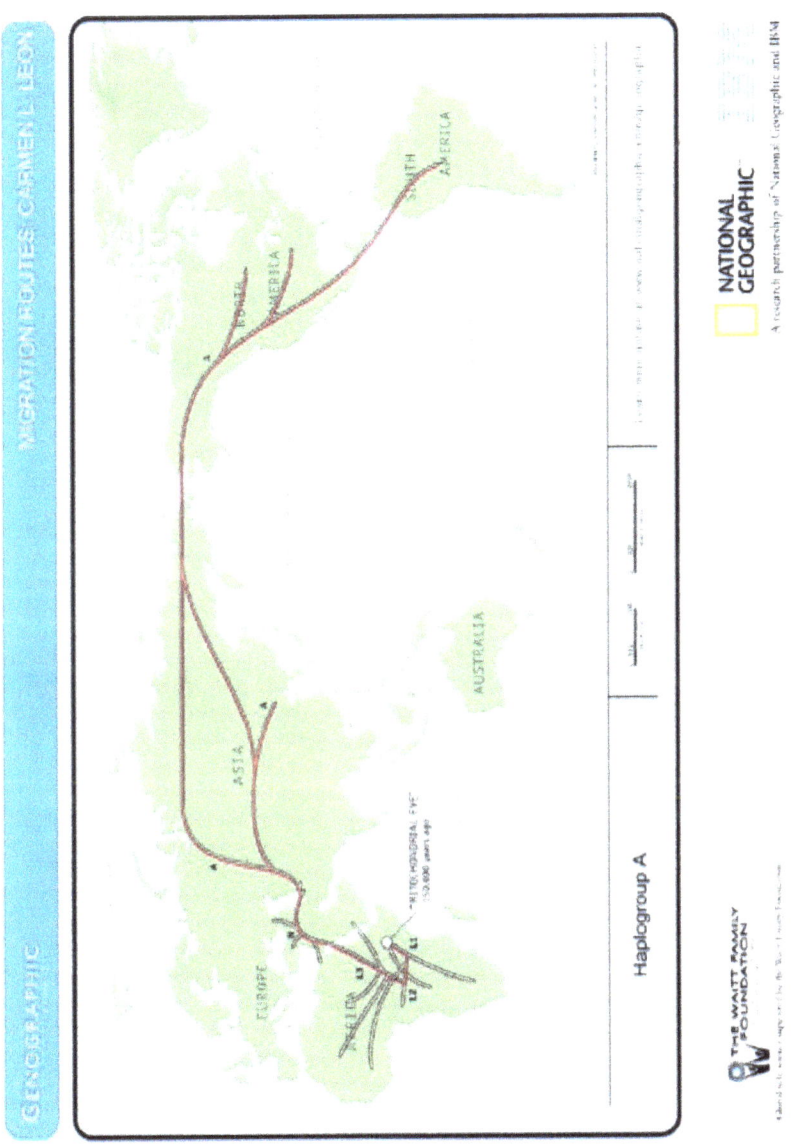

Appendix IV – León-Cordero-Bills Family Milestones

This appendix has two sets of charts with informational dates for the León-Cordero-Bills family. The first chart lists chronological information beginning with Jesús and Chelo's birth year, 1944, and continuing through 2019. The second chart shows milestone dates (birth, baptism, confirmation, marriage, schools) for each member of the León-Cordero-Bills family.

Year	Milestone(s)
1944	Chelo & Jesús are born
1960	Jesús leaves Cuba
1961	Chelo leaves Cuba. Chelo and Jesús meet
1967	Chelo graduates with BA from Barry College Jesús graduates with BS from University of Florida Chelo and Jesús marry
1968	Consuelo Beatriz is born Chelo first job as teacher at Bradford High School in Starke, Florida.
1969	Jesús completes Master's degree at UF. Chelo and Jesús move to Atlanta
1970	Cristina is born
1973	Chelo starts part-time teaching job at St. Pius X Catholic High School
1974	Jesús starts first professional engineering job in December at Scientific-Atlanta
1975	We make our first trip to Europe (Spain, Italy, France) with the ACU in Ruta Ignaciana that includes a Holy Year peregrination to Rome We bought our first home at 5659 Fern Creek Drive in Lilburn, Georgia

Year	Milestone
1976	Miracle to Consuelo Beatriz thanks to the intercession of Our Lady of Lourdes Consuelo Berdasco visits Atlanta
1978	Foundation of ACU Atlanta (Manny Antón, José Batlle, Alex Saker, John Alarcón)
1979	First ACU "lechón" to celebrate the arrival of Rembé's parents & brother
1983	Lorenzo is born
1984	Sold first house. Second house was designed by Rembe Rodríguez, built by Walter Chewning. We moved into house at 2850 Cravey Trail in December.
1986	Jesús leaves Scientific-Atlanta and joins start-up DTS
1990	Jesús goes to work for Alcatel in Spain. Chelo, Lorenzo and Cristy visit during the summer Consuelo Beatriz marries on September 8
1991	Chelo and Jesús have car problems near Brive, France. Jesús is a suspect in a double-execution-murder. Lorenzo's first communion at ACU in Miami. Jesús returns from Spain and starts work at Americom.
1992	Cristina marries on July 25. Jesús joins AT&T Tridom founded by ex Scientific-Atlanta employees.
1993	Jesús accepts position in Alcatel. Chelo, Lorenzo and Jesús move to Madrid. Sold Cravey Trail house. Jorge Guigou dies the week of the closing.
1994	Cordero visits Spain and travels to visit relatives in Alicante and to the hometown of his father, Torrelavega. Alexandra joins us in Madrid to do her last year of high school. Argentina visits Spain and travels extensively there including to Lourdes and Fátima

Year	Milestone
1996	Consuelo Alina Bills is born in February. Jesús accepts position with Ciena. Chelo, Lorenzo and Jesús move to Maryland
1997	Argentina Marta Núñez de León dies in September
1998	Ethan Daniel Bills is born in August. Lorenzo graduates from elementary school. Lorenzo's confirmation. We moved into house at 11537 Manorstone Lane, Columbia, MD.
1999	Cristina's divorce
2000	Discovery that Alina has diabetes
2001	Jesús commutes to California starting August 15 and lasting one year. Jesús arrives in California for one of his weekly trips a few hours before the September 11 terrorist attack. Jesús is inducted into the Georgia Tech College of Engineering's Academy of Distinguished Engineering Alumni.
2002-3	Jesús has Polymyalgia Rheumatica. Lorenzo graduates from high school
2004	Alina's First Communion. Rigoberto Amado León Díaz dies November 24
2005	Consuelo Beatriz's divorce. Consuelo Beatriz, Alina and Ethan move to Atlanta
2006	Ethan's First Communion. Trip to Paris & Pilgrimage to Lourdes. Lorenzo Secundino Cordero Alcade dies November 15
2007	Chelo and Jesús decided to move back to Atlanta and buy a lot at 239 St. Nicholas Circle NW. They asked Architect David Cabarrocas to design the house. Father Llorente blesses the lot in November during his last visit to Atlanta. Lorenzo completes Associates Degree and moves to Atlanta. Jesús receives the GSU Robinson College of Business Technology Leadership Award.
2008	We sold Maryland house and moved to Atlanta. Jesús retires from Ciena. Chelo and Jesús take Western Mediterranean Cruise

Year	Milestone
2009	Moved into new house at 239 St Nicholas Circle NW. Eastern Mediterranean cruise
2010	Father Llorente dies. Trip to Punta Cana. Jesús has mild PMR relapse. Alina graduates from IHM and starts at St. Pius X. Baltic cruise. Family travels to Puerto Rico for Maritere's wedding.
2011	Trip to Punta Cana to celebrate Gigi's 15th Birthday. Trip to New York City and to Carlos/Lauren's wedding in New Jersey.
2012	Alina's confirmation. Ethan graduates from IHM and starts at St. Pius X. Chelo, Cristy, Ana Silva & Jesús' trip to Italy, Venice and Adriatic cruise. Trip to Los Angeles for Ana Tere's graduation recital. Sudden deaths of Jean-Marie Finison & José Fetzer, SJ.
2013	Ethan's confirmation. Alaska and Caribbean cruises
2014	Alina graduates from high school. Trip to London and around British Isles. Alina begins college at Fordham. Chelo has Transient Global Amnesia.
2015	Trip to Rio de Janeiro and Rio-to-Miami cruise. Rhine River Cruise plus travel in Provence and Burgundy finishing in Paris. Trip and cruise to New Zealand and Australia.
2016	Trip to Western Caribbean. Consuelo marries John Ecuyer. Ethan graduates from Pius and starts GT. Problems with: elevator, pool, Jesús' iPhone, espresso machine, and MB E320.
2017	Cruise around Cape Horn, then Machu Picchu. Golden Anniversary Tuscany trip.
2018	Alina graduated Summa cum laude from Fordham University. Consuelo S. Redruello died on 28 October.
2019	Chelo, Cristy and Jesús travel in Spain with Alina. Chelo and Jesús continue to Paris. Lorenzo had benign Schwannoma tumor removed via surgery on 30 June and underwent rehab. Alina returned from one-year teaching in Spain and started work at Emory Goizueta Business School. Henry "Hank" Ecuyer died in July.

		Jesús León	**Consuclo L. Cordero**
Birth date	Date	23-Oct-1944	28-Dec-1944
	Location	Calle Morales Lemus 64, Holguín	Clínica Católicas Cubanas, La Habana
Baptism	Date	12-Nov-1944	18-Feb-1945
	Location	At the house on Calle Morales Lemus. Recorded San José Church Holguín	Monserrate Church, La Habana, Cuba
	Celebrant	Fr. Germán Lence González	Fr. Juan José Lobato
	Sponsors	Fr. José Lence & María del Carmen Núñez Berro (aunt)	Francisco Redruello Berdasco (grandfather) & Rosario Cordero Salcines (aunt)
First Communion	Date	25-Mar-1952	2-Apr-1952
	Location	Col. Verbo Encarnado, Victoria de las Tunas	Col. Domínicas Americanas, La Coronela (La Habana)
	Celebrant	Fr. José Lence (Godfather)	Cardenal Manuel Arteaga
Confirmation	Date	8-Dec-1945	
	Location	S. José Church Holguín	
	Celebrant	Bishop Fray Valentín Zubizarreta Unamunsaga	
	Sponsor	José León González	

		Jesús León	**Consuelo L. Cordero**
Wedding	Date	26-Aug-1967	26-Aug-1967
	Location	Corpus Christie, Miami	Corpus Christie, Miami
	Celebrant	Fr. Amando Llorente	Fr. Amando Llorente
	Spouse	Consuelo L. Cordero	Jesús León
	Sponsors	Argentina Núñez	Lorenzo Cordero

		Jesús León	**Consuelo L. Cordero**
Elementary school		Colegio Verbo Encarnado	American Dominican Academy
		Belén (boarding)	
	Graduation	1957	
High School		Escolapios Camagüey	American Dominican Academy
		Academia Alfa, La Vibora, Havana 1958	St Patrick Academy (Momence Illinois) June-December 1961
		Northeast Catholic 1960-61 Archbishop Curley 1961-62	Notre Dame Academy (Miami) January 1962-June 1963
	Graduation	1962	1963

	Jesús León	**Consuelo L. Cordero**
College	Miami-Dade	Barry College 1963-1967
	University of Florida	Georgia State Univ. 1984-1988
	Georgia Tech 1969-74	
	Georgia State Univ. 1983-85	
Graduation	UF: BSEE 1967; MSE 1969	Barry: BA 1967
	GSU: MBA 1985	GSU: MAT 1988

		Consuelo Beatriz	**Cristina**	**Lorenzo Javier**
Birth	Date	8:20 A.M. 5/30/1968	~Noon 2/5/1970	4:09 P.M. 1/6/1983
	Location	Alachua General Hospital Gainesville, FL	Dekalb General Hospital Atlanta, GA	Northside Hospital Atlanta, GA
	Doctor	Dr. Ike Ganey		Dr. Robert Kral
Baptism	Date	1-Jul-1968	21-Jun-1970	13-Mar-1983
	Location	St. John Bosco Miami	St. John Bosco Miami	IHM, Atlanta
	Celebrant	Fr. Amando Llorente	Fr. Amando Llorente	Fr. Amando Llorente
	Sponsors	Adolfo Fernández & Mary Trujillo	Enrique L. León & Carmen L. León	Drs. José & Virginia Balbona

		Consuelo Beatriz	**Cristina**	**Lorenzo Javier**
First Communion	Date	8-May-1976	13-May-1978	10-Aug-1991
	Location	IHM Church Atlanta, GA.	IHM Church Atlanta, GA.	ACU, Miami Florida
	Celebrant	Fr. Richard Kieran	Fr. Richard Kieran	Fr. Amando Llorente
Confirmation	Date	1981	1983	30-May-1998
	Location	IHM Church Atlanta, GA.	IHM Church Atlanta, GA.	St. John Evangelist Columbia, MD
	Sponsor	Mary Trujillo	Carmen L. León	Joel Higgins
Wedding	1st marriage	8-Sep-1990, IHM	25-Jul-1992, IHM	
	Celebrant	Frs. Richard López & Amando Llorente	Frs. López, Mario Dilela, Terry Young	
	Spouse	Robert Todd Bills, divorced 2005	Joel Higgins, divorced 1999	
	Other	Annulment 2008		
	2nd Marriage	John Ecuyer 6-Aug-2016 Jesuit High School New Orleans		

		Consuelo Beatriz	Cristina	Lorenzo Javier
Elementary		IHM	IHM	Howard School, IHM American School Madrid OLPH, MD
	Graduation	1982	1984	1998
High School		St. Pius H. S.	St. Pius H. S.	Archbishop Spalding H. S.
	Graduation	1986	1988	2002
College				Howard Community College, MD
		Georgia Tech Purdue	GT Univ. South Carolina	Georgia State Univ.
	Graduation	Purdue BISYE 1991 & MS Mgmt. 1997	GT: B. Mgmt. 1992 USC: JD 1995	Howard: Associate 2007 GSU: B.B.A. 2015

		Consuelo Alina	Ethan Daniel
Birth date	Date	10-Feb-1996	16-Aug-1998
	Location	Methodist Hospital Indianapolis, Indiana	Methodist Hospital Indianapolis, Indiana
	Doctor		

		Consuelo Alina	**Ethan Daniel**
Baptism	Date	7-Apr-1996	1-Nov-1998
	Location	St. Monica Indianapolis, Indiana	St. Malachi Brownsburg, Indiana
	Celebrant	Rev. Clement Davis	Rev. Daniel Staublin (pastor)
	Sponsors	Lorenzo & Alexandra León (Jesús' niece)	Cristina León (aunt) & Joel Higgins (uncle by marriage)
First Communion	Date	8-May-2004	13-May-2006
	Location	Sacred Heart Church Wadsworth, Ohio	IHM Church Atlanta, Georgia
	Celebrant	Fr. Joseph L. Labak	Fr. James A. Schillinger
Confirmation	Date	7-May-2012	2-Nov-2013
	Location	IHM Church, Atlanta Arch. Wilton Gregory	IHM Church, Atlanta Bishop Luis Rafael Zarama
	Saint Name	St. Therese de Lisieux	Tarcisius
	Sponsor	Consuelo L. León	Jesús León
Elementary school		Sacred Heart Wadsworth, Ohio	Sacred Heart Wadsworth, Ohio
		IHM 2005-2010	IHM 2005-2012
	Graduation	2010	2012

	Consuelo Alina	Ethan Daniel
High School	St. Pius X High School	St. Pius X High School
Graduation	2014	2016
College	Fordham University Bronx, New York City	Georgia Institute of Technology Atlanta, Georgia
Graduation	19 May 2018	

Summary of Jesús' and Chelo's professional careers
Consuelo L. León, Spanish Teacher
(Certifications from Florida and Georgia)

Organization	Position
Starke High School Starke, Florida	Spanish Teacher
Fulton County System (part-time) Atlanta, Georgia	Teacher of English as a second language
DeKalb County System (part-time) Atlanta, Georgia	Teacher of Spanish
Berlitz Corporation Atlanta, Georgia	Teacher of Spanish
St. Pius X High School Atlanta, Georgia	Spanish Teacher Chair of the Language Department

Jesús León, Professional Engineer (registered in Georgia)

Organization	Position
Scientific-Atlanta Atlanta, Georgia	Senior Engineer. Leader of Systems Group Engineering Manager. Manager of Programs
Digital Transmission Systems (start-up) Atlanta, Georgia	Vice President Engineering
Digital Wireless (start-up) Atlanta, Georgia	President and CEO
Americom and AT&T Tridom Atlanta, Georgia	Director of Engineering and Services Director of Sales Engineering
Alcatel Standard Electrica, S.A. Madrid, Spain	Director, joint Spain-Belgium development project Director, Spain-Belgium-France development project Vice President, Access Systems Division
Ciena Corporation (start-up) Linthicum, Maryland	Vice President, Access Products Senior Vice President, Engineering Senior Vice President and Chief Development Officer

Appendix V –
Anecdotes and interesting information

This appendix contains supplementary information about our lives. We did not include this information in the main body of our memories because we felt that the amount of detail would distract the reader from the main point of the story. On the other hand, this appendix contains anecdotes that provide interesting additional information about our lives.

Incident in France in 1991

We described in Book V that Jesús was questioned regarding the execution style of two persons in the area of Brive-la-Gaillarde, about one hour south of Limoges, France. Below is a copy of the document that Chelo requested and received from a member of the Gendarmerie de Donzenac in case the police would stop us again— fortunately, we did not need the document.

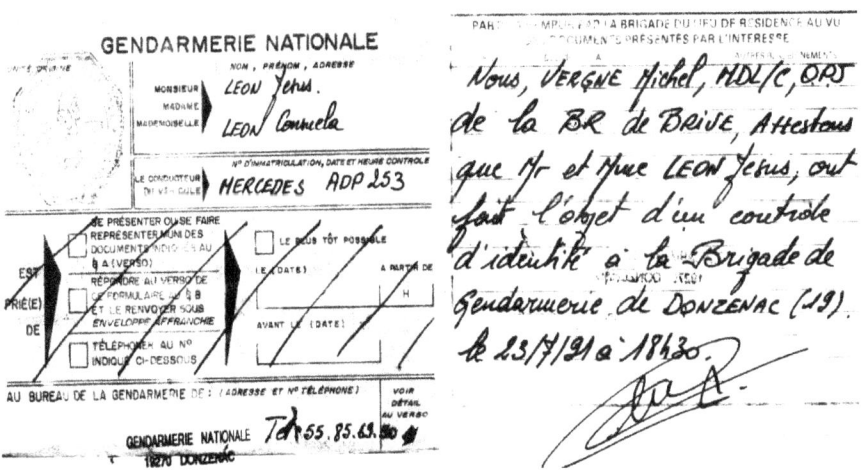

Translation from French: "We, Vergne Michel, MDL/C, OPJ de la Brigade de Brive, attest ("declare, assert") that Mr. and Mrs. ("Madame") LEON Jesus, were the object of an identity control by the Gendarmerie Brigade of Donzenac (19) on July 23, 1991, at 18 hours 30 minutes."

There is an extensive article about the whole affair in the Atlanta Business Chronicle issue of January 3, 1992, World's largest treasure hunt: $1.5 trillion, an Atlanta investment firm, murder and a global investigation. Atlanta Business Chronicle, January 03, 1992, Thomas, Emory, Jr. We downloaded and read it with interest.

A peculiar experience at a NYC Greenwich Village Restaurant

This incident illustrates some aspects of our personalities, and at the same time is peculiar, somewhat funny and has a happy ending.

In the early 1980s, we went to New York City for a business trip and then took a few days off to enjoy the city. We rented a car at the airport and parked it on the street of Manhattan the first evening. The next day, Jesús went to the AT&T offices in Bedminster, NJ, to show our potential customer the prototype of a new instrument. Unfortunately, when Jesús opened the trunk to get the equipment box he found that the prototype had been stolen! Someone broke into the trunk of the car and stole the device. This was an embarrassment to Jesús and a disappointment to the customer. Jesús reported the theft to the NY Police Department and the company filed a claim with the insurance company.

In any case, after reporting the incident, we spent a couple of days sightseeing. On Saturday, our last full day in NYC, after sightseeing, we went to a Broadway show and decided to go to Greenwich Village for dinner. It was raining on-and-off when we came out of the Subway, and unfortunately, we did not have reservations at any restaurant. Since it was Saturday night, almost every restaurant was packed. By this time, we were tired because of our full day of sightseeing and because Jesús had started walking in the wrong direction out of the subway exit requiring us to walk more than necessary. Chelo told Jesús, "Tonight I want to eat a steak." Chelo does not usually want to eat beef, but Jesús thought it would be very simple to meet her request because "most restaurants in America had beef in their menus."[171]

---

[171] Remember, this was the early 1980s— vegetarian fare was not common yet.

After stopping at several restaurants, we found one that was not full. Chelo looked at the menu posted outside and mentioned to Jesús that it did not have beef. However, it had duck and chicken, so Jesús said, "I am sure they have steaks," and we went in and were seated. The waiter gave us the menu... and there was no beef in the menu. We proceeded to have an argument along the following lines. Chelo: "I told you I wanted beef." Jesús: "Well, let's get up and go somewhere else." Chelo: "I am tired and don't want to continue walking." Jesús: "Well, make up your mind."

While this argument is going on, the waiter comes to our table to ask if we wanted to order. Jesús told him, "Come back in ten minutes; we are having a fight." We decided to stay and ordered wine. Jesús was not a happy person and told the waiter to bring the appropriate wine glasses for the wine we had ordered. We asked the waiter about the specialty of the restaurant and he told us that the breast of duck was superb. Chelo did not want to order the duck and she ordered sardines instead, but Jesús ordered the duck. The sardines were OK, but the duck was outstanding and Jesús gave the duck to Chelo and ate the sardines. When we finished with the sardines and duck, Jesús ordered another serving of duck! (And "we lived happily ever after.")

The following day we had brunch with Bertha, Owen and Owen Miguel before heading to La Guardia Airport.

How we met Placido Domingo

Alexandra called us one day while we lived in Maryland to tell us that the daughter of a good friend of her mother-in-law would be singing with Placido Domingo in the zarzuela Luisa Fernanda. This zarzuela was to be the last event of the Washington Opera season at the Kennedy Center. Alexandra told us we should go and see her friend perform. We had seen Luisa Fernanda in Madrid and were not enthusiastic about attending the Washington Opera performance. At the end, we agreed and Alexandra arranged for us to meet her mother-in-law's friend after the performance.

Chelo, Lorenzo and Jesús bought tickets and proceeded to our seats at the Kennedy Center. We noticed several Latin American couples sitting in the row directly ahead of us. After the performance, we tried to find Juanjo's mother's friend and had a hard time locating the dressing room area. After asking several people, Jesús decided to go backstage and found a side door that eventually led to the stage. When we arrived, we noticed they were setting tables at the stage. A few minutes later we saw Placido Domingo and his wife come from backstage and about to pass next to us, so we said in Spanish, "magnífico, excelente." Placido and his wife came to us, shook our hands and then proceeded to the stage where there were now thirty or so people.

It turns out that the people sitting in front of us were ambassadors from Latin America with their spouses. They were invited by the Washington Symphony to the last performance of the season followed by a reception and dinner. Chelo, Lorenzo and I stayed and ate with the ambassadors— the one from the Dominican Republic gave us his card and asked us to contact him before we traveled there. Placido probably thought we were part of the diplomatic corps!

Abella-León-Sorondo dinner reunions

In 2009 we began a tradition with our very close friends Ignacio and Lourdes Abella and Victor and María Sorondo. We call it the Abella-León-Sorondo dinner reunion and we have feasted together several years during an August weekend. The reunion starts on Friday with the arrival of the out-of-town travelers in time to go to a Miami Marlins vs. Atlanta Braves baseball game at either the Braves or Marlins stadium. On Saturday, the women may stay at home or go shopping before starting to prepare the Saturday evening dinner. The Saturday dinners are major culinary affairs served with Champagne and fine wines. The entrees have included Boeuf a la Mode, Osso Bucco a la Milanesa, and Rabo Encendido. We have served great wines: 1989 Champagne Louise (Wine Spectator, WS, 95), 2002 Joseph Phelps Insignia (WS, 96), 1996 Château Lafite Rothschild (Wine Advocate, WA, 100), 2000 Château Lynch Bages (WS 96), 2005 Chassagne Montrachet, Sauternes, Oremus 5 Puttonyos; 2005 Muga Reserva

(WA 94) and 2004 Viña Mayor (WS 93) for the Rabo Encendido. However, the highlight of these dinner reunions is the interaction among all of us who have been extremely close friends for more than forty-five years.

Vacations and dining in restaurants have evolved over the years

We have had the opportunity of enjoying many great vacations with our children, grandchildren, friends and family. The flavor of the vacations, but not necessarily the quality of our enjoyment, has changed over the years as our financial situation has improved.

When Disney World opened in 1971, we visited the park the week after Christmas. We stayed at the Sorondo's house, brought our lunch with us, arrived at the park very early in the morning and stayed until it closed. For the next few visits, we either stayed at the Sorondo's house or at inexpensive motels outside the park, and we continued to bring our lunch and remain until the park closed. In later years, we were able to stay inside the park in one of Disney's hotels (Key West, Beach Club, Boardwalk and our favorite, The Floridian).

We experienced similar improvements in the quality of accommodations since our first trip to Europe in 1975, a trip organized by the ACU as "La Ruta Ignaciana." The cost of that trip was $675 for 15 days and included the airfare from New York, the hotels, most meals and most of the tours. Obviously, the hotels were modest; almost all two stars (out of a maximum of five stars), and the meals were basic. The quality of the hotels and meals for the second ACU trip, a peregrination to the Holy Land in 1978, was a lot better. On later trips, we were able to stay at better hotels, often using "points" that Jesús had earned while traveling for business. Jesús traveled so often for work that he reached platinum level at both Delta Airlines (obtaining free airline travel and upgrades) and also with Starwood Hotels (earning free stays at Westin, Sheraton and the Starwood Luxury Collection hotels).

We have enjoyed great trips. We visited the Holy Land, traveled extensively in Spain and Europe while living in Madrid. Among the countries we visited in Europe are Portugal, Belgium, The Netherlands, France, Italy, Norway, Switzerland, Austria and the Czech Republic. We traveled several times with our children and grandchildren: Paris and Lourdes, Punta Cana in the Dominican Republic, New York City, London, Italy (Tuscany, Cinque Terre, Rome) and a cruise around the British Isles. After retirement, we began taking cruises to the Mediterranean (Italy, France, Malta, Tunisia, Sicily, Monaco, Greece, Istanbul and Ephesus), the Baltic (Denmark, Germany, Russia, Finland, Estonia and Sweden), to England, Scotland and Ireland. We made a memorable trip in 2012 with Cristy and Ana Silva to northeast Italy (Padova, Verona, the Dolomites, Lake Garda, Ferrara, Bologna, Modena, Parma, Padua, Venice) and a cruise in the Adriatic. We cruised in 2015 to Brazil and the Caribbean, a river cruise from Holland through France and Germany, and to Australia and New Zealand. We also traveled from Argentina to Chile, around Cape Horn and then went to the Sacred Valley and Machu Picchu—where Jesús completed his "bucket list."

One of our favorite hobbies is eating excellent meals at very good restaurants. We started this hobby during our honeymoon when we did not have a lot of money. Later, we became gourmets. We have eaten in more than twenty restaurants with three Michelin stars, the highest rating of the Michelin Guide. These restaurants include, in France at Le Buerehiesel (Strasbourg), and in Paris at Alain Ducasse, L'Ambroisie, Arpège, Le Bristol, Ledoyen, Le Cinq, Lucas Carton, Le Pré Catelan and La Tour d'Argent. In Belgium at Comme Chez Soi. In Spain at Arzak (San Sebastian) and Zalacaín (Madrid). In Italy at La Antica Osteria del Ponte (near Milan), La Pergola (Rome) and Le Calandre (Padova). In the USA at The French Laundry (Napa), Le Bernardin (NYC), Daniel (NYC), The Inn at Little Washington (Virginia), Gary Danko (San Francisco), Chez Panisse (Berkeley), and Le Bec-Fin (Philadelphia). We have also had great meals at scores of two and one stars restaurants in France, Belgium, Italy, Switzerland, Germany, Norway, and the USA. We had great experiences at La Casa degli Spiriti (Verona), Ca' Matilde (Quattro Castella) and La Terrazza of the Danieli Hotel in Venice. Also, at 't Fornuis ["the stove"] (Antwerp) and several Paris Restaurants: Lasserre, La Grande Cascade and others; at la Enoteca Pinchiorri (Florence), Il Convivio Troiani (Rome), Atrio in Caceres, and many of the excellent restaurants in Madrid (El Landó, El Paraguas, Viridiana, Santceloni, etc., etc.).

Information about Jesús' family and friends in Tunas

Jesús lived at 108 Maceo Street in a house flanked on one side by the house of his uncle Rodolfo and aunt Lolín, and on the other side by the house of the Corella family. On the other side of the Corella's house was the house of Anita, Grecia, Ana María and Alicia Núñez. At the end of the street was the Colegio Victoria de las Tunas. Across the street from the León-Núñez family lived the Villoch family: Guillermo and Caridad, their daughter Cristina, and their sons "Bebo" (Guillermo Junior) and "Niño" (Salvador)— the two boys were very close friends of Jesús and Ticó. Continuing on Maceo Street beyond the Colegio Victoria de las Tunas, there was a multistory garage and then the house of the García family: Don Manuel and Marciana were the parents of Toñico, Manolo, Elena and the uncle/aunt of Benedicto González. These four persons married Jesús' first cousins Luisita, Bertica, Segisberto and María de los Angeles, respectively. Marciana, Argentina, Lolín and another Tunas lady, Nena Amado, were rock solid Catholics who transmitted their faith to their children and worked together on a number of missionary and charitable activities in Tunas.

Several of Jesús' relatives lived in houses facing the Maceo Square in Tunas located a couple of hundred feet from Jesús' house. They included Encarnita (aunt) and her husband Eladio Patallo; Laura (aunt); Clarita, a cousin, daughter of Encarnita; Ethel, another daughter of Encarnita, who was married to Guillermo Hernández— both of them were dentists and had their home and practice on a house facing the square.

ACU members who lived in Gainesville

Many of the ACU members who lived in Gainesville and their spouses became very close life-long friends of Chelo and Jesús: Lorenzo (Cuso) and Estrella Pérez; Orlando and Yolanda Carneiro; Ignacio and Lourdes Abella; Arsenio and Elena Milian; Victor and María Sorondo; Juan Luis and Mary Porro; Enrique (Kike) and Clarita Baloyra; and, Sergio and Laly Rodríguez.

Close friends in Atlanta

We were also blessed with many close and wonderful friends in Atlanta. We mentioned in our memoirs the Balbona family: José (Peque), Virginia, their children Virgie, Teresa, Eddie, José and Georgie; Virginia's niece, Virgilou; Peque's Madrid nephew Luis Pire Méndez de Andes, his wife María José and their children Inés and Alfonso.

Other good friends in Atlanta included Francisco (Paco) and Carmín Macias, their daughter Carmencita, and Carmín's nephews Rafael (Toti) and Reemberto (Rémbe). René and Rosa López. El "Gallego" Pagoaga and María del Carmen. El "Tigre" César and Carmen Berenguer and their children, especially "La Nena." Luisa and Hernán Blanco. Galo and Marta Cimadevilla. Pepe and Berta Irastorza and their children, especially Lizzie and Aida. Alberto and Margarita Bolet. Carlos and María Victoria (Toti) Navarro. Andy and Selene López. Sergio and Yolanda Magadan. Pepe and Zenaida López. Gonzalo and Grace Saldaña. Armando and Juanita Rodríguez.

Our Atlanta friends include the ACU "boys" and their spouses: José and Alina Batlle. Jorge and Clarita Guigou. Alex and Ana Saker. Alfredo and Melba Trujillo. Gorka and Jackie Zurinaga, and others.

Appendix VI –
Excerpt of Argentina Marta Núñez Berro History

Prologue

Jesús' mother, Argentina, wrote a very personal narrative about her family during the last few years of her life. The narrative was addressed to Carmen Luisa León Núñez and was not intended for publication or general distribution. Jesús translated the document to make it available to the grandchildren and future generations.

Argentina's narrative is fascinating and provides further background on Jesús' family and also on a period of Cuban history beginning in the second half of the 19th century and concluding in the first half of the 20th century.

The document describes the background of Argentina's parents, how they met and how they eventually moved to their cattle ranch on the Cauto River. We have selected to include in this appendix two small portions of Argentina's narrative: the first is a very brief note about her parents and childhood; the second, is of crucial importance to our family: Argentina's conversion to Christianity.

Argentina's parents and childhood

Argentina's maternal grandparents, Miguel Berro and María del Carmen Reyes, were born in the city of Manzanillo, Cuba. Her paternal grandparents were José Manuel Núñez Cándamo, a Spanish immigrant from Galicia, and María de la Luz Parra Oliva, who Argentina believed was born in the small village of Cauto Embarcadero, the last town accesible by small ships traversing the Cauto River.

Argentina's parents were Manuel Ladislao Núñez and María del Carmen Berro, who were born, probably, in Cauto Embarcadero and Manzanillo, respectively. They met while teaching in the village of Media Luna, located about 30 miles from Manzanillo along the coast bordering the Gulf of Guacanayabo. They married in Media Luna, later lived in Manzanillo and eventually moved to a cattle ranch named "Tiguabos" on the Cauto River.

Argentina was the sixth of seven surviving children; three died as children, two of meningitis and one due to typhus. María, Manolo and Germán were born in Media Luna while Regilio, René, Argentina and Rubén were born in Tiguabos.

The family lived in very rustic, some would say primitive, dwellings that had no running water and floors of packed dirt. On the other hand, her parents, both teachers, created an environment of learning and culture. It is notable that both of the girls, María and Argentina, earned college degrees, in an era where few women were, at most, educated at the secondary level.

Argentina remembered her childhood in Tiguabos as a happy time period, although recognizing that they lived like "poor people." The family moved to Victoria de las Tunas when Argentina was twelve years old. Argentina married Rigoberto Amado León Díaz in Holguín in 1943 and later lived in Tunas for over ten years before immigrating to the United States in 1961.

Argentina's account of her encounter with God

One item from my childhood that I need to describe is MY ENCOUNTER WITH GOD.

My father was a mason and anticlerical, but he was not an atheist. If he believed in anything it was on "scientific spiritualism" (nothing to do with common spiritualists of the time in Cuba) and maybe something about theosophy.[172] My mother said that she practiced the Catholic faith when she was young. I do not know when she stopped practicing, if it was before or after marrying my father. She spoke vaguely about God but never taught us anything about religion nor about how to pray. During the summer of 1927,[173] I went for the first time to the house of the Revuelta family, the grandparents of José Manuel.

---

[172] The Concise Encyclopedia of the Merriam-Webster Online Dictionary defines theosophy as a "Religious philosophy with mystical concerns that can be traced to the ancient world. It holds that God, whose essence pervades the universe as an absolute reality, can be known only through mystical experience."

[173] Argentina had turned 11 on March of that year.

My sister María had been the roommate of Vicenta Revuelta at the boarding house (the only boarding house for women in Havana at the time) while they studied at the University of Havana. Vicenta was the sister of Gonzalo, the father of José Manuel. María and Vicenta had hit if off perfectly and Vicenta invited María to spend part of her summer vacation with her in Bayamo and also asked María to bring me. I entered a Catholic church when I was 9 years old because I had asked to be baptized and my parents took me to the small village of Cauto Embarcadero, located about 4 or 5 kilometers from the ranch, where I was baptized in the village church. But I want to make it clear that at the time of my baptism, I had no idea what the sacrament meant and did not have any idea about Christ or the church. The reason I asked to be baptized was because of the teasing of my schoolmates at the Cauto del Paso public school, the district school that included the ranch, and where my mother was a teacher. We attended this school as students when the road was passable. In any case, the schoolboys fought with me and called me "heretic" because I was not baptized, and since this was the greatest insult that you could receive in Cuba at the time, I asked to be baptized so they could not call me a heretic anymore.

After the day I was baptized, probably in either 1924 or 1925, I did not enter another Catholic Church until the summer of 1927. But I can say:

> "Me miraste a los ojos, sonriendo
> dijiste mi nombre, en la arena he
> dejado mi barca…"[174]

Whenever I think about that time of my life and the significance it had for my future, I remember a "guajirita" in Tiguabos, playing with my brothers, and I ask myself, every time more amazed and grateful, why did God look me in the eyes and say, with a lot of love,

---

[174] The song, "Pescador de hombres" is sung commonly at Mass during Communion. The citation is to the refrain: "Oh Lord, in my eyes you were gazing, Kindly smiling, my name you were saying; All I treasured, I have left on the sand there; Close to you, I will find other seas."

my name? A mystery of faith, a faith that has been the cornerstone in my life journey, the ray of light that has always illuminated my life. I could not understand my life today without this pillar that has been my source of strength.

During the days that I spent with the Revuelta family that summer, I went to Mass and said the Rosary for the first time. I also went to a convent of nuns and friars, both of the Franciscan Capuchins order. I was given and read a Sacred History (histories from the Old Testament) and was told about Christ and the Virgin. In my next visits to Bayamo in 1927 and 1928, I continued to learn about the Catholic Religion, saw a procession, went to Adoration of the Blessed Sacrament and heard Micaela Revuelta (Vicenta's sister) sing with her beautiful voice in Latin the Litany of the Saints, the Ave Maria and other sacred hymns. I have not forgotten the prayers and especially, the hymns. They have stayed in my memory from the very first time I heard them sung in the wide naves of the beautiful church of El Salvador (Our Savior) in Bayamo.

In September 1928, we passed through Bayamo in the direction of Tunas as we prepared to move to Tunas. We stopped to visit the Revuelta family and Micaela took me aside and told me: "You are now going to live in a city with a Catholic Church. Remember that you should go to church every Sunday, and attend catechism classes so you can soon make your First Communion." Whether it was because God had lovingly looked into my eyes, or because I looked up to the Revuelta family, it is clear that God used Micaela to guide me. When I arrived in Tunas, I started to go to Mass on Sundays and to attend catechism classes, so that on May 9, 1929, on the Feast of the Ascension, I made my First Communion. Since then, whenever I could, I went to daily Mass and received Holy Communion, and I became very involved in every aspect of the Catholic Religion: Catholic Action, Spiritual Exercises, Parish Missions, Rural Missions, Parish Schools, etc. I cannot fail to mention that God was the source of the brightest moments of my life since "He gazed into my eyes."

www.ingramcontent.com/pod-product-compliance
Lightning Source LLC
Chambersburg PA
CBHW061753070526
44586CB00023B/2602